COOPERATIVE CAPITALISM

JAPAN BUSINESS AND ECONOMICS SERIES

This series provides a forum for books on the workings of Japan's economy, its business enterprises, its management practices, and its macroeconomic structure. Japan has achieved the status of a major economic world power and much can be learned from an understanding of how this has been accomplished and how it is being sustained.

The series aims to balance empirical and theoretical work. It also implicitly takes for granted that both the significant differences between Japan and other countries and the similarities between them are worth knowing about. The series will present a broad range of work on economics, politics, and systems of management, in analysing the performance of one of the major players in what may well be the largest economic region in the twenty-first century.

Series Board

Cooperative Capitalism

Self-Regulation, Trade Associations, and the Antimonopoly Law in Japan

ULRIKE SCHAEDE

OXFORD
UNIVERSITY PRESS

OXFORD
UNIVERSITY PRESS

Great Clarendon Street, Oxford OX2 6DP

Oxford University Press is a department of the University of Oxford.
It furthers the University's objective of excellence in research, scholarship,
and education by publishing worldwide in

Oxford New York

Athens Auckland Bangkok Bogotá Buenos Aires Calcutta
Cape Town Chennai Dar es Salaam Delhi Florence Hong Kong Istanbul
Karachi Kuala Lumpur Madrid Melbourne Mexico City Mumbai
Nairobi Paris São Paulo Singapore Taipei Tokyo Toronto Warsaw
and associated companies in Berlin Ibadan

Oxford is a registered trade mark of Oxford University Press
in the UK and certain other countries

Published in the United States
by Oxford University Press Inc. New York

British Library Cataloguing in Publication Data

Library of Congress Cataloging in Publication Data

Schaede, Ulrike, 1962–
Cooperative capitalism : self-regulation, trade association, and the antimonopoly law in
Japan / Ulrike Schaede.
p. cm – (Japan business and economies series)
Includes bibliographical references.
I. Industrial policy–Japan 2. Capitalism–Japan 3. Trade regulation–Japan I. Title. II. Series
IID3616.133.833.2000   338.952–dc21   00-024722
ISBN 0–19–829718–1

1 3 5 7 9 10 8 6 4 2

Typeset by Kolam Information Services Pvt Ltd, Pondicherry, India
Printed in Great Britain
on acid free paper
by TJ International Ltd
Padstow, Cornwall

To Charles

CONTENTS

PREFACE

'*Shōji to shōbai wa massugu da to tatanai.*'
Shoji screens and merchants don't work if they are entirely upstanding.
(Old Japanese merchants' saying)

After 50 years of fast economic growth, Japan's developmental state has outlived its usefulness. Industries that can be nourished through industrial policy alone, such as those based on manufacturing prowess, will not be sufficient to sustain the country's growth into the 21st century. As the Japanese government becomes less central and deregulation continues, some propose that Japan's markets must surely become more open to foreign competition. But is this necessarily the case? Where is "post-developmental" Japan really headed? Anyone who is familiar with Japan will likely agree that the country is characterized by many systemic and institutional features that clearly run counter to a full "convergence" with the U.S. market system. These features include major differences in politics, markets, companies, laws, and society—all of which may augur a future very different from the default U.S. model of market capitalism.

This book argues that Japan is on its way to a cooperative market system based on self-regulation by trade associations; i.e. independent rule-making by the industries themselves. As the strong state declines and deregulation proceeds absent the establishment of a large number of supervisory regulatory agencies, industries are assuming the role of formulating and enforcing their own rules. While this is a major change within Japan, the net result for the world economy is that many Japanese markets will not become more open and accessible to foreign competitors. This book presents a careful institutional, legal, and empirical analysis of the activities and organization of Japan's trade associations, of the country's antitrust laws, and of its antitrust enforcement in the postwar period. The evidence is manifest: self-regulation is on the rise, and it is contained by neither domestic antitrust enforcement nor foreign pressure. This new system is likely to characterize Japanese government–business relations for the foreseeable future. One important consequence for the Japanese economy is that the division of Japan's industry into efficient and non-efficient sectors will become more pronounced. Whereas the most competitive companies will remain world market leaders and reemerge strongly after the recession of the 1990s, some of the inefficient, domestic sectors will continue to operate under domestic protection.

The study specifically focuses on a legal-institutional analysis of self-regulation in Japan. Although I have included occasional comparison with the U.S. and Germany, a full-fledged comparative analysis is left for further research. Naturally, Japan in general and its system of self-regulation in particular are evolving rapidly. The interviews which provide a foundation for this book were conducted between 1993 and 1998, and case studies and data analysis span through the end of 1997. In my research, I have included trade associations from all sectors, including finance and services. Although the food and drink industry is part of the analysis, I exclude the agricultural cooperatives, or *Nōkyō*. These cooperatives are influential, yet so different from all other associations that they warrant a study of their own. I do not believe, however, that excluding the *Nōkyō* alters the conclusions of this study. Rather, were these cooperatives included, I believe that the picture of self-regulation would be even stronger.

This research is an outgrowth of my long-held interest in Japan's political economy and government–business relationships. When I began studying Japan's financial markets in the 1980s, I realized how important it was to fully understand the role of industry in the regulatory process: rather than being passive "regulatees", Japanese firms were actively involved in shaping their own regulation. Compared with other countries, this seemed to occur in highly institutionalized and organized ways, not through fragmented lobbying efforts as seen in the U.S. In the 1990s this trend became ever stronger. In trying to make sense of this phenomenon, I was very fortunate to find myself at the Graduate School of International Relations and Pacific Studies (IR/PS) at the University of California, San Diego. With its interdisciplinary faculty, IR/PS has provided the ideal intellectual environment for this research project. Being exposed to the varied perspectives and theoretical frameworks of my colleagues has encouraged me to continuously sharpen my arguments. While occasionally this exchange pulled me in opposing directions, in the end the manuscript has been greatly improved by it. In particular, I am indebted to John McMillan, Peter Gourevitch, and Takeo Hoshi for being great mentors throughout. Many of my colleagues read and commented on parts of the manuscript at various stages, and I am grateful for insightful comments from Stephan Haggard, Takeo Hoshi, Miles Kahler, Ellis Krauss, Andrew MacIntryre, David McKendrick, John McMillan, Masao Miyoshi, Barry Naughton, and Peter Timmer. Outside IR/PS, Jennifer Amyx, Michael Gerlach, James Lincoln, Leonard Lynn, Daniel Okimoto, Frank Upham, and Tom Roehl all provided helpful suggestions.

Most importantly, I have benefited greatly for many years from the insights, comments, and encouragement from Hugh Patrick. His 1962 book on monetary policy first triggered my interest in Japanese financial matters and government–business relationships when I was an undergraduate student in Germany. Although it took a long time until we finally met, over the years I have learned enormously from letters and conversations with him. At a conference in the early 1990s, he pointed out that one of the more interesting current issues in the field was the role of business in Japan's economic development. When, several years later, this manuscript landed on his desk, he ploughed through it, cover to cover, with amazing patience and outstanding insight. Thanks to Hugh's comments, many loose ends in this book could be connected.

This research project would have been impossible without the generous support of the Abe Fellowship by the Center for Global Partnership (Japan Foundation), the U.S.–Japan Friendship Commission, and the UCSD Hellman Faculty Fellowship. Through this funding, I was able to receive the help of a group of excellent research assistants. Jessica Jensen provided incisive comments and insights; without her support, the manuscript would not be nearly as coherent. Jeffrey Rector and Kuk-Soo Choi were critical in putting together the unique databases on which this study is based. Arbora Johnson helped finishing it all up.

The financial support also allowed me to conduct extended research in Japan and interview executives in 37 trade associations, as well as many government officials, academics, and businessmen. All of these interviewees requested anonymity, which I happily promised in return for their insights. After one extended interview at a small-firm association, the official ended by pointing out that there are three critical things one needs to know when trying to understand the processes of interest alignment in Japanese trade associations: "First, if something needs to get done, we start with *nemawashi*—to lay the groundwork, and then *jingi ni kiru*—to make the formal greeting. Second, if we need to accelerate an issue, we practice *atamagoshi*—to jump over someone's head in the hierarchy. And third, in extremely difficult situations one has to *seishin seii uso o tsuku*—to tell a lie faithfully." And he added smilingly: "*Gijutsu desu yo*—That's an art."

In sticking with more traditional Western practices, I have tried in this book to tell the truth to the very best of my knowledge. It is my hope that by carefully disentangling the "faithful lies" from the real facts, I have been able to report fairly and without distortion the recent changes in Japan's political economy. All remaining errors are mine alone.

I thank my friends and family around the world for support and cheerful encouragement throughout the process of putting this research together. Above all, it is thanks to Charles A. O'Reilly III that I had a happy smile on my face as I was typing along.

US

La Jolla, CA, January 2000

Following the Japanese practice, throughout the book Japanese names are rendered with last name first (e.g., Tanaka Kakuei). Macrons that indicate long vowels (ō, ū) are included for all Japanese terms with the exception of Americanized words and well-known city names (e.g., Tokyo).

LIST OF FIGURES

LIST OF TABLES

LIST OF ABBREVIATIONS

AML	Antimonopoly Law
BOJ	Bank of Japan
CEO	Chief Executive Officer
DIL	Depressed Industries Law
FDI	Foreign Direct Investment
FSA	Financial Supervisory Agency
FTC	Federal Trade Commission (U.S.)
GATT	General Agreement on Tariffs and Trade
GDP	Gross Domestic Product
IMF	International Monetary Fund
JASD	Japan Association of Securities Dealers
JFTC	Japan Fair Trade Commission
LDP	Liberal Democratic Party
MAC	Ministry of Agriculture and Commerce
MCI	Ministry of Commerce and Industry
MITI	Ministry of International Trade and Industry
MM	Ministry of Munitions
MOF	Ministry of Finance
NASD	National Association of Securities Dealers
OBs	Old Boys
PARC	Policy Affairs Research Council
PIG	Private Interest Government
R&D	Research and Development
SCAP	Supreme Commander of the Allied Powers
SDIL	Structurally Depressed Industries Law
SEC	Securities and Exchange Commission
SEL	Securities and Exchange Law
SIC	Standard Industry Classification
SII	Structural Impediments Initiative
SME	Small- and Medium-Sized Enterprise
WTO	World Trade Organization

1

Introduction

1.1. The Argument: Toward a "Cooperative System" Based on Self-Regulation

'Trade associations are increasingly adopting their own self-regulation codes
or standards with respect to such matters as the variety and quality of goods,
representations and advertising, and methods of business operation.'

(JFTC 1995: 17)

Deregulation will not necessarily lead to increased competition across all Japanese industries. Rather, as Japan's postwar industrial policy regime crumbles and the regulating ministries become less potent, many industries rely more than ever on the practice of "self-regulation" (*jishu kisei*)—using trade associations to enforce trade rules and market controls. As argued here, "post-developmental" Japan will be characterized by increasing self-regulation through trade associations. As a result of self-regulation, many markets will remain as restricted as they are today, but this restriction will be based more on trade practices established by trade associations and less on government intervention in the marketplace. Thus, the demise of ministerial regulatory power and the process of deregulation are unlikely to have a positive impact on Japan's trade relations with other nations, because most associations remain exclusive in nature. Many Japanese industries will continue to use their domestic markets as profit sanctuaries.

In this book, I argue that self-regulation through trade associations will become an even more important characteristic of Japan than it has historically been. I support this thesis with an exploration of the evolution and mechanisms of self-regulation as well as an institutional and legal analysis of Japan's trade associations. While industries differ significantly in both the degree and the ways in which they self-regulate, it will become clear that in general all Japanese trade associations self-regulate more than their counterparts in other countries. Japan's antitrust system needs to undergo significant changes before it can contain self-regulation. Therefore, this system of self-regulation will be stable in the medium term, and ultimately, its effect on Japan's economy will be an increase in the bifurcation between primarily domestically oriented and largely inefficient sectors on the one hand, and export-oriented and internationally competitive industries on the other hand. Self-regulation is an efficient regulatory system from industry's perspective, and its dominance will continue as long as Japan's society as a whole, and its politicians in particular, prove unable or unwilling to curb industry's influence on regulation. In the medium run, most sectors of Japanese industry will benefit from self-regulation—since naturally they attempt to structure their rules to their own advancement—at the expense of Japan's consumers and trading partners, as domestic prices and profits will remain high and markets will remain closed.

During the 1970s and 1980s, one dominant paradigm among scholars studying Japan was the notion of the "developmental state" (Johnson 1982). Yamamura (1997: 296) defines the developmental state system as one in which institutions are shaped by the belief that a developing economy can best achieve growth by adopting promotional and protective industrial policies that enable its manufacturing firms to adopt successively new technologies as rapidly as possible in order to increase productive capacity and efficiency.[1] To be sure, there has been a great debate in the field of Japanese Studies over both the mechanisms and the economic effects of this system. For instance, analysts remain divided in their interpretations about whether Japan's industrial policy programs had any posit-ive effects on economic growth (e.g., Weinstein 1993, Beason/Weinstein 1996, Noble 1988). Moreover, too much emphasis may have been placed on the bureaucracy, at the expense of elected politicians, when both groups were involved in the varying stages of designing and implementing policy programs (see, e.g., Ramseyer/Rosenbluth 1993, Muramatsu/Krauss 1987, 1990, Calder 1988, McCubbins/Noble 1995a, 1995b, Kernell 1991). One obvious shortcoming of the original "developmental state" concept was that it did not include industry as an independent actor, and looking at only one side of the equation led to an exaggeration of state power. Many studies of the 1980s and 1990s have therefore addressed the issue of coexistence of a "strong state" with "strong business", stressing the necessity of negotiation and cooperation between the public and private sectors (e.g., Samuels 1987, Okimoto 1989, Haley 1991b, Upham 1996). Yet another group of scholars maintains that while the Japanese state may have attempted to exert strong leadership, it was ultimately industry that was driving the political and business agendas (e.g., Patrick 1967, Friedman 1988, Uriu 1996). Once industry as an independent actor is included in the revised developmental state concept, and once it is agreed that industrial policy was not always success-ful, most analysts concur that, compared with other countries, Japan's postwar political economy is best characterized as a vast system of rules and regulations administered by a relatively strong bureaucracy aiming to spur economic growth.

Remarkably absent among studies of industry's role in Japan's postwar economic growth is an institutional analysis of the regulatory role of trade associations.[2] This is astounding, given that throughout Japan's economic history

---

[1] For details on the developmental state proposition and the political consequences for Japan, see, for instance, Johnson (1982), Prestowitz (1988), Fallows (1994), Hadley (1970). Gao (1997) offers a detailed historical analysis, while Tilton (1996) highlights the workings of the mechanism through industry case studies. For theoretical analyses of the "strong state" concept, see Evans et al. (1985), Krasner (1978, 1984), Zysman (1983), Katzenstein (1978).

[2] See Section 1.2 for a discussion of Tilton (1996) and Upham (1996), and how the concept of self-regulation differs from their approaches.

industry has played a paramount role in structuring markets and formulating trade rules. Yet, economic developments in the 1980s and 1990s are bringing trade associations once again to the fore. The emerging consensus in the field of Japanese social studies in the mid-1990s was that the bureaucratic influence on economic growth has been declining and will continue to decline further in the future: once economic development was achieved, the developmental state, with its emphasis on goals such as fostering infant industries and promoting exports, had outlived its usefulness and feasibility (e.g., Vogel, S. 1999, Pempel 1998). Industrial change, deregulation and the 1990s recession have combined to undermine the bureaucracy's strength in setting incentives for business. At the same time, the absence of a well-established system of process regulation through independent supervisory agencies (i.e., the monitoring of incumbent firms, as opposed to entry regulation, the licensing of new firms in an industry) has created a regulatory void. Therefore, deregulation has triggered greater efforts at industry self-regulation to maintain previous protective patterns owing to two simultaneous forces: (1) through ending official government protection for many industries and introducing a more competitive environment; and (2) through creating a regulatory void in terms of process supervision and monitoring. The question, then, is: Where is Japan going from here? How will Japan's political economy be organized and function in the post-developmental era?

In general, one can conceive of two major directions that a "developmental" country can take once it has achieved its goal of economic development: (1) toward a competitive system (Anglo-American style) that, while based on a significant number of laws and regulations, has little room for discretionary deal-making by government or business, and is primarily characterized by market competition and strict antitrust rules; or in contrast (2) toward a cooperative system (Asian and continental European style) in which competition is complemented by collaboration even among fierce competitors and where regulators allow a significant exchange of information among competing firms.[3] The primary

---

[3] Chandler (1990) has used the term "competitive managerial capitalism" to describe the U.S. system that developed after the 1890s, whereas he chose the term "cooperative managerial system" to describe prewar Germany, following Kocka's (1978) notion of prewar Germany as a system of "organized capitalism". While there is debate whether the "cooperative" concept fully captures the German situation (Herrigel 1996), the dominant features of Germany's prewar system as described by Chandler (1990: 395)—"strong support given to cartels and other interfirm agreements,... shared belief in the value of cooperation,... larger role played by trade associations,... and close attention to the needs and welfare of [the]... working force"—describe postwar Japan very well. Chandler also argues for prewar Germany that "the cooperation that developed between and within industrial firms can be considered as part of a larger system". Procassini (1995) uses the term "collaborative capitalism" for Japan to underscore the cooperation between government and business. For a discussion of the main features of the postwar continental European political and economic system, see Zysman (1983), Gourevitch (1982). For discussions of the various systems in Asia, see Haggard (1990), MacIntyre (1994a), Wade (1990), Kim (1997), World Bank (1993). Finally, for an introduction to the literature and varying viewpoints concerning "convergence", see Berger/Dore (1996). Yamamura (1997) and Anchordoguy (1997) offer perspectives why convergence is unlikely to occur in the Japanese case.

differences between the two systems are (a) the propensity of competing firms to collaborate; and (b) the degree to which cooperation among competitors is considered legal; i.e., the logic and effectiveness of antitrust enforcement. A high propensity of firms to collaborate is obviously the first and necessary condition for a cooperative system. Whether firms agree to cooperate is often path-dependent, i.e., based on their previous interactions. Game theory offers one explanation for this logic: cooperation is easier in a repeated game setting (see Section 1.2). Industries for which the government has created a negotiation framework to allow for repeated interactions over time are likely to show a higher propensity to collaborate and have more institutionalized processes of cooperation than industries without government coordination. However, the propensity to collaborate is itself significantly influenced by the lenience of the country's antitrust enforcement. A permissive antitrust system is therefore the sufficient condition for the cooperative system.

Japan in the 1990s fulfils both the necessary and the sufficient conditions for the emergence of a cooperative system. Throughout history, Japanese firms have often agreed to cooperate and self-regulate. In fact, Japan's economic development since the Middle Ages has built on industrial self-regulation (see Chapter 7). But not only have Japanese companies a long history of cooperation independent of their government; postwar industrial policies, especially those resting on cartel agreements within industries, have also created or buttressed institutionalized processes of cooperation through well-established trade associations, even in highly competitive industries (see Chapter 3). Regardless of whether these cartels were ultimately successful or not, by building on cooperation with industry, industrial policies have reinforced negotiation frameworks in many industries, domestic and export-oriented, and have led to an overall high propensity to cooperate as well as an institutionalized role for trade associations. Meanwhile, Japan's antitrust authorities, while certainly not inactive, have allowed for considerable exchange of information across firms and industries; moreover there is no evidence that this will change any time soon (see Chapters 4 and 5).

In the 1980s and 1990s, the combination of deregulation, recession and the relative loss in authority by the bureaucracy pushed Japan clearly onto the path toward a cooperative system based on self-regulation by industry. Although industries differ in the degree to which they self-regulate, Japan's industrial policy and lenient antitrust enforcement have combined to result in a higher propensity to cooperate across virtually all industries than is observable in other industrialized countries; in addition, industries with specific structural and product characteristics are particularly active in self-regulation (Chapter 6). Due to the absence of independent supervisory agencies, and the time it would take to create such institutions, this system of self-regulation will be stable in the medium run. Trade liberalization, too, is unlikely to undermine self-regulation in the foreseeable future: while in the past, government regulation has limited competition through imports, after liberalization it is through self-regulation that industries have substituted the former official rules and can thus uphold entry barriers to foreign competition.[4]

The implications of this shift from the developmental state to a system dominated by industry self-regulation are enormous. There are at least four major areas of impact:

1. *The reshaping of power structures toward industry.* With the end of the developmental state and its attempted micro-management of corporate strategies, the bureaucrats' role in Japan's political economy shifts from that of a proactive supporter-regulator to that of a responsive adviser (similar, for instance, to the role of government in Germany). In their place, the relative role of trade associations in structuring regulation is becoming more dominant, as more and more business decisions are made without government input, support, or oversight. Since business interests are more diverse than the hitherto dominant government interest of economic growth through protection, the shift toward self-regulation blurs economic policy goals.

2. *An increase in private process regulation and non-transparency of market rules.* The shift toward a cooperative system reinforces Japan's opaque deal-making system, and many markets will remain closed. As self-regulation replaces government rules, official deregulation programs are being rendered largely irrelevant. Japan's regulatory system builds primarily on entry regulation through licenses and permits; once licensed to enter an industry, companies are typically regulated through informal processes of administrative guidance. "Deregulation" refers to a reduction in the number of licenses and permits required to enter a business. While the cognizant ministries might attempt to "retrench and re-regulate" by substituting discretionary business licenses and entry permits for formerly official rules (Vogel, S. 1996), trade associations fill in where deregulation eventually opens markets. Meanwhile, deregulation is creating a void in process regulation (i.e., monitoring the behavior of firms established in an industry), and trade associations are filling this regulatory void through self-regulation. For instance, in 1987 and 1995, the Federation of Bankers' Associations created its own guidelines on banking disclosure (see Chapter 5). Rules, standards, and market access differ across industries, making it difficult to penetrate the market. Trade relations with other nations are unlikely to improve, as process regulation will remain non-transparent.

3. *An increase in the "bifurcation" of Japanese industry.* Not all industries are the same, and neither do they self-regulate in the same ways. Some sectors may want to open up to competition. Therefore, market access will become more disparate, reflecting the differing needs and rules across various industries. Similarly, the effect of self-regulation on competitiveness will differ across industries: industries characterized by only limited cooperation in the past

---

[4] See Encarnation (1992) for an analysis of impediments to trade in Japan throughout the postwar period, and Kahler (1996) for a discussion on how the forces of trade may affect domestic regulatory systems.

may reach only few industry-specific agreements and therefore will create a rather competitive market for themselves. In contrast, industries characterized by frequent interaction are likely to agree on more and more self-regulatory protection for their member companies. Competitive industries will become even more competitive, whereas some of the collusive industries may lose out in the long run.

4. *An additional competitive edge for export-oriented industries.* Permissive antitrust rules and self-regulation facilitate a regular and open exchange of information among competing firms. The more detailed and open the information exchange is among competitors, the more this exchange will afford the participating firms a competitive advantage, both over domestic industries that do not cooperate in the same way, and over foreign competitors that are not allowed to self-regulate in their domestic markets in the same way. Moreover, as expanding self-regulation helps limit competition in particular Japanese markets, it allows some industries to use the domestic market as a "profit sanctuary" for more forceful competition in international markets.

Trade or industry associations (*jigyōsha dantai*) provide the platform for business agreements and rule-setting among firms. While associations have played critical roles in shaping the industrial policies of the high-growth era, the shift toward industry self-regulation places them at the center of Japan's regulatory system. Trade associations are thus the key to a complete understanding of Japan's political economy in the 21st century. This book explains how trade associations shape Japan's emerging self-regulatory system. How many associations are there, and what are their characteristics? What do they do, and how do they differ from each other in form or function? What are their specific functions in Japan's political economy? Further, how do we know self-regulation when we see it, and how is it realized? What is the system of antitrust enforcement for self-regulatory activities? What is the evidence that self-regulation through trade associations is on the rise, replacing state regulation and guidance? And finally, how stable is this system likely to be, and what are the likely ramifications for Japan's economy of this shift toward self-regulation?

In answering these questions, this book focuses on the institutional and legal analysis of the regulatory role played by trade associations in Japan; an in-depth evaluation of the economic effects of those self-regulatory activities amounting to cartels is left for further study. The remainder of this chapter will lay the groundwork for this institutional and legal analysis. After considering in more detail the nature of self-regulation, the decline of Japan's industrial policy system, and why antitrust policy is unlikely to curtail cooperation between Japanese firms, we will examine the standing and function of trade associations within the larger picture of Japan's political economy. Section 1.2 highlights various theoretical approaches to trade association analysis, and Section 1.3 outlines the structure of this book.

Definition of "Self-Regulation"

The term "self-regulation" (*jishu kisei*) describes a process by which a trade association, comprised of the leading firms in an industry, designs rules of trade for that industry and enforces those rules through self-designed sanctions. While self-regulation is certainly not an activity that is unique to Japan's trade associations, the scope and depth with which Japanese associations pursue it are much more significant than in other countries, due to the confluence of a lenient antitrust system, the particular evolution of Japan's political economy, and the process of deregulation in the 1980s and 1990s. As a result of these factors, self-regulation in Japan encompasses a broad spectrum of activities, and it is important to note that not all self-regulation is illegal.

In general, the boundaries between trade-facilitating cooperation and collusion are not clear. In an early study of the benefits of cooperation, Machlup (1952: 85–6) found:

No lines, certainly no clear lines, can be drawn between cooperation, collusion, and cartelization. For purely informal, self-imposed restraints on competitors and without any set pattern for pricing or selling practices the term *cooperation* may be most fitting. For less informal limitations in competitive conduct, involving direct or indirect communication among competitors or compliance with a set pattern of pricing or selling, the term *collusion* may be more appropriate. For arrangements involving more frequent communication among competitors or some sort of permanent organization such as a trade association ... the term cartel may be most suitable. Since there is an air of suspicion and illegality attached to the terms "collusion" and "cartel"—in the United States at least—"cooperation" is the widely preferred term for all forms of restraint or non-aggressiveness in competition.

Self-regulation entails both the positive (trade-enhancing) and negative (trade-restricting) aspects of cooperation. To capture these differences in an analysis of Japanese trade associations, it is useful to group self-regulation into two main categories:

1. *Administrative self-regulation.* This category includes activities that aim to structure the rules and regulations of the industry, with the primary motive to facilitate or enhance trade in the industry. Examples include: setting standards or minimum quality requirements, conducting quality inspections, setting rules on advertising and ethical standards, controlling mutual trade credit financing, or providing mutual management support. Often, these activities increase the overall quality reputation of the industry and enhance economic performance. While some of these activities may have anti-competitive effects, most types of administrative self-regulation are considered legal in many countries.

2. *Protective self-regulation.* This category refers to all activities ultimately aimed to shield the industry from competition by creating defensive boundaries to trade. Activities include agreements on prices, entry barriers, exclusive trade tie-ups, boycotts and refusals to deal with nonmembers of the association. The

legal interpretation of these activities differs across countries; while price fixing is considered illegal almost everywhere, countries diverge in how they consider, for example, the competitive effects of restrictions in the distribution system. Thus, whereas from the U.S. perspective much of the protective self-regulation looks like collusion, not all of it is interpreted as such in Japan.

The boundaries between administrative and protective self-regulation are blurred, which is why the increase in self-regulation cannot easily be halted in Japan. Many self-regulatory activities simultaneously affect regulatory structure and competition, and sometimes administrative self-regulation evolves into protective self-regulation over time. For instance, an association could set industry standards so high that only incumbent firms can indeed meet these standards; whereas setting standards is generally considered a trade-enhancing activity, setting them out of reach for competitors is not. Another outstanding example of blurred legal boundaries concerns the so-called "trade habits" (*shōkankō*) that are common practice in the Japanese distribution system. Consisting of a system of rebates, returns, exclusive wholesaler relations, and retail price maintenance—which each by itself is not necessarily illegal—these "trade habits" have developed over years into an intricate, interwoven system that in fact typically results in restraints to competition. Moreover, price rules in the distribution system are often related to collusion among the product manufacturers, who then use restrictions on their exclusive retailers to force their price agreements through the retail system (see Chapters 4 and 5). Still, as I will argue in this book, the situation of antitrust enforcement in Japan is such that even if the authorities wanted to take a tougher stand in defining "trade habits" and other protective self-regulation as illegal, the necessary legal doctrine for such a move has yet to be established, and the law to be rewritten. As it stands, there are only few legal deterrents to most forms of administrative and protective self-regulation in Japan.

  Protective self-regulation differs from a cartel by being a continuous process nested in the trade association and connected to other, long-term industry activities, such as lobbying. Self-regulation is an institutionalized, ongoing process, and it is thus inherently much more stable than a cartel, where companies get together with the singular purpose of fixing prices. While cartels typically build on self-regulation and are often organized through trade associations, self-regulation is not based on a cartel, and it may not constitute a cartel. Self-regulation is therefore more stable and predictable than a cartel.

  Self-regulation also includes the self-enforcement of rules by the association. Having outlined the competitive behavior for their industry, companies often negotiate business plans, or divide markets either by territory or product category. They may agree to refuse to deal with companies that are not association members, and monitor their members' behavior by requesting detailed trade statistics from each member. They may create a fund, so that should one company deviate from the agreed-upon plan, its contribution to the fund can be confiscated by the group as a penalty. Associations meet regularly and frequently to assure constant interaction and mutual monitoring. Just as the original structuring of the rules and agreements, supervising adherence to trade habits is enforced in the marketplace, usually without interference or oversight by the government.

Frequent interaction and agreements with industry competitors come at an immense cost for a company, of course, and time expenses and constraints to individual corporate strategy are only the most visible of these. Why, then, would Japanese companies be interested in participating actively in administrative and protective self-regulation? There are five primary reasons and motives why a company can find self-regulation beneficial over time:

1. As for administrative self-regulation, companies may have three prime objectives with self-regulation: (a) to complement or augment existing official regulation in fast-changing markets where the government cannot structure rules fast enough, e.g., in high-technology industries such as biotechnology or investment banking; (b) to create a reputation of fairness and sound business by self-enforcing ethical standards and launching social responsibility campaigns, such as in many medical or other professional associations; and (c) to increase the bargaining power of the association's members vis-à-vis large customers, especially in intermediate product markets. These types of activities are common to trade associations in many countries, and they are typically considered legal, unless adherence is coerced or rules are used to limit competition in the industry.

2. As for protective self-regulation, companies may aim to increase profits through collusion with their competitors; this objective is typically achieved through price fixing. One challenge for price cartels is the monitoring of cartel members to insure adherence with the price limits. Self-regulation through constant meetings and through distribution rules is the ideal tool for carrying out price agreements. Yet, while price fixing may be the most obvious motive of self-regulation, and the one practice that is easiest to observe, it is not necessarily the most common: price cartels are inherently unstable and are typically considered illegal.

3. In combining administrative and protective self-regulation, companies may strive to reduce uncertainty through extensive exchange of information, including investment plans and costs. The primary goal is to lower variance in profits. The means to achieve this goal are plentiful, including agreements to reduce capacity, to keep dividend payments low, to allocate customers and markets, or to require exclusive trade rules in the distribution system (e.g., boycotting discount stores) and other "trade habits", as previously mentioned.[5]

4. Related to the objective of stabilizing profits over time is the use of self-regulation to construct a "sanctuary strategy". This strategy aims at building a

---

[5] The motive of reducing the variance in profits has also been observed for the logic of Japanese *keiretsu* affiliations; see Nakatani (1984), Hoshi et al. (1990a, 1990b, 1991).

predictable profit cushion in the home market that allows companies to compete forcefully through price discounts abroad. Lower profits in export markets are counterbalanced by higher profits in the domestic market. To implement this strategy, self-regulation may include price fixing, retail price maintenance, and other means to restrain competition in the home market.

5. Most importantly, a group of companies may self-regulate because of inertia or "dynamic conservatism", whereby organizations actively seek to preserve the status quo (Morison 1966). As specified in Section 1.2 below, there is ample evidence from studies in organizational ecology and institutional theory that companies often continue doing what has worked for them in the past. In the case of self-regulation, throughout Japan's economic history trade associations have cooperated and self-regulated. In the postwar period of active industrial policy, the propensity to cooperate was further nourished, even among fierce competitors, through government-organized cartels and research consortia. Thus, in the 1950s and 1960s the newly emerging Japanese companies, too, learned that it often paid to cooperate, especially when the agreement left enough room for competition on quality, service, or other issues.

A variant of this motivation for self-regulation comes in the form of group pressure. Because self-regulation often pertains to access to the distribution system, sometimes companies have no choice but to participate in the cooperative agreements of the industry, lest they be excluded from business. Examples abound of how self-regulation can be structured such that undermining the agreement becomes bad corporate strategy. Moreover, promotion systems in Japanese companies set incentives for individuals to go along rather than be labeled a "renegade", thus limiting the efforts of individuals to resist the pressure in the industry to self-regulate (see, e.g., the introductory case to Chapter 5).

The obvious problem with self-regulation is the danger that it may result in collusive practices that harm the efficiency of the industry and its firms. To be sure, if companies block market entry and rig prices, over time they are likely to become cost-inefficient, and several of Japan's domestic industries have succumbed to this slack. Yet, some of Japan's export-oriented industries, such as automobiles and electronics, have successfully avoided the pitfalls of collusion. There are three major ways in which industries can benefit from self-regulation while escaping potential pitfalls: (1) by focusing on their international competitors, besides their domestic ones, as the measure for competitiveness and benchmarking, companies can avoid being blindsided; (2) by sharing cost and other strategic information for the domestic market, companies can make more informed business decisions and reduce waste of resources; and (3) by limiting self-regulation to those activities that do not harm efficiency, companies can leave room for competition: e.g., even under price agreements they can agree to compete on quality. Therefore, while domestically oriented industries may suffer a loss in efficiency from increased self-regulation, competitive industries can use self-regulation to structure the rules of trade such as to enhance their competitive standing.

Why the "Developmental State" is History

Although many more industries enjoyed rather than rejected strong government guidance during the postwar period of strong state guidance, the postwar alliance between the central government and big business was never a truly stable one. For instance, Japan's automobile makers resisted MITI guidance and refused to merge in the 1950s and 1960s (e.g., Kaplan 1976). In the famous Sumitomo Metals incident of 1965, MITI needed support from the big steel companies and intervention by the largest trade associations to bend Sumitomo Metal into a steel production cartel (Johnson 1982, Upham 1987, 1996). The most glaring marker of disunity, which gave maverick firms an excellent excuse for resisting government guidance, occurred in the oil cartel after the "oil shock" of 1973 (see Chapter 3). Petroleum companies agreed to set limits on prices, output, and sales, allegedly under guidance from MITI; the Supreme Court found the firms guilty of collusion nevertheless. For the first time after the U.S. occupation, senior executives from the colluding companies were convicted on criminal charges for, as they claimed, following the directions of the government in colluding on price.

Such government directions are often referred to as administrative guidance (*gyōsei shidō*). Administrative guidance is a form of non-codified, extralegal regulation. A ministry or agency attempts to induce specific firm behavior with the aim of realizing an administrative goal through industry cooperation. The process is typically not transparent and involves delicate conversations between ministry officials and industry representatives. Rules may be invoked or revoked at the discretion of the ministry, without need of cabinet or parliamentary approval, which gives administrative guidance a strong situational character. Enforcement of administrative guidance is based on a *quid pro quo* approach: corporations know that by following the ministry's "advice" they may reap rewards later, whereas refusal to comply may lead the ministry to obstruct future business opportunities. Because compliance is "voluntary", there is effectively no legal recourse for firms subjected to administrative guidance. Neither is there a legal means for the regulating ministry to enforce its guidance. "Carrots" and "sticks", rewards and punishments, are thus the most important tools of administrative guidance.

However, administrative guidance is not usually a one-way street, with the ministry unilaterally designing all the rules. Precisely because administrative guidance is extralegal, ministry officials have to ensure that the regulation garners a sufficient amount of industry support to be meaningful. The process of designing guidance therefore often entails sending a draft of a new rule to the trade association concerned, whereafter the presidents of the leading companies discuss the proposal and may suggest modifications. The association then reports the presidents' decision to the ministry.[6] In this sense, administrative guidance often emerges out of public–private discussions between bureaucrats and trade associations.

Yet, the oil cartel conviction was a first harbinger of the shift away from administrative guidance. Three major currents combined to diminish governmental sway over industry in the 1980s: (1) the "carrots" of administrative guidance became less appealing to industry; i.e., firms became less interested in what the government had to offer; (2) the "sticks" of administrative guidance were undermined by the opening and partial deregulation of financial and other markets; i.e., government lost some of its extralegal leverage over firms; and (3) the shift in industrial focus with the emergence of information technologies left the regulators in a futile search for new policies for the unfamiliar strategic sectors.

The primary "carrots", or rewards, that ministries used to induce companies to implement industrial policies in the postwar period came in two forms: (a) access to and allocation of imported or otherwise scarce raw materials; and (b) opening of new business opportunities through such means as granting licenses, subjecting product innovation and new strategies to approval, furnishing low interest loans through public financial institutions, or facilitating mergers. The allocation of raw materials and foreign technology worked well until 1965, when the revision of the Foreign Investment Law diminished MITI's control over foreign reserve allocation. The revision of the Foreign Exchange and Trade Law in 1980 further curtailed MITI's command over trade flows, and the 1998 revision completely abolished all trade controls. No longer could MITI reward cooperative firms through allocation of scarce raw material imports. In addition, in the late 1980s leading companies in some strategic industries (automobiles, electric machinery and electronics) began to turn the tables on their regulators and threatened them with a "hollowing out" (*kūdōka*) of Japanese industry by shifting more of their operations abroad. This threat overturned the power structure in the regulation of Japan's internationally competitive industries. Rather than coercing the leading firms, the ministries then tried to appease them by transferring regulatory decisions to their associations.

Second, changes in financial markets in the 1980s seriously undercut the ministries' ability to punish manufacturing firms and banks that resisted administrative guidance. As manufacturing firms became more able to raise funds abroad, the government's threat of punishing mavericks by blocking access to loans became meaningless. With the development of the bond and stock markets, firms became less dependent on banks for financing, so that banking

---

[6] Interview, Japan Securities Dealers' Association, summer 1995; the notion of discussing administrative guidance prior to its issuance was confirmed by all trade associations interviewed. When administrative guidance is carried out vis-à-vis single firms, for instance in cases of government-orchestrated mergers, the trade association may not be involved or may be a passive observer.

regulation no longer translated into manufacturing guidance.[7] For the banks, on the other hand, deregulation forced the difficult choice of whether to introduce strict monitoring and risk evaluation techniques or to rely on the implicit bailout contract that they had held with the Ministry of Finance (MOF) during the postwar period. Most banks paid lip service to the former, yet opted to rely on MOF and continued to furnish loans without thorough risk assessment. In addition, virtually all banks began to invest their surpluses in risky real estate ventures during the stock market bubble of 1987–91. When the bubble burst in the early 1990s, the banks could not retrieve major portions of their loans, which were enmeshed in real estate pyramid schemes. In 1995 and 1997, MOF had no choice but to let even major banks fail. By reneging on the bailout promise, MOF undermined the *quid pro quo* mechanism of administrative guidance and thus destroyed the "carrot-and-stick" logic in banking. Therefore, the liberalization of trade rules and access to financial markets in the 1980s undermined government guidance of both the manufacturing and the financial sectors.

Third, the change in industrial structure beginning in the mid-1980s rendered ministerial guidance of corporate strategies largely ineffective. Why exactly MITI and the other regulating industries could not find recipes for the newly emerging industries such as information technology, telecommunication, or biotechnology is likely to be the subject of future debate. One reason may be that the increasing technological complexity in these new sectors has forced government officials to rely on the knowledge of the regulatees and thus deprived them of the ability to reach independent evaluations of the regulatory demands. Regulators therefore have become increasingly dependent on industry opinion on these matters. Another constraining factor lay in the difficulty of managing innovation in general, and newly emerging innovative industries in particular. While Japanese industries could excel during the high-growth period by designing smart applications for technologies invented elsewhere, the accomplishment of the technological "catch-up" now called for new methods in R&D and management of human resources. Related to this, advances in technology also blurred the regulatory turf of the various ministries, such as witnessed in the "telecommunications war" fought between MITI and the Ministry of Post and Telecommunications over responsibility of telecommunication equipment manufacturers (Johnson 1989). Whatever the reasons, MITI and the other ministries were not effective in responding to the policy challenges of the new strategic industries in the 1980s, and lost their position as the proactive policy adviser to these industries. In the 1990s, most of the work left for MITI and the other industry-regulating ministries were the declining industries, and industrial policy was pushed out of the spotlight.

To be sure, Japanese bureaucrats have not been happy to give up power. The deregulation process of the 1980s and 1990s was widely criticized for being too

---

[7] See Zysman (1983) for a comparative analysis of how "credit-based systems" like Japan's are more amenable to industrial policy than equity-based systems, such as in the U.S.

slow, unfocused, and ineffective. Often, when a law or rule was scrapped in the name of deregulation with a big fanfare, a new set of licenses, approvals or other administrative regulation was quietly introduced in its place, in an effort by the government to entrench its regulatory control (Vogel, S. 1996). Yet, none of these efforts could obscure the reality that the government was not as powerful as it had been in the 1950s and 1960s in helping Japanese corporations enhance their international competitiveness. The competitive Japanese firms of the 1990s, such as Toyota and Honda, Sony and Matsushita, NEC and Toshiba, and Canon and Nikon, had thrived because of, among other factors, the government support (such as import restriction and export promotion) they received throughout the 1960s and 1970s. However, these firms continued to be competitive in the 1990s not so much thanks to government-initiated programs, but because of their own astute business strategies. Increasingly, their success has become attributable to their efforts to coordinate their strategies through self-regulation.

The process of deregulation and the recession of the 1990s have thus changed Japanese political economy. Following the strong state system, there is now a shift toward strong business leadership in regulatory matters. As argued above, the new cooperative system based on self-regulation has two prerequisites: well-organized trade associations and lenient treatment of self-regulation in antitrust enforcement. To see how these forces play out, we will turn to an analysis of these two prerequisites.

Japanese Antitrust Enforcement and Self-Regulation

While the Japanese Antimonopoly Law (AML, *Dokusen kinshi-hō*) of 1947 was originally drafted by the U.S. Occupational Forces as an improved version of U.S. antitrust laws, the Japanese government revised the law as early as 1953 and relaxed virtually all of its critical restrictions (see Chapter 3). Additionally, during the years of rapid economic growth and strong state guidance of industry in the 1950s and 1960s, the interpretation of the remaining antitrust restrictions was clearly overpowered by the growth agenda promoted by the industrial ministries. To support national economic growth, ministries encouraged the companies they were supposed to regulate to merge (to increase industry concentration) and to cooperate (to form cartels).

With the AML revision of 1953, Japan began to differentiate between "good" (legal) and "bad" (illegal) cartels.[8] In the U.S., any collusion or cartel activity is "*per se* illegal", meaning that the activity will be considered a violation of antitrust statutes whatever its impact on the competitive situation of the industry concerned (Greer 1993). In contrast, in Japan two broad categories of cartels are deemed legal. The first category consists of policy-induced cartels, i.e., cartels

---

[8] In Japanese, a differentiation is made between *karuteru* (meaning "good", legal cartels) and *yami karuteru* (lit.: "shadow cartels", meaning illegal cartels).

designated and encouraged by the cognizant ministry. Such cartels can be exempted from the antitrust law because they are deemed beneficial for the economy.[9] The second category consists of cartels that, even if not specifically exempted from the AML, might be legal if they are considered to be in the public interest. According to Section 2(6) of the AML, collaboration among business-men to restrict markets constitutes an "unreasonable restraint of trade" (i.e., a cartel) if it is "contrary to the public interest".[10] This means that a cartel may be legal if it does not restrain competition substantially, or if it does so without hurting the public interest. The ambiguity of this language is compounded by the fact that "public interest" is not clearly defined. In various battles between MITI and the JFTC (Japan's Fair Trade Commission), the term "public interest" has come to include the interests of consumers, producers, and government alike. This ambiguity has allowed the government to adopt a utilitarian approach to antitrust enforcement throughout the postwar period: when the government has viewed it necessary to achieve a certain economic policy goal, such as steep economic growth in the 1950s and 1960s, it has tried to encourage cartels to speed up the growth process. However, if firms cooperate in a way that obstructs a specific government policy goal, or if a cartel harms an industry considered important for achieving growth, this can be considered counter to the public interest and companies can be prosecuted. In Japan's environment of "situational regulation", antitrust policy has played an integral role in supporting the nation's developmental policies.

Some argue that this situation has begun to change in the 1990s (e.g., First 1995, Iyori 1995). While MITI is becoming weaker in terms of guiding certain industries, the JFTC has allegedly become more independent from political pressures not to prosecute certain sectors of the economy. Officials at the JFTC claim that the "public interest" clause has become irrelevant, because cartels are now generally considered illegal.[11] However, antitrust authorities in any country are subject to political pressure, and in Japan many activities that might be considered collusive elsewhere continue to be tolerated. For instance, so-called "unfair trade practices" such as boycotts or exclusive trade relationships, many of which are the basic tools of self-regulation, are typically not prosecuted strid-ently. Neither is there convincing evidence that the JFTC has indeed increased

---

[9] Exemptions from the AML usually require special legislation, such as that for small- and medium-sized industries or the "depressed industries laws" of the 1970s and 1980s. Most studies of cartels in postwar Japan are concerned with these legalized "recession" and "rationalization" cartels; see Chapter 3 for details and literature.

[10] The text of Section 2(6) is as follows: "The term 'unreasonable restraint of trade' as used in this Act shall mean such business activities, by which any entrepreneur, by contract, agreement or any other concerted actions, irrespective if its names, with other entrepreneurs, mutually restrict or conduct their business activities in such a manner as to fix, maintain, or increase prices, or to limit production, technology, products, facilities, or customers or suppliers, thereby causing, contrary to the public interest, a substantial restraint of competition in any particular field of trade." See Chapter 3 for background, and Chapter 5 for current applications. Iyori/Uesugi (1994: 74–5), Iyori (1995: 79–80), and Kawagoe (1997: 76–7) offer legal interpretations of this Section.

[11] Interviews with the JFTC and with one JFTC adviser, 1995 and 1997, Tokyo.

its enforcement activities in the 1990s (as detailed in Chapter 5). Self-regulation is a common practice.

Trade Associations within the Institutions of Japan's Political Economy

Trade associations lead the self-regulation that takes center stage in Japan's cooperative system. In the U.S., strict antitrust rules circumscribe association activities very narrowly, and lawyers are typically present at all meetings. In contrast, Japanese trade associations not only have a long history of facilitating forms of information exchange that would be outlawed in many other countries, but have been actively encouraged by the government to foster cooperation among firms. Therefore, companies that want to engage in self-regulation do so through their trade association, which is the easiest and most obvious forum for any interaction among competing firms.

During the postwar period of rapid growth, the Japanese system was structured to support frequent exchange of information among industry. Government was usually participating in this flow of information both informally and through several institutionalized mechanisms, such as standing deliberation councils or frequent transfer of personnel. The underlying notion was to ensure informal involvement of all concerned interests before reaching policy decisions. Given this concept, it is not surprising that as the power of the government bureaucracy began to wane in the 1980s, companies assumed the task of maintaining and directing this system of information exchange. While the institutions of Japan's postwar political economy—the councils and the personnel exchange—still remain in place today, their functions have gradually shifted from state-guided to self-directed activities. This is especially true for trade associations. During the strong state years, trade associations were one of several central institutions directing the flow of information, and the self-regulatory function of trade associations was subordinate to their information-exchange function. In contrast, in the new cooperative system, self-regulation has become the core function of trade associations, while the various mechanisms of information exchange remain important complements to self-regulation.

To understand fully the impact of the shift toward self-regulation, it is helpful to review briefly three primary institutions of information exchange in Japan's political economy: the deliberation councils, the dispatching of employees, and the hiring of former government officials into the private sector. Deliberation councils (*shingikai*) are advisory groups established by a ministry to discuss and formulate a policy position on a current issue facing the bureaucracy. In 1995, Japan had a total of 215 standing councils, with a varying but large number of subcommittees and sub-subcommittees. The members of a council are chosen by the ministry, and there has been criticism that the *shingikai* system simply serves to co-opt the public and government policy critics. That is, critics are sometimes invited so that they become part of the policymaking process and thereby are less likely to speak out against the policy after it has been formally adopted. A less cynical assessment of *shingikai* sees them as the one institution that allows industry representatives, the media, and occasionally the public at large to participate in the policymaking process (cf. Tōyō Keizai 1995, Schwartz 1993, 1998, Harari 1988). As data analysis in Chapter 2 will show, industry representatives are typically represented in the *shingikai* and can thus directly influence government policies. Trade associations also regularly dispatch representatives to almost all *shingikai* to ensure the associations' influence on the decision-making process.

A second formalized mechanism of information exchange through personnel movements is the *shukkō* system, i.e., secondment of company employees into a government agency or a trade association for a two-year term. *Shukkō* can occur early in a career, when an employee is sent to participate in a ministry's in-house education program for its officials, or at higher levels. For example, many companies regularly send employees to work for one of the relevant trade associations, where the employees take over staff functions. They conduct industry analyses, compile data on all companies, organize meetings, and participate in those association committees that consist of firm representatives of their rank (see Chapter 2). Regular staff *shukkō* from the various companies are expected to get to know each other during their stint at the association, so that they have a contact in the other companies whenever they need one in their future careers.

The third mechanism that ties trade associations, corporations and ministries together is the "Old Boy network" based on the process of *amakudari* ("descent from heaven"). In the Japanese system, career bureaucrats retire relatively early, at around age 55, and then move on to take jobs in other government agencies, public corporations, or trade associations. After a two-year waiting period, many ex-bureaucrats assume positions in private companies. By casting a net of retired government officials over the private sector, the *amakudari* process ensures two primary objectives: first, a smooth flow of information among firms and between firms and ministries; and second, a two-way feedback mechanism through which the "Old Boys" can advise a company on the government's views, and inform the government of industry's desired corporate strategies.[12]

Trade associations operate at the center of this system of information exchange. Representing their respective industries, associations negotiate with the regulating ministry, which in turn uses the associations to disseminate administrative information and administrative guidance, discuss future policies, organize joint research, or design new international trade strategies. At the same

---

[12] Japan analysts remain divided as to whether the *amakudari* bureaucrats control and regulate the company, whether they simply offer their expertise to the company, or whether they are captured rent-seekers who, rather than strictly regulating their industries, seek to complement their lifetime income. Whatever the motivation in individual cases, one underlying effect of the widespread OB network is an increased exchange of information between ministries and their regulated industries that replaces more formal mechanisms of process regulation. See, e.g., Johnson (1974), Calder (1989), Schaede (1995).

time, associations contribute to politicians' campaigns, so that the industry can lobby Diet members effectively in case it disagrees with the bureaucrats' position. Moreover, the association is the chief location for the intra-industry exchange of information. Customarily, the directors (i.e., presidents of the leading member firms) meet monthly, and almost every association has a large number of committees, with numerous subcommittees, in which middle and lower level managers hold regular meetings. The staff on secondment (*shukkō*) from the association's member firms further increase the flow of information among companies. Moreover, many trade associations hire former bureaucrat "Old Boys" (OBs) on a long-term basis, almost invariably from the regulating ministry. Associations also help to increase the general flow of information among firms within an industry: they perform marketing functions for the industry (e.g., trade shows); sometimes they provide financing for their members; they conduct seminars and courses; they provide guidance on management; and they hold end of the year parties to increase friendship among member firms (see Chapter 2).

The *shingikai* and regular association meetings, the *shukkō* stints, and the *amakudari* officials in private companies combine to create a system of constant inter-firm/government interaction. The regular exchange of information in this system facilitates cooperation among Japanese firms, and between the firms and the government. These institutions have assured corporate influence on the regulatory process not seen in other industrialized countries. Thus, even under strong state guidance during rapid growth, the formulation and implementation of regulation were not unilateral processes. And now, with the waning state role, industries are making more decisions by and for themselves. The institutions of tight government–business relationships that used to assure business influence on the regulators' decision-making now serve increasingly to keep the government informed of industry self-regulation.

1.2. Paradigms for Studying Trade Associations and Self-Regulation

While many theories help explain partially what trade associations do, no one body of theory covers the complete spectrum of activities that result in self-regulation. An interdisciplinary approach that brings together insights from economics, political science, organizational sociology, law, and management is thus needed. Insights from the economics of industrial organization and game theory reveal how trade associations overcome collective action problems in self-regulation. The concept of "private interest government", developed in political sociology, clarifies the differences between delegated regulation and autonomous self-regulation. Recent advances in legal studies guide the analysis of Japan's antitrust system as well as of structural and normative issues related with self-regulation. And finally, insights developed in the strategy and management literature suggest what the ramifications of self-regulation might be for corporate strategy and the competitiveness of Japanese firms. This section briefly summarizes the basics of these different bodies of theory to lay the groundwork for the analysis of self-regulation and the empirical studies conducted in this book.

Economics: Self-Regulation and the Theory of Cartels

One important issue regarding the shift toward increasing self-regulation is how companies structure their agreements, and how these agreements can be stable over time, especially without the government as a "referee" to structure bargaining situations. While cartels are structurally different from self-regulation, theories of collusion in micro-economics and game theory, as well as insights from the economics of industrial organization, nevertheless help us understand better under what economic conditions self-regulation is most likely to occur, and when it is likely to be successful.

In game-theoretic terms, firms face problems in cooperating due to what is called the "prisoners' dilemma". This "dilemma" refers to a situation where, for example, two companies can choose to cooperate or to compete. If one company decides to cooperate and give up valuable information, it is prone to being exploited by the other. Without some initial mutual exchange to overcome this vulnerability, no cooperation will occur.[13] Game theory has identified three primary ways to attain cooperative outcomes in the face of a "prisoners' dilemma" situation. First, the companies could form a legally enforceable agreement against exploitation that covers all contingencies; however, this is usually not feasible. Second, the companies can identify a mediator that monitors compliance by all parties. Examples of such an arrangement are the recession cartels or joint R&D consortia that used to be encouraged by the Japanese

---

[13] The original explanation of this situation uses as an example two prison inmates who can choose either to cooperate (i.e., deny any misdeed) or cheat (fink) on the other. They face the following pay-off matrix:

		Prisoner A	
		cooperate	cheat
Prisoner B	cooperate	4, 4	−3, 7
	cheat	7, −3	0, 0

If both cooperate and deny any wrongdoing, they both get free (in this matrix, each gets a payoff of 4); if one cooperates and the other cheats, the cheater gets free with a reward, while the cooperator gets punished with a long-term prison stay; and if both cheat, both stay in prison for a while. While both would be better off cooperating, unless they are allowed to ensure that neither will cheat, both will settle for the medium-term prison stay. The so-called Nash Equilibrium i.e., the dominant strategy that trumps all other courses of actions, is for both to cheat. See McMillan (1992) and Kreps (1990) for introductory explanations; Axelrod (1984) for the logic of cooperation through repeated interaction.

government. Finally, cooperation is possible if companies engage in "repeated games". This means that companies are more willing to cooperate if they expect to have a long-term trade relationship with repeated transactions. With long-term expectations, neither side is likely to take short-term advantage because the other side can threaten reciprocal action. Relating this logic to Japanese trade associations, it becomes obvious how associations can sustain self-regulation by tying various corporate agreements into a long-term institution that pursues multiple functions.

Two conditions must be fulfilled for cooperative equilibria to occur. First, the companies must be quite sure that they will interact repeatedly in the future. Second, the stakes (i.e., the expected payoffs or outcomes) must be constant over time; if the stakes increase suddenly and dramatically, the short-term gain of cheating may outweigh the benefits of the long-term relationship. As long as the future relations matter enough, any outcome better than any player's worst "punishment" can be obtained. That is, for agreements to be stable, the benefits of a long-term cartel must outweigh the benefits of a short-run attack on the competitor to take over control of the market. A firm's short-run interest in competing aggressively is balanced by its long-term interest in survival: if the other firms retaliate, the cartel breaker may be worse off than if he had continued to collude.[14]

Besides high stakes, two additional conditions help sustain collusion: participants must have a propensity to cooperate, and the economic situation and industry structure must be supportive. "Propensity to cooperate" simply refers to how well people in the industry know each other and whether there is a willingness to interact on both sides. Company and industry history as well as personalities loom large here. For instance, most oligopolies that form long-term explicit or implicit cartels have a long history of amicable dealings with each other.[15] "Supportive economic conditions and industry structure" relate to the economics of industrial organization. Four primary aspects are worth noting here: (a) the number of firms (i.e., how easy it is to reach an agreement in the group); (b) entry barriers (i.e., how easy it is to keep potential cartel breakers out); (c) industry characteristics (i.e., whether product characteristics support cartels); and (d) the "stake structure" and business cycles. While the first three conditions contribute to the inherent stability of a cartel, the last affects its

---

[14] This insight is referred to as the "Folk Theorem", so called because the insight is so intuitive that no one wanted to take credit for it. "Punishment", i.e. the max-min payoffs in the previous footnote, again refers to the inmates: any outcome that is better than the long-term prison stay can be accomplished if the future matters sufficiently to both. If both inmates want to live a happy life together after their punishment, any outcome that is better than the longest prison term is a preferred outcome. They are therefore likely to cooperate. For a formal exposition, see Tirole (1988: 245–7).

[15] "Implicit" (tacit) collusion refers to cartel agreements that are not based on a specific "contract", but function because of the threat of all players to revert to competition whenever a single firm does not cooperate. "Explicit collusion", in contrast, is based on an intra-firm agreement which specifies penalties for cartel breakers. While both are illegal in most countries, the latter is usually easier to prosecute and therefore is more likely to trigger investigations by antitrust authorities.

viability over time. For instance, research on cartels during boom and recession periods has revealed that cartel agreements are more likely to occur during periods of economic downturn (see Chapter 5).

One critical issue in reaching cooperative agreements that the "prisoners' dilemma" logic does not explain, however, is how the parties will divide the pieces of the pie. This division of the pie necessitates frequent meetings, a forum for negotiation, and some basic rules on how the negotiations will be carried out (McMillan 1991, McAffee/McMillan 1992). This is where trade associations become important in Japan's system of self-regulation. By structuring the association in particular ways, the member firms can predetermine the rules for the division of the pie. Thus, providing a setting for these negotiations for self-regulation and helping their smooth implementation is one of the central roles of trade associations in Japan.

Finally, even after an agreement has been reached and the rules have been established, there is still the issue of monitoring and enforcement. This is particularly problematic in industries where manufacturers sell to a few big buyers, so that they make individual deals rather than quoting explicit, generic prices. In Japan, this is very common under the system of "after-sales price adjustment" (*atogime seido*) in intermediate products, where the price between the manufacturers and the wholesalers is established only after the product has reached the end user (see Chapter 4). Because price behavior can be observed only with a lag, a maverick can get away with undercutting the cartel price for quite a while, which makes it more tempting to cheat (Stigler 1964). To overcome the problem of sustaining cooperative agreements in adverse situations, the cooperating firms can do a number of things, including:

1. meet in their trade association to collect and publish information on all transactions and prices and allow members to check on each others' price quotations; if the collusion is explicit, they may also require members to give advance notice to the association of price changes;
2. establish a system of retail price maintenance on wholesalers and retailers, i.e., a system in which the manufacturers determine the product's ultimate retail price, to enforce the agreement through the distribution system and facilitate the monitoring of the manufacturers' pricing behavior (Telser 1960; as we will see in Chapter 4, this is exactly what many Japanese industries do to enforce self-regulation); or
3. in industries that sell many different products, e.g., in specialized retailing such as department stores, require the cartel members to establish a uniform profit margin on all products, again with the goal of facilitating the monitoring of the retailers' pricing strategies (cf. Tirole 1988: 241).

In sum, the combined application of game theory and the economics of industrial organization suggest that the formation of a successful cooperation is highly dependent on the structure of the industry and the future relationship between firms. In an industry dominated by a few large firms, with high barriers to entry and low imports, successful cooperation is more likely if companies are certain of future dealings and compliance can be easily monitored. Mature and stable industries are more likely to fulfil these conditions than either young growth industries (which attract much new entry) or declining industries (which face an endpoint of the game). Therefore, when analyzing the economic functions and possible collusive activities of Japanese trade associations, one needs to consider both the organizational characteristics of the industry and the internal forces within the industry that shape the incentives and relations of the competing firms.

Political Science/Sociology: Private Interest Government

As interest groups, trade associations have long received attention in the fields of political science and sociology, typically under the heading of "corporatism". Early studies of corporatism date back to the beginning of this century (see Almond 1990 for a review). While primarily empirical, these early studies tried to explain business cooperation and its effects on the political economy of a country. In the 1950s, a pluralist approach added more analytical structure to interest group research. This approach sees associations as autonomous, competitive pressure groups with fluid borderlines, resulting from and reflecting societal movements. Groupings vary with issues and thus cooperation is limited in time and does not develop into consistent alliances with iteration.

The various "shocks" of the 1970s (the end of Bretton Woods, the phenomenon of stagflation, the oil crisis, etc.) triggered further advances in the study of interest groups. For instance, the introduction of "concerted action" after the 1967 economic crisis in the Federal Republic of Germany gave trade unions and trade associations the right to negotiate directly with the Chancellor during annual wage discussions. The new role of interest groups in policy formation led to a refinement of the concept of corporatism, which now focused on the interaction of the major interest groups, including politicians and the bureaucracy, in a bargaining process over major policy issues. Schmitter (1979: 13) defines corporatism as

a system of interest representation in which the constituent units are organized into a limited number of singular, compulsory, non-competitive, hierarchically ordered, and functionally differentiated categories, recognized or licensed by the state, and granted a deliberate representational monopoly within their respective categories in exchange for observing certain controls on their selection of leaders and articulation of demands and supports.

In the corporatist model, trade associations are seen as one central institution, located at the interface of government and business. The most important concept that resulted from the corporatist approach is that of "private interest governments", or PIGs. The underlying notion is that of "unburdening of the state"

(*Staatsentlastung*), a widely used term in Germany in the 1970s when increasing government expenditures and deficits in maturing social welfare programs led many to believe that the role of the state had to be curtailed. To shift part of its burden to the private sector, the state gave some interest groups, especially labor unions and trade associations, a monopoly right of representation for their particular industry and made membership in the organization compulsory to ensure full implementation of the rules. In exchange for allowing a certain degree of state control over their activities, these PIGs received state recognition, so that their activities had official standing (Berger 1981, Streeck 1994, Streeck/Schmitter 1985, Czada 1994).[16]

The important difference between the PIG concept and that of self-regulation in Japan lies in the degree of delegation of regulatory authority and state recognition of association activities: self-regulation is broader than the PIG concept in that it encompasses both industry regulation delegated by the state to an association and self-regulation completely independent from the state. The PIG concept restricts analysis to activities by associations that are clearly delegated by the state so that the private sector overtakes a state task. Self-regulation, in contrast, means that trade associations take over regulatory functions and powers by either going beyond what is delegated, or by acting without any delegation or authorization.

Legal Studies: Self-Regulation as a Dominant Regulatory System

While there has long been recognition in legal studies of the fact that industries often self-regulate and occasionally collude, utilizing self-regulation to complement state regulation has recently been proposed as an alternative government approach to regulation. Ayres and Braithwaite (1992) argue that the 1990s mark an era not so much of deregulation but of "regulatory flux". According to these authors, the solution to this situation of flux is to transfer more regulatory powers to the regulatees themselves. Based on the notion that sound policy analysis begins with an understanding of private regulation and how it interacts with government regulation, Ayres and Braithwaite extend the notion of "private interest government" to promote a regulatory system in which the government delegates as much rule-making as possible to the regulatees. In addition, the government enforces adherence to basic guidelines primarily through a tit-for-tat strategy of mixing punishment and persuasion, rather than through non-discretionary punishment strictly by the books. In instances where complete self-regulation is at odds with overall government strategies, they propose a compromise between strictly private and entirely public regulation in the form

---

[16] An example of a PIG in Germany is the Chamber of Commerce, which runs, among others, the general schools that apprentices attend during their two-year apprenticeship programs. All schools in Germany are public, except for these apprenticeship schools. The schools are, however, under government supervision, and in turn the state recognizes the degrees these schools award.

of "enforced self-regulation". In "enforced self-regulation", the government ratifies the rules that industries have written and acts as a "fire department" ready to intervene should an industry prove unable to self-enforce its own rules. The resulting mixed regulatory system is best described as a pyramid of enforcement strategies, with "command regulation" and non-discretionary punishment at the top, and complete self-regulation at the bottom. In between is a large area of delegated self-regulation with the government as the ultimate enforcement agent.

The notion of self-regulation of individual markets has been proposed before, and in some instances even implemented. For instance, stock exchanges—which are run by associations of stock brokers—are by law authorized to regulate themselves in many countries, including the U.S. and Japan. Likewise, the legal and the accounting professions are guided by their own rules (e.g., Willmott 1985).[17] However, in all of these examples there is still an initial delegation of regulatory powers from the state to the regulated group, as suggested in the "private interest government" concept. Likewise, while Ayres and Braithwaite suggest that pure self-regulation ought to take over a larger share of the regulatory market, they do not develop a precise outline of that system.

Japan offers an example of how a regulatory system with a large portion of self-regulation and private enforcement looks. As the discussion of Japan's antitrust policies in the postwar period in Chapters 3 through 5 will show, the Japanese interpretation of antitrust poses much less of a legal problem for pure self-regulation than is the case in the Anglo-Saxon legal systems. To allow for pure self-regulation without delegation in the Anglo-Saxon system requires a tremendously strong belief in market forces: namely that, if on their own, companies will produce optimal regulatory outcomes due to competition. While Japan's antitrust system is very different from the one envisioned by Ayres/Braithwaite, the Japanese case of self-regulation adds empirical evidence of feasibility for the new legal concept of self-regulation.

Management: Self-Regulation and Competitiveness

The study of self-regulation by trade associations also benefits from insights provided by organization theory and management strategy. One major reason why Japanese companies may join trade associations and actively participate in self-regulation is that there is a tradition of cooperation and self-regulation in Japan, and this tradition has been further entrenched by the incentives set by industrial policy in the postwar period. Inertia, that is, a reluctance to change from something that has worked in the past to something new that entails uncertainty, is a dominant characteristic of organizations (e.g., Tushman/O'Reilly 1997, Pfeffer 1978). Within organizational behavior, two main schools of thought

---

[17] The concept of "privatized regulation" in Japan will be discussed below.

explain inertia: organizational ecology and institutional theory. A decade's research on organizational ecology demonstrates how inertial organizations are, with individual organizations typically being unable to adapt to significant environmental shifts (e.g., Hannan/Freeman 1989, Hannan/Carroll 1992). Conducted on a wide variety of types of organization, this research has also shown that, under some circumstances, organizations are mutualistic—helping each other rather than being competitive—and that mutualism is associated with survival (Barnett/Carroll 1987). A separate line of research on institutional theory documents how organizations often imitate each other, adopting similar structures and processes (DiMaggio/Powell 1983, Scott 1995). Zucker (1983: 5) notes that "institutionalization operates to produce common understandings about what is appropriate and, fundamentally, meaningful behavior". Thus, organizations often implicitly or explicitly cooperate in determining the form and nature of the interactions that, once determined, can be stable over long periods, even in the face of significant exogenous change. For Japan's trade associations, this implies that exogenous shocks, such as deregulation, will not necessarily cause change in cooperative behavior. What has worked well in the past will likely be continued into the future.

Studies in corporate strategy help address the issue of what kinds of strategic benefit accrue for an individual firm from membership in a trade association. As we will see in Chapter 2, association membership in Japan is more expensive than in the U.S., and meetings occur in large numbers at high frequencies. Yet, while membership is costly, most large Japanese companies are members in several associations. One explanation is suggested by the literature on information and knowledge transfer. Increasing the frequency of exchange can be beneficial because it can reduce friction and noise in sending and receiving information. Just as markets work better with a free flow of information, companies may operate more efficiently the less friction or noise in the information they receive (Nonaka/Takeuchi 1995). As markets become more complex, fast, and noisy, owing to forces such as internationalization, product differentiation, and technological change, even small reductions of noise can translate into substantial advantage. Yet, the more complex markets become, the more difficult it gets to convey and receive information. Ashby's Law of Requisite Variety tells us that to decipher a message, the receiver needs to have the same amount of complexity as the message (Ashby 1956, Weick 1969). Therefore, the more extensive and regular the information they receive, the more companies may benefit.

Cooperation among firms within one industry, and across industries, helps reduce noise and make information exchange regular. The management literature suggests that, to the extent that such exchanges result in a coordination of business strategies and activities, the formal and informal mechanisms of information exchange afford competitive advantage to those Japanese firms that actively participate in associations (Galbraith 1973). Specifically, competitive advantage might result from two separate factors. First, absent any intentional collusion, simply knowing details about the state of the domestic industry will give companies an advantage over firms that do not know as much about their competitors. Likewise, cost savings through joint market research can easily translate into international competitive advantage. Second, if information exchange results in price fixing or other collusive agreements, Japanese firms can engage in a "sanctuary" strategy (Baron 1995, 1997): by using their home market to make above-normal profits through collusion, Japanese firms can undercut competitors in foreign markets.

Japanese Studies: Self-Regulation and Trade Associations

In spite of their long and important history, Japanese trade associations remain understudied. While there are a number of case studies on individual industries, there is a surprising lack of an encompassing, systematic analysis of their activities (see, for instance, Samuels 1987 on energy; Friedman 1988 on machine tools; Saxonhouse 1977, Young 1991, and Fletcher 1996 on cotton spinning; Tilton 1996 on basic materials; Uriu 1996 on declining industries; Noble 1998 on steel). Lynn/McKeown's (1988) comparative study on U.S. and Japanese trade associations is the only English-language overview study concerned with the role of trade associations in the Japanese political economy. In Japanese, Muramatsu et al. (1986) and Tsujinaka (1988) have studied the influence of interest groups on Japan's policymaking processes. However, they treat trade associations as only one of many interest groups and do not analyze them *per se*.

In Japan legal studies, concepts of business empowerment and a strong role of industry in the regulatory system have been suggested by several scholars. For instance, Haley (1991b) argues that the regulatory function of industry is strong simply because the bureaucracy lacks enforcement power and thus will give in to business demands in its formulation of rules. The notion of self-regulation was first specifically raised in Japanese studies by Upham (1993, 1996) who observed patterns of "privatized regulation". Upham describes a process in Japan's regulatory system that allows businesses to shape the interpretation of laws and regulations through private implementation. Outstanding examples where the regulating ministries delegated allocation of licenses, approvals and other kinds of regulations to competing companies are the Large-Scale Retail Store Law (which allows local shopkeepers to vote on admitting a new store in the neighborhood) and television broadcast licensing (where competitors divided the licenses among themselves). In analyzing this process, Upham is primarily concerned with the regulatory environment and stresses the delegation of regulatory power to regulated industries. In his view, privatized regulation depends on ministerial power to delegate, and is therefore bound to decline together with strong state guidance. In a way, the notion of "privatized regulation" is one variant of the "private interest government" concept: the government delegates regulatory powers to the affected industry that takes over the design and implementation of the regulation. According to Upham (1996), delegation will decrease with bureaucratic powers and, presumably, a regulatory system will eventually be formed in which the legal statute and court procedures will fill the void created by the decline in regulatory discretion by both ministries and industries.

In contrast to Upham's view, the concept of self-regulation does not rest on the notion of delegation of regulatory powers, but rather of their replacement. As the developmental state regime abates, industry self-regulation increases. Rather than the legal statutes and the courts, rules designed by trade associations shape the Japanese marketplace. To argue this point, this book will provide evidence for both the behavior of trade associations and the logic of Japanese antitrust enforcement. Taken together, these two blocks of evidence support the notion that industry, rather than the legislative branch within Japan's government, has assumed regulatory control.

In a different approach, Tilton (1996) argues that all cartels in Japan, in particular those in the basic materials industries, are tools of public policy because they have the tacit blessing of the government and fulfil public policy goals by affording protection to the colluding companies. Thus, Tilton does not differentiate between regulation delegated by the government (i.e., "private interest government") and self-regulation. This is similar to Johnson's (1982: 310) definition of "self-control" as a state licensing of private companies to achieve developmental goals. However, by assuming that all cartels have state authorization, these authors have deliberately excluded from their analyses any purely private initiative to cooperate or to collude. The critical difference of the interpretation presented in this study is that self-regulation is considered as an autonomous process, independent of the government's public policy goals. This adds a dimension to Japan's political economy that has until now been ignored: the notion that private business may regulate its own markets without delegation or authorization, thus shaping the market rules according to its own needs.

Finally, this study proposes that deregulation has contributed greatly to the marked increase in self-regulation in the 1990s. Vogel S. (1996) has convincingly argued that deregulation has proceeded neither as fast nor as effectively in Japan as it may seem on paper, because many previously formal rules were replaced by new informal entry regulation in the form of licenses and other approvals still controlled by the cognizant ministry. Yet, this does not contradict the observation of an increase in self-regulation. There is a crucial difference between entry regulation and process regulation: the former refers to permits allowing businesses to enter an industry, while the latter describes government oversight once firms have entered the industry. Vogel's argument refers to the former, while the increase in self-regulation pertains more prominently to the latter. Moreover, even re-regulation through permits and licenses necessitates more self-regulation, because whatever formal process regulation may have been included in the official laws is not replaced by new mechanisms of process regulation. Thus, the argument of increased self-regulation complements Vogel's study in that it explains what happens in a regulatory system that lacks process regulation when deregulation is attempted.

1.3. Structure of the Book

Given the many functions that trade associations perform, no single approach could offer all of the tools required to tell a coherent story of Japanese trade associations. This book therefore employs a dual approach of qualitative and quantitative analysis, whereby the qualitative analysis consists of two components, institutional and historical.

Chapter 2 introduces the general characteristics and functions of Japan's trade associations. How many trade associations are there, how big are these associations, how are they structured, and what, in general, do they do? Following this introduction to trade association activities, Chapters 3 through 5 provide the main evidence for the argument. Chapter 3 analyzes the relation between industrial policy and the propensity to cooperate among Japanese companies by reviewing the development of antitrust policy between 1947 and the 1980s. Under the paradigm of industrial policy geared toward increasing exports and "catching-up" with the industrialized Western countries, antitrust enforcement was pushed aside and many cartels were legalized. The chapter shows how the government's encouragement of cartel formations resulted in a widespread understanding in Japan of cooperation among competitors as a positive activity. Chapter 4 analyzes the legal doctrine of antitrust enforcement that developed during the period of rapid growth, and shows in detail how the Japanese antitrust system works. It becomes clear that both the structure of the law and the existing legal doctrine mean that self-regulation by trade associations is typically either not considered illegal, or prosecuted in extremely lenient ways.

Adding to this qualitative discussion of the legal situation, Chapter 5 presents data on the actual record of antitrust enforcement in Japan for the 50 years between 1948 and 1997 by analyzing all 1,007 formal cases that the JFTC prosecuted during this period, as well as an even larger number of so-called informal cases. A longitudinal study of all formal cases shows only a slow increase of JFTC activities over time. More importantly, the number of formal cases prosecuted by the JFTC is negatively correlated with the business cycle, i.e., it increases during recessions but decreases during booms. However, the full extent of self-regulation cannot meaningfully be measured by looking only at the "collusive" type of activities that are prosecuted. In fact, a much larger portion of self-regulation in Japan is not considered to be in violation of antitrust laws. To get a better understanding of this situation, the second part of Chapter 5 presents case study evidence of self-regulation in the 1990s to complement the analysis of JFTC cases. A picture emerges of how self-regulation is structured, how it is set up, and how remarkably widespread it is.

Chapter 6 looks into the internal characteristics of Japan's trade associations, connects their functional characteristics with their activities, and identifies those elements of industry structure that are most conducive to self-regulation in the Japanese context: product homogeneity and a rapid rate of technological change.

The analysis builds on a database containing 1,153 associations, with data on membership, budget, staff, etc. and also on industry characteristics (concentration, exports and imports, product type). A model is developed that shows how different organizational features of associations and structural characteristics of their industries are related to above-average levels of self-regulation. The analysis identifies predictors of self-regulation in both product characteristics and organizational patterns of Japanese trade associations, thus offering a set of tools with which to identify strong self-regulating associations.

Chapter 7 examines self-regulation and trade associations in Japanese economic and business history to underscore how trade associations have assumed an institutionalized and solid role in Japan's political economy. Beginning in the Middle Ages, and in particular through the Tokugawa period (1603–1868), trade associations were instrumental in designing and enforcing market rules and thus enabling trade and credit. The government at times tried to utilize associations for public policy purposes, but often left market regulation to the business. Over time, trade associations assumed a much more firmly established role in Japan than in other Asian countries. This institutionalized role of business helps explain the phenomenal success of postwar Japanese industry, and it also adds the key element in understanding why industrial policy worked. Chapter 8 concludes with a discussion of the stability of the cooperative system based on self-regulation in the medium run, the implications of the shift toward this system for the Japanese economy, and the implications for U.S.–Japan relations.

2

Japan's Trade Associations in the 1990s

'People of the same trade seldom meet together, even for merriment and diversion, but the conversation ends in a conspiracy against the public, or in some contrivance to raise prices. It is impossible indeed to prevent such meetings, by any law which either could be executed, or would be consistent with liberty and justice.'

(Adam Smith, *The Wealth of Nations*, 1776, Book 1, Chapter 10)

To understand fully why self-regulation is so important and how it is administered, it is necessary to take an in-depth look at the structure and function of Japan's trade associations. This chapter outlines how many trade associations there are in Japan, how large they are, how they are organized, and what they do. The Japanese Fair Trade Commission defines a trade association (*jigyōsha dantai*) as "a combination (or federation of combinations) of two or more firms that has as one of its principal purposes the furtherance of common business interests" (JFTC 1995: 7). The definition's focus on business interests excludes scientific societies, public service organizations, and religious organizations from this group.

Trade associations perform a variety of functions that can broadly be divided into three categories: (1) information exchange and administration; (2) political influence; and (3) participation in the regulatory process, including self-regulation. In performing the three categories of function, trade associations face a participatory dilemma related to size: the larger they are, the more effective they are likely to be in terms of political influence, but the less effectively they can arrange regulation or the exchange of strategic information. In other words, trade associations operate on a continuum between effective political lobbying through large size on the one end, and effective self-regulation in small-sized units on the other end (cf. Figure 2.1). Japanese industries have addressed this tradeoff between size and effectiveness by creating a pyramidal structure, with focused, small associations at the bottom for purposes of self-regulation and mutual aid, and umbrella or peak associations at the top for political interest representation (see Figure 2.2). In this way, different types of association perform different functions within the political economy. While other countries display similar hierarchies, in Japan these layers are much more pronounced and the smaller associations are more focused on narrowly defined industries.

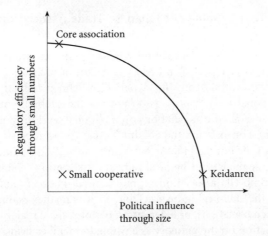

Figure 2.1. The Tradeoff between Size and Regulatory Efficiency

This chapter will begin by introducing a typology of Japanese trade associations and their legal and functional specifications. It will then look at three
broadly defined functional areas to analyze the internal organization of trade
associations and the processes of information exchange, political participation
and regulatory activities. It will become clear that self-regulation is predominantly the domain of the focused associations at the bottom of the hierarchy,
whereas political activities are primarily conducted by the larger umbrella organizations.

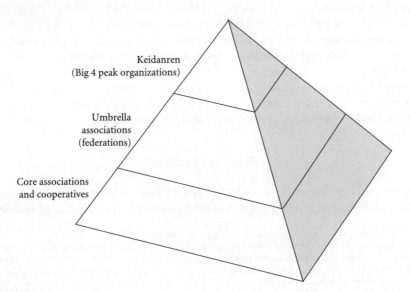

Figure 2.2. The Pyramid of Japanese Trade Associations

2.1. A Typology of Japanese Trade Associations

The first important distinction for understanding Japanese trade associations is the difference between peak (umbrella) and core associations. While a core association is the central group for a narrowly defined industry at either the national or regional level, a peak association is the umbrella organization, or federation, for several core associations on a national level or in a more broadly defined industry. For instance, the Sulphuric Acid Association of Japan (*Ryūsan kyōkai*) and the Calcium Carbide Association (*Kaabaido kōgyōkai*) are both core associations, while the Japan Chemical Industry Association (*Nihon kagaku kōgyō kyōkai*) is the umbrella association representing all national and regional core associations in the chemical industry. Table 2.1 lists further examples.

The umbrella associations, or federations, perform three major functions: they provide information on the industry as a whole to member firms, provide access to the ministries and facilitate "*o-tsukiai*"—the forming of relationships with executives from other parts of the industry.[1] A large company can be a member of both the core association and its umbrella. In highly diversified but interrelated industries, such as the chemical industry, large firms are on average members of ten to 12 associations; in more focused industries with no overarching federation, such as automobiles, this number decreases to one or two.

The second dimension for differentiating Japan's trade associations is the size of a group's member firms and the association's regional scope. Japanese industry is characterized by a so-called "dual structure" (*nijū kōzō*) in that only 1.4% of all corporations account for the production of roughly 50% of all manufactured goods and employ some 30% of the workforce, while the remaining 70% of the workforce works in small- and medium-sized enterprises. Reflecting this dual structure, Japanese trade associations are divided into associations dominated by large companies, and cooperatives (*kyōdō kumiai*) which consist exclusively of small- and medium-sized enterprises.[2] Geographically, associations can be either national or regional. Regional associations sometimes form intermediate umbrella associations that cover a larger region, and in such cases regional, intermediate umbrella associations are usually represented by a national umbrella association.

Legal Specifications

There are three different types of legal status for Japanese associations, which are somewhat abstruse but very important for regulatory purposes. First, an associa-

---

[1] Interview with an association representative, Tokyo, summer 1995.

[2] Agricultural cooperatives perform similar basic functions as those in the manufacturing and service industries, but in addition also provide mechanisms of joint machinery purchase and utilization, banking and financing, and distribution. The agricultural sector is so large, and different along so many dimensions, that it warrants a study of its own. In this book, agriculture is included in the analysis of industry case studies, but an examination of the functioning of cultural cooperatives is left for further study.

Table 2.1. Typology of Japanese Trade Associations

	Core association	Umbrella association	Cooperative	Peak cooperative	Other
Suffix in Japanese	*-kyōkai* *-kōgyōkai* *-kyōgikai* etc.	*-rengōkai* (sometimes *-kyōkai*)	*-kyōdō kumiai*	*-kumiai rengōkai*	Various
Definition	Central association for large companies in a narrowly defined industry	Intermediate peak or peak association for core associations, in a more broadly defined industry	Core association for small companies in a narrowly defined industry	Peak association for a group of cooperatives, in a more broadly defined industry	Regardless of industry; usually has a special purpose such as research
Examples	Japan Association of Steel Bridge Construction; Flat Glass Association; Beer Association; Japan Bicycle Manufacturers' Association; Japan Macaroni Association	All Japan General Contractors' Association; Japan Federation of Taxicab Associations; All Japan Business Hotel Association; Federation of Bankers' Associations	Nihon Ball Pen Cooperative; Hiroshima Needle Manufacturers' Cooperative; Kanto Plastic Manufacturers' Cooperative	Japan Stationery Industrial Association; All Japan Tatami Manufacturers' Association; Japan Federation of Photo Dealers Association; Federation of Japan Plastic Manufacturers' Cooperatives	Japan Fine Ceramics Center; Japan Mining Promotion Foundation; Kansai Electronic Development Center
Legal standing	May be voluntary or incorporated	May be voluntary or incorporated	Based on special law for small- and medium-sized companies; usually exempted from AML rules	Based on special law for small- and medium-sized companies; usually exempted from AML rules	May be based on a specific law that grants special treatment; often a foundation
Scope	May be national or regional	Usually national	Usually regional, but may be national	Usually national	National or regional

tion may be a "voluntary association" (*nin'i dantai*), in which case it is not a juridical person (i.e., it is not legally attributable and liable before the law, and therefore cannot own or rent a building, receive subsidies, etc.). Similar to the U.S., voluntary associations are quite independent from regulating agencies. While not required to disclose internal data, Japanese voluntary associations, like all other associations, have to notify the JFTC of their existence and organizational changes within 30 days.

Second, an association may assume full legal status, which requires registration and an "approval license" by the regulating ministry. Incorporated associations cannot be free-floating, but have to come under the jurisdiction of one ministry. For instance, MITI issues an annual approval license for JAMA, the Japan Automobile Manufacturers' Association. "Approved associations" are subdivided into so-called non-profit *shadan hōjin* (usually translated as "incorporated associations") and *zaidan hōjin* ("foundations"). The primary legal difference is that foundations are based on funds dedicated to a particular purpose, such as a joint R&D project, and members gather around that purpose. In contrast, incorporated associations represent a set of firms that share similar interests; there is no money at the time of establishment, but the association is financed through a constant income stream in the form of membership dues (for details, see Nagasawa 1989, 1996).

There are three major differences between an incorporated association and a voluntary association. First, an incorporated association must have bylaws or articles, delineating the group's purpose (including non-profit status), provisions for the appointment and removal of officers and directors, and requirements for membership. While voluntary associations may also have bylaws, for incorporated associations these bylaws are re-approved annually by the regulating ministry. Second, because only incorporated associations can receive subsidies, own a building or run a joint research facility, industries that want to engage in such ventures have to register with their regulating ministry. Finally, only incorporated, not-for-profit associations enjoy a tax-preferred status, so that dues are deductible. Thus, the benefits of being incorporated come at the cost of being regulated and monitored closely; the tradeoff lies in the association's desired degree of closeness to the regulator. Some associations deliberately forgo the tax exemption for freedom from a direct connection with the regulating ministry.

While all incorporated associations are closer to their regulators than are voluntary associations, there are differences among the *shadan hōjin* as to how tightly they are tied to the ministries. The degree of connectedness depends on why, when and by whom an association was established. During the postwar years, regulating ministries sometimes created new associations for policy purposes, such as in the emerging computer industry in the 1980s. But not all incorporated associations were founded by their regulators. Many have long histories as trade associations but changed to a non-profit status only in the postwar period for such purposes as to construct an association building.

According to one official, associations created by the ministry to meet a policy purpose tend to be very close to that ministry, and in 95% of all cases, their leading staff people include retired ministry officials. The number of such officials (the so-called OBs, Old Boys) employed by an association is one indicator of intimacy between an association and its regulating ministry. In contrast, associations established by private initiative have OBs among their staff in only about half of all cases (interview, Tokyo, summer 1995).

A third possible legal status for a trade association in Japan is that of a "cooperative" (*kyōdō kumiai*). Cooperatives can be based on Section 7(1) of the "Small- and Medium-Sized Enterprise Etc. Cooperative Law" (*Chūsho kigyō-tō kyōdō kumiai hō*) if they consist of small- and medium-sized companies only. As such they are exempted by the JFTC from the Antimonopoly Law (AML Section 24(1)), and except for flagrant price fixing, cooperatives cannot usually be pursued for antitrust violations. If a cooperative has members that exceed the legal limits of a "small- and medium-sized enterprise" (capital of less than ¥100 million and fewer than 300 employees), the JFTC decides whether the AML exemption remains valid on a case-by-case basis.[3]

By combining the differences in legal standing and "peak" versus "core" versus "cooperative", we can group Japanese associations into five categories (cf. Table 2.1). The first and most basic type are the core associations for large companies in narrowly defined industries. In Japanese, these usually carry the suffix *kyōkai*, *kyōgikai* or *kōgyōkai*, although at least five alternative terms are occasionally applied. Examples include the Electronic Industries Association of Japan, the Japan Golf Goods Association, or the Tape-Recorder Association. The second category contains the umbrella associations for core associations (often *rengōkai* or *renmei*), although not all core associations necessarily have an umbrella association. The third category is the cooperatives (*kyōdō kumiai*), which are core associations for small-sized companies. The fourth category of associations is that of the "peak cooperatives" (*kumiai rengōkai*), the umbrella organizations of the cooperatives. Finally, the fifth category, "others", consists primarily of foundations, research institutes and research consortia, which typically have very close ties to the government.

These various legal categories and the complex pyramidal structure of associations bespeak a large overall number of trade associations in Japan. Table 2.2 shows that in 1996, of Japan's total of 15,391 trade associations, 3,127 were national and 12,264 were regional. Of the total, 9,655 associations were "voluntary", while 2,107 were "incorporated" (*shadan hōjin*), 116 were foundations, and 3,513 were cooperatives (JFTC 1991). Aldrich et al. (1990) found for the U.S.

---

[3] Cooperatives may admit large-firm members for several reasons, including to increase the cooperative's creditworthiness for loan applications, to increase the image of the cooperative, to receive management guidance from a large company, or simply because long-term members have grown large over time. The JFTC looks at the reason why a large firm is a member of a cooperative in order to decide whether the AML exemption has to be revoked (JFTC Annual Report 1988: 90, 1994: 198–9).

Table 2.2. Number of Trade Associations by Type and by Industry in 1996

	All associations	*Of which:* nationwide
Total number	15,391	3,127
1. By kind of association		
Voluntary (*nin'i dantai*)	9,655	1,987
Incorporated (*shadan hōjin*)	2,107	715
Foundation (*zaidan hōjin*)	116	78
Based on special laws of cooperatives	3,513	347
2. By industry		
Sector I (Agriculture, fisheries, forestry; mining; construction)	1,524	341
Sector II (Manufacturing; food; etc.)	4,433	1,793
Sector III (Wholesaling & retailing;	6,383	514
other services)	3,051	479

Source: JFTC Annual Report 1996, Appendix 6–1.

that the number of national trade associations in the 1980s was stable at around 2,100. Therefore, Japan, with half the GDP, has more national associations than the U.S. One explanation for Japan's comparatively large numbers is that associations are organized by a very detailed differentiation of industries. For instance, there are separate associations for each of the following writing utensil industries: ball pens, fountain pens, pencils, highlighting pens, erasers, and white-out ink.[4] By dividing industries into sub-markets like these, the number of associations naturally increases.

Yet, Table 2.2 does not even report all of the associations that exist in Japan, but only those that have notified the JFTC of their existence. The JFTC has no means by which to enforce the notification rule. There are many groups of business executives that do not file reports but clearly function as groups aimed at furthering their mutual business interests. These range from highly informal industry discussion groups (often with names ending in -*konwakai*) to the Presidents' Councils of the *keiretsu* groups (*shachōkai*). One outstanding example of a powerful "shadow association" is the *Toginkon* (*Toshi ginkō konwakai*, lit.: "City Bank Discussion Council"). The category of city banks includes Japan's money-center banks, and whereas all other bank categories, such as regional banks, credit unions, etc., have their own core associations, the city banks lead the Federation of Bankers' Associations but see after their own focused interests in the unofficial group. According to one

---

[4] These are, respectively, the *Nihon booru pen kyōdō kumiai, Tōkyō mannenhitsu jigyō kyōdō kumiai, Nihon enpitsu kōgyō kyōdō kumiai, Nihon maakingu pen kōgyōkai, Nihon jishō kōgyōkai,* and *Nihon shūsei-eki kōgyōkai.*

banker, the *Toginkon* is the most powerful of all the bankers' associations in terms of setting interest rates and agreeing on market rules.[5] There are no data on the total number and scope of activities of these "shadow associations".

Returning to the official data, Table 2.2 also breaks Japanese associations down by industry. The sectors with the highest number of associations by far are the wholesaling and retailing industries. One explanation for this phenomenon is that while there is usually one core association per manufactured good category, there are multiple layers of distribution for any given product. In each geographical market and at each distribution layer, trade merchants establish their own association to negotiate their interests against both upstream suppliers and downstream customers in their particular region or industry segment.

One often-cited reason for the large number of Japanese trade associations is that they are leftovers from the control associations of WWII. These control associations supervised input rationing and therefore existed in every narrowly defined industry segment (see Chapter 7). After the war many of these associations did not dissolve, but simply renamed and stayed in place. While it sounds quite plausible, the argument does not explain why the numerous associations did not dissolve over time if they did not serve a particular function. More importantly, the broad base of the pyramid suggests that the many core associations perform specific functions within their narrowly defined industries. The structure fulfils a purpose: it exists to accommodate self-regulation through focused, compact associations.

Membership and Budget of Trade Associations

The JFTC does not publish data on membership, size, and staff of all trade associations. For the purpose of exploring the internal organization of Japanese associations, a database consisting of 1,153 associations in 28 industries was created based on the biannual publication *Dantai Meikan*, the "Association Directory", for 1990/91 (Shiba 1991; see Chapter 6 on how the data set was constructed). This handbook collates data on location, foundation date, number of members, budget, etc. While the data will be analyzed in more detail in Chapter 6, we can use them here for a brief, aggregate overview.

Table 2.3 summarizes average data for the most basic organizational features of Japanese trade associations. The large variance in these makes the median (i.e., the midpoint of the distribution) a more meaningful measure than the average. As of 1991, the median membership for the 1,153 associations was 78, while the

---

[5] The *Toginkon* has long been a thorn in the side of the JFTC, and following the scandals in 1997 and 1998 related to both the bad loan clean-up and the alleged bribery of Ministry of Finance officials, the city banks agreed to report their group to the JFTC as a voluntary association.

Table 2.3. Average Size and Membership of Japanese Trade Associations

	Average	Median	Core average	Coop average	Japan nationwide avg. (1990)	U.S. nationwide avg. (1983)
Regular members	695.5	78	642.8	112.8	897	951
Annual budget (¥ millions)	374.4	70	423.0	106.9	449	$623,000
Staff	13.7	4	12.9	4.4	15.7	14.5
Directors	25.6	20	24.7	16.7	—	—

Source: database consisting of 1,153 trade associations; *Dantai Meikan*, 1990–1.

median annual budget amounted to ¥70 million (roughly $650,000 at the time). A median of 20 directors (i.e., presidents of the member companies dispatched to serve on the association's board of directors) was supported by a median of four staff employees.

Probably one of the biggest differences in the roles played by Japanese associations and those in the U.S. lies in the continuity of membership. In the U.S., members often leave the association in times of recession and declining profits, or at least reduce their commitment (Lynn/McKeown 1988: 57). In Japan, a withdrawal in times of crisis runs counter to the whole idea of association membership: the exchange of information and cooperation among competitors is even more important in recessions than it is in profitable times. To be sure, Japanese firms may choose not to join an association or may splinter off, but not only is this rare, it is also typically not caused by the immediate economic situation. Because the JFTC only began to publish coverage data (i.e., membership in the association expressed in total output or sales in the industry) in 1995, we do not know how inclusive membership in Japanese associations has been over time. However, data from 37 interviews suggest that coverage ratios are generally in the 90% range of all companies (and even higher in terms of total sales), and all large firms in an industry are typically members of the association. The nonmembers are mostly small-sized companies that cannot afford to pay membership dues.

Japanese trade associations have three types of member. The first type is "regular members" (*sei kaiin*), i.e., the companies in the industry represented. The second type is association members; for instance, federations have primarily associations as members. Finally, there are "supportive members" (*sanjo kaiin*), who pay only a fraction of the regular membership dues. While they benefit from the association's publications and external affairs activities, they typically cannot vote in the general meeting, nor are they represented on the board of directors. Most Japanese associations in the manufacturing sector require that members produce in Japan. This requirement precludes Japanese sales offices of foreign firms from becoming regular members and participating in the information exchange in Japanese associations.[6] Because of the legal restrictions on foreign direct investment into Japan during most of the postwar period, most foreign firms do not manufacture in Japan—unless their activities in Japan predate WWII.[7] As a result, Japanese firms often remain undisturbed by foreign competitors in conducting their various activities, including self-regulation.

Reflecting the differences in size and number of association members, budgets differ significantly across the different types of association. Since an association's budget is based on membership dues, which are calculated as a percentage of either a member's profits or sales, the smaller number of members and the smaller firm size translate into much smaller budgets for cooperatives. Table 2.3 shows that the budgets of core associations are on average four times as large as those of small-firm cooperatives.

Comparable data for the U.S. are available only for 1983 (Aldrich et al. 1990: 24). Even if a decade of economic growth and inflation is accounted for, the average numbers appear to be similar except the budget: Japan's 1990 average association budget of ¥450 million (roughly $4 million) compares with an average $623,000 for U.S. associations in 1983 (cf. Table 2.3). Given the similarity in numbers of member firms, association dues are therefore much higher in Japan than in the U.S. This begs the question what benefits Japanese associations offer to their member companies. Why are Japanese companies willing to pay such high dues, and become members of several associations? Before we address the issue of what trade associations do for their members, it is important to look briefly at the ultimate peak associations.

Keidanren and the "Big Four" Peak Associations

At the top of the association hierarchy are big business's four peak organizations: the Keidanren (*Keizai dantai rengōkai*, "Federation of Business Associations"), Nikkeiren (*Nihon keieisha dantai renmei*), Keizai Dōyūkai (lit.: "Economic Friendship Club", but officially rendered as "Japan Committee for Economic Development"), and the Japan Chamber of Commerce (*Nisshō, Nihon shōkō kaigisho*) (for their historical roots, see Chapter 7). The Japan Chamber of Commerce is the umbrella organization of all regional chambers of commerce that list as their main function providing advice and management guidance for

---

[6] This does not mean that there are no foreign member firms in Japanese associations at all. The chemical and pharmaceutical industries (with active participation by German and U.S. firms) and the automobile tire industry (French representation) are prime examples. In contrast, the Federation of Bankers' Associations denied foreign banks until 1999. In some industries, this discrimination has led to complaints that foreign firms cannot participate in the exchange of industry information, "friendship" creation (as explained below), or have easy access to regulatory information from the government. See JFTC (1996b) for a recent survey on foreign firms and trade associations in Japan.

[7] See Chapter 3 for a brief explanation of the Foreign Investment Law (*Gaishihō*); Encarnation (1992) offers a complete analysis of the implications of restrictions on FDI for trade and economic growth.

small- and medium-sized enterprises. When it comes to broad political issues, the Chamber often sides with the other big organizations to represent business interests. Yet, the Chamber has been very effective in helping to push through special legislation for small- and medium-sized companies, at times against the interests of the large-scale companies.

The Nikkeiren is the employer's central peak association and thus the counterpart to the labor unions' peak organizations, and it represents about 30,000 companies in labor issues. The Keizai Dōyūkai has as its members individuals, rather than associations, who are executives in Japan's blue-chip companies. Founded as a forum for young, upcoming company executives in 1946, the leaders of the Keizai Dōyūkai have historically recruited from newly emerging, important industries, such as investment banking, retailing, and non-life insurance companies. As these industries have become more important within Japan's economic structure, so has the Keizai Dōyūkai in terms of voicing big business interests.

Even more powerful than these three groups is the ultimate peak organization, Keidanren. The chairman of Keidanren is sometimes referred to as the "Prime Minister of Japanese business", and for a large portion of the postwar period, and again in the late 1990s, was a representative of the steel industry (Lynn/McKeown 1988: 79). Keidanren has a total of ten vice-chairmen, who traditionally were the presidents of the leading firms in Japan's six early strategic industries: steel, energy, banking, petrochemicals, automobiles, and electronics. Only in the 1980s was this group of vice-chairmen diversified to include the increasingly important large retailers (department stores) and life insurance companies.

Keidanren has about 900–1,000 corporate members, which are all very large, industrial companies and financial institutions, and about 120 trade association members. In addition, famous executives can become individual members to serve as advisers (*komon*). The representatives of the top member firms are in charge of running the 45–50 standing committees. These committees are sometimes called the "headquarters of the *zaikai*" (Tsuda 1990: 259). The term *zaikai* refers to the business leaders that formulate and represent the interests of big business in the policy process. The word was in use even before WWII, but at that time referred to the leaders of the biggest *zaibatsu*; nowadays, it simply refers to the most powerful businessmen in the country.

Keidanren's primary function is to mediate differences of opinion among its members, and in particular among the six key industries. Keidanren attempts to represent a unified business interest in official proposals to the government on policy issues such as the course of deregulation (e.g., Keidanren 1993, 1994a). In the 1990s, this has become increasingly difficult, as the internationally competitive industries have priorities that differ greatly from those of the domestic, protected ones. In spite of these increasing differences, Keidanren remains the most powerful political forum for big business.[8]

---

[8] Keidanren's role in political campaign financing will be discussed in Section 2.4, below.

General Functions of Trade Associations

The activities of trade associations can be divided into three categories: (1) administrative, including the exchange of information; (2) economic, including self-regulation and other regulatory participation; and (3) political, narrowly defined to mean lobbying and contacts with politicians. Japanese associations split these three functions among categories of associations, so that different types of association focus in on one of these areas of activities. Following a general overview, we will see that the execution of the political function is usually left to the top of the association pyramid, whereas the regulatory functions are concentrated in the core associations and cooperatives.

Table 2.4 juxtaposes the results of a questionnaire on trade association activities conducted by the respective antitrust authorities in the U.S. in 1987 and in Japan in 1992. In the U.S., the most frequently cited activities are those related to "liaison" functions between industries and the government, including information on regulation, lobbying in the broadest sense, and political funding. While the Japanese associations, too, are actively involved in lobbying, they do much more than that and most often describe themselves as service and self-regulatory institutions: they provide information to the government and to the members, cooperate with the regulators, conduct market research, and "create friendship" among their members. Of the 17 categories listed in Table 2.4 for the U.S., 11 were directly related to political functions, whereas of the 18 categories listed for Japan's associations, only four were directly political, while five were related to administration and information, and the remaining ten to government regulation and self-regulation.

Among the various activities of Japanese associations, two deserve special attention. The first is the "provision of administrative information" (line 1, 83.5%). As we saw in Chapter 1, the regulatory environment of extralegal administrative guidance lends this category a special subtext, as this activity includes an association's advising the regulator on guidance. Therefore, rather than just coordinating the information exchange of its members, this activity includes aspects of regulatory cooperation and self-regulation to a degree that is not entailed in the U.S. activity of *post hoc* provision of "information on congressional developments". The second outstanding category in the Japanese case is that of "promotion of friendship" (*shinboku*). *Shinboku* is a rather broad term that refers to everything from holding an "end-of-the-year-party" (*bōnen-kai*) to going out together to drink, so that the member firms' employees and executives get to know each other well and are more likely to be able to form a unified opinion. Yet, the *shinboku* category contains all activities that Adam Smith had in mind when he observed that two or more businessmen rarely meet for merriment alone. When asked what *shinboku* meant in real terms, one association official answered: "*Shinboku* means drinking beer and talking about cartels" (*karuteru no hanashi o suru*; interview, Tokyo, summer 1995). Interestingly, many Japanese trade associations even list *shinboku* as the group's primary

Table 2.4. Activities of Trade Associations in the U.S. and Japan (in % of associations reporting that they perform this function)

United States		Japan	
Information on congressional developments	92	Provide administrative information	83.5
Help members express views to Congress	87	Public relations	71.4
Inform members of federal and state/local administrative actions	87	Conducting market research	67.5
Testify before Congress and state legislatures	76	"Administrative activities" (holding regular meetings with regulators)	64.0
Make recommendations on legislation	71	Promotion of friendship (*shinboku*)	62.7
Provide data to federal and state governments	66	Cooperating with public administration (standards, permission and approval procedures)	55.3
Include speakers in convention programs	57	Legal studies	55.2
Draft legislation	55	Presentation of opinions to public administration	53.7
Lobby and inform Congress of industry views	54	Other overseas activities	45.4
Report federal court decisions	46	Technical training	43.5
Train members to become active in politics	29	Handling of international affairs (*Kokusai mondai taiō*)	38.0
Collect and distribute funds to political candidates	27	Voluntary regulations	25.2
Arrange plant tours to help government expose foreign visitors to U.S. industry	23	Formulation of vision	22.4
Sponsor courses on political participation	15	Labor problems	20.7
Assist members with tariffs and trade agreements	12	Technical research (*gijutsu kenkyū*)	19.1
Represent industry in tariff negotiations	9	Designation of programs (*shikaku nintei*)	17.9
Assist government in foreign trade participation	8	Voluntary product standards	16.6
		Guidance on management	16.5
		Finance and debt guaranteeing	4.4

Source: for the U.S., based on 1987 report of American Society of Association Executives, as cited in Weidenbaum (1990); for Japan, based on a 1992 questionnaire conducted by the JFTC ($n = 844$).

function in the association's bylaws. The fact that 63% of all associations self-report this activity evidences Japan's rather lenient interpretation of antitrust rules and the importance of associations as the locations for intra-industry cooperation and exchange of information.

2.2. Internal Organization and Information Exchange

'The exchange of information is probably the associations' biggest function. It is not so much information on the products they directly compete in, but fundamental market information. They meet twice or three times a week at the *buchō* (section chief) level, and hold informal lunches, and sometimes [our ministry's] people join them... And then there is of course the famous brainstorming over *sake*'.

(Interview with a MITI official, Tokyo, summer 1995)

Studies in corporate management and strategy have attested to the importance of information and knowledge for business. The more extensive and regular the information they receive, the more companies benefit. To the extent that information exchange results in coordination of business strategies and activities, it affords competitive advantage to the firms involved. Economists have long argued that frequent exchange of information is the most important condition for a sustainable inter-firm agreement, because it facilitates monitoring; the more secretive the members to an agreement are allowed to be, the more tempted they are to cheat the other parties to the agreement (Stigler 1964, Dolbear et al. 1968). Scherer (1980: 176) even argues that the paramount problem in business co-operation is to devise and maintain communication systems, and concludes that "collusion is communication par excellence". Exchange of information is thus the most obvious and basic function of any trade association. The term refers to both general information regarding domestic and foreign markets and government rules, as well as more detailed issues best referred to as "competitor intelligence".

Understanding this, Japan's trade associations have crafted a system of institutionalized information exchange through meetings at various executive levels and through mechanisms of personnel exchange. Associations provide opportunities, both formal and informal, to interpret complicated signals from competitors and related markets and respond to them. The more powers an association has to process information on its members, the easier it is to structure and enforce self-regulation. It is generally and widely acknowledged that Japanese associations are much more active in exchanging critical and strategic information about member firms than their U.S. counterparts, owing to the different ways in which antitrust rules are enforced in the two countries. We will see in detail in Chapters 4 and 5 how exactly the JFTC enforces the Japanese law, and what kinds of activity are permitted in Japan. Note here that lawyers are not usually present at association meetings in Japan, and that the exchange of critical data including information on price and costs appears to be quite customary. Besides lenient antitrust enforcement, there are also internal organizational features of trade associations that support and enhance the constant flow of information.

Organization

While Japanese associations differ in minor ways as to how they organize their activities and administration, there is a common pattern in their organizational structure.[9] First, the governing body of every trade association is the "general meeting" (*sōkai*). Once (sometimes twice) a year, all association members meet for about two hours to vote on general issues such as changes in the bylaws or appointments of new officers. Very large associations also hold annual *taikai*, or conventions. These high-profile events are typically held in the Keidanren Hall and attended by the leading politicians, bureaucrats, and representatives from related industries. To ensure *shinboku*, the meeting is generally followed by a reception and banquet. For instance, at the 1995 Annual Meeting of the Regional Banks' Association, the Governor of the Bank of Japan, a politician from the "finance group" within the LDP, and a high-level representative from the Ministry of Finance all made appearances. Likewise, the 1994 convention of the Japanese Association of Securities Dealers had 790 attendees, including Japan's Prime Minister, the Governor of the Bank of Japan, the Minister of Finance, and the chairman of Keidanren. The high level and the frequency of such conventions attest to the important political role played by trade associations in Japan.

Within the association, substantial policy decisions and discussion of positions and interests are delegated to the board of directors (*rijikai*), which meets monthly. The directors (*riji*) are member company presidents and represent the interests of their company at the industry level. While officially these directors are elected by all association members at the general meeting, in practice these positions typically rotate among the presidents of the largest firms in the industry. In associations with few members, the presidents of all member firms are directors. In some very hierarchical industries dominated by one or two firms, the leading firms may dispatch several executives to the board and thus have significant power to influence the association's actions. At their monthly meetings, the directors discuss current challenges to the industry, pending regulatory changes and other matters of mutual interest.

The head of the board of directors (*kaichō*) is the chairman of the association. In most large industries, the leading four or five companies take turns filling this position. For instance, the chairmanship of the Bankers' Federation rotates regularly among the top six city banks. Again, while the directors supposedly

---

[9] The following is based on interviews with 37 trade associations in 20 different product and service sectors, as well as monthly publications of a large number of associations.

elect their chairman, the rotation order is usually predetermined. In this way, the large firms in the industry are assured of playing the leading role in the association, and there is little haggling over successions.[10]

Directly under the president, the staff of the association is headed by one senior director (*senmu riji*, lit.: "special administrative director") who is also a member of the board of directors. This person acts as a liaison between the members and the administrative office of the association. In those associations that hire retired government officials for closer contacts with regulators and politicians, the OB often assumes the *senmu riji* position.[11] Thus, the retired bureaucrat both serves on the board and is available on a daily basis to handle administrative matters for the association. In contrast to the president of the association, the *senmu riji* does not rotate but is typically a long-term employee who provides stability in leadership in a system of frequent changes in the top position of an association.

Below the senior staff, a number of staff people are in charge of administrative functions. These administrative tasks include: organizing committee and subcommittee meetings; running the association's publications (usually a monthly magazine); collecting and publishing industry statistics; doing research on domestic and foreign market access; collecting opinions on policy issues and contacting related associations on these matters; furnishing the regulators with current industry information; processing information from the regulating ministries for distribution to member firms; running the associations' finances; organizing educational programs and seminars for industry employees; and overseeing operations of joint computer networks and similar shared facilities. To promote their industries or products, associations often organize trade shows and engage in joint advertising. They also staff representative offices in foreign countries.

Probably the most important external function in this long list is industry promotion. This joint industry promotion often focuses on advertising the generic product category, exemplified by the successful "Got Milk?" advertisements in the U.S. in the 1990s. For example, the Japan Electrical Manufacturers' Association (JEMA, *Nihon denki kōgyōkai*) has established four days in the year for special product category promotion: May 30 is "garbage day", promoting waste recycling equipment (this is based on a pun: "go-mi-zero" can be read as

---

[10] The major exception from the automatic succession system is Keidanren, whose chairman is elected from among the leading firms of the major industries. During the period of rapid economic growth (i.e., in the 1950s and 1960s), these were electric power and steel. In more recent years, the focus has shifted to automobiles and electronics. In the 1990s, there has been a heated discussion within Keidanren as to the appropriate industrial pecking order.

[11] In associations that are particularly close to their regulating ministry, the OBs may assume the position of chairman or vice-chairman. For instance, in the Japan Paper Association (*Nihon seishi rengōkai*) the chairman has traditionally been a retired MITI official, while the vice-chairman is a retired official from the Ministry of Agriculture, Fishery, and Forestry (MAFF; related to pulp imports). See Schaede (1995) for a discussion of the "Old Boy" and *amakudari* ("descent from heaven") system, and the reasons why companies or associations might employ retired government officials in the Japanese system.

both "May 30" and "zero garbage"); June 23 is "refrigerator day" to promote the cleaning or replacement of fridges (marking the beginning of the hot weather season); August 1 is "laundry day" to promote water-saving efforts at the beginning of the dry season by replacing old washers; and November 9 is "*danbō day*" (heating system day, again based on a pun, as "ichi ichi kyū", November 9, is abbreviated into "*ii kūki*", "nice air"). Such generic product promotion can be quite effective if conducted as a complement to the individual manufacturers' advertisements, and it is particularly common for intermediate products and in industries with little product differentiation, such as glass or paper.

Another important staff task in large associations is the publication of a monthly or quarterly journal. While the journal serves the two primary purposes of reporting on technological developments in other countries and chronicling personnel movements in the industry, it sometimes also contains minutes on meetings, summaries of industry agreements (including some that would be considered suspicious in other countries), and policy speeches by ministry officials. For instance, the Winter 1994 issue of the *The Glass*, which all glass product manufacturers subscribe to, contains full translations of three articles on technological advances in glass production (two from Germany, one from the U.S.) as well as five short summaries of other such articles. These are followed by a few essays and articles on the Japanese glass industry, detailed statistics on glass product output through the calendar year, and a list of promotions and personnel movements with the new phone and fax numbers of company employees (GMAJ 1994).

In large associations, several of the staff are *shukkō*, i.e., employees of member firms working on a two-year secondment to the association. Often, the chairman of the association is accompanied by an employee as his personal assistant. Companies also send employees to the association to establish *shinboku* (friendship) among junior employees of the leading firms and the regular association staff. The young employee meets representatives from other firms, has regular contact with the bureaucrats in the ministry in charge of regulating the industry, and learns how the association operates. During his ensuing career with his company, this employee is likely to remain in job areas that involve negotiations with other companies or the regulators. Overall, an association that has no *shukkō* is considered more neutral and independent, because no member firm has preferential access to industry data or information through its *shukkō*. Therefore, associations in competitive industries, such as automobiles, tend to have fewer or no *shukkō* than collusive industries, to prevent competitor intelligence.

Committees and Information Exchange

In addition to the board of directors, which meets once a month to discuss large-scale regulatory issues and decide on future strategies in politics and business, there are typically very many committees and subcommittees that meet frequently both to prepare the directors' discussions and implement their decisions. These committees consist of middle- and lower-level employees whose task it is to negotiate with the other companies regarding specific areas of cooperation. Typical areas for committee work include: contact with regulators; joint R&D; marketing; foreign trade; environment/recycling; and special projects, such as introducing new central computer systems or the formulation of industry standards.

For example, in the early 1990s, the directors of the Department Stores Association decided to introduce a joint gift certificate (i.e., a gift certificate that is valid in all participating stores). The technicalities of this idea were discussed in a large number of the association's committees and subcommittees, which finally submitted a draft for how to organize this venture to the directors.[12] In some associations that conduct market research for their regulating ministry, a ministry official may be a regular committee member. In fact, the regulating ministries can ask associations to form special committees. For instance, trying to push environmental awareness, in 1994 MITI asked the Japan Plastics Industries Federation (*Nihon purasuchikku kōgyō renmei*) to conduct a study on environmental measures in the plastics industries; a special committee to design new policies met 25 times in 1994, and 80% of the committee members came from various ministries, especially MITI.[13] Because committees are often the "pipe" for information exchange, both among companies and between the industry and MITI, the number of committees run by an association is one indication of the activities of this association and its involvement with the government.

While discussing the specifics of joint projects, company employees are likely to exchange strategic information on their companies. Therefore, it is through the middle- or lower-level committees that the most critical information is exchanged. In cases where associations attempt to collude, e.g., by fixing prices, it is the lower-level committees that are in charge of structuring and implementing the agreement. For example, when the Money Market Broker Association was raided in 1995 on suspicion of colluding on fees, it was found that the agreements had been reached in the "R&D subcommittee". In another case, the association representative explained: "Of course we would not talk about prices in the board of directors meeting, because we have to keep minutes of such meetings. Therefore, we ask the lower-level committees to prepare and implement price agreements."[14]

While committees vastly enhance the exchange of information and support the network of personal relations at various managerial levels, it is of course possible that the companies within an association are fierce competitors, and employees therefore do not easily trust each other. Certainly not all trade associations in

---

[12] Interview, Tokyo, summer 1995.
[13] Interview, Tokyo, summer 1995.
[14] Interview, Tokyo, summer 1995; the legal issues involved with frequent meetings are discussed in Chapter 4.

Japan are "friendly" and networked, and many are highly competitive. But even in these cases, information exchange can be beneficial to member firms. For instance, information on regulatory changes, foreign competitors, or foreign markets is expensive to gather individually but easy to share with other firms. By holding monthly meetings at various levels of the corporate hierarchy, even among competitors, the exchange of information is eased significantly.

Table 2.5 gives a broad overview of committees for a set of 37 core associations. Note that the number of associations for which these data are available is limited, and the variance in the number of members in committees and subcommittees is high, so that average numbers may give the impression of regularity where there is indeed a great deal of fluctuation. Still, even accepting these caveats, Table 2.5 offers some insights into committee frequency and size. The average association has 25 directors that meet once a month. Given that there are about 15,000 associations, the number of corporate presidents that meet once a month in Japan is truly amazing. Further, we know for 53 core associations that the average number of OBs is about two (for umbrella organizations, it drops to 1.5), while there are on average nine *shukkō* employees on the staff. Both these numbers are much smaller for cooperatives: neither are cooperatives very interesting destinations for retiring bureaucrats, nor can small firms usually afford to send an employee to the association. The associations interviewed for this project had, on average, 20 committees with 17 members each, and 75 subcommittees with about ten members each. Table 2.5 shows the numbers of employees that meet monthly (a total of almost 1,100) just for these 37 associations. If we visualize this traffic for all meetings held by only the 3,000 large, national associations, we get an idea of how much time, effort, and money companies are willing to expend for information exchange and cooperation with other firms.

Besides the internal committee structure of Japanese trade associations, the exchange process within and among industries is further enhanced by frequent meetings up and down the "pyramid" of trade associations. Meetings organized similarly to the internal committee gatherings are routine among associations in various industries. And ultimately, just as committees at various levels meet at the core associations of one industry, so do whole industries meet at Keidanren. Core associations therefore exchange information in three directions: (1) within the association; (2) with other associations in related industries, either vertically in the federation (umbrella association), or horizontally with other core associations; and (3) with all other industries at the Keidanren level.

2.3. Economic and Regulatory Functions of Trade Associations

The economic and regulatory functions of Japan's trade associations can be divided into three broad sets of activities: (1) the associations' involvement in

Table 2.5. Meetings and Personnel Exchanges in Core Associations

	Core associations				Umbrella associations average	Cooperatives average
	Average	Standard deviation	Maximum	Sample size		
Directors	24.63	19.91	177	784	35.26	16.75
OBs	2.13	3.22	20	53	1.57	0.29
Shukkō	9.95	22.15	80	21	7.00	3.67
Committees	19.26	27.46	150	27	22.08	8.00
Committee members (Members × committees)	17.04 (328)	7.51	30	20	21.67	6.50
Subcommittees	75.36	175.94	600	11	n.a.	n.a.
Subcommittee members (Members × subcom.)	10.00 (754)	n.a.	n.a.	15		

Source: based on interviews with 37 trade associations and their publications as well as database based on *Dantai Meikan* (1991).

The high values for standard deviation reflect the great diversity among even the core associations. See Chapter 6 for an analysis of the relation between internal organization and the likelihood of self-regulation. In terms of maximum values, the outliers are:

177 directors = Japan Dye & Mold Manufacturers' Associations (*Nihon kinkei kōgyōkai*; machine tools)
150 committees, 600 subcommittees = EIAJ (Electronic Industries Associations of Japan, *Nihon denshi kikai kōgyōkai*); the number of committees was reduced in 1995.
80 *shukkō* = The Life Insurance Association of Japan (*Nihon seimei kyōkai*); this association has only 31 members, so each member firm has an average of 2.6 employees dispatched to the association at all times.
20 OBs = The Second Association of Regional Banks (*Daini chihō ginkō kyōkai*); reflecting the crisis in this banking sector in the late 1990s.

industrial policy implementation; (2) participation in administrative guidance and other informal government support; and (3) formulation and enforcement of self-regulation, ranging from straightforward trade facilitation to collusion. It is in this last category of economic activities that Japanese associations differ most from those in other countries.

In general, the term "industrial policy" refers to governmental policies aimed at protecting certain domestic industries, developing strategic industries, and adjusting the nation's economic structure to enhance its international competitiveness (Ozaki 1972, Johnson 1982; cf. Chapter 3). In macroeconomic terms, industrial policy involves the allocation of financial and human capital across industries to achieve goals of economic growth or industrial restructuring, and protecting "infant industries" from imports. This has resulted in limited market access for both domestic and foreign competitors in these industries. Observers agree that Japan's industrial policy has been built on two assumptions: (a) that efficiency is associated with firm size, so that the higher the market concentration, the greater the effective use of resources (e.g., Hadley 1970: 391); and (b) that price competition destroys "orderly growth" and that the investment race among large firms has to be coordinated by the government (Yamamura 1982: 84). Pro-cartel policy was an integral part of this system, for cartel agreements reduced the risks associated with highly leveraged investments. Still, the primary reason why the industrial policy paradigm was effective in orchestrating Japanese economic growth is probably not so much that MITI's coercive powers did not leave the regulated businesses any choice (e.g., Johnson 1982), or that the policies were geared toward specific industries that would least resist them (Okimoto 1989). Rather, the primary reason for success was that the affected industries were directly involved in designing and implementing them. It has been shown that industrial policy programs were effective only if they built on cooperation and input by the affected industries and companies (e.g., Samuels 1987, Upham 1987, Uriu 1996). This is where trade associations have played a crucial rule.

At the most basic level, there has always been a constant flow of information and discussion between Japan's government officials and the associations of the industries they monitor. Activities that formalize this information exchange include: the long-standing deliberation councils, holding joint seminars on special policy issues; inviting association representatives to ministry meetings and vice versa; or paying associations to conduct a certain policy feasibility study. These committee meetings often end with social outings, which account for significant traffic in the more upscale restaurants in central Tokyo. It is also very common for regulating bureaucrats to attend the "end-of-the-year" parties (*bōnenkai*) or anniversary parties of trade associations to establish personal relations with the industry leaders. More specifically, the economic role of trade associations and their involvement in industrial policy can be evaluated by looking at the various ways in which government and business mutually support each other; namely, in terms of how the bureaucrats support associations, how associations support regulation, and how associations at times operate completely outside the influence sphere of their regulating ministries.

What the Ministries do for Trade Associations

In general, by asking competing companies to outline their positions on a certain policy issue, the ministries structure a bargaining situation and assume the role of referee for the negotiation (Young 1991). The insights of game theory suggest that the logic of the prisoner's dilemma can work to inhibit cooperation among competitors, in the sense that one company cannot easily believe that it will not be taken advantage of if it discloses proprietary information on its cost structure. In such a situation, it takes a third party—such as the regulating ministry—to overcome the informational deficiencies and reduce the risk associated with disclosing information.

Probably the best-known examples of the Japanese government's structuring of bargaining situations are research consortia (*kenkyū kumiai*). Upon discussion with all affected industries, MITI may formulate the basic rules and offer subsidies as incentives for a group of firms to establish a research consortium. The consortium is often established as an association of its own, typically a foundation. If the subsidies are of sufficient interest, competing companies may agree to engage in some technology transfer. The joint effort may result in new technological advances that the individual firms may not have achieved without the intermediation by the ministry.

It is important to note that Japan's ministries typically do not offer subsidies to individual companies, but rather to a group of companies or to the trade association, with the explicit order to divide the amount and the research activities among themselves.[15] This underscores why membership in the focal trade association is so important for Japanese companies. During the preliminary *nemawashi* (consultation) process, members of the trade association decide whether they can agree on a joint project. Only after they reach an agreement will MITI announce the new consortium; should the association's members be unable to agree, MITI will drop the plan. This prior, private consultation process in the associations is the reason that we rarely see open disagreement or haggling about research consortia either within the association or between the association and the government, for the public is only involved after everything has been settled. Further, while the outward impression may be that MITI is guiding the industry into a joint research project, in reality there is significant input or even initiative by the industry in the initial stages of formulating the policy. Often the industry, through its association, suggests joint activities which the ministry then sets up.

---

[15] According to one MITI official, "MITI is a public entity, and as such we must not favor one or two companies over the others. So we never give money to specific firms, we never do that. We use the trade association for money allocation." Interview, Tokyo, summer 1995.

Another example of how the government structures bargaining situations within industries can be found in maturing, or so-called "structurally depressed" industries. By creating negotiations among firms regarding capacity reductions, a ministry can fulfil its own goals of phasing in unemployment. Also, the ministry enables the firms to reach a joint decision on how to structure the turnaround process such that the industry as a whole, and each individual player in it, will emerge more efficient.[16]

There are two inherent problems in the government's "referee role". For one, bureaucrats cannot force their programs onto unwilling industries, but have to build on a joint decision-making process. That is, the bureaucrats cannot simply identify one industry as being in need of joint research or some other project, and then throw a subsidy at it; rather, the structuring of the bargaining situation needs to be preceded by a consensus among the affected and related industries on the particular policy. The second problem with the "referee role" is that there will always be firms that do not wish to participate in the bargaining process; i.e., in the above examples, firms that are uninterested in joint R&D or refuse to follow an industry-wide capacity reduction. While the ministry can use administrative guidance to help trade associations control their members, it cannot invoke any legal powers to rein in mavericks but must revert to indirect means of enforcement. Examples abound that show how garnering support for programs is often difficult. It is this resistance of private companies to some policy programs that has kept a healthy balance among the various industrial policy measures adopted in the 1950s and 1960s, and the relative power structure between bureaucrats and industry. For MITI, trade liberalization over time undermined its control over imports and thus its power in forcing companies to go along with industry agreements. The less impact MITI has had on the supplies of raw materials, technology or other input factors, the less important has the ministry become for enforcing industry agreements. Thus, in the 1980s, trade associations increasingly structured their negotiations without the ministerial referees.

What Trade Associations do for Their Ministries

From the perspective of the regulating ministries, trade associations are very important both in formulating and implementing regulation. At the most basic level, ministries need associations to provide them with aggregate information on industry, such as sales, investments, or inventory. While these data are available from the individual firms, the understaffed ministries prefer having the associations do the clerical work for them. Moreover, the regulators, being generalists, often lack the industry-specific knowledge to evaluate the situation of a company or industry as a whole. Further, because associations collect data on foreign

---

[16] Such arrangements were very frequent under the "Depressed Industries Law" and the "Structurally Depressed Industries Law" of 1978–88 (cf. Chapter 3). See Upham (1987), Young (1991) for discussions.

markets and competitors, the regulators also often use them as informants in international trade negotiations.

Just as it is easier, and less costly, for a regulating ministry to collect data through the associations, it is also easier and cheaper for the ministry to negotiate policy issues with the association rather than with individual firms. This is particularly useful when the ministry is contemplating a new regulation for an industry, which it might deliver in the semiformal form of a written administrative guidance (*tsūtatsu*). In such a case, the ministry typically sends a draft of the guidance to the association, where it is discussed by the board of directors. The industry's response to the draft is incorporated in the guidance, which is then re-announced to the industry. Again, what the public observes is just the outcome and smooth implementation of a rule that resulted from negotiations between ministries and regulatees.[17]

As important as their input in regulatory policy creation is the association's function in monitoring the implementation of rules. After a new rule has been issued by the ministry, the regulatees themselves often assume the task of ensuring adherence. It is much easier for the firms in an industry to observe the market behavior of their competitors. In contrast, if a ministry were to monitor rule compliance, it could typically only do so by looking at data post hoc, and reconstructing the context of a violation after it has occurred. And because there are only very few independent supervisory agencies and process regulation is in the hands of the industry ministries, staffing is a problem. Self-monitoring is therefore both more effective and, from the ministry's perspective, more efficient.

The ministries are especially dependent on industry self-monitoring for purposes of administrative guidance. Because it is extralegal and informal, administrative guidance potentially invites cheating, and without group pressure and group controls by the industry concerned there is no way for the ministry to ensure compliance. Precisely because administrative guidance builds on self-regulation for enforcement, it can be either extremely effective (if all companies agree to comply) or completely ineffective (if they choose to ignore the ministry's guidance). For instance, in the wake of the yen appreciation to an exchange rate of below ¥100 = US$1 in 1993, MITI reportedly called up several trade associations with a request to lower domestic prices (to alleviate the price differential for basic goods between New York and Tokyo). However, without the support of the companies in the affected industries, this guidance amounted to no more than hot air.[18]

---

[17] The trade association is important in this process because an individual company cannot easily reject a ministerial guidance, whereas an entire industry certainly can. Interviews, Tokyo, summers of 1993 and 1995.

[18] Interviews with various associations, Tokyo, summer 1995. Upham (1987) argues that the involvement of the regulatees in the government's rule-making process and their role in compliance monitoring are in fact related. As a result of the informality of Japan's regulatory system, based on numerous meetings and discussions involving all affected parties, all regulatees have a prior commitment to the rule. All competing firms know who has committed to the rule to what extent, and it would be a bad decision for a company to first sign off on a new regulation and then not to comply with it. Certainly this trickery would undermine the company's credibility in the industry, and its weight in the next round of negotiations for a new policy would be severely diminished.

In sum, trade associations are important for the bureaucrats because they help lower the cost of policy implementation by (a) ensuring commitment by all members of the industry in the negotiating process, and (b) by assuming self-monitoring tasks. This makes implementation more speedy and less demanding for the bureaucrats, and increases compliance by the regulatees. However, there is one significant downside for the regulating ministries implicit in the self-monitoring system. Naturally, the regulated industry may choose to implement its own rules instead of, or in addition to, the official ones. Over time, as industries grow stronger and become less dependent on ministerial subsidies and other forms of protection, the tendency for firms to assume regulatory tasks will become stronger. The less dependent an industry is on the ministry, the more autonomous will its association become, not only in monitoring compliance with governmental rules, but in drafting its own rules. This blurs the boundaries between delegated monitoring and entirely independent self-regulation.

What Trade Associations do Independently of Their Regulators: Self-Regulation

Trade associations also engage in completely independent activities that have neither the explicit blessing nor the oversight of the regulating ministries. Although not all of these are necessarily collusive, most of them are conducted surreptitiously because they border the illegal, especially when the boundaries between administrative and protective self-regulation are crossed. Collusive behavior can originate from two types of activity: (1) anti-competitive agreements and cooperation within trade associations unknown to and independent of the government; and (2) the extension of government-delegated regulatory tasks into purely private regulation.

The first of these two types contains simply illegal agreements within an association to collude on price, quantity, or restrictions on market access. Collusive agreements cover a wide range of activities. For instance, price-fixing can take the form of an implicit price leadership agreement (whereby one company takes the lead in setting the price for base models in each product category and other companies follow suit), or it can be a straightforward agreement on a percentage or absolute price increase. Trade associations can also stage boycotts to block non-member firms from the market or close up the distribution system. These activities will be studied in detail in Chapter 4.

To understand the second type of self-regulatory activity, we must differentiate between delegated regulatory authority and autonomous self-regulation. Most governments delegate certain kinds of rule-making to industry, particularly when industry-specific knowledge is required, such as the design of standards. Moreover, trade associations are often asked to formulate and enforce "soft rules", such as for the appropriate types of advertisement in an industry. Two areas where Japanese associations assume delegated regulatory functions are quality inspections and safety registration checks. The idea of checking product quality at the industry level originated in the 1960s in export industries that suffered from a reputation for poor quality associated with the "Made in Japan" label. To ensure that all exported products were of high quality, some of Japan's trade associations set up specialized sister associations to administer a quality approval system. For instance, the camera industry established the Camera Inspection Institute, JCII.[19] All cameras were inspected; those that passed received a golden "JCII passed" sticker for exports, while faulty items had to be sold on the domestic market. Likewise, the Japan Toy Association maintains the "Japan Recreation and Miscellaneous Goods Safety Association" (*Nihon kikai gangu kensa kyōkai*) which conducts safety checks on toys and umbrellas. The Japan Pasta Association (*Nihon makaroni kyōkai*) entrusts its quality checks to the Japan Grain Inspection Association (*Nihon kokumotsu kentei kyōkai*) which is also in charge of monitoring the quality of rare but increasing rice imports.

Regulatory activities like these, which follow an official government mandate, are often called the "private interest government" function. As seen in Chapter 1, this term describes a situation in which the government delegates rule-making and rule-enforcing authority to associations, and in return, the government grants the associations a monopoly on the described functions (e.g., there is only one inspection association for cameras), grants special status before the antitrust laws, and may even allow a system of compulsory membership to enhance the association's effectiveness. The system of delegating some regulatory functions has the advantage of lowering the government's monitoring cost and achieving a socially desirable outcome.

In countries with strict antitrust rules, the only regulatory functions that associations perform are delegated. The reason is obvious: if left alone, constituent firms might be tempted to create rules that restrain competition, and such activities would be outlawed. For instance, quality inspection associations could stipulate special requirements that favor incumbents over new entrants. The monopoly right of representation could be used to bar competitors from certain markets by denying membership to the association. In Japan, however, antitrust authorities have long acquiesced to trade associations by allowing them to self-regulate to a significant extent, and a large portion of rule-making is based on private initiative. Accordingly, Japan's self-regulation is broader than the concept of "private interest government", because it includes both delegated and independent self-regulation. Delegated regulation is part of public policy, and by definition it is legal. In contrast, self-regulation is based on purely private initiative, and the primary intent is to serve the interests of the members of the trade association.

---

[19] The official name is JCII, Japan Camera and Optical Instruments Inspection and Testing Institute (*Nihon shashinki kōgaku kiki kensa kyōkai*).

It is difficult to differentiate between delegated regulation and self-regulation when trade associations overstep their regulatory mandate and extend delegated functions into the realm of self-regulation. This "gray area" also implies that not all self-regulation necessarily entails cartels and collusion. For instance, the setting of standards by a trade association may not transgress the antitrust law, if this activity merely involves the setting of some explicit industry standards, the publication of these standards, and the subsequent monitoring of compliance by all producers. However, some associations design standards or prescribe minimum quality rules outside the government's official JIS (Japan Industrial Standard) system, and often such rules become the stepping stones to collusive agreements on output or price. These so-called "self-standards" (*jishu kijun*) are stricter than the JIS rules and typically have the intended effect of excluding small competitors from the market. If the association skews the standards such that only market incumbents can achieve the requirements, or keeps those standards private and disseminates them only to trade association members, then the association is likely to block competition.

Self-regulation, therefore, refers to an association's taking over regulatory functions either by going beyond the scope of regulation delegated by the government, or by cooperating and colluding without any authorization. In both cases, the industry sets its own rules through its associations and describes codes of behavior for its member firms. The industry members then enforce these rules by ensuring that membership affords vital benefits and threatens to exclude mavericks from the association. These rules may or may not include collusive actions or price fixing; the incidence of collusion depends critically on the nature of competition in the industry concerned. In some cases, even if the association agrees on prices for end products, such as has been the case for many years in the electronics industry, the association still leaves room for competition among its members along dimensions other than price, such as quality, features, after-service, etc. (see Chapter 4).

The widespread practice of self-regulation in Japan is related to the country's antitrust enforcement regime. In general, enforcing laws against self-regulation is difficult for the Japan Fair Trade Commission. First, standard-setting is delegated to the associations because it requires specific industry knowledge not typically shared by the ministry officials. Therefore, industry transgressions are sometimes difficult for the regulator to recognize. Second, antitrust enforcement has traditionally been lenient regarding association meetings, informal gatherings, and other fora for the exchange of critical information. Moreover, as we will see in Chapter 4, the logic of Japanese antitrust law puts industrial self-regulatory activities into a legal category for which there is little effective legal action. As a result, Japan's Fair Trade Commission has not prosecuted self-regulation stridently. In the 1980s and 1990s, as the regulating ministries' powers began to decline and industries' self-regulatory activities began to rise, the antitrust system has not had the power to stem the tide that shifted regulatory power to the associations' self-regulation.

2.4. Political Functions of Japanese Trade Associations

The political function of associations, narrowly defined, consists of interest intermediation and internal consensus-building on specific policy issues; the lobbying of politicians and regulators; and participation in the policymaking process. The two primary sources of association power in these activities are votes and money. For instance, Japan's textile industry used to have very many employees who were influenced in their voting behavior by their employers, which afforded the industry leaders a significant political impact. Likewise, the banking industry has long been the biggest financial backer of conservative politics (Rosenbluth 1989). Overall, large Japanese trade associations are generally better known than their U.S. counterparts, because there is no independent lobbying industry in Japan; associations combine the functions of lobbying with all their other tasks. While measuring and evaluating the influence of business on Japanese politics is beyond the scope of this study and has been attempted elsewhere (e.g., Muramatsu et al. 1986, Tsujinaka 1988), a brief overview of the political functions of trade associations is in order here to provide a complete picture of their activities.

As described earlier, Japanese industry is characterized by a "dual structure" in terms of a few large, dominant firms on the one hand versus a large number of very small firms on the other hand. The leaders of the large firms, the *zaikai*, are the dominant political representatives of business, and they exert a pro-active and immediate influence over policy programs. Yet, this does not mean that small business is void of political influence: the very large number of small- and medium-sized enterprises in manufacturing, distribution and services translates into a substantial block of voters. The existence of this powerful group explains the long list of special legislation for small- and medium-sized firms, including the exemption of cooperatives from antitrust provision (cf. Whittaker 1997). The need for appeasing small firms, which after all employ 70% of the workforce, makes it difficult for politicians to push through sweeping deregulation programs or other measures to increase productivity and efficiency in Japanese manufacturing.

Broadly speaking, there are four ways in which the *zaikai* and the Chamber of Commerce can influence policy decisions: (1) formal and semi-formal councils and reports through the trade associations; (2) informal meetings with government officials; (3) highly informal meetings and personal gifts; and (4) party financing and political donations.

Shingikai—Deliberation Councils

Japanese firms seek formal representation of their interests mainly through participation in government deliberation councils, the *shingikai,* and through filing official reports through their trade associations and Keidanren. In contrast to the more *ad hoc* character of U.S. advisory councils, Japan's *shingikai* are long-standing committees that ensure continuous private sector input into policy decisions. Of the 215 *shingikai* that were convened in 1995, 162 were founded in or prior to 1970, and only nine were established after 1990 (Sōmuchō 1994). For instance, MITI's Industrial Structure Council (*Sangyō kōzō shingikai*) was formally established in 1964 based on the MITI Establishment Law. The councils have, on average, 20 members who are not politicians or bureaucrats. These private members serve two- to three-year terms, and they are nominally invited as "learned people" (*gakushoku keikensha*) rather than on account of their professional positions, although their affiliations—such as being the chairman of a major trade association—are clearly key to their council appointments. In 1995, of the 48 members of MITI's Industrial Structure Council, 13 were corporate executives, while 7 were representatives from trade associations. Besides its main group, this council has at least 20 subcommittees and a great many sub-subcommittees with an even higher percentage of business representation. This council therefore assures that a large number of corporations are involved in formulating industrial policy, and through their participation become committed to specific policy measures that they have helped to formulate (cf. Komiya 1988: 18; Schwartz 1998).

To be sure, many Japanese have a rather cynical view of the *shingikai* as mere fora for the ministries' co-optation of its critics. In this view, actual business input occurs through informal routes, whereas at the formal meetings the "mavericks" and system critics are enticed into signing off the bureaucrats' plans. This interpretation, however, cannot explain why busy corporate executives would agree to serve on a deliberation council if there is nothing in it for them. Executives, and especially corporate chairmen, face high time costs, and their willingness to participate in the deliberations suggests that their participation translates into some benefits for their corporation or their industry.[20]

One can test the proposition that *shingikai* discussions are relevant—and hence, that trade association representation on *shingikai* is relevant—by looking at the composition of members in the total group of *shingikai*. If councils are merely meant to appease the various interest groups, one can assume a rather regular and similar composition of businessmen, journalists, and consumer and labor representatives in all councils. If, however, there is something to be gained from these councils, then businessmen would be more involved in councils concerned with business matters and regulation, whereas consumers and journalists would be more dominant in councils on cultural and educational affairs. In other words, if the cynical co-optation interpretation holds, then the number of representatives from various parts of society should be similar across councils. In

---

[20] Participation in *shingikai* may also benefit the executives personally, as it may enhance their chances of being awarded an imperial order (*kunshō*). While this may help explain the behavior of some executives from second-tier companies, it is doubtful whether the presidents of Japan's leading companies consider serving on *shingikai* the most efficient means to self-promote for this award.

reality, however, *shingikai* membership shows a clear pattern to the contrary of this interpretation.

To test the proposition that *shingikai* matter for industry input and to identify the role of trade associations on these councils, I analyzed the composition of the 215 councils in 1994 (excluding subcommittees). Table 2.6 summarizes the results. On average, all *shingikai* have 20 members of whom 2.2 are from the business world, only 0.1 are company chairmen, and 2.3 are representatives from trade associations. Of the 215 councils, 95 were of no immediate interest to business (such as the Cultural Heritage Council, *Bunka zaihogo shingikai*, or the Animal Protection Council, *Dōbutsu hogo shinkgikai*), whereas 56 councils had marginal or possible relevance to business interest, and 64 were of immediate regulatory relevance. In looking at the composition of these three groups of councils, it is obvious that corporate executives do not waste their time on general affairs, but are indeed represented in large numbers on councils relevant to their interest. With 5.5 business executives and 4.3 association representatives per council, the corporate world comprised almost half (9.8 of 23.9) of all members of business-related *shingikai*. This finding suggests that *shingikai* are not just vehicles for co-optation of corporate mavericks by the bureaucracy; rather, businessmen dominate the *shingikai* with regulatory relevance to their industries, outnumbering by far the bureaucrats and politicians on these committees. At the end of their deliberations regarding a certain topic, *shingikai* have to file a report that is usually published. It is hard to imagine that a group of ten corporate executives and chairmen of leading trade associations would sign off on a report drafted by the bureaucrats that did not reflect their industries' interests. Thus, in drafting the reports, bureaucrats have to consider the members' interests carefully. Clearly, then, the *shingikai* system gives the business world a forceful, if often indirect, voice in Japan's policymaking process.

Besides the formal *shingikai*, the *zaikai* also influences public policy debates through more informal groupings. Probably the most important of these in the postwar period was the *Sanken* (*Sangyō mondai kenkyūkai*, lit.: "Industrial Problems Research Group"). Some consider this group to have been the "bridgehead" for *zaikai* lobbying in the 1960s (Tsuda 1990: 283). The *Sanken* was founded in 1966 as an informal meeting of the most important business leaders and, interestingly, is assumed to have been behind many big corporate mergers at the time, including those of Dai-Ichi Bank and Nihon Kangyō Bank into Dai-Ichi Kangyō Bank, and of Yawata and Fuji Steel into New Japan Steel against the advice of the JFTC in 1968.[21] Other examples of informal "shadow" groupings include the "Monday Club" of the iron and steel industry, where the top eight presidents of the industry regularly met with industry officials (Yamamura 1982: 83). Therefore, in evaluating the influence of *zaikai* groups on the policymaking

---

[21] The *Sanken* and its policy-oriented affiliate *Shinshinkai* are also said to be the source behind Tanaka Kakuei's introduction of the small district electoral system after a poor election in 1972, which was to help assure a continued LDP rule. See Tsuda (1990) for details.

Table 2.6. Business Participation in *Shingikai* in 1994

	Number of councils	Members per council	Zaikai members	Zaikai members per council	Corporate chairmen	Chairmen per council	Members from trade associations	Association members per council	Members from *zaidan* and public corporations
All *shingikai*	215	20.0	469	2.2	28	0.1	495	2.3	596
No business interest	95	15.9	66	0.7	0	0.0	58	1.1	155
Marginal business interest	56	22.5	135	2.4	4	0.1	162	2.9	188
Strong business interest	64	23.9	354	5.5	24	0.4	275	4.3	253

Source: compiled from data in *Shingikai Sōran Heisei 6nenpan* (Sōmuchō 1994).

process, one needs to consider both their formal participation through official deliberation councils and the influence of informal groups on individual politicians and bureaucrats.

Informal Meetings and Gifts

A more informal means for the *zaikai* to influence politics is through personal contacts with regulators and politicians. In Tokyo's colloquial parlance this activity is sometimes subsumed under the subtly nuanced term *"tsurumu"* (lit.: "to couple, pair, mate", usually used for animals) (Ebata 1990: 256). The word describes the tight relationship between officials from the regulating ministries and corporate employees on the one hand, and between politicians and *zaikai* leaders on the other hand.

It has often been pointed out that Japan's policymaking processes are highly informal. Time-consuming consultation mechanisms lay the groundwork for policy formulation and implementation by commitment rather than law enforcement. Constant contacts and personal ties are at the heart of this process, so that anyone who wants to be influential has to be well-networked (e.g., Upham 1987: 202–14). While informal influence-peddling is certainly a major *forte* of all lobbyists around the world, the informality of Japanese policymaking is often assumed to be much more extensive than in Western industrialized countries. Images abound of a host of characters cutting deals in smoke-filled private rooms, undisclosed and impenetrable by the media or the public, and seemingly oblivious to various legal statutes. Evidence of such deals occasionally surfaces as bribery scandals involving politicians and bureaucrats alike. For instance, the Recruit scandal of 1988 was only one of many cases in which politicians were found to have received shares of a company prior to its placement on the stock exchange, complete with a tip of exactly when to sell. The 1998 raids of the Ministry of Finance and the Bank of Japan, following scandals with similar implications in the Ministry of Health and Welfare and others in the early 1990s, provided evidence that bureaucrats, just like politicians, were lobbied on a continual, informal basis by business representatives.

In addition to "wining and dining", Japan's large core associations—such as those in banking, steel, paper, cement, glass, and automobiles—all have one employee, usually in the "Public Relations Department", whose specific job it is to procure valuable entry tickets to theater (*kabuki* and *nō*) performances and *sumō* wrestling bouts. The associations regularly give these tickets as gifts to politicians and bureaucrats who hold influence over their industry.[22] In those

---

[22] LDP politicians usually specialize in one policy area or industry and then become members of the "PARC" (Policy Affairs Research Council), which has 17 divisions that correspond to the major ministries and agencies, with more than 100 subcommittees. This system groups politicians clearly into areas of expertise, and streamlines the lobbying efforts of the regulated industries (on PARCs, see Inoguchi/Iwai 1987).

associations that have hired a former government official as the senior staff person, the OB is often in charge of allocating the tickets based on his understanding of relative power structures within the government. The OB typically also determines how much commitment is made to fund-raising parties and other gift-giving occasions.[23] In return for their generous gifts, trade associations expect an open ear by the gift recipients on policy matters.

Political Donations

Most importantly, the *zaikai* can influence politics through political funding. This system is separate from the smaller gift-giving, as it involves both larger amounts of money and a more centralized process of donation. Japan's political funding system is markedly different from that of the U.S., both in terms of the rules concerning political donations and the proportion of contributions made by business. In Japan, corporations and trade associations account for most of the political funding. Companies can directly donate to parties or candidates up to a limit of ¥100 million per year, though only donations exceeding ¥50,000 within one fiscal year must be reported and indirect donations through associations are substantial.[24] In 1995, total reported political donations in Japan amounted to ¥170.7 billion (or $1.65 billion at 1995 exchange rates), while in 1996, the figure was ¥178 billion ($1.68 billion); thus, the total for the two years was $3.33 billion. Of this total, roughly 45% were raised through contributions, 10% through party dues, 32% through activity fees (such as fund-raising dinners), and 13% were other indirect donations. The 45% of "contributions" in turn break down in equal parts to corporations/associations and so-called "political associations" (*seiji dantai*), which each account for 45% of contributions (or 21% each of total party financing); individuals account for the remaining 10% of contributions, or 5% of total party financing. The political associations are primarily funded through indirect donations by corporations through their associations, as well as Keidanren. Most corporations donate through their trade associations, i.e., it is the industries rather than the individual companies that are the biggest donors to political parties in Japan (Keidanren 1994b, Washio 1996, Nikkei Weekly 1/16/1995).

In contrast, in the U.S., total political donations in the two years 1995 and 1996 amounted to $2 billion, of which $129.3 million, or only 6%, were given by corporations and their employees (Vartabedian 1997). While trade associations

---

[23] Interview with various trade associations in Tokyo, 1993–5.

[24] Prior to a revision of the system in 1994, only donations exceeding ¥1 million in a fiscal year needed to be reported, leading to a huge amount of unreported donations. It is therefore difficult to observe the development of political donations over time. However, the official data suggest that throughout the 1990s, annual political donations to all parties totaled about ¥175 billion a year, of which on average 45% were provided by corporations, trade associations and labor unions (Keidanren 1994b).

certainly are huge donors in the U.S. system as well, such as in the firearm and tobacco industries, statistics are difficult to gather and observers suggest that individuals remain the biggest source of political financing (Weidenbaum 1990). Therefore, not only are total donations in the U.S. smaller, but most political contributions are given by individuals.

In the 1980s and 1990s, the most generous Japanese associations have been in the automobile, steel, petroleum, and banking/finance industries. Table 2.7 lists the 15 largest donor associations for the period 1980–97. The table suggests that, as one would expect, the largest donors are those that seek government support, e.g., through changes in regulation. While there was some fluctuation over the two decades, in many years the automobile and steel associations made donations up to the legal limit of ¥100 million. The automobile industry has been the subject of numerous trade problems with both the U.S. and Europe, and was also facing issues of domestic deregulation pertaining to the *shaken* (inspection) system, subcontractor system, and many more (e.g., Yayama 1998). As for the finance industry, during the "bubble recession" of the 1990s, the Tokyo Stock Exchange Members' Associations, i.e., the large investment banks, were the most generous lobbyists. During the 1990s, the Securities and Exchange Law was revised four times to account for the securities compensation scandal, the abolition of the "firewall" between the banking and securities business, the stepwise deregulation of fixed commissions in stock trades, and the change of the trade association into a designated "self-regulatory association" (see Chapter 5). During this process, the major investment banks were obviously concerned about political protection at a time when the public was much in favor of stricter regulation of the financial industry. Likewise, donations by other associations seem to fluctuate with political events: the chemical fibers' manufacturers were active during the U.S.–Japan textile agreement negotiations in the early 1980s, the Osaka Stock Exchange Members were very generous in the mid-1980s when they were lobbying hard for the introduction of futures contracts at their exchange to attract trading volume away from Tokyo, and the department stores were concerned about the revision of the Large-Scale Retail Law in the early and mid-1990s.

Given the relatively large amounts of funds funneled through the associations in Japan, as compared with the U.S., trade associations and their deep pockets play a more important role in Japan's party politics than in the U.S. The underlying logic of political donations is, of course, similar in all countries: the industries support the party for political favors. Japan is just one further example in this process. However, in the comparison with the U.S., two differences stand out: first, the amount of money that trade associations and individual companies give to the LDP are larger than in the U.S., and second, the role of trade associations is relatively much more important in the Japanese process of party financing.

From the early 1950s until 1993, Keidanren was at the center of this process of political funding, and of large-scale political lobbying by business. Keidanren collected corporate contributions and funneled them to the LDP, which was consistently seen as the pro-business party, and to a lesser extent to other parties. For instance, in 1992, the total Keidanren contribution to the LDP amounted to ¥12 billion, while the Social Democratic Party received a mere ¥1 billion. In 1991, the LDP had received a total of ¥29.3 billion, of which Keidanren accounted for ¥13 billion (_Jurisuto_ 1993/9/15: 6).

Under the mediation system, which had been established in 1955, Keidanren had routed political donations to parties and their funding organizations, primarily to the LDP's "People's Politics Group" (_Kokumin seiji kyōkai_).[25] The declared goal with these joint donations was to curb bribery and increase transparency as much as possible during a period in which most of Japan's political funding was contributed by businesses and trade associations (Keidanren 1994b). However, when the LDP lost the majority in the Lower House and the new Hosokawa government began a brief interlude of Social Democratic administration in 1993, Keidanren officially ended its traditional role of a mediator in September 1993: the system had outlived its usefulness. Some Keidanren members shifted their donations to the new government party, rendering a joint payment structure unfeasible. Moreover, the political financing scandal involving Kanemaru Shin and the big general construction companies in the same year had outraged the public regarding the non-transparency of political financing. This required a move by big business to distance itself from the image of cozy tie-ups between big business and big politicians. The new Prime Minister had already announced a revision of the Law Concerning Rules on Political Donations (_Seiji shikin kisei hō_), and so it made sense to preempt the public scrutiny this revision would necessarily entail with a change in the Keidanren donation system.

Yet, Keidanren continues to play a prominent role in influencing politics through lobbying. This central role is reflected in the fact that Keidanren owns a large building in central Tokyo's Marunouchi district, where LDP and other politicians and bureaucrats regularly attend daily meetings. As the policymaking organ of the _zaikai_, Keidanren's major task is to influence government policies to the benefit of big business. However, in this task, too, Keidanren finds itself increasingly caught between diverging business interests. In contrast to the postwar years of rapid economic growth, when big business was largely aligned in its calls for market protection and subsidies, the processes of deregulation and internationalization have created conflicts of interests among Japanese firms. For instance, in the early 1990s the petrochemical companies vehemently opposed a move to deregulate rules on gas stations so that consumers could opt for self-service. The automobile manufacturers, however, very much favored this deregulation, hoping that lower gas prices would increase the demand for new cars. Over time, as the gap in international competitiveness among Japan's leading

---

[25] The Social Democratic Party (SDP) and its _Seiwa kyōkai_ also received some token funding from business; according to Keidanren (1994), less than 10% of business donations were directed to the SDP. The SDP's primary campaign contributor during the postwar period were the labor unions.

Table 2.7. Trade Association Donations to Political Parties—The 15 Largest Donors, 1980–1997 (in millions Yen)

Trade association	Rank 80–97	Rank 80–89	Rank 90–97	1980	1981	1982	1983	1984	1985	1986	1987	1988
The Kozai Club (steel)	8	2	12	100.0	100.0	100.0	100.0	100.0	100.0	100.0	100.0	68.0
Petroleum Association of Japan	3	4	4	n.a.	100.0	100.0	100.0	100.0	100.0	100.0	97.0	97.0
The Japan Iron & Steel Federation	2	3	3	100.0	100.0	100.0	100.0	100.0	100.0	85.0	85.0	68.0
Japan Automobile Manufacturers' Association (JAMA)	1	1	2	90.0	90.0	90.0	95.1	95.0	95.0	100.0	95.0	95.0
Osaka Stock Exchange Members' Association	9	7	11	65.3	71.0	75.7	69.9	83.9	86.8	93.0	95.7	65.5
Japan Chemical Fibers Association	5	5	9	100.0	100.0	100.0	100.0	100.0	80.0	80.0	80.0	60.0
National Association of Sogo Banks*	11	6	—	86.0	87.0	83.0	78.0	78.0	78.0	68.0	80.0	80.0
The Second Association of Regional Banks*	11	—	8	n.a.	n.a.	n.a.	n.a.	n.a.	n.a.	n.a.	n.a.	n.a.
Real Estate Companies Association in Japan	6	9	7	72.8	60.0	83.4	71.0	80.1	77.3	74.5	82.2	75.3
Japan Petrochemical Industry Association	7	11	6	60.0	65.3	65.3	65.3	65.3	74.1	65.3	65.3	65.3
Tokyo Stock Exchange Members' Association	4	8	1	92.0	90.0	80.0	67.8	52.8	72.0	62.0	62.0	97.0
The Cement Association of Japan	10	10	—	88.0	90.0	90.0	100.0	90.0	50.0	50.0	50.0	50.0
Japan Electrical Manufacturers' Association (JEMA)	12	13	5	n.a.	n.a.	92.5	n.a.	n.a.	n.a.	n.a.	n.a.	n.a.
Japan Department Stores Association	15	—	13	n.a.	n.a.	55.0	n.a.	n.a.	n.a.	n.a.	n.a.	n.a.
The National Association of Shinkin Banks	13	—	10	54.0	51.0	n.a.	n.a.	n.a.	n.a.	n.a.	n.a.	n.a.
Japan Shipping Association	14	12	—	75.0	81.0	80.0	52.5	n.a.	n.a.	n.a.	n.a.	n.a.

Table 2.7. Cont.

Trade association	1989	1990	1991	1992	1993	1994	1995	1996	1997
The Kozai Club (steel products)	58.0	58.0	58.0	58.0	58.0	n.a.	n.a.	n.a.	n.a.
Petroleum Association of Japan	97.0	100.0	100.0	100.0	100.0	100.0	77.5	n.a.	60.0
The Japan Iron & Steel Federation	68.0	90.0	98.0	100.0	100.0	67.0	n.a.	84.5	100.0
Japan Automobile Manufacturers' Association (JAMA)	95.0	95.0	95.0	95.0	95.0	95.0	80.0	82.8	100.0
Osaka Stock Exchange Members' Association	61.1	57.7	60.0	60.0	60.0	65.3	33.0	n.a.	n.a.
Japan Chemical Fibers Association	60.0	60.0	60.0	70.0	70.0	60.0	n.a.	30.0	50.0
National Association of Sogo Banks*	80.0	n.a.	n.a.	n.a.	n.a.	n.a.	n.a.	n.a.	n.a.
The Second Association of Regional Banks*	n.a.	80.0	80.0	80.0	80.0	65.0	41.2	32.0	n.a.
Real Estate Companies Association in Japan	75.2	82.0	83.0	85.2	85.2	85.2	n.a.	37.0	30.0
Japan Petrochemical Industry Association	70.0	76.0	80.5	86.5	86.5	76.6	n.a.	39.9	52.3
Tokyo Stock Exchange Members' Association	92.0	92.0	91.5	91.5	96.3	99.9	96.8	93.2	77.0
The Cement Association of Japan	50.0	n.a.	n.a.	n.a.	40.0	40.0	30.0	34.0	55.0
Japan Electrical Manufacturers' Association (JEMA)	50.0	50.0	50.0	50.0	50.0	50.0	50.0	99.0	100.0
Japan Department Stores Association	n.a.	n.a.	61.5	n.a.	51.5	48.0	n.a.	n.a.	41.0
The National Association of Shinkin Banks	n.a.	55.0	55.0	55.0	51.3	52.0	48.0	36.5	35.0
Japan Shipping Association	n.a.	n.a.	n.a.	n.a.	n.a.	n.a.	n.a.	n.a.	n.a.

Source: Nihon Keizai Shinbun, various issues.

n.a. = The association was not among the top donors in that year, and therefore data are not available.

* = The "sogo banks" were transformed into "second-tier regional banks" in 1990, so the association changed its name.

businesses increased, the interests that Keidanren was supposed to represent became ever more diverse. In response, beginning in the late 1980s Keidanren became more timid in its political demands and policy reports (e.g., Keidanren 1994a).

2.5. Conclusions: Trade Associations and Self-Regulation

Trade associations face a tradeoff between political influence through large size on the one hand, and effective internal self-regulation through focused membership on the other hand. Japanese associations have addressed this problem by forming basic "core" units around narrowly defined industry segments for effective industry governance. These core groups unite in several layers of regional and topical intermediate umbrella organization, which in turn link up under large national umbrella federations that lobby for political representation. Due to this multilayered structure, there are an unusual number of trade associations in Japan.

The umbrella organizations, headed by Keidanren and the large industry federations, are in charge of overall business interest representation in the policy-making process. They represent business interests through three primary routes: *shingikai* participation; informal interest group pressure on politicians and bureaucrats; and contributions to political campaigns. At the level of core associations and cooperatives, the primary associational function is in the economic and regulatory realm. The logic here is that of "small is beautiful": the smaller the industry segment, the easier it is for the association to formulate a unified opinion on regulatory matters, and the easier it is for the regulating ministry to communicate with this industry segment. Yet, not all of Japan's core associations are the same in terms of how close they are to their regulating ministries or how tightly knit the industry is. Indicators that signal the closeness to the regulator include the number of retired government officials employed by the association, and the number of *shukkō* (member firm employees) on the staff. The organization into small, focused units also facilitates the exchange of information within the industry, including both the exchange of fundamental economic data and competitor intelligence. Numerous regular committee meetings support this exchange, and other than in cases of flagrant price fixing these committees are generally left alone by the antitrust authorities.

Most core associations are primarily concerned with self-regulation, partially due to the evolution of delegated regulatory functions. Over time, associations extended these boundaries, and when the regulating ministries began losing their powers to ensure industry compliance, associations were able to adopt rules that allowed them to restrict entry by outsider firms and generally favor the incumbent firms over others.

Thus, while umbrella associations primarily lobby, core associations primarily self-regulate. They do this through constant interaction at various levels: company presidents meet monthly, and various ranks of executives have their special committees for frequent exchange of information. In competitive industries, their agreements may amount to no more than the basic rules of trade, leaving the rest to market competition. In less competitive industries, the institution of the core association with its predetermined meeting schedule and organizational setup provides the ideal ground for cooperative agreements—administrative, protective, or collusive. Still, self-regulation has not been curtailed by the antitrust authority in the 1990s. Why and how antitrust cannot contain trade associations will be the topic of the following three chapters.

3

Antitrust Policy and Industrial Policy in the Postwar Period

The economic development of Japan in the postwar years can be divided into three major parts: the period of "rapid growth" (1955–72), the period of "moderate, stable growth" (1977–87), and the "bubble and post-bubble recession" (1987–97). The goals of economic policy and the ways in which these policies were implemented changed significantly during these phases. Moreover, while antitrust policy was clearly trumped by the goals of industrial policy between 1955 and 1975, the "oil shock" of the early 1970s and the subsequent revision of the Antimonopoly Law in 1977 gave the Japan Fair Trade Commission (JFTC)[1] more power to object to MITI-sponsored cartels. Yet, even in the 1990s the JFTC was not an independent, strong antitrust watchdog. To understand how the forces between the industrial ministries and the JFTC played out in the 1990s and how these developments influenced industry self-regulation, it is important to examine the background of the current situation.

This chapter shows how the logic and implementation of industrial policy fostered a propensity to cooperate within trade associations that formed the basis of increasing self-regulation even in competitive industries. The conflicts between Japan's emerging antitrust policy in the postwar period and the diametrically different goals of industrial policy highlight just how the system of self-regulation was cultivated by providing strength and institutional legitimacy to trade associations. One thrust of industrial policy was the encouragement of both mergers and cartels, initially in order to increase the competitiveness of Japan's export industries but later also to support small- and medium-sized firms, declining industries, and capital-intensive industries facing temporary decline in demand. Trade associations were the primary vehicles of implementing these policies, as the government tolerated or even encouraged their cartels and other protective arrangements.[2] To be sure, the ministries', and in particular MITI's, efforts to foster economic growth through mergers and cartels were not necessarily all successful. For instance, Rotwein (1964, 1976) and Uekusa (1987) show that

---

[1] Following the Washington D.C. custom, the Japanese Fair Trade Commission (*Kōsei torihiki iinkai*) is abbreviated here as "JFTC" to differentiate it from the U.S. Federal Trade Commission (FTC).

[2] One indicator of the dominant role of trade associations in facilitating cooperative agreements is that more than two-thirds of all cartel cases prosecuted by the JFTC in the postwar period involve trade associations; see Chapter 5 for a detailed analysis.

market concentration in Japan in the 1960s and 1970s was only slightly higher than in the United States. Weinstein (1995) demonstrates that neither price levels nor profit margins increased significantly in cartels formed in the early 1960s.[3]

Still, whatever the outcomes of industrial policy, there is no denying that the various ministries actively encouraged the formation of cartels. In the early 1960s, more than 40% of all manufacturing output at the four-digit level was produced with some cartel activity[4] (Yoshida 1964, Weinstein 1995). Ultimately, MITI's persistent efforts to structure cartels fostered a propensity to cooperate due to repeated cooperation in many industries. In the context of self-regulation, whether these cartels in fact achieved the original industrial policy goals is not nearly as relevant as the "cooperative heritage" that was thus formed: companies learned that antitrust was not a significant threat and that it paid to cooperate. In the process of trial and error, trade associations also learned what it took to structure successful agreements, how to set incentives for small firms to abide by the agreements, and how to structure monitoring and punishment systems. Furthermore, even at the heyday of industrial policy some portion of policy-making was left to autonomous self-regulation. Over time, these two character-istics—the propensity to cooperate and the habit to self-regulate through trade associations—became more pronounced and led to the shift toward the co-operative system based on industry self-regulation in the 1980s and 1990s.

Overview: Economic Cycles during the Postwar Period

During 40 years of postwar economic growth, Japan experienced four major boom periods. After the "Korean War Boom" (also called the "investment boom"), which was spurred by demand for U.S. military supplies during the Korean War, Japanese journalists began to name these boom periods after figures from Japanese mythology. The first such home-grown boom period was the Jimmu boom of 1955–6. This was followed by the Iwato boom period of 1958–61, and the Izanami boom of 1966–70.[5] The Izanami years were the Japanese

---

[3] Since the thrust of cartel policies occurred throughout the 1960s, Weinstein's (1995) data may have been somewhat limited. Moreover, data are not available for informal cartels (*kankoku sōtan*, as described later in this chapter) and the investment cartels of the late 1960s. Nevertheless, the track record of industrial policy in the early stages is mixed at best. Beason/Weinstein (1996) argue that for the later cartels, which aimed to reduce the impact of structural recession, results are equally refutable.

[4] To give one example of how the classification of sectors into digit-levels works, the "chemical industry" overall is a two-digit category, "organic chemicals" is the four-digit categorization, and the "soda ash" industry is a six-digit level subcategory. In the early 1960s, 50.4% of the shipments in chemicals (at the two-digit level) were produced under cartel agreements, while almost 20% of all four-digit subcategories of chemicals were. Japanese documents that count "cartelized industries" typically refer to the six-digit-level.

[5] Jimmu was the first goddess to descend to earth to become the first emperor of Japan. Officially, until 1945, all *tennō* (emperors) were considered to be his descendants. Iwato, according to mytho-logy, was a goddess who performed a mesmerizing dance that enticed the sun goddess Amaterasu to leave a cave where she had been sulking and shine back on earth. Izanagi and Izanami were goddess siblings who are thought to have created Japan.

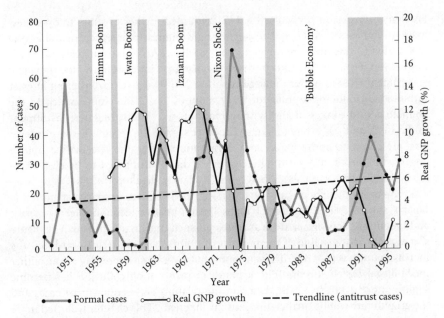

Figure 3.1. Number of Cartel Prosecutions and GNP Growth in the Postwar Period
Sources: EPA 1996, JFTC Annual Reports, 1948–1997.

equivalent to the consumer boom of the 1950s in the U.S., and they ended abruptly with the Nixon Shock of 1971 (when Nixon introduced a 10% tariff on U.S. imports, primarily from Japan, and ended the dollar–gold convertibility), the end of the Bretton Woods system, and then the oil shock of 1973 (cf. Figure 3.1.).

The 1970s were a decade of large-scale industrial restructuring from heavy, energy-consumptive, high-pollution industries to light, energy-saving, high value-added industries. The decade also brought to light the wide scope of political corruption (e.g., the Tanaka–Lockheed scandal of 1974), the recognition that economic growth had been achieved at the expense of ordinary people and the environment, and huge government deficits caused by low-interest rate financing and preferential taxes for the fastest-growing "designated industries". The policy changes required to address these issues—ranging from creating a social security system to enforcing environmental rules and trying to stem the growing budget deficit—cut the average annual growth rate of 10% witnessed during the 1960s roughly in half.

The 1980s in Japan were characterized by *"gaiatsu"* (foreign pressure) to deregulate market access, financial deregulation, and the "financial bubble". The changes in fiscal and monetary policy in the wake of the 1970s recession (including the new foreign exchange pressures, the financing of the newly introduced pension system, and the sharp increase in issues of government bonds) necessitated a relaxation of the tight rules governing financial markets.

Foreign countries, in particular the U.S., mounted further pressure to open new market segments and deregulate Japan's rigid interest rate structure. When the U.S. added to this pressure through the 1985 Plaza Accord, to increase the value of the yen vis-à-vis the dollar through currency interventions, the Japanese government tried to buffer the negative effect of a strong yen by lowering interest rates and introducing a policy of "easy money". These interventions led to the "bubble period": excess liquidity soon found its way into speculative investment in the stock and real estate markets. The price tag for the speculative investments was presented to most banks and corporations after the speculative bubble "burst" in 1991–2. The ensuing recession of the 1990s proved to be even more devastating than the oil shock had been 20 years earlier.[6]

Throughout these boom and bust periods, the JFTC was in charge of enforcing Japan's antitrust laws. Figure 3.1 maps Japan's postwar economic growth path and the number of formal antitrust cases pursued during this period. This figure shows that the trend line of the number of cases slopes slightly upward, but the increase is not very steep. This suggests that over time there have been either more illegal cartels, or the JFTC's stance in prosecuting collusion has become slightly more aggressive. The data and the relation between antitrust cases and the growth rate will be further analyzed in Chapter 5. This chapter will shed more light on the role of antitrust policy in the period of rapid growth, the system of "exempting" certain cartels from antitrust statutes, the concept of "legal cartels", and the battle between antitrust and industrial policy in postwar Japan.

3.1. The 1947 Antimonopoly Law and its 1953 Revision

'Businessmen with a long tradition of cartels and trade associations can understand regulations arrived at after discussions among the competitors much more readily than they can the bizarre notion that concerted actions constitute an unreasonable restraint of trade...

In the Japanese literature on Occupation changes in the business world one even—astonishingly enough—comes upon the phrase "nostalgic longing" of businessmen for "the prewar days of laissez-faire"... The term "laissez-faire" in such references means the freedom of the government to favor some business and the freedom of businessmen to contract for a wide variety of restrictive practices—which should surely stand as the all-time classic in definitions of "laissez-faire".'

(Hadley 1975: 372–3, partially citing Ariga/Rieke 1964: 459)[7]

---

[6] On the process of financial deregulation in the 1980s, see KZJK (1986), Saijō (1986), FAIR (1991), Vogel, S. K. (1996), Schaede (1990, 2000). Murphy (1996) gives an account of the policy processes triggered by the Plaza Agreement in 1985.

[7] Eleanor Hadley was one of the members of the SCAP cartel division in Tokyo.

In 1945, the Supreme Commander of the Allied Powers (SCAP), under the leadership of General Douglas MacArthur, set up headquarters in Tokyo and began its work to "democratize" Japan by abolishing those institutions identified to have played an integral part in the war effort. Among the major reforms accomplished in the first three years of the Occupation was a new Constitution, land reform, tax reform, the creation of labor unions, the dissolution of the *zaibatsu*, and the introduction of antitrust legislation.[8]

One of SCAP's major challenges was its dual task of both preventing a resurgence of a war aggressor and trying to reconstruct Japan's economy. Around 1948, the U.S. changed its strategy regarding Japan due to increasing fear that Japan might go Communist and the growing desire to make Japan a buffer against Communism in Asia. The biggest hindrance to rebuilding the economy was considered high inflation, and in 1948 SCAP drafted an "Economic Stabilization Plan" which was enforced through the so-called "Dodge Line". This was a set of policies designed by Joseph Dodge to balance the budget, set one exchange rate for foreign trade, and stop all subsidies and reconstruction moneys. While these policies were eventually helpful in putting Japan on the right footing for the ensuing "Korean War Boom", initially they led to recession and an increase in market concentration because many small firms went bankrupt.

As one of their earliest measures, in August 1946 SCAP ordered the Japanese government to dissolve all wartime control associations (*tōseikai*) within 90 days (see Chapter 7). However, some leading control associations, such as in iron and steel, rubber, and lumber, had already been disbanded, and SCAP was concerned that a dissolution of all control associations at once would disrupt government allocation controls in the face of increasing inflation and a severe shortage of goods. Therefore, while the roughly 1,200 wartime control associations were dissolved beginning in 1946, some of them were used for product allocation until 1949. Moreover, before long most of the dissolved control associations reappeared under different names but with the same member firms and, in many cases, the same staff.

In 1947 SCAP passed the new "Law for the Elimination of Excessive Concentration of Economic Power" (*Kado keizai shūchū haijo hō*). This "*zaibatsu* breakup law" designated 325 companies to be broken up by the Holding Company Liquidation Committee. Yet, while the *zaibatsu* family members were dispossessed and purged, the shift in U.S. policy stance soon thereafter meant that eventually only 18 corporate groups were disbanded, and most of these reorganized through mergers during the 1960s. In 1948 and 1949, SCAP also conducted purges to remove military and political leaders. However, this purge left bureaucrats firmly in place and thus assured a continuance of wartime bureaucratic power into the postwar period.[9] Moreover, since SCAP placed the

---

[8] For details on land, labor, tax and *zaibatsu* reforms, see Bisson (1954), Hadley (1970), Yamamura (1967).

[9] See Chapter 7 for an analysis of wartime economic controls, and Johnson (1982), Noguchi (1995) and Nakamura (1989) for analyses of the transfer of wartime controls into the postwar period.

Japanese bureaucrats in charge of administering the *zaibatsu* purges, they fulfilled the SCAP order by removing the top corporate leaders— with whom they had communicated closely through the war years—while leaving their protégés in public office to continue the personal connections with the corporations (Cohen 1958: 197, Lynn/McKeown 1988: 25). Yet, all these measures were considered "one time" policies to change the old system, with little assurance how long their effects would be felt. SCAP sensed a need to ensure the long-term continuity of free markets and fair trade by creating permanent antitrust legislation (in 1947) as well as a law on trade associations (in 1948) which aimed to prevent the resurgence of wartime-style control cartels for good.

The 1947 Antimonopoly Law

Although Truman himself was not pushing hard for antitrust policy, the SCAP staff in Japan, and in particular the SCAP Cartel Division, consisted of a group of "zealous New Dealers" (Misonō 1987: 10) who saw it as their mission to create for Japan an antitrust law that was even more strict than the U.S. laws. Yet, by overshooting in the direction of "strictness", the SCAP officials may have caused more resistance to the law than they would have with a more lenient set of rules. First, the Japanese business world did not consider cartels to be a negative force, and neither did the bureaucrats in the ministries. The process of "catch-up" industrialization of the Meiji and Taishō periods and the early Shōwa years, while initially triggered by competition, had rested on the notion of creating a few large industry leaders that would spearhead the development process. Japan had achieved industrialization quite successfully, so why were cooperation and market concentration suddenly wrong? More important, during the war companies had been asked to cooperate on input, output, and price, and this cooperation had helped them to do relatively well, given the general scarcity of raw materials and labor. Therefore, even before the 1947 antitrust law was passed, there was a good deal of misunderstanding and ill-will among the Japanese about SCAP's intent to impose this new legislation. The notion that a market economy based on free competition would be more beneficial to Japan than cooperation and market allocation ran counter to the nation's experience and was not an attractive option in the immediate aftermath of a destructive war.[10]

The process of formulating the new antitrust law began in January 1946, when SCAP asked the Ministry of Commerce and Industry (MCI, soon to be reformed into MITI) to prepare a draft. Since the Japanese had no experience with antitrust policy, the MCI bureaucrats dug out the 1931 Important Industries Control Law (*Jūyō sangyō tōsei hō*; cf. Chapter 7) and slightly revised it to include a notifica-

---

[10] In addition, Marxist ideology of monopoly capitalism was very popular both during and immediately after WWII, and Marxist economists formed an odd alliance with businessmen in opposing a system of free market economy (Gao 1997).

tion system for cartels (i.e., if corporations formed a cartel, they had to notify the MCI) and a special price approval system for firms in highly concentrated industries. One can imagine the long faces in SCAP's Cartel Division when they saw this draft, and SCAP immediately turned around and crafted their own proposal. This proposal was essentially a translated amalgamation of the U.S. Sherman Act, FTC Act, and Clayton Act, only with fewer loopholes. The new SCAP conception also included a prohibition of holding companies and limitations on cross-shareholdings, interlocking directors and international cartels. Moreover, it prescribed the establishment of a politically independent sole agency for enforcement of the antitrust law (Misonō 1987: 19).

With significant U.S. pressure, the draft passed the Diet in March of 1947, and became effective in April 1947, as Law No. 54 of 1947, "Law Concerning the Prohibition of Private Monopolies and the Assurance of Fair Trade" (for short: the Antimonopoly Law or AML; *Shiteki dokusen no kinshi oyobi kōsei torihiki no kakuho ni kansuru hōritsu*, short: *Dokkinhō*). The 1947 AML made all cartels and trusts *per se* illegal (i.e., illegal regardless of whether there is a demonstrable negative effect on market competition), and defined in great detail and prohibited unfair trade practices such as boycotts or selling at overly discounted (dumping) prices. It contained preventive rules, procedural regulations, and specifications on the establishment and legal rights of Japan's Fair Trade Commission. The biggest difference from the U.S. arrangement was that all antitrust enforcement rights resided with the JFTC (rather than being shared with the Justice Department), so that the JFTC came to be in charge of all violation cases, international cartels, merger approvals and merger notifications. The logic behind this centralization was that if the system functions well, one institution in charge of all antitrust issues is better than a division and possible overlap of functions between agencies. However, if there is political pressure to undermine the system, one single institution will wither and sink much more easily than two, which is exactly the fate that the JFTC was to face during the period of rapid growth (Misonō 1987: 21, 30).

Ironically, the new JFTC was initially housed in the headquarters of the former Mitsui *Zaibatsu*, and its first Commissioner was a former Industrial Bank of Japan Director. The initial JFTC staff of 284 consisted of repatriated officials from the Manchurian Railways and other government institutions in territories occupied during WWII, such as the Bank of Korea, as well as a large number of "loaners" from other ministries (i.e., bureaucrats from MITI, MOF and other ministries sent to the JFTC on a two-year *shukkō*–secondment stint). Since these staff members were inexperienced in antitrust matters, SCAP's cartel division had to teach them how to identify and prosecute an antitrust violation.

The first case brought by the new JFTC in 1947 describes well the difficulties encountered by the new antitrust policy in the Japanese setting. The case concerned interest rate collusion by a group of 27 banks. The agreement by these banks to charge the same loan rates was in violation of the brand-new AML. When the JFTC issued a cease-and-desist order, the banks were taken by surprise: not only had they agreed on these interest rates since prewar times, but both the Ministry of Finance (MOF) and the Bank of Japan (BOJ) had encouraged them to do so (because controlling monetary flows is easier if the interest rate is not a strategic variable for banks) (Misonō 1987: 32). The solution to this problem would serve as a precedent for many future cases when antitrust enforcement clashed with economic policy: after discussing the issue with MOF and the BOJ, the banks agreed to end their agreement. At the same time, MOF set out to draft the Temporary Interest Rate Adjustment Law (*Rinji kinri chōsei hō*) of 1949 under supervision by Joseph Dodge, who sought to curb inflation through interest rate controls. The law pegged all major interest rates to the official discount rate, and in contrast to the original intention this law was in effect until 1993. Therefore, while the banking industry complied with the JFTC order, MOF drafted a special industry law that resulted in the same non-competitive outcome as the previous cartel agreement.

Under SCAP guidance, in the first nine months of its existence the JFTC initiated a total of 66 investigations; in 1948, this number increased to 200. While some of these involved simply ignorance of the new law or international agreements of cooperation that predated the law, many cases referred to self-regulation in trade associations. In 1950, the JFTC launched a total of 59 prosecutions (cf. Figure 3.1.), which was to remain the record high for a single year until the 1973 oil shock. Twenty of these cases involved trade associations that had forced their members to conform to certain restrictive actions or collude on price. However, with the shift in U.S. priority to rebuilding Japan's economy around 1948, even within SCAP some considered the new AML as a hindrance to Japan's reconstruction. Large Japanese firms, through the newly formed Keidanren, tried to exploit this change in U.S. attitude and submitted a report requesting a revision of the rules on international agreements, stockholdings by banks and corporations, and Section 8 of the AML. This section had been a thorn in the side of big business from day one, as it stipulated that firms with excessive bargaining power could be forced by the JFTC to spin off large portions or split into several independent companies. This "breakup clause" was a threat to all large firms, and it remains a touchy issue to the present day. SCAP rejected this request, but in 1948 agreed to introduce emergency measures that watered down both the rules on international agreements (allowing exclusive cooperative agreements between firms in different countries) and on stockholdings. These changes paved the way for a formal revision of the AML in 1953.

The 1948 Trade Association Law

Even with the AML in place, SCAP was worried that Japanese industry was traditionally so "cartel-minded" that control associations would resurface or trade associations would surreptitiously assume cartel functions. The outstanding case that triggered these concerns involved the "Glorious *Bōren*"("*Kagayaku*

Bōren"; it was called this because it was so powerful). In the Meiji period, the Cotton Spinning Federation (*Dai Nihon menshi bōseki dōgyō rengōkai*, short: *Bōren*) had been one of the first associations to form, and with direct government assistance had created a very stable, long-term output restriction cartel, supported by a transportation and shipment agreement (cf. Chapter 7). During WWII, the "Glorious *Bōren*" had assumed control and allocation functions. SCAP ordered *Bōren* to dissolve in 1947, so the federation and its member associations reorganized into a new core association, the *Nihon bōseki kyōkai*, and a new umbrella federation named the *Nihon bōseki rengōkai*, likewise abbreviated as *Bōren*. The member firms of the federation did not change at all, and neither was the staff replaced. As early as in 1948, the concept of self-regulation was clearly alive and well in this federation, and as we will see below, after SCAP left in 1952 the "Glorious *Bōren*" was the first association to effectively and efficiently launch a production and output cartel (Misonō 1987: 24).

But cotton spinning was by no means a singular case, and SCAP's concern about the continuity of existing association practices intensified. In December 1947, SCAP announced a law intended specifically to limit the activities of trade associations. From the Japanese perspective this law was entirely superfluous, but SCAP firmly rejected all proposals for modifications. In July 1948, the Trade Association Law (*Jigyōsha dantai hō*; Law No. 191 of 1948) passed the Japanese Diet, again under considerable U.S. pressure. In the preamble, the law placed all trade association activities unequivocally under the auspices of the JFTC (rather than the ministries in charge of supporting and regulating the industries) and introduced a notification system. The law limited trade association activities to the areas of exchange of technical information; quality and standard regulation; and negotiation with labor unions. It made all price fixing through associations *per se* illegal, and regulated all activities concerning mutual financing, right to patents, management advice, and stockholding. The law even outlawed the "inappropriate influence of government and bureaucrats", a rule that threatened the *raison d'être* of trade associations. Finally, the new law contained a list of activities that, while not specifically prohibited, would require JFTC approval. In short, the law was a knockout for most trade association activities: in order to wipe out any possibility of cartels in trade associations, the law limited trade association functions to a minimal set of almost meaningless activities (Misonō 1987: 25–6, 42–3).

To make the new arrangement foolproof, SCAP formulated an extremely broad definition of a "trade association" in the law: a "group of two or more businessmen who gather to further their joint business interests" were deemed to constitute an association. This nomenclature included all "presidents' councils" (*shachōkai*), not-for-profit foundations, joint financing groups (cooperative-like setups), and the umbrella organizations such as Keidanren or the Chambers of Commerce. In the end, this blanket definition turned out to be the straw that broke the camel's back: by evoking fierce resistance from the *zaikai* (leading industrialists), the law's primary effect was to heighten the general resistance to antitrust regulation. In engendering such virulent opposition, SCAP's new law proved ineffective in changing the *zaikai's* "cartel state of mind". In September 1948, Keidanren submitted a first proposal to modify the Trade Association Law as well as the AML. However, SCAP denied all requests for a revision of either law. The Japanese would have to wait until SCAP left the country before abolishing the association law and revising the AML.

The 1953 Revision of the Antimonopoly Law

It is not surprising that large Japanese firms and bureaucrats alike detested the new antitrust legislation. Traditionally, they had based policies and strategies on close cooperation and exchange of information, and this approach had proven successful in creating a set of large companies that thrived on high and stable profit margins (HKKK 1977: 120). Many Japanese industrialists thought that antitrust regulation had to be a temporary Occupation policy, just like the *zaibatsu* dissolution, which was never completed. When SCAP changed its basic attitude toward Japan's postwar political role, it further fed the hope that cartel restrictions were only temporary. SCAP gradually allowed the Japanese staff in the JFTC to take over. To address the new issues of Japanese dumping practices in foreign trade, SCAP also allowed special export associations, which could agree on prices in export goods (see below, this section). Several original "democratization officers" were called back to Washington D.C., as was General MacArthur himself. His successor, General Matthew Ridgway, declared a "re-evaluation of occupation policies" in his inauguration speech. The September 1951 San Francisco peace treaty put Japan firmly under the U.S. security umbrella, making Washington believe that it was time to give the Japanese government more leeway in running its country.

Upon hearing Ridgway's speech in May 1951, the Japanese government promptly established a "Legal Inquiry Council", which had many *zaikai* representatives as its members. The council's first move was to push for a major revision of the AML and the Trade Association Law. This led to a huge discussion within the government itself, with the JFTC and MITI submitting their own, diametrically different revision drafts. It became obvious in this process that the JFTC was subject to immense pressures from politicians and MITI bureaucrats, and was anything but the strong, independent organization that SCAP had hoped to create. In December of 1951, SCAP intervened one more time to, again, reject all revision plans and drive a hard line against the pro-business ministries (Misonō 1987: 66–8).

As SCAP withdrew from overseeing the daily activities of the JFTC, the number of cases prosecuted by the JFTC dropped sharply (see Figure 3.1). While the JFTC conducted 68 investigations in the year 1951, only 14 resulted in formal cases, whereas 49 were dropped because of "insufficient evidence". This is surprising considering that the AML at that time defined cartels as *per se* illegal, so that simple evidence of an agreement, without a discussion of its effects on competition, should have been sufficient to bring a case. The JFTC ended most cases with a rather inconsequential "warning" (see Chapter 4), primarily because it was pushed by MITI and other ministries to be lenient. In public, the JFTC declared that the primary reason for dropping these cases was an uncertainty as to whether prosecution would have been in the "public interest". This set a precedent of MITI and the *zaikai* manipulating the meaning of "public interest" for many years after. Thus, even while SCAP was still in Japan, the JFTC shifted to a much more flexible application of the AML than the U.S. lawmakers had ever imagined possible.

The major reason industry was regaining influence was the first postwar boom period, triggered by the "special demand" of military supplies such as trucks, blankets and foodstuff during the Korean War. As they resumed earning profits and accumulating funds to give to politicians, large corporations re-established their influence on politics. However, when the war ended in July 1953, the economy again fell into a recession. The Bank of Japan channeled money into the economy, and many industries again benefited from subsidies and other supportive measures. In particular, the products that had enjoyed the biggest demand push during the Korean War, such as sugar, fats and oils, leather, cotton, wool, synthetic fibers, and rubber, all badly needed a weed-out or capacity reduction. It was at this point that the prewar propensity to cooperate in times of crisis resurfaced.

The occupation ended in April 1952, when the San Francisco Peace Treaty went into effect and SCAP was formally abolished. In December of 1952, Keidanren resubmitted its request for a major revision of the AML. One primary concern to the *zaikai* was the definition of "public interest", which according to Keidanren included the interests of producers. Cartels could thus not possibly be "against the public interest". Instead, cartels should on principle be allowed, the *zaikai* argued, with an obligation for the cartelists to notify the JFTC of their agreements. The JFTC had to be reorganized to include representatives of consumers and producers, and the Trade Association Law, according to Keidanren's proposal, had to be abolished. Finally, industry argued for cutting the original Section 8, which empowered the JFTC to order large firms to break up if they had "dominant bargaining power" (Misonō 1987: 75, Keidanren 1978: 51).

MITI soon joined the industrialists, but in contrast to Keidanren's idea of simply allowing all cartels, the ministry pushed for the new concept of "exempting" certain cartels from the AML. Following the logic of administrative guidance, everything that empowers a ministry to approve or license an activity translates into leverage in terms of "carrots and sticks"; i.e., something that it can promise to give or threaten to withhold. Accordingly, rather than pushing for a complete abolition of cartel rules, MITI suggested a licensing system for cartels. In particular, MITI had two kinds of cartels in mind: "recession cartels" (*fukyō karuteru*) and "rationalization cartels" (*gōrika karuteru*). The former would be authorized when supply and demand in an industry were temporarily imbalanced because of recession, when the market price of the commodity had dropped below average costs in the industry, or under similar temporary conditions. No exact definition or benchmark measures were offered as to what would constitute an "imbalance", or how to define a "recession". Rationalization cartels were to be approved if an industry needed to upgrade its technology, quality, efficiency, or cost structure, and would allow firms to agree on investments or capacity reductions, output curtailment, price and quantity. MITI argued that in these cases an exemption from the stipulations of the AML was appropriate because such improvements in industrial efficiency were clearly in the interest of economic growth and would therefore benefit, rather than hurt, Japanese consumers (Yamamura 1967: 54–61, Johnson 1982: 215).

Upon receiving the Keidanren and MITI proposals, the JFTC adopted a very passive stance. Keidanren was lobbying the politicians heavily, and major ministries (including MITI and those of Finance, Transportation, Construction and Agriculture) were all for a revision of the AML. The JFTC's lone supporter, the U.S., had departed and Japanese forces united to unravel what the Americans had wrought. The JFTC had to be realistic about its weak position vis-à-vis the other ministries and so sought to retain what vestiges of power and autonomy it could. In an attempt to keep at least the pillars of the AML standing, the JFTC settled for preserving the spirit and basic principles of the new antitrust policy, and it issued a revision draft that was rather similar to that proposed by Keidanren. The AML revision of 1953 led to four fundamental changes:[11]

(1) It stripped the JFTC of its major weapon against concentration and market domination, through the abolition of the old Section 8 and the increase in shareholding limits by corporations and financial institutions in Section 11.[12] Abolishing Section 8 meant that large firms could now become dominant market leaders without fearing antitrust investigation; subsequently, this led to an increase in market concentration. Increasing shareholding limits paved the way for the formation of *keiretsu* and vertical corporate groups (*kigyō shūdan*).

(2) It dropped the very strict rules on trade association behavior, by abolishing the 1948 Trade Association Law. The revised AML adopted some of the old law's restrictions on unfair trade and trade association activities; these were now split up across three clauses, in particular in a new Section 8. Yet, many former restrictions were lifted without replacement, leading to a revival of cooperation within trade associations.

(3) It relaxed the "trade rules" (of the old Section 2(7)), by redefining the concept of "unfair competition" and dropping most of the detailed definitions of what forms "unfair restraint of trade". This had severe implications for the prosecution of self-regulation, because it became much more difficult for the JFTC to establish evidence of "unfair trade". The old prohibitions of agreements on price, output, technology, etc., were subsumed in less rigid wording under Section 3, which prohibited "private monopolies" and "trade

---

[11] See Yamamura (1967) for the full text of the law before and after 1953.
[12] The shareholding limit for banks was raised from 5% of outstanding capital of a company to 10%. Because capital was very limited at the time, a bank holding 10% of a company's equity would typically be the largest shareholder.

restrictions". The revised AML also allowed for retail price maintenance in many designated industries. Overall, the revised AML lost most of its bite in reference to pricing because of more ambiguous wording.

(4) It divided cartels into "good cartels" and "bad cartels", and allowed the formation of "good cartels" based on a government license. If an industry in economic trouble could be supported by forming a cartel, collusion was considered to serve the "public interest". Following MITI's concept, the new Section 24(3) allowed for the licensing of "recession" cartels, and therefore a temporary exemption of an industry from antitrust stipulations. Section 24(4) allowed for exemption for the purpose of "rationalization" (i.e., capacity adjustment) of an industry.

One consequential effect of this AML revision came in how it demonstrated to the *zaikai* that they could count on the government (especially the LDP and MITI) to fight for their interests against the JFTC. By agreeing to a revision that cut the old Section 8, increased stockholding limits, and watered down the restrictions on "unfair trade", the JFTC lost most of its powers and public recognition. Contrary to the JFTC's intentions, the basic principles of antitrust policy had been recast.

The most important factor was arguably the change in cartel definition. By dropping the *per se* illegal clause from the AML and introducing a "rule of reason" in its stead, cartels became permissible if firms could convincingly argue that cooperation was necessary for economic growth, i.e., if this cooperation served the "public interest". This introduced two loopholes: (1) the definition of "significant" restraint of competition, and (2) the definition of "public interest". In general, by allowing for a case-by-case interpretation, a "rule of reason" may be a better rule if the law enforcement agency is strong enough to uphold its legal interpretation against corporate interests. But if the agency is weak, as with the JFTC, then vague wording opens all kinds of possibilities to cooperate without doing something, strictly speaking, illegal.

The new Section 24 allowed for licenses (*ninka*) for cartels under special economic circumstances, which raised the issue of who would have the right to grant such a license—the ministry in charge of the industry or the JFTC? MITI thought that the cognizant ministry had to issue the license. After all, MITI argued, it was in charge of industrial policy. The JFTC submitted that such licenses were an exemption from the AML, and only the JFTC, as the agency responsible for the AML, could grant such exemptions. In this battle between industrial policy and antitrust policy, government gave the right to license AML exemptions to the JFTC.[13] The JFTC had dodged a bullet, or so it seemed. In the end, however, the 1953 revision changed the basic character of the AML, and the licensing right turned out to be a Pyrrhic victory. By introducing the notion of a "good cartel"

---

[13] The Economic Stabilization Committee (*Keizai antei iinkai*) was in charge of the legal revision and sided with the JFTC on this issue. This Committee was part of the Economic Stabilization Board (*Keizai antei honbu*), which was the predecessor of today's Economic Planning Agency (*Keizai kikaku-chō*) and very powerful in designing Japan's postwar economy; cf. Tsuru (1993).

based on a rule of reason, even if the JFTC did not license a certain recession or rationalization cartel, before the law such a cartel technically could still be legal. MITI soon began to exploit this loophole for its industrial policy purposes.

Cartels Under the Production Curtailment System

The *zaikai*, still convinced that antitrust policy was an American innovation that Japan did not need, was facing a recession in 1953–4. To support suffering industries in this first postwar recession, MITI adopted two new means to circumvent antitrust restrictions: (1) the formation of production curtailment cartels based on administrative guidance; and (2) the formulation of special industry laws to exempt an entire industry from antitrust rules.

During the post-Korean War recession in the early 1950s, two types of cartel had emerged, both of which were typically administered by trade associations. The first were unauthorized, illegal price cartels. These were most common in industries with a few large firms (that could overcome the collective action problem more easily), such as steel, aluminum, chemicals, petroleum, auto tires, cement, flat glass, and dairy products. A subset of these cartels was characterized by tacit agreements of price leadership by one firm, which were observed in rubber, ammonium sulfate, chemicals and some non-ferrous metals. However, undercover cartels did not function in the fragmented industries that were, in MITI's view, most in need of capacity reduction, such as natural and synthetic fibers. Therefore MITI and the industry leaders designed a scheme to bypass the AML and establish a second, new type of cartel. In February 1952, the first so-called "recommended reduction" scheme (*kankoku sōtan*; from *kankoku sōgyō tanshoku*, lit.: "recommended curtailment of operation") was formed by MITI together with the "Glorious *Bōren*", the Federation of Cotton Spinners. Through this scheme, MITI issued a "ministerial recommendation" to all companies in the industry (i.e., to the federation) to reduce capacity by 25%, and because this warning was based on extralegal administrative guidance, it was not, in MITI's view, a violation of the AML.

The logic of MITI's administrative guidance at that time functioned as follows. In 1949, the Diet passed the Foreign Trade and Foreign Exchange Control Law which, together with the Foreign Investment Law, introduced extensive government controls of foreign reserves and prohibited all international trade transactions not explicitly allowed by MITI.[14] The controls included the purchase and

---

[14] These were the *Gaikoku kawase oyobi gaikoku bōeki kanri hō* ("*Gaitamehō*") and the *Gaishi ni kan suru hōritsu*. The combined goal of the two laws was to achieve an optimal allocation of foreign reserves. The Foreign Investment Law regulated the inflow of foreign capital, and while the initial intent in 1947 was to encourage such inflows, after SCAP left in 1952 it was used to protect Japanese industry from foreign direct investment and foreign takeovers. The law was abolished in 1965, when its major clauses were subsumed in the amended Foreign Exchange and Foreign Control Law. Prior to 1980, the Foreign Exchange Law prohibited all outflows of currency unless they were specifically approved. A 1980 revision allowed all cross-border capital flows unless they were explicitly prohibited,

import of technology, the payments of licensing fees to foreign firms, and other transactions necessary for the technological catch-up that Japanese firms would embark on in the following two decades. This law therefore was the basis of MITI's postwar industrial policy, and it provided for an ideal "carrot and stick" mechanism: it allowed MITI to threaten with quota curtailments or entice cooperation by promising future rewards in the form of technology imports. For instance, in the "Glorious *Bōren*" scheme, the cotton spinners needed to import raw cotton, and just how much cotton they could get hold of determined their market share in cotton products. By being in charge of foreign reserves and import allocations, MITI could effectively control the market share of each company in the industry. As long as every company obeyed the 25% capacity reduction agreement, no one lost market share. In this way, a law designed to regulate foreign trade and administer Japan's scarce foreign reserves became a tool to enforce cartels among competitors aimed to adjust domestic production capacities and output (Misonō 1987: 58–61).

The 1952 *kankoku sōtan*, and many similar arrangements administered by MITI, were bitter pills to swallow for the JFTC. Formally, MITI consulted with the JFTC, but often MITI simply informed one of the JFTC staff on *shukkō* assignment from MITI after the fact. When non-MITI personnel from the JFTC questioned an arrangement, MITI excelled in creating excuses for its actions. For instance, with the textile *kankoku sōtan*, MITI explained that it was not based on cooperation among the firms, but on unilateral MITI orders to each company in the industry. In any event, MITI claimed, this was only an emergency measure. And finally, the ministry threatened that the JFTC would be responsible for the recession, chaos and panic that would result should these agreements be outlawed. Since the official policy goal at this point was technological catch-up and economic growth, the JFTC could not afford to be blamed for causing a recession.

Interestingly, at least the first of MITI's arguments was untrue. MITI did not unilaterally set and issue the quota of each firm in the cotton spinning industry. Instead, the quotas were based on a prior agreement among the firms themselves, reached in the *Bōkyō kamei* (lit.: the "Spinners' Union"), an unofficial industry group consisting of the CEOs of the largest firms. The Union agreed to base the reduction rates on their existing market shares, to submit the agreement to MITI, and to comply with these ratios. While the firms agreed on their quotas by way of self-regulation, MITI was the administrator of the agreement (Misonō 1987: 62).[15]

---

but MITI initially maintained a long list of restrictions. The Foreign Exchange Law was again significantly amended in 1998, and now allows free inflow and outflow of capital.

[15] Uriu (1996) reports this and similar events and argues that in general MITI did not unilaterally impose quotas on industry. Rather, in many cases industry initiated an agreement and MITI simply ratified it. MITI did not always get away with such transgressions. For instance, the JFTC did not accept the "unilateral quota setting" argument in the case of MITI's intervention in the rubber industry, and the Japan Automobile Tire Association was ordered to stop its behavior. The staple fibers industry, in contrast, was allowed to follow up on the MITI order. These differences in prosecution soon gave rise to criticism by the media and academics that Japanese antitrust was a system of "application when convenient" (*tsūgō no yoi hō no tekiyō*) (Misonō 1987: 64).

Once the *kankoku sōtan* was successfully accomplished by the spinners' association, one industry after the other agreed to quasi-legal capacity reductions to alleviate the effects of economic recession. During 1957, MITI arranged for such agreements in, among others, textiles, paper and pulp, chemicals, petroleum, coal, iron and steel, and cement. The two alternatives to the *kankoku sōtan*—an illegal cartel or an official JFTC license—were much more difficult for firms to accomplish. A MITI-administered *kankoku sōtan* trumped an official JFTC exemption license for a recession cartel for three main reasons. First, the procedure was easier, as MITI was ever eager to encourage cartels. Having detailed data on all firms through close contacts with the associations, MITI did not require special filing of material. Second, because MITI's "recommendations" were enforced by the carrot-and-stick mechanism of administrative guidance, MITI usually tied compliance to import or export support. This was a mutually beneficial arrangement: the firms wanted cartels and were rewarded for complying with the agreement. Third, MITI was usually highly effective in barring new entry that could undermine the cartel, which was certainly not so for JFTC-licensed setups. Therefore, in the mid-1950s, the number of JFTC-licensed recession and rationalization cartels remained low, whereas MITI's *kankoku sōtan*-type cartels proliferated. In 1957, the JFTC identified 22 industries as guided by a total of 40 "visible cartels". Of these 40 cartels, only six were JFTC-licensed cartels, whereas 23 were *kankoku sōtan*. In addition, the JFTC identified 18 "probable" cartels. In 1958, another 15 "recommended curtailments" were set up; in 1959, this number reached 28; and the year 1960 added another 15. In addition, during those same three years, 23 industries were asked to establish joint sales or purchase companies to allocate markets and set prices (JFTC Annual Report 1957: 35–7, Yoshida 1964).

Still, the *kankoku sōtan* had one major shortcoming: the JFTC could legally challenge them anytime, and MITI would then have to carefully construct an argument why these were not really cartels. This was an unstable situation, and MITI began to look for additional ways to bypass the AML. The solution was to draft a specific industry law that contained a clause exempting an industry from antitrust legislation and gave the ministry the right to allow cartels in this industry. In addition, MITI drafted plans for special technology imports and subsidies to make special legislation attractive to industries. Other regulating ministries—such as in transportation, construction, or health and welfare—soon copied MITI's idea, and the number of special industry laws grew fast. Industries covered by such laws in the 1950s included fertilizer, coal, machine tools, textiles, electronics, electric machinery, iron and steel, sugar, milk, sea transportation, harbor docking, and air transportation.[16]

---

[16] See Appendix 7 of the JFTC Annual Report, any year; see also Figure 3.2 below. Some of these industry laws explicitly put the trade association in charge of self-regulation and monitoring of compliance with industry rules.

MITI's active encouragement of cartels through trade associations as a countermeasure to recession signaled to industries that cartels were not only permissible but desirable. As cartel administrators, the ministries created bargaining situations even in competitive industries that might otherwise not have cooperated. Companies learned that the default reaction to an economic problem was to talk to the other companies in the industry. Over time, the repeated negotiations among firms resulted in an increasing propensity to cooperate in many industries. The "cartel-mindedness" of the Japanese *zaikai*, which SCAP had tried to expunge, was revived.

The Export–Import Trade Law and Export Associations

Writing laws that would exempt a specific industry from the AML stipulations was not originally MITI's idea, but indeed was inspired by various "special industry measures" adopted by SCAP around 1947. The first of these was the export association legislation of 1952 that originated partially in the 1890s (see Chapter 7.3) and partially in the U.S. In the late 1940s, dumping on foreign markets by Japanese exporters became a problem, especially in exports of canned crab and tuna to the U.S. Based on pressure from U.S. industry, SCAP requested that exporters practice self-regulation (*jishu kisei*) in terms of prices and shipping quotas on export markets. This delegated self-regulation was soon pursued in industries as diverse as cotton products, sewing machines, binoculars, cameras, plywood, bicycles, cigarette lighters, flatware, and automobiles. SCAP suggested elevating this practice to a more permanent, legal format, by drafting a law similar to the U.S. Webb–Pomerene Act. In 1952, the Export Trade Law (*Yushutsu torihiki-hō*; renamed the Export–Import Trade Law, *Yushutsu yunyū torihiki hō*, in 1953) was passed to allow price fixing and quota setting for exports to ensure "orderly marketing" abroad. This law was specifically meant to apply only "beyond the beach" (*mizugiwa kara saki no karuteru*; or "offshore cartels") (Misonō 1987: 74).

The law was amended four times to allow more joint activities. Export associations soon mushroomed, and typically they were simply departments of existing domestic trade associations. By 1960, a total of 172 export association cartels in 65 industries were in effect (cf. Figure 3.2). While this accounted for almost 50% of all export product categories, most of the industries covered by this law consisted of small- and medium-sized firms, and the basic idea behind allowing cooperation in these industries was infant industry protection and an increase in quality. Over time, large-scale strategic industries, including paper, vinyl chloride, chemical fertilizers (ammonium sulfate), cement, steel products, and synthetic fibers also formed export cartels as a means to overcome recession. Still, the effect of export associations on export activity and economic growth was probably less than the high number of instances indicates (Dick 1992). Moreover, many industries that grew through this protection, such as electronics and cameras, disbanded or inactivated their export associations when they had achieved competitiveness. Therefore, while there were 209 such export associations in operation in 1969, this number dropped to 56 in the 1980s.

Yet, the application of this law was and is much more active than in the U.S., and some industries, such as steel, have occasionally re-established their export association in times of economic recession (Iyori 1986: 81, Lynn/McKeown 1988: 130, Misonō 1987: 128). Moreover, contrary to SCAP's initial idea, the export associations soon began to extend their delegated regulatory task to areas of independent rule-making. In particular, rather than setting "fair prices" only for export products abroad, many associations began to agree on export prices together with much lower domestic prices; i.e., they agreed to dumping their products abroad. Yamamura (1967: 63) estimates that goods were often dumped on foreign markets at prices that were 20–30% lower than the domestic prices.[17]

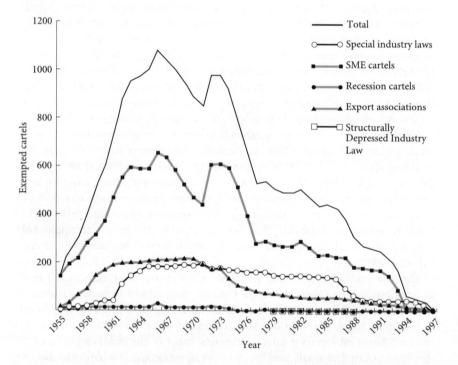

Figure 3.2. Cartels Exempted from the Antimonopoly Law, 1955–1994
Source: JFTC Annual Report, Appendix, 1997: 80–5.

[17] For a study of export association behavior during the postwar period, see Dick (1992). However, Dick only considers foreign markets—rather than the domestic cartel effects of these associations—and his sample excludes the strategic export industries that dropped out of export association activities after the 1970s. In an interview with a trade association official in Tokyo in 1998, I asked what export associations do. The answer was: "They are cartels, of course" ("*Karuteru desu yo*").

Upon receiving an application for an export association from a group of firms, MITI was in charge of its administration. When MITI assumed the role of a mediator in forming and supporting price agreements, it often used this position to promote domestic price cartels by export industries. In this way, export associations were used not only to prevent practices of unfair competition in foreign markets, but to align domestic producers to set quality standards (to counter the image of "cheap" Japanese products), establish rules on trademark violations,[18] and discuss prices for domestic and foreign markets. While the export associations were also in charge of research on overseas markets and the lobbying of foreign governments, their domestic functions were at least as important as their activities in international markets.

MITI's extension of the Export–Import Trade Law to domestic price agreements seriously undermined antitrust enforcement. Practically no restraint remained for an association to form a cartel, as long as it received MITI's consent to form an export association as a subgroup of the existing trade association. Almost all agreements by export associations, be it on price, capacity, investment, or output, could be justified as being in the interest of export promotion, which after all was a major component of the country's growth policy. Therefore, when export industries petitioned to form an agreement, MITI's default advice was to form an export association rather than go through the more complicated process of applying for a JFTC exemption license. The Export–Import Trade Law was the first blanket law that exempted industries from antitrust rules.

A typical example of an export association cartel is the cement cartel active in the second half of the 1950s. Note that cement is an industry with large economies of scale effects, where adjusting production in response to market fluctuations is difficult, the product cannot be stored for long periods, and transportation costs are high. The Cement Export Cooperation Association agreed to set an export volume for each firm annually based on the domestic market situation, usually at about 15% of output for each firm. Simultaneously, a domestic market standard price and an export price were established; for instance, in 1956 this domestic price was set at $17.40 per ton, and the export price was determined to be a much lower $16.98 per ton. Next, each member of the industry had to contribute to an "export adjustment account" (*Yushutsu chōseikin kanjō*). The contribution of each member was determined to be ¥30 per ton produced; i.e., it was scaled by domestic market share. Not all firms, however, were located on the coast or close to the major export markets (Korea, Taiwan, South East Asia). Firms not well located for export strategies were asked not to export, but they still benefited from the export cartel because exports were adjusted to domestic demand, such that domestic supplies were kept scarce

---

[18] One outstanding example of this is the camera industry. When the camera manufacturers began to export, they suffered from high variance in product quality. Also, they chose English-sounding brand names and used logos that often looked very similar to that of the market leaders in foreign countries.

enough to ensure the high domestic price of $17.40 per ton. When selling abroad, the exporting firms necessarily suffered losses relative to domestic sales, but they were then reimbursed from the "export adjustment account" according to the loss suffered, at a rate of ¥186 per ton exported (at an exchange rate of $1 = ¥360, this equaled the difference between the domestic and the export standard price). This scheme thus pursued two goals simultaneously: securing foreign markets by setting a below world-market average price; and maintaining domestic prices by using exports as a buffer to adjust production and inventory such that excess production would not jeopardize domestic prices (Yamamura 1967: 63, Misonō 1987: 127–8, JFTC Annual Report 1957: 104).[19]

The Export–Import Trade Law thus had four major ramifications for the development of Japanese industry in the postwar period. First, it offered a convenient and widely used loophole to the new antitrust law. Second, for a while, export associations became the primary *modus operandi* for exporting industries, whether they included price fixing or not. In this way, Japanese exporters built a joint history of cooperation under competition, which increased the long-run propensity to collaborate even in more competitive industries such as cameras. Third, export associations also served to increase the quality of Japanese products, which in combination with the price agreements over time resulted in a new international reputation of Japanese products as being both well-made and well-priced. Finally, the Export–Import Trade Law also was an early instance of the extension of delegated regulation to independent self-regulation. While MITI was involved in the extension of export associations into the domestic realm, it lacked formal means to enforce the domestic agreements concealed under this law. Export associations over time assumed more and more functions of independent self-regulation, including the monitoring and enforcement of the export agreements.

The Small- and Medium-Sized Enterprise Associations Law

Besides generic exemption of exporters, MITI pushed for another blanket law specifically to exempt small- and medium-sized enterprises from antitrust rules. MITI had come to realize that the guidance-based output reductions in cotton spinning were necessarily unstable unless the firms in related industries, most of which were small-sized, could form agreements as well. For instance, as the spinners' cartel began to work, prices for cotton yarn went up whereas prices for knitted cotton products were still set competitively, causing a negative spread for knitters. The situation was sustainable only if the knitters could also rig their prices, and given the large number of tiny firms in the knitting industry, this

---

[19] For the developments in the cement industry after the 1950s, its cartels in the 1960s and 1970s, and its designation as structurally depressed and thus needy of a rationalization cartel in the 1980s, see Tilton (1995, 1996).

required an officially induced and enforced price cartel (Misonō 1987: 72–3). The "Temporary Small- and Medium-Sized Enterprise Stabilization Act" (*Tokutei chūsho kigyō no antei ni kan suru rinji sochi-hō*) of 1952 allowed small companies to form official cartels. In this way, one cartel—the original 1952 cotton spinners' *kankoku sōtan*—begot a law exempting an entire range of small-sized firms from antitrust legislation. By 1953, 41 cartels were authorized under this law, but as Figure 3.2 shows, their number was soon to increase, as MITI was extremely eager to encourage and foster what it called "cooperative market behavior" (*kyōchōteki shijō kōdō*).

MITI's pushing of a blanket exemption for small companies met the support of politicians. More than 70% of Japan's workforce was employed in small- and medium-sized enterprises, defined as having less than 300 employees and ¥100 million of capital. The LDP was concerned about this large number of employees as voters and had embarked on an active small company policy in the late 1940s. The "Small- and Medium-Sized Enterprise Cooperative Law" (*Chūsho kigyō-tō kyōdo kumiai-hō*) had been passed in 1949 to facilitate cooperation among small firms through tax incentives. Moreover, while politicians welcomed special legislation for small companies for securing electoral votes, MITI was in favor because this law allowed MITI to support agreements among large firms in the strategic industries.

The 1949 and 1952 laws were combined and replaced by the much more encompassing "Small- and Medium-Sized Enterprise Associations Law" (*Chūsho kigyō dantai no soshiki ni kan suru hōritsu*) of 1957. This law permitted the formation of cooperatives for the specific purpose of establishing recession cartels without antitrust constraints as long as the associations consisted of small-sized firms only. Its most outstanding feature is a "two-thirds" rule: if two-thirds of the small-sized firms in an industry apply to their cognizant ministry to form a cartel through their association, the ministry can order both members and nonmembers in the industry to observe the restrictions, and can also order firms to join the association.[20] This two-thirds rule made it easier to form cartel agreements even in fragmented industries. Figure 3.2 shows that "SME cartels" accounted for more than half of all exemptions in the 1960s and were the largest category of exempted cartels throughout the postwar period. While the law is still valid today, the relevance of SME cartels has been largely diminished; in 1997, no such cartels were in existence.

Figure 3.2 also shows that, including all official recession and rationalization cartels and export association cartels, during the 1960s more than a thousand AML-exempted cartels were registered. Two things are noteworthy about this

---

[20] This is the same "two-thirds" rule as was embodied in the 1884 "Regulations for Local Trade Associations" and the 1931"Important Industries Control Law"; see Chapter 7. Similar to the prewar laws, this clause could have been found to violate the Constitution, which in Art. 21 guarantees freedom of association. Therefore, an additional clause was inserted saying that those who refuse to join in the face of an administrative order may stay out by seeking a special permission from the ministry in charge.

figure. First, while it accurately describes the relative importance of small-firm and trade cartels over AML-exempted large-firm cartels, it tells only half of the story: the *kankoku sōtan* of the 1950s and early 1960s were never officially legally exempted. Further, the chart shows the declining trend of these AML-exempted cartels over time, especially after the oil shock. Yet, prior to a discussion of the 1970s, we need first to look at what happened to industrial policy in the 1960s.[21]

3.2. Antitrust Policy in the 1960s: The *Tokushinhō* Controversy

'There is hardly any industry left in Japan that does not have a cartel.'

(JFTC Annual Report 1957: 35)

In the late 1950s, MITI's increasing use of *kankoku sōtan* and bypass laws began to worry the JFTC. In an attempt at retrenchment, so as not to lose control of the AML entirely, in 1955 the JFTC had announced a "more flexible application" of the AML. But in the end, liberalizing AML exemptions only undermined the standing of antitrust policy further, and voices calling for an additional attenuation of the AML became louder. Antitrust policy had only few public supporters who could hardly challenge the "iron triangle" of *zaikai*, politicians and bureaucrats. The JFTC Commissioner had no power against the LDP or its support base. The *zaikai* leaders were elders who had been in the same industries in the prewar and war periods. Their "cartel-mindedness" seemed immutable. This tradition was particularly strong in industries such as chemicals or iron and steel, which were susceptible to swings in the business cycle and grew up with the understanding that an intra-industry agreement is the best way to cope with such swings (Yamamura 1967: 68).

---

[21] The Small Business Associations Law spawned numerous other laws based on a similar logic of facilitating cartels among small firms and exempting these cartels from antitrust rules. The most important of these was the 1957 "Law for Business Related to Environmental Health" (*Kankyō eisei kankei eigyō no unei no tekiseika ni kan suru hōritsu*), which covered six service industries, including barber shops, beauticians, and public bath houses. The Ministry of Health and Welfare has remained in charge of enforcing this law, and through the 1980s more than 120 cartels were exempted from the AML via this law. The 1959 Liquor Law ("Law Concerning the Preservation of Liquor Tax and Liquor Business Associations", *Shuzei no hozen oyobi shuruigyō kumiai-tō ni kan suru hō*) initially aimed to support *sake* brewers by allocating markets and creating barriers to entry such that each brewer and each liquor store was profitable enough to pass on liquor taxes to the Ministry of Finance (which is in charge of regulating the alcoholic beverages industries). The primary impact of this law, however, has been on the beer industry which surpassed *sake* sales in the 1960s. Other laws for the small- and medium-sized enterprises were the 1962 Shopping District Promotional Law (*Shōtengai shinkō kumiai-hō*), the 1963 Small- and Medium-Sized Enterprise Modernization Law (*Chūsho kigyō kindaika sokushin-hō*), and the 1967 Small- and Medium-Sized Enterprise Promotional Association Law (*Chūsho kigyō shinkō jigyō dantai hō*). All of these encouraged the formation of cartels and cooperative agreements to support small businesses.

Table 3.1. JFTC Cartel Cases in the Period 1951–1964

	By initiation of case (new cases only)			By type of procedure (new and pending cases)				Carried over to following year
	Private complaint (*shinkoku*)	JFTC identification (*shokken tanchi*)	Total	Formal recommendation (*kankoku*)	Full adjudicative procedure (*shinketsu kaishi*)	Insufficient evidence	Total	
1951	26	42	68	4	10	49	63	13
1952	24	27	51	3	9	38	50	14
1953	32	36	68	5	8	53	66	16
1954	17	19	36	0	3	23	26	26
1955	13	12	25	5	2	24	31	20
1956	22	5	27	5	2	10	17	31
1957	41	4	45	7	0	26	33	43
1958	28	2	30	2	0	26	28	44
1959	17	0	17	2	0	20	22	36
1960	12	1	13	2	0	14	16	33
1961	11	13	24	2	1	8	11	46
1962	13	11	24	7	11	40	58	12
1963	28	13	41	15	3	16	34	19
1964	21	13	34	18	2	14	34	19

Sources: Misonō 1987: 83, JFTC 1977: 356–7.

Indicating the decline in its authority, the number of cases brought by the JFTC decreased sharply after the departure of SCAP (see Table 3.1). After the JFTC brought a total of 68 cases in 1951, this number fell to 25 in 1955. Between 1957 and 1960, when MITI's *kankoku sōtan* were mushrooming, the JFTC did not fully prosecute a single case. While these low numbers could be simply due to a decline in illegal behavior during the Jimmu boom, Table 3.1 suggests otherwise: JFTC investigation declined. Of all cases investigated by the JFTC in the late 1950s, 80% were dismissed for reasons of insufficient evidence. The increasing number of pending cases carried over to the following year further underscores the JFTC's indecisiveness. Perhaps the best example that highlights the JFTC's decline in power during those years is the 1959 newspaper case.

The 1959 Newspaper Incident

On April 1, 1959, 30 central and local newspapers simultaneously raised their prices by the same margin. The JFTC began an investigation in May, but by August concluded that in spite of a seemingly orchestrated price increase there was no evidence for a coercive threat that obliged newspapers to raise prices. The JFTC dropped the case for "insufficient evidence". This was an odd finding indeed, for the 30 newspapers had announced prior to April 1 that they had all agreed to raise prices on that day, by the same amount. The background plot to these events runs as follows. In April, the JFTC received a private complaint from the *Shufuren* (Housewives' Association) and other consumer groups. It then began the investigation at the Newspaper Association (*Shinbun kyōkai*) where it collected tons of material, including minutes of a meeting in which the association detailed the price hike agreement. The JFTC then found similarly compromising documents at local newspaper associations, and in June filed a report to this effect. It is unclear what happened next, other than that between April and July, there were three changes in leadership at the JFTC: Commissioner Naganuma retired in April 1959, followed by an interim Commissioner Nakamura, who was replaced in June by Commissioner Itō, who resigned in August. It is very rare for the Commissioner of the JFTC to change so frequently. Coincidentally, in August the Commission dismissed the newspaper case due to insufficient evidence that the companies had indeed been forced to increase prices (evidence of coercion is necessary to bring a price fixing case; see Chapter 4). The evidence gathered from the associations' offices was discarded on a technicality. Although it sounds absurd, the JFTC concluded that the papers' concerted action was not an agreement, and no "unfair restraint of competition" had occurred (Misonō 1987: 120–1). Not surprisingly, the newspapers did not report about this case in detail at the time, but the confluence of events suggests that there was significant pressure by the newspapers on the politicians not to pursue further—presumably bolstered by a threat to report scoops on the politicians. In turn, the politicians pushed the JFTC to drop the case. The fast succession of Commissioners suggests some futile resistance on the part of the JFTC.

This strange case set a bad precedent. The JFTC lost the trust of the consumer groups who had filed the initial complaints, as well as what little respect it may have had from the business world. Firms concluded that if the newspaper agreement did not constitute a violation, then nothing would. The newspaper case established legal doctrine: the only acceptable evidence for "pressure to collude" was a written agreement specifying the penalties for dissenting firms; therefore, if there was nothing in writing, the JFTC would be unable to prosecute. Not surprisingly, the case opened the flood gates to a wave of price agreements set by trade associations. In its Annual Report of 1959, the JFTC presented a list of "*de facto*/real cartels", which included copper, aluminum, nickel and most other non-ferrous metals, soda and soda ash, benzol and others, and what the JFTC labeled "large oligopolies" such as auto tires, chemicals, pharmaceuticals, rubber and many more. The JFTC called these "*de facto*" cartels, because most of them were implicit price leadership agreements.[22] Following the newspaper incident, the JFTC was unable to prosecute such schemes because there was no evidence in writing. In the late 1950s, the activities of the JFTC were thus curbed by three forces: the AML bypass laws, including the large number of small-firm exemption and trade promotion cartels; the administrative guidance-based *kankoku sōtan*; and the legal doctrine, presumably pushed by political pressure, not to enforce censure even in the face of obvious price collusion.

The Tokushinhō Debacle and Investment Cartels

With the JFTC sitting hamstrung in the mid-1950s, in 1958 MITI launched yet another attack on the AML. The campaign was supported by the LDP, whose patience was considerably strained with the burgeoning number of special industry laws that MITI was pushing through the Diet. Politicians wondered, why not change the AML itself, instead of going through this cumbersome process of exempting one industry after the other from the AML? In 1958, MITI submitted a draft for a new AML that was a 180-degree turn from the existing law, in that it allowed all cartels in principle other than those that were

---

[22] After the newspaper incident, many industries created a price leadership system to avoid frequent meetings for their regular price increases. Following the newspaper example, such arrangements were referred to as *samidare* ("early summer rain") schemes. This term marked a system whereby companies agreed to raise prices on the first day of a given seasonal cycle, such as the first rain in May. The leading company in an industry determined the amount of the price increase in its first move, and all other companies followed. The logic is similar to that employed in the U.S. "moon phases" bid-rigging cartels among turbine generator and high voltage switchgear manufacturers in the late 1950s, where the conspiring firms predetermined the winners of an upcoming public procurement by the phase of the moon at the time of the auction; cf. Smith (1961).

specifically prohibited. The opposition parties called this proposal the "revival of the Important Industries Control Law" of 1931 (cf. Chapter 7).[23]

However, with this approach MITI had gone too far. The proposal was very much at odds with the *zaikai*'s objective, which was simply to remove the AML altogether. Some large companies became increasingly resentful of MITI's efforts to manipulate their corporate strategies. Cartels were most certainly fine with the *zaikai*, but they wanted to control these cartels themselves, without government interference. Suddenly, the JFTC found itself with an odd assortment of industrial allies against MITI. The group was headed by the steel industry (whose long-term influential leader and president of Yawata Steel, Inayama Yoshihiro, was dubbed "Mister Cartel" in the 1950s[24]). The steel industry, more than any other, was synonymous with "cartel" in the 1950s and 1960s. MITI was very much involved in the industry, and the companies received huge subsidies in return for compliance with MITI's efforts to induce "cooperative market behavior". But as MITI suggested extending the range of cartels through a revision of the AML, the steel leaders got worried. It was one thing for them to agree on prices and have MITI applaud, but being under government price control was a different matter. The steel industry began to resist MITI's laws, even those that had already passed the Diet. The power of the steel industry was so great that it shifted the entire *zaikai*. The industrialists concluded that a complete abolition of the AML, or at least a relaxation of the cartel rules, would have been highly desirable, but that MITI's design to increase ministerial control over industry was not (Yamamura 1967: 74, Misonō 1987: 97–101, 137). In addition to large industry opposition, small-sized firms, agriculture interests and consumers also protested against the revision plans. The 1958 proposal to revise the AML was dropped.

The defeat of the 1958 proposal was a blow to MITI in terms of being betrayed by the *zaikai*. MITI was also worried about upcoming trade liberalization. At the 1959 IMF General Meeting and the 1959 GATT Conference, Japan was sternly criticized for its heavy import controls and received substantial pressure to change to an "Article 8" status in the IMF (which, among others, required liberalizing cross-border capital flows[25]), and an "Article 11" status in GATT (which prohib-

---

[23] The opposition parties identified as the proposal's prime victims consumers, farmers and small-sized enterprises. While these groups initially showed little interest in the matter, in 1958 they became active; indeed, the farmers were so outraged that the LDP politicians related to agriculture turned against the proposal to placate their constituents (Misonō 1987: 111).

[24] Inayama began his career at the MCI (MITI's predecessor) in 1928, was section chief for steel, and began to work for Yawata Steel in 1950. He became the CEO of Yawata Steel in 1960, presided over the 1970 merger of Yawata and Fuji Steel into New Japan Steel, and became the new company's chairman in 1973. He also was the chairman of Keidanren, Nikkeiren, and of the Japan Steel Federation and the Coal Mining Deliberation Council.

[25] The key issue regarding Article 8 status at the IMF was whether balance of payments problems could be used as a reason for temporarily restricting imports beyond previously existing import levels—a proviso that applied to developing countries. Thus, in accepting Article 8, Japan agreed not to use balance of payments to justify import protection. In 1964, the balance of payments issue was much more critical for Japan than that of liberalizing cross-border capital flows, which only gained importance in the 1970s and 1980s.

ited levying heavy tariffs). To change its status in both organizations—which Japan eventually did in 1964—it was necessary to abolish a number of market access restrictions and, more important, to revise the two trade control laws, i.e., the Foreign Exchange Control Law and the Foreign Investment Law. While it turned out later that MITI was able to remain in control of some major restrictions on trade through administrative guidance, prior to 1964 this was not clear. Therefore, in 1961 MITI began circulating proposals for a "New Industrial System" and a "New Industrial Order" in an attempt to solidify its hold on trade policy.

The underlying logic of the "New Industrial Order" can be summarized as follows. According to MITI, the three major problems plaguing Japanese industry as of the early 1960s were small industrial scale, an overabundance of companies, and excessive entries (startups) and exits (bankruptcies). MITI identified scale as the most pressing issue, as small scale led to inferior quality that blocked the growth of companies. Combined with the threats of market liberalization and higher imports after assuming new status in GATT and IMF, MITI believed both policies to increase productivity and a re-ranking of the "designated growth industries" to be necessary. In MITI's view, Japan could utilize three routes to guide the economy efficiently at this critical juncture: (1) industry self-regulation in the trade associations; (2) fund allocation through a highly regulated financial system; and (3) close cooperation between government and business in the form of *kyōdō chōsei*, "cooperative regulation". Via the third option, which MITI favored most, government and business were to cooperate in setting output levels. Industry was to implement these, while the government would take care of preferential taxes, preferred financing and other support measures.

The most significant component in MITI's logic was the notion of "excessive competition". MITI held that there was a tendency among Japanese companies to compete excessively in terms of investing too much to undercut others' prices but then being left with highly leveraged excess investment. This behavior, MITI claimed, had to be turned into "effective competition", but the AML offered undesirable protection for competition. In order for Japan to achieve full economies of scale, MITI argued that cartels were imperative. Competition had to be curtailed by the creation of barriers to entry, investments and output had to be coordinated to cut duplication and waste, and raw materials had to be purchased through joint purchase institutions to cut input costs. To introduce the "New Order", MITI effectively suggested that the AML be either revised or ignored.[26]

In MITI's vision, the primary tool to create the new system was to be a new "Special Industry Promotion Temporary Measures Law" (*Tokutei sangyō shinkō rinji sochi hō*, short: "*Tokushinhō*"). The idea behind the *Tokushinhō* was to substitute MITI's foreign capital allocation powers with new MITI

---

[26] Misonō (1987: 156–9) explains the "New Order" ideas in detail; also, see Hadley (1970: 396–8) for quotes from the 1962 paper by Morozumi Yoshihiko, a leading MITI official involved in shaping these ideas, and Yamamura (1967: 77–86). Johnson (1982: 255–61) offers a detailed analysis of the legal draft, its creation and the political processes leading to its defeat.

powers to manage production and output through guiding mergers, intra-firm cooperation and cartels. In effect, the entire effort was driven by the intent to create a single AML bypass law and to further increase MITI's powers in guiding industry.

But as with the 1958 proposal to change the AML, the *zaikai* was extremely alarmed by MITI's "New Order" idea: to their taste, this new "cooperative system" could quickly devolve into a "control system". Rather, as before, the *zaikai* lobbied for a revision of the AML such that industry cooperation would be left to "self-alignment" (*jishu chōsei*). Based on deliberations led by the banking industry, which was at the heart of MITI's control scheme and was thus most skeptical of it, Keidanren publicly stated that it was "fundamentally against" the *Tokushinhō* (Keidanren 1978: 373). Upon hearing industry's staunch opposition and criticism from parts of the government, the LDP politicians, who had initially signaled support to MITI, began to drag their feet. The *Tokushinhō* idea was history.

However, MITI would not give up so easily, and in 1963 came up with yet another plan to undermine antitrust policy: investment coordination cartels (*tōshi chōsei karuteru*). This one was more successful because it did not pose a direct threat to either banks or large manufacturers. The idea behind investment cartels was to prevent duplication and leverage each single investment through integrative agreements among firms in one industry as to who would invest how much in what type of production line. MITI would administer such agreements, and use preferential financing and taxes as inducements. Having fended off MITI's previous attempts, the JFTC Commissioner was pressured by the government to agree that investment cartels should be licensed as being in the "public interest" (Misono 1987: 164). MITI and the JFTC agreed that the MITI Minister was to be in charge of such cartels and that the JFTC would grant AML exemptions. They also concurred on a rather broad definition of an "investment cartel". The definition included activities ranging from straight investment coordination among competitors, to joint investment, to curtailing excessive investments and allowing large-scale mergers, especially in industries facing the competitive threat of imports. Investment cartels thus became the third category of MITI-organized, AML-exempted cartels, following recession and rationalization cartels.

The new investment cartels rendered superfluous MITI's extralegal *kankoku sōtan*, guidance-based cartels. In 1966, the Cabinet passed a decision that all *kankoku sōtan* were to be transformed into investment cartels formally exempted from the AML through a JFTC license; since this decision contained a "grandfather" clause, the JFTC had no choice but to issue licenses all around. In the second half of the 1960s, designated growth industries such as steel, chemical fibers, paper and pulp, all ended their *kankoku sōtan* and applied for a regular JFTC license instead (Misono 1987: 165–6, 220–3).

Thus, while MITI had to give up the extralegal agreements, it gained new powers through the investment cartels. In MITI's view, the more official standing of investment cartels meant it had achieved something very close to the objectives it had sought with the *Tokushinhō* proposal. In the wake of "over-investment" during the Tokyo Olympics Boom of 1964, industries such as ethylene and petrochemicals, synthetic fibers, paper and pulp, and ferro-alloy all formed investment cartels. While the *Tokushinhō* draft had failed, the agreements were considered legal nonetheless. But just when the JFTC looked as if it had been sidelined for good, it was rejuvenated by the Japanese public during the oil shock recession.

3.3. The 1977 Revision of the Antimonopoly Law

The Izanami Boom of the 1960s was driven by strong exports, especially to the U.S., of steel products, electric machinery, electronics, cars, precision mechanics, chemical products, and textiles. It came to an abrupt end when Nixon announced on August 15, 1971, a 10% surcharge on U.S. imports and the end of the gold–dollar convertibility at the old rates. Since Japan was highly dependent on both exports to the U.S. and the fixed exchange rate, this resulted in a panic often called the "Nixon Shock". The 1972 Textile Agreement with the U.S., which forced Japan to restrict its textiles exports to the U.S., only added to the crisis mood. Production and investment cartels among large-scale producers increased, and small-sized companies cartels, which had decreased during the 1960s boom, resurfaced in high numbers (cf. Figure 3.2). Government economic policies further exacerbated the situation. First, in reaction to the end of the ¥360/$1 fixed exchange rate in 1971, the Japanese government inflated domestic price levels so that the yen would not have to appreciate too much. In 1972 the Tanaka Kakuei Cabinet began to implement Tanaka's ideas of "restructuring the Japanese Archipelago", which required huge public work outlays to construct new high-ways and railroads, and to begin a social security and public pension system. While these public investments caused an upsurge in the economy in 1972, they put additional pressure on prices. When the Bretton Woods system of fixed exchange rates collapsed and the OPEC oil embargo hit in 1973, Japan, being 99.7% dependent on oil imports, fell into its then biggest postwar recession, which marked the end of the "high growth" era. Inflation reached double digits in 1973, wholesale prices surged by 40% in 1974, and consumer prices rose by more than 30%. Finance Minister Fukuda Takeo labeled this the period of "mad prices" (Misonō 1987: 224).

The 1970s Oil Cartel

Five primary reasons account for the severity of Japan's "oil shock" inflation, which was much worse than that of any other industrialized country at the time.

First, in macroeconomic terms, a policy of easy money to support the Tanaka investment plans had led to surplus liquidity, and during the 1974 spring labor negotiations (*shuntō*) wages were adjusted fully for inflation. Second, the policy of easy money also led to real estate speculation by large firms. In the early 1970s, corporations purchased large areas of land, feeding into a speculative boom. Third, a real fear that petroleum would become a scarce commodity led consumers to panic and hoard toilet paper and other daily-life products. The trading companies jumped on this opportunity and started to corner the market for these and other products, such as lumber, cotton, raw materials for textiles, and *mochi*-rice (glutinous rice used for rice cakes). The goal of this attempt to control markets was, of course, to exploit the public panic by holding back these commodities until they could be sold at an even higher price. Fourth, both legal cartels and private self-regulation became ubiquitous, and most manufacturing industries found themselves under some production restriction agreement or another; by limiting supply, these agreements further increased the pressure on prices. Agreements of cooperation and collusion became stronger as the recession continued and companies tried hard to "maintain prices" through price and/or quantity agreements with their competitors. Finally, many smaller companies faced bankruptcy and were acquired by large companies, causing a reduction in competitive threat and the number of firms in many industries (Misonō 1987, Nakamura 1985, Ishikawa 1985, HKKK 1977).

To deal with the trading houses, in July 1973 the Diet passed a law that explicitly prohibited activities aimed at cornering the market in daily-life products.[27] This law partially reflected the public outcry over the opportunistic behavior of trading companies and large firms in this national emergency. The *zaikai*, through outlets such as Keidanren, issued statements on corporate morale, business ethics, and the social functions of corporations, and announced corporate self-discipline on these matters. Nevertheless, after October 1973, prices for most oil- and petrochemical-based products skyrocketed, and some items disappeared from the shelves altogether. The result was an overall consumer panic. In December 1973, the government passed the first of several emergency laws to deal with inflation through government price controls for basic commodities, including kerosene oil, propane gas, toilet paper, and detergents. In spite of these measures, the price increases in these products continued, and by far exceeded the oil price increases triggered by the OPEC cartel. This stimulated further expectations of inflation and opportunistic price hikes in most industries. Then it became clear that most of the price hikes were triggered by price fixing in private cartels.

The situation was so grave that the JFTC was inspired to take action. In 1973, the number of cartel investigations climbed to 184, of which 66 ended in a warning or formal sentencing (cf. Figure 3.1). In 1974, a total of 176 investiga-

---

[27] "Temporary emergency law against the cornering and hoarding of daily-life and other products"; *Seikatsu kanren busshi-tō no kaishime oyobi urishime ni tai suru kinyū sochi hō.*

tions resulted in 58 formal cases, the highest number of JFTC cases since 1947.[28] Not only did the JFTC become more active, it also changed its targets. In the 1960s, the JFTC had primarily prosecuted small-sized firms. Doubtless, this was due to MITI's pressure and the various tools it had designed to bypass the AML, and the political strength and influence of the large firms. Large-firm cartel schemes were also often more intricate and clever than those of small companies, making it harder for the JFTC to prosecute. In contrast, of the 66 cases brought in 1973, 70% involved large firms, some of which manufactured intermediate products. Buoyed by its successes in these cases, the JFTC was ready to bring its first criminal cartel case after it gained independence from SCAP: the oil cartel.

The JFTC can bring its cases as administrative violations, which end in a cease-and-desist order, if the colluding parties accept the recommendation. If the parties do not accept it, the JFTC can start an administrative legal procedure (cf. Chapter 4 for details on the legal process). In severe cases the JFTC can launch a criminal investigation, which makes the cartel a criminal offense and thus may end in prison terms to individuals representing the colluding parties. While this is not at all unusual in the U.S., the JFTC has only brought ten criminal cases in the 50 years between 1947 and 1997, and four of these cases occurred only in the 1990s. Therefore, some observers have argued that the years 1973–4 were the most important years in Japanese antitrust policy history (e.g., Misonō 1987: 226).

In the early 1970s, 12 companies held 95% of market share in total domestic sales of petroleum. Between May and November 1973, these companies met five times in the conference room of the Petroleum Federation (*Sekiyū renmei*, the leading trade association of the industry), where they agreed on price increases in all of the various categories of oil (light, heavy, etc.). The price hikes were especially pronounced in gasoline, where the price increased by 93%, from ¥14,000 to ¥27,000 per kiloliter. Rates for increases were carefully orchestrated, and this was clearly a price cartel. In addition, all companies (except Taiyō) arranged for a "gasoline *kachōkai*" (division chief meeting) in May 1973, when they agreed on monthly sales restrictions (i.e., volume quotas) for each cartel member in each region of Japan to support the price agreement; the group also specifically spelled out penalties for various types of transgressions. Prior to this, the Petroleum Federation in its November 1972 meeting of the "Demand and Supply Committee" (*jukyū iinkai*) had established crude oil processing quotas for all members. Thus, the petroleum industry had cartels on price, sales volume and production.

When first presenting the case, the JFTC stressed that the petroleum industry had repeatedly violated the AML even before the oil crisis, but that the oil

---

[28] Industries subpoenaed and raided by the JFTC in these two years include: milk, instant *ramen*, vinyl wrap, resin, polyethylene, petroleum, paint, concrete, aluminum, slate, agricultural machinery, ethylene, auto tires, large-scale freezer storage, glass bottles, pesticides, rubber plates, plastic overcoats, boiler, tissue paper, toilet paper, and many more; JFTC Annual Reports (1973, 1974, 1975).

companies would rig prices in times of a national economic crisis was particularly heinous (HKKK 1977: 161). The Petroleum Federation had repeatedly received cease-and-desist orders in the 1960s, and one as late as in 1971 which was still pending. Operating in the spirit of the 1959 newspaper incident, when it was first confronted with the 1971 order the Federation denied it ("we did not agree on this"), then blamed MITI ("we only followed MITI orders in setting prices"), and finally turned themselves into the victimized parties ("with the OPEC cartel, we got dragged into the oil price hikes") (HKKK 1977: 161). The public was decidedly unsympathetic. The Diet opposition parties pushed for a criminal investigation, and on February 19, 1974, the JFTC filed a criminal charge against the Petroleum Federation, the 12 companies, and 17 individuals representing these companies. On May 28, the Tokyo Police Department began collecting evidence from the companies and the trade association. The case went to court, and the companies argued that MITI had asked them to collude on price, sales quotas, and output. MITI testified that it had not mandated specific prices. The court acknowledged that the industry had followed ministerial guidance to some extent, but the companies were found guilty of price fixing nevertheless. The defendants appealed, but ultimately all parties were found guilty of illegal collusion by the Tokyo High Court in 1980 (Upham 1987: 184–6, Ramseyer 1982, 1983).

The case had obvious negative implications for MITI's status. First, a cartel MITI had encouraged was found to be illegal, and therefore by implication MITI was also guilty. Second, the Supreme Court had upheld antitrust policy before industrial policy, and this was the first time that the JFTC received full-fledged support within the Japanese political economy. Third, with the verdict, the JFTC now had a precedent with which it could potentially challenge MITI's administrative guidance. Companies were not immune if ministerial guidance led to behavior that violated the antitrust law. Blindly following ministerial administrative guidance was suddenly rendered a dangerous proposition. In 1981, the JFTC published its first Guideline on Administrative Guidance and the AML (JFTC 1981a). Furthermore, the oil cartel case, which was in court and therefore in the media for many years, also had an immediate impact on the revision of the AML in 1977. The public had been outraged by corporate behavior to begin with, and hearing the details of how the companies colluded to profit from the crisis of the early 1970s further infuriated people.

The Strengthening of the Antimonopoly Law

As the public's anger still simmered, the JFTC and the media brought a revision of the AML onto the agenda, with the goal to increase the AML's power regarding illegal cartels. Although Keidanren claimed that blaming big business for the 1970s inflation was unfair, in the eyes of average consumers, illegal cartels were culpable for the insufferable price explosion. The public realized that the JFTC had been unable to stop these cartels and people became interested in antitrust. The JFTC decided to ride on the wave of public unrest and in early 1974 submitted a detailed proposal to revise the AML to give the JFTC more teeth. The focal points of the proposal were: (1) to enable the JFTC to order the breakup of dominant firms, oligopolies or conglomerates; (2) to abolish price cartels; (3) to increase penalty provisions such that a criminal fine was a meaningful threat, and to introduce a new administrative surcharge fee to cream off the profits made by companies over the duration of a cartel; (4) to lower the requirements of what constitutes "sufficient evidence" for a cartel to be prosecuted; (5) to strengthen disclosure and accounting rules for large firms, including cost data; (6) to strengthen the rules on unfair trade restrictions; and (7) to limit stockholdings in one corporation by banks and trading companies (JFTC Annual Report 1971: 15, 1975: 280–2).

In the midst of this debate, the Lockheed corruption scandal broke loose and brought down the Tanaka Cabinet. This seriously limited the LDP's opposition to the JFTC proposal. The only "clean" politician that the LDP could suggest for the replacement of Tanaka Kakuei was Miki Takeo, from the smallest and least relevant LDP faction. The entire party and its public image were thrown into a major crisis, and the public was now upset at both the *zaikai* and the politicians. In his inauguration speech, the new Prime Minister Miki promised swift cleanup action and a revision of the AML.

Keidanren rushed to counter the JFTC with a public statement that there was "absolutely no need to change the AML" (HKKK 1977: 168). A Keidanren study group soon followed with a report arguing that breaking up large companies or demanding cost disclosure for large firms were all against the concept of free markets. Further, Keidanren argued, the JFTC's independent standing was probably unconstitutional to begin with, and antitrust policy should be part of the larger concept of economic policy. Finally, limiting corporate stockholding would incapacitate Japanese corporations and hurt their international competitiveness (Keidanren 1978: 774, Misonō 1987: 230–3).

While none of this sparring was new, in the midst of the post oil-shock panic, when some Keidanren leaders themselves were entangled in a criminal probe of illegal cartel behavior, their arguments carried no weight. The media had a field day, lashing out at industry. The Consumer Association (*Nihon shōhisha renmei*) conducted an opinion poll on the Keidanren statement, and in the public's eye the image of big business was even worse than that of the LDP, which was at the lowest in the postwar period. In July 1974, Keidanren backpedaled but submitted a new seven-point proposal that rejected all JFTC suggestions for a revision of the AML. MITI and most other ministries also became vocal opponents of the JFTC proposal, especially because it encroached the agreement on MITI's investment cartels. Further, MITI asked, what exactly was the damage caused by cartels or concentrated industries? And finally, not to be outdone, MITI claimed that the JFTC's proposal to empower it to break up market-dominant firms (similar to the U.S. FTC's right) was a tool of "planned market economies", and MITI was in principle against any interference with free market forces other than through its own industrial structure policies (Misonō 1987: 243, HKKK 1977: 177).

The LDP, upon hearing the negative consumer reaction, officially adopted a "neutral" stance. The only public statement that the LDP dared to make in this situation was that the issue was important and required considerable study and reflection. The LDP's objective was to win time and hope that the public would calm down when the economy finally picked up again. Yet, in reality, the LDP was heavily lobbied by the *zaikai* and most likely agreed with MITI. When it came to voting on draft proposals, the party sided with the large pressure groups, and its true intention was to take as much beef out of the JFTC's original proposal as possible. The Prime Minister's Office prepared a legal draft which was submitted to the Diet in April 1975. While this draft adopted some of the JFTC's proposals, such as the new surcharge and an increase in fines, it differed from the JFTC draft in important respects, such as on the split-up issue and limits on stockholdings by corporations and financial institutions.

However, the LDP had clearly underestimated the outrage of the Japanese people. In September 1974, the Nationwide Federation of Consumer Groups (*Zenkoku shōhisha dantai renrakukai*, "*Shōdanren*") publicly endorsed the JFTC proposal, embarked onto a two-month public initiative, and began to lobby the opposition parties heavily. The opposition parties saw a chance to utilize this public outrage against the LDP, and each party drafted its own bill proposal for a revised AML (JFTC Annual Report 1977: 175–6). But even more surprising than the consumer groups was another source of protest: academics. Professors from the fields of economics and law formed groups, each comprising about 250 of the leading scholars in the country. The economists, led by the top ten economists at the time, formed a study group that fully endorsed the JFTC draft and publicly criticized both the LDP and the *zaikai* for undermining antitrust policy. Likewise, the leading law professors fully supported the JFTC draft. The primary effect of these activities was to give academic backing and logical reasoning to the consumer groups' arguments; both academic groups hugely affected journalists and the public.

As a result of all this uproar, the Prime Minister's 1975 AML revision draft was rejected by the Diet. The Prime Minister's Office revised the draft to include some suggestions made by the opposition parties. The academics issued another "protest memo" against this second draft, and it, too, failed to pass the Diet in 1976. In the December 1976 elections, the LDP lost 22 seats, which meant that opposition parties and the LDP were equally strong. The new Fukuda Cabinet promised swift action on the AML revision, and when a third version was submitted to the Diet in 1977, it finally passed in the same year after two years and eight months of haggling.

The final, third draft was close to the JFTC proposal, but contained some important restrictions. First, the original "breakup provision", which had been dropped in 1953, was re-instituted to empower the JFTC to order spinoffs or breakups of companies with overly dominant market power; however, per the proposal the JFTC was obliged to notify and cooperate with the cognizant minister before taking such measures. Maximum fines were increased from ¥500,000 to ¥5 million—while still low and therefore symbolic, this made it somewhat more costly to break the law. Also, a surcharge system for fining illegal cartels even without a criminal trial was introduced, but less stringent than originally requested (see Chapter 4). The law contained new limits on corporate stockholdings by banks, limiting stockholdings by one bank to 5% of the out-standing capital of a corporation (down from 10%); this was still higher than the JFTC had suggested. In sum, with these changes the AML remained quite harmless to dominant firms and monopolists, but at the margin the revised AML gave the JFTC additional means to prosecute cartels, and in particular price agreements.

3.4. "Structural Depression" after 1977

The grass roots movement that had backed the revision of the AML, and the unlikely coalition between the public, academics and opposition parties, had taken the "iron triangle" of *zaikai*, LDP politicians and bureaucrats by surprise. Even more surprisingly, however, after the revision of the AML and the senten-cing of the oil companies and the Petroleum Federation, MITI returned to "industrial policy as usual". The Antimonopoly Law had been circumvented, if not ignored, before, and there was no change in attitude after the 1977 revision. Consequently, there was no obvious, significant increase in cartel prosecution by the JFTC (cf. Figure 3.1). While the law had been changed, the *zaikai*, MITI and the LDP maintained their effective alliance against any real prolonged threat from the antitrust watchdog.

Yet, in the 1970s MITI began to face changes in the thrust of its industrial policy. Until then, industrial policy had been driven by the one goal of promoting growth, and import controls had been the Ministry's primary tool. MITI's major policy actions were the encouragement of informal cartels and merger policies to increase Japan's international competitiveness. This changed after the two oil shocks. First, the steep increase in energy costs changed MITI's set of designated growth sectors: energy-intensive industries were replaced as "strategic industries" by high-tech, high value-added, capital intensive industries. The shift to new flagship industries meant that many industries were identified as being "structur-ally depressed", i.e., demand and growth prospects were maturing.[29] To be sure, even in the period of rapid growth, industrial policy had been divided into growth-promoting policies on the one hand, and structural reorganization and

---

[29] For models framing industrial policy in industry growth cycle terms, see Okimoto (1989: 50–1), Vestal (1993: 62–8), Young (1991).

capacity reduction policies on the other; the latter were much harder to do as they required sacrifices by the companies concerned. However, until the 1960s, most of the "troubled" industries considered their problems to be temporary, and were therefore happy to cooperate for future gain. Japan's 1970s recession marred that optimism, because companies figured that there could be an endpoint to the "repeated game". Agreements in the new "troubled industries" therefore had to be organized and enforced by MITI as a mediating agent with some skill and considerable enticement in the form of subsidies.

Further, MITI now had fewer tools at its disposal with which to persuade firms to cooperate. The outcome of the oil cartel case meant that companies could reject administrative guidance on the grounds that they feared JFTC prosecution, even if that was only a convenient excuse not to have to conform to MITI's guidance. Moreover, MITI's leverage in administrative guidance was curtailed from two ends. Continuing trade liberalization was undermining the effectiveness of the "carrot and stick" of import controls, and the 1980 revision of the Foreign Trade and Foreign Exchange Control Law further truncated MITI's leverage. At the same time, growing industries were beginning to self-regulate, in particular in structuring their new markets and distribution systems. MITI decided that it was more important to look out for the troubled industries than the growing ones, and in order to do so, MITI sought a new law that would give it renewed power to intervene in declining sectors.

Following the basic ideas of the failed 1960s *Tokushinhō* draft, MITI suggested a law that would allow the ministry to encourage capacity reduction cartels in structurally depressed industries. What followed was a replay of the 1960s discussions; the only difference was that the JFTC's public standing had significantly increased since then. After considerable haggling, in May 1978 the Diet passed the "Depressed Industries Law" (DIL).[30] The law had a five-year time limit and focused on excess capacity only, and thus was specifically designed as a countermeasure for the oil shock recession.

Initially, four industries were designated under this law: aluminum, synthetic fibers, shipbuilding, and steel. Soon, the group was extended to ten other industries, all of which had been allowed to form cartels repeatedly in the past.[31] The designation of an industry as "depressed" was done either by MITI, or followed the prewar principle of a "two-thirds" rule; i.e., if two-thirds of the firms in an industry wanted to be designated, they could apply at MITI for enforcement of their cartel (see Chapter 7). Per the DIL, MITI would draft a Stabilization Plan for the designated industries jointly with the companies in the industry, detailing what facilities to scrap, how, and when. If firms were unable to meet the plan's target, MITI had the explicit legal authority to form a "voluntary"

---

[30] "Temporary Measures Law for the Stabilization of Designated Depressed Industries"; *Tokutei fukyō sangyō antei rinji sochi hō*.

[31] These were: nylon filament, polyester filament, polyester staple, ammonium, urea, phosphoric acid, cotton spinning, wool, ferro-silicon, and corrugated board.

(non-coercive) cartel which was exempted from AML provisions. While MITI could not force firms to participate, one feature of the law was the "Depressed Industries Credit Fund" of initially ¥10 billion, from which subsidies would be distributed to participating companies. This made it expensive for any one company to refuse to participate in the industry-wide cartel.

Although the 14 industries covered by the DIL had achieved a substantial reduction of capacity by 1982, their economic situation did not improve. This was primarily due to the second oil shock of 1979, which, while much less traumatic than the first, had vitiated the comeback attempts of the energy-intensive industries. By 1982 it was apparent that many of these industries were in chronic, rather than temporary, distress. MITI therefore began to lobby for a legal means to continue support of these industries. To deal with the chronic issues, it argued, more extensive measures of cooperation beyond a simple reduction of capacity were required. MITI wanted to be able to orchestrate mergers and encourage joint activities. This re-opened the old debate about who should be in charge of exempting cartels from the AML—MITI or the JFTC? Moreover, should MITI be allowed to force outsiders into cartel agreements so that they could not foil the cooperative attempts, or should such coercion be considered an "unfair restraint of trade"?

A new public debate emerged which revived the economists' group and the media. Finally, in 1983 the "Structurally Depressed Industries Law" (SDIL, *Tokutei sangyō kōzō kaizen rinji sochi hō*) was passed; it was a classic compromise between the JFTC, public opinion, and MITI. First, the law again was limited to a five-year period, and was to expire in 1988. The JFTC retained the cartel licensing right, and MITI (and any other ministry in charge of a "structurally depressed industry") was denied a *carte blanche* to exempt any designated industry from the provisions of the AML. Neither did MITI gain the right to coerce resistant firms into joining cartels. However, the law allowed coordination of virtually all business activities in the designated industries. Companies could coordinate joint production, storage, sales, joint investments, R&D, and shifts in production among firms, i.e., market allocation by product, so that each firm would have a niche for a certain product category. To entice cooperation, the SDIL also contained many new preferential tax measures and government loan guarantees. On the whole, the SDIL was the direct successor to the 1978 DIL, but it vastly expanded the scope of cooperation.

Initially, 15 broadly defined industries were designated under the SDIL.[32] As with the previous law, MITI (or other cognizant ministries) and the firms in these industries would draft a "Structural Reform Plan", and MITI would encourage the cooperation necessary to reach the targets of this plan. Most of the

---

[32] These were: polyolephene, phosphoric acid, compound fertilizer, ethylene, polyvinyl chloride, ethylene oxide, paper, cement, electric furnace steel production, aluminum, synthetic fibers, chemical fertilizers, ferro-alloys, petrochemicals, and shipbuilding. Over time, other industries joined the club, such as sugar, hard PVC pipes, and wool spinning.

fundamental decisions as to what kind of capacities to curtail, and by how much, were left to business executives who would meet in their trade associations and draft the initial plan. Likewise, implementation and monitoring were left to self-regulation, not so much because MITI would not have liked to monitor the cartels, but because it was clearly understaffed and undertrained to fulfil these functions. In this way, the SDIL gave legal cover to industry self-regulation in times of distress, to be organized through the trade associations.[33]

The SDIL expired in 1988, just at the onset of the "bubble years" (1987–91), with increasingly speculative investments in real estate and the stock market. The rise in land value improved the financial situation even of those enterprises that were unprofitable in their main lines of business. Companies did not lobby for further protection, and MITI had little grounds to claim that it needed an extension to the depressed industries' legislation. The SDIL therefore elapsed without being immediately replaced by other legislation.[34] Thus, Japan entered the 1990s with no special legislation for the troubled industries, but with a history of 40 years of cartel encouragement and government-guided circumvention of the AML.

3.5. Summary: Industrial Policy and the Propensity to Cooperate

The postwar years were not a period of unchallenged, smooth MITI guidance of economic policy. Rather, between the 1950s and 1980s, as Japan experienced fast corporate development and technological catch-up, the ministries and industry rode a see-saw of opinion swings as to whether the fast-growing industries should be supported and cartelized, or regulated. Per their Establishment Laws, MITI and the other ministries were responsible for both the protection and regulation

---

[33] There is a substantial amount of research on the DIL and SDIL, the ramifications of these laws for Japan's economic structure, and the evaluation of the effectiveness of industrial policy (e.g., Yamamura 1982, Uekusa 1987, Upham 1987, Uriu 1996, Vestal 1993, Saxonhouse 1979). It is important to note that the intent of the DIL and SDIL was not necessarily always to increase productivity in the designated sectors, but to smooth out the decline of these industries. Moreover, in addition to these blanket laws, MITI still used specific industry laws to promote growth and support maturing industries. For instance, the 1978 Law for the Promotion of Designated Machinery and Information Industries (*Tokutei kikai jōhō sangyō shinkō rinji sochi hō*) was instrumental in promoting Japan's computer industry (cf. Anchordoguy 1989).

[34] While not a direct successor, the 1995 Business Reform Law picked up on the SDIL measures ("Temporary Law to Promote Business Reform of Specific Companies", *Tokutei jigyōsha no jigyō kakushin no enkatsu-ka ni kan suru rinji sochi-hō*). This law allowed MITI to designate a company for the purpose of collaboration on a "business reform plan", including joint product development, cost reduction efforts and changes in distribution practices in the industry concerned. MITI designation also qualified a company for support measures such as special depreciation allowances, low interest loans, and government subsidies. Within six months of the passing of this law in 1995, 50 companies were designated. The law had a seven-year life span and was designed to support companies facing structural problems in the 1990s recession.

of the industries in their domains, but all ministries were typically weak on supervision. The JFTC was therefore the only government agency that would challenge cartel agreements.

In the 1950s and early 1960s, when the economy was still struggling, the JFTC was obviously unable to stand up against the "iron triangle" coalition of ministries, politicians, and industrialists. The national economic growth objective overrode any concerns for fair trade. Little attention was paid to what the JFTC was saying or doing, except when the watchdog encroached upon politically sensitive terrain. In such cases, the JFTC was generally told to withdraw. The outstanding, but certainly not the only, example of this process of silencing the JFTC is the 1959 newspaper incident: in spite of large amounts of compromising papers and minutes, the JFTC dropped the case under pressure from politicians and other ministries.

In addition to supporting economic growth in designated, large-scale export industries, MITI had also pushed for a blanket exemption from the AML for all small-sized companies and their cooperatives. Just as large companies were important contributors to LDP finances, small firms were important LDP voters. The politicians therefore wanted both groups kept happy. MITI's response was to exempt all industries as much as possible from antitrust constraints. Thus, a significant portion of the postwar growth of both large and small enterprises was built on intra-industry cooperation, price agreements, joint management strategies, investment "adjustments" and protection from outside competitors. Examples of means adopted by industry and MITI to disguise or legalize cartels include: implicit collusion through price leadership schemes or other covert collusion; special industry laws that granted exemption from the AML; blanket "AML bypass laws"; and administrative guidance-based schemes that MITI claimed were based on unilateral ministerial orders but *de facto* were based on agreements by the industry representatives and therefore constituted cartels. Over time, these multiple means of circumvention of the AML established a cooperative system that the JFTC was too weak to change. All the JFTC could try to do was to influence the ways in which the inter-firm cooperation was structured by threatening to prosecute the most egregious cases and to report names of violating companies to the media.

With the achievement of economic growth and the first *bona fide* postwar consumer boom in the late 1960s, the Japanese approach to antitrust policy began to change slowly. The public became interested in how Japan's growing economic pie would be divided between the producers and consumers, and many citizens felt they were losing out to industry. The students' protests of the late 1960s, the pollution incidents of the early 1970s, large political corruption scandals, and corporate market cornering schemes during the "oil shock" all combined to arouse the public's anger to a point where they organized to support the AML and its enforcement agency, the JFTC.

This public support was critical in shaping the 1977 revision of the AML that gave the JFTC more powers to prosecute cartels; at the same time, however, the "iron triangle" (LDP, ministries, and *zaikai*) managed to block stricter rules. While the 1977 AML revision and the 1980 oil cartel case served to increase the JFTC, MITI was granted the legal right to encourage "structural depression cartels" in 1978, which increased MITI's powers to bypass the AML. In the 1980s, the JFTC stepped up its efforts to be a respected force by publishing so-called Guidelines designed to remind corporations of the AML and signal to industry that it would be vigilant in its monitoring.

However, the JFTC is still anything but a strong, autonomous agency. It is part and parcel of the Japanese government and political economy and must operate within the confines prescribed by the various ongoing power struggles. Many leaders in government and industry do not consider antitrust policy to be an independent regulatory policy, but view it as an integral part of economic policy. In addition, throughout almost the entire postwar period, the JFTC Commissioner has been a retired high-ranking bureaucrat from the Ministry of Finance, who after 30 years of ministerial service was firmly tied into the network underlying government–business relations and far from immune from political interference.

From the corporate perspective, the subordination of antitrust policy to industrial policy had two major strategic implications. First, companies learned that it paid to cooperate. When agreements were difficult to reach or enforce because of the competitive nature of an industry, the cognizant ministry jumped in to mediate and structure the bargaining process. Therefore, the 1950s and 1960s witnessed repeated instances of cooperation even in industries that were traditionally rather competitive. This led to an overall high propensity to co-operate among Japanese companies: there was a past experience of cooperation through the association on which new agreements could be built. Second, the government's active encouragement of cartels, and the large number of cartels, necessarily meant that a large portion of the structuring and enforcement of these agreements was left to the industries themselves. Since MITI and the other ministries did not have the resources to regulate all industry agreements, the job was left to trade associations. In the process, companies learned what it took to structure an agreement and monitor its compliance. They also learned that unless the agreements were effected in obviously and flagrantly illegal ways, there was little cause to fear intervention, let alone punishment, by the JFTC. Administrative guidance to self-regulate therefore laid the groundwork in many industries for an extension of the delegated tasks into the realm of independent self-regulation.

4

Self-Regulation and the Antimonopoly Law

'There is no legal problem with self-regulation, as long as it is voluntary.'
(Interview with a JFTC adviser, March 1995)

The political prerogatives established by industrial policy and the national effort to "catch up" have limited the political standing and independence of Japan's Fair Trade Commission (JFTC) over time. In addition to the political constraints, the JFTC's power to enforce antitrust policy is also constrained by the wording of the Antimonopoly Law (AML) itself, and the interpretation and processes of implementation that developed around the law during the postwar period. By explaining the logic of the Japanese antitrust system, this chapter shows how and why existing legal doctrine makes it difficult for the JFTC to prosecute anti-competitive behavior, in particular regarding the multifaceted activities of self-regulation. While protective self-regulation aims at closing markets and restraining competition, and is thus largely outlawed by the antitrust law, many parts of administrative self-regulation, too, can easily result in entry barriers or other restrictions of exchange. Thus, even the rule-making activities of trade associations sometimes entail boycotts, refusals to deal with nonmembers and similar market constraints. Antitrust law calls such market restrictions "unfair trade practices", and while they are outlawed in Japan, these practices have not been prosecuted stridently.

This chapter looks at the details of Japan's antitrust system to analyze the legal context of self-regulation. It will become apparent that the established legal doctrine inhibits a more authoritative or autonomous stance by the JFTC. Compared with other countries, the JFTC needs to provide strong evidence to bring a case, and penalty provisions and other deterrents are not as powerful. The combined result of lax treatment of "unfair trade practices" and comparatively lenient punishment of cartel violations is that the JFTC has been unable to contain self-regulation.

The difference in prosecuting antitrust violations in Japan is due to the general interpretation of the AML, and the standing of the antitrust authority within the larger political economy. Specifically, three factors combine to work against an empowerment of the JFTC and the AML over time: (1) a lack of public awareness of antitrust; (2) the absence of private suits; and (3) the Japanese legal and regulatory culture in general. First, there is little common understanding of the AML's content. The general public is not sure what exactly the law permits or prohibits, offering little support for stricter AML enforcement (Kawagoe 1997: 2). Second, in stark contrast to the U.S., where private damage action is a primary deterrent to cartel formation, private antitrust lawsuits are extremely rare in Japan. Whereas a total of 31,745 private antitrust suits were brought in the U.S. between 1945 and 1988, only 15 such suits were filed in Japan in that same period (see Chapter 5 for data). The primary reason for this discrepancy may lie not so much in a different attitude toward litigation, but in a combination of high costs and a low probability of success in Japan (Ramseyer 1985). Private parties can file two different civil damage suits: based on Section 25 of the AML in conjunction with a JFTC case, or independent from the JFTC based on Section 709 of the Civil Code (*Minpō*). AML Section 25 suits are inconvenient for companies not located in Tokyo, because they are in the exclusive jurisdiction of the Tokyo High Court.[1] More importantly, in both AML and Civil Code cases, the plaintiff has the full burden of proof and must provide evidence both of a causal relationship between collusion and the injury suffered, and of the extent of damages incurred. There are neither double or treble damages nor punitive damages, so that there are only few financial incentives for bringing a private suit. Because class action suits are not allowed in the Japanese system, potential plaintiffs cannot pool their litigation cost. Lastly, the chances of winning a private antitrust charge are small, as courts have in the past sided with the defendants in most instances.[2]

The third factor inhibiting the reach of the JFTC in enforcing antitrust rules are the imprecise wording and inconsistent application of the Japanese AML, combined with a lack of precedents. Businessmen cannot always be certain what the law prohibits. Japan's general legal and regulatory culture, which rests on informal and situational enforcement, compounds this uncertainty: some argue that the wording of the AML, as well as other laws, is designed to be ambiguous to afford the government flexibility in administrative guidance (Iyori 1986: 62, Upham 1987). In a similar vein, First (1995: 143–4) contends that in spite of the seeming similarities in the letter of the U.S. and Japanese antimonopoly laws, the differences in the legal cultures of the two countries translate into highly divergent applications of the antitrust statues. He describes the U.S. as a "legalistic" system that works by prohibitory rules and aims to protect the law's primary beneficiaries, the consumers. In contrast, Japan's "bureaucratic" regulatory culture is principally concerned with overall economic welfare and growth, and

[1]   Moreover, private suits based on the AML can only be brought for violation of Section 3 (cartels) or Section 19 (unfair trade practices) of the AML, and only after the JFTC has initiated an administrative case against the violators. As explained below, this excludes violations by trade associations. However, between 1947 and the 1980s, 75% of all antitrust cases brought by the JFTC involved trade associations. Because the JFTC has to initiate the case before a private suit can be filed, the restriction on Section 3 and 19 cases *de facto* has restricted private suits.

[2]   See Ramseyer (1985, 1992) for an analysis of cases and a complete argument why and how private antitrust suits are not a significant deterrent to price fixing or other violations of the antitrust law in Japan; see Iyori/Uesugi (1994: 237–43) for procedural details.

consumer protection is an afterthought at best. This "bureaucratic system" is based on consensual (or negotiated) decision-making between government and business, and in this system antitrust policies are carried out in a utilitarian way to match broader policy issues. For this to function properly, the law has to be ambiguous. Yet, the more ambiguous the wording, the more difficult it is for the JFTC to push for a stricter interpretation of the statute over time.

As a result of these three factors, which result in a profound lack of institutional backing for rigorous antitrust, the JFTC has found itself unable to strictly enforce the AML in general, and to halt the increase in self-regulation by trade associations since the 1980s in particular. Based on an analysis of the organization of the JFTC and the content and current interpretation of the AML, this chapter evaluates the implications of antitrust enforcement for the Japanese system of self-regulation. What, exactly, is the legal situation, and why is the JFTC unlikely to increase prosecution of self-regulation in the foreseeable future? Examples of formal and informal cases and their means of settlement highlight how the AML is applied. Based on the legal discussion in this chapter, Chapter 5 will then provide evidence of how this legal situation is reflected in the JFTC's actual record of prosecution in the postwar period.

4.1. The JFTC and the Enforcement Process

The Japan Fair Trade Commission

The Japan Fair Trade Commission (JFTC, *Kōsei torihiki iinkai*) is in charge of enforcing four related but separate laws: the Antimonopoly Law, the AML Exemption Law, the Subcontractor Law, and the Labeling Law.[3] The JFTC formulates rules related to the administrative procedures of these laws, such as notifications by trade associations on their formation or change in bylaws, and it is in charge of investigations and adjudicative procedures related to violations of these laws.

The JFTC is an independent administrative commission belonging to the Prime Minister's Office, so that the head of the JFTC reports directly to the Prime Minister but is not a member of the cabinet. The Prime Minister appoints the JFTC Chairman and four subordinate commissioners with the consent of both the Upper and Lower Houses of the Diet. The commissioners

---

[3] In Japanese, these are the: *Dokusen kinshi hō*, as discussed below; *Tekiyō igai hō (Shiteki dokusen no kinshi oyobi kōsei torihiki no kakuho ni kan suru hōritsu)*, which exempts certain cartels from AML enforcement; *Shitauke hō (Shitauke daikin shiharai chien-tō bōshi hō)*, which protects subcontractors from late payments and other abusive practices by powerful customers; and *Keihin hyōshi hō*, which prohibits unjust labeling and improper premia. See Chapter 4.2 below for a brief discussion of these laws.

are thus political appointees. They are supported by a secretariat consisting of lifetime bureaucrats headed by a secretary-general, the highest-ranking civil servant in the JFTC.

While on paper it may be a strong agency, six systemic factors combine to limit the JFTC's power. First, under the National Public Service Law (*Kokka kōmuin hō*), the JFTC's secretary-general is one rank below an Administrative Vice Minister (*jimu jikan*) in a ministry, and therefore the JFTC is of lower bureaucratic standing than the industry-regulating ministries (Iyori 1995: 87). Second, the position of JFTC Chairman (or head commissioner) is not of high political standing, because it is not a cabinet post. Also, the JFTC Chairman is closely connected to the industry-regulating ministries, because between 1947 and 1998, with three exceptions this position has been occupied by a retired Administrative Vice Minister from the Ministry of Finance. Third, the JFTC staff continues to be augmented by *shukkō* (secondments) from the regulating ministries, including senior officials from MITI. While this may be helpful in building relations and possibly convincing the *shukkō* officials of the relevance of antitrust policy, it curbs the JFTC's independence in its decision-making. Fourth, per the stipulations of the AML, the JFTC can only take administrative actions upon identifying a legal transgression, whereas all criminal prosecutions have to be launched by the Prosecutor's Office in the Ministry of Justice. Although a similar system works well in the U.S., in Japan the Prosecutor's Office is severely understaffed, so that support from the Justice Ministry is slim. Fifth, while the JFTC has the right to launch on-site investigations when it detects anti-competitive activities, its enforcement powers are limited: never has an obstruction of a JFTC investigation been prosecuted, and it is widely assumed that companies and associations are informed in advance of an upcoming JFTC raid.[4] Finally, the already-mentioned lack of private suits means that the JFTC shoulders all responsibility of enforcing the AML (Lynn/McKeown 1988: 43–5, Iyori 1995: 86, Haley 1995: 313).

In spite of being the sole enforcer of antitrust, the JFTC's workforce is not very large. To be sure, the JFTC's staff has grown over time, from 237 in 1954 to 529 in 1996. As of June 1996, of these 529 employees, 181 were on-site investigators, 143 were "trade and market researchers" (including monitoring trade associations and unfair trade practices), 76 worked in the secretariat, and 129 were in the regional offices in Hokkaidō, Tōhoku, Chūbu, Kinki and Kyūshū (Kawagoe 1997: 50). Adjusted for the relative size of the economies, the total JFTC staff is similar to the roughly 1,000 FTC employees in the U.S. However, the Antitrust Division of the U.S. Department of Justice, which accounts for about half of U.S. antitrust investigations, has a staff of roughly 600, while the Japanese Ministry of Justice

---

[4] During the 1998 scandals involving the Ministry of Finance, public prosecutors found evidence that banks were informed prior to upcoming investigations by the ministry. While no such evidence is explicitly documented for antitrust investigations, journalists have pointed out that JFTC investigations are typically announced in the economics daily newspaper *Nikkei* one day *before* they occur (interviews, Tokyo, summer 1995).

has no specialized antitrust staff, leaving all investigative tasks with the 500 staff at the JFTC (Iyori 1995: 86).

When the U.S. occupation forces designed the legal standing of the JFTC in 1947, they had the U.S. political system in mind and did not realize that in Japan, an independent agency would be less, rather than more, powerful. Further, since a system of political appointees is largely unknown in Japan, the Japanese opted to staff the JFTC with career bureaucrats from the regulating ministries, thus significantly compromising the thrust of antitrust enforcement against industries. The JFTC is part and parcel of the Japanese bureaucratic system. Yet, being of lower institutional standing than the industry-regulating industries such as MITI, the JFTC is rarely able to push its position against the will of these other ministries.

The Legal Processes of Antitrust Enforcement

The JFTC can choose to prosecute a violation in various ways, each of which has different legal consequences and thus implies differing degrees of deterrent or actual punishment. While these differentiations are somewhat legalistic, they are important to see just how much power the JFTC can exert over industry, and whether there have been qualitative changes over time in the ways in which the JFTC has sought to enforce the AML. There are four broad categories of AML enforcement: informal settlement, formal administrative procedures, criminal investigation, and preventive consultation. Of these, the preventive consultation system is the least studied and yet probably the most critical for a thorough understanding of Japan's antitrust system.

An administrative investigation can be started from two primary sources: by initiation of the JFTC itself, or based on a report to the JFTC by the general public. While the JFTC does not disclose the original source of a case, possibly to protect "whistle-blowers" (i.e., cartel breakers who report), most cases are triggered by complaints from the general public.[5] Upon receiving a report, the JFTC's Investigation Bureau begins a preliminary investigation. If suspicion of a violation is confirmed, it will launch a formal investigation during which it may order persons to testify, confiscate documents, and inspect business offices without prior notice. Following the investigation, the JFTC has six options for how to proceed (see Figure 4.1): drop the case; issue a "warning" or "caution"; issue a "recommendation"; issue a "complaint"; file for criminal prosecution with the Ministry of Justice; or file for an injunction with the Tokyo High Court. Among these, issuing warnings, recommendations, and complaints are the most common and important procedures.

---

[5] Interview, JFTC, Tokyo, winter 1998. The law also enables the General Prosecutor and the Agency for Small- and Medium-Sized Enterprises (affiliated with MITI) to file reports with the JFTC, but not a single case has been initiated by either of these institutions.

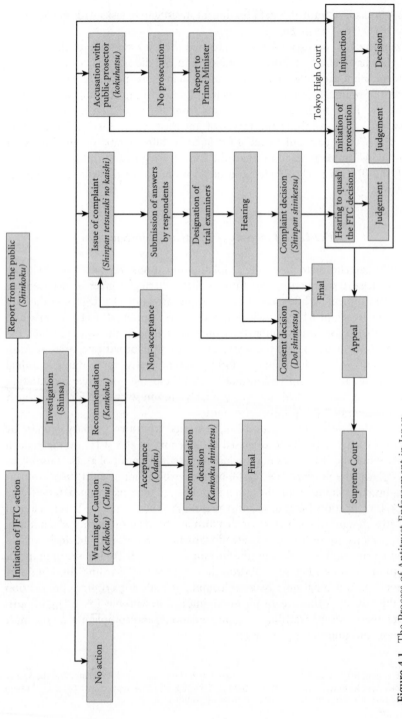

Figure 4.1. The Process of Antitrust Enforcement in Japan

Source: adapted from Kawagoe 1997: 393.

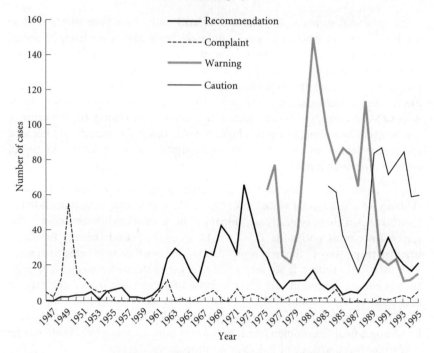

Figure 4.2. Formal Enforcement versus Informal Enforcement, 1947–1996
Source: database built from JFTC Annual Reports, 1947–1997.

Informal settlement of violations. If during the investigation the JFTC finds insufficient evidence to launch a case, it can choose to take no action. If the JFTC nevertheless suspects a strong violation, it can issue the antitrust equivalent of administrative guidance. The weakest form of this is a "caution"(*chūi*), while the "warning" (*keikoku*) is a stronger, written version of guidance.[6] In a warning, the JFTC advises the firms or association under suspicion that they are close to a violation of the law and should terminate the described behavior. There is no legal basis for such a warning, and no punishment will ensue. Companies that receive a warning can either comply, guard their activities more carefully, or simply shrug it off. The JFTC began publishing statistics on the content of these highly informal means of enforcement only in 1978. Yet, Figure 4.2 suggests that the JFTC uses warnings and cautions very frequently (see Chapter 5 for a detailed analysis).

[6] More precisely, the JFTC uses a "warning" in one of the following four situations: (1) the facts of a violation cannot be proven; (2) the illegal conduct was voluntarily discontinued and occurred more than 12 months in the past; (3) if a trade association was involved, this association was voluntarily dissolved; or (4) the JFTC considers the impact of the illegal actions to be minor, so that an informal settlement is sufficient to correct the conduct (Iyori/Uesugi 1994: 218). The difference between a "caution" and a "warning" is similar to oral administrative guidance and a *tsūtatsu*, i.e., a written note containing the guidance. A warning thus insinuates more of a violation than a caution.

Informal settlements economize on staff work and yet are quite effective: while the JFTC does not have to prepare a full case, businessmen are likely to accept and comply, because they prefer to keep the accusation low profile and avoid a report in the media. As Iyori/Uesugi (1994: 218) argue, if the JFTC's goal is simply to terminate the behavior, rather than punish the violator, informal means may be sufficient in many cases. However, because informal settlement does not carry strong deterrent effects, it is unlikely to change the behavior of corporations over time. Using this logic, the U.S. raised the issue during bilateral trade negotiations in the late 1980s and pushed for more formal means of curbing antitrust violations.

Formal administrative procedures. If during its investigation the JFTC finds evidence of a substantial violation of the AML, it can issue a recommendation (*kankoku*), which is typically accompanied by a cease-and-desist order.[7] The respondents must notify the JFTC within a certain period (usually ten days) whether they "accept" this recommendation, i.e., whether they agree to comply with the JFTC's orders. If so, they must take the prescribed remedial measures, such as ending the conduct, deleting a clause of unfair trade from a contract, or dissolving an association. If the JFTC receives an acceptance, including agreement to take the remedial measures as recommended, the JFTC will close the case by issuing a final "recommendation decision" (*kankoku shinketsu*). There will be no further investigations or adjudicative procedures.[8]

If, however, the respondents deny the alleged conduct and refuse to accept the recommendation, the case is turned into a "complaint" (*shinpan*). For flagrant violations, the JFTC can also issue a complaint directly. In either case, the respondents have to submit in writing their reasons for not accepting the recommendation or their position on the complaint. Trial examiners will then open a hearing. During the hearing, the investigators present their evidence, which is typically the same as that detailed in the original complaint. The violators then have the option to either accept the complaint (*dōi shinketsu*; this is rare, because no new evidence is produced during the hearings), or continue to deny the wrongdoing. If they deny the JFTC's complaint, the examiners have to reach a decision on the case. If the examiners find the respondents in violation of the AML, they issue a complaint decision (*shinpan shinketsu*), which means that the respondents are found guilty even though they

---

[7] In general, evidence is considered to be substantial if there are both written materials and witnesses. If the JFTC has only one of those two, it is likely to issue a "warning" only, because the recommendation has to stand up to further investigation should it be rejected by the respondent (see below). This means that a whistle-blower alone, without evidence of a cartel in writing, may be insufficient for launching a formal procedure.

[8] In legal terms, a recommendation decision is simply based on the respondent's willing acceptance of a recommendation issued by the JFTC, and therefore this decision does not legally establish a factual violation of the law. However, contravening a JFTC decision can be punished with a fine or imprisonment. See Iyori/Uesugi (1994: 220) for legal interpretation, Kawagoe (1997: 396) for criticism of the dominance of informal settlement of AML violations.

deny the wrongdoing. If the violators are unwilling to accept this decision, they can appeal to the Tokyo High Court and, if necessary, to the Supreme Court.

Of 1,007 total formal cases brought by the JFTC between 1947 and 1996, 77.8% were recommendations, and most of these cases were immediately accepted by the respondents (cf. Figure 4.2). The reason for this high acceptance ratio is that the JFTC cannot add to the case once the recommendation is issued, and is therefore careful to issue a recommendation only if it could stand up in a hearing. Without sufficient evidence, the JFTC will opt to issue an informal warning only.[9] Thus, the systemic constraints on recommendations further increase the bias toward informal settlement of cases: only the truly tight cases will be brought formally.

Nonetheless, the formal recommendation system is actually very lenient. It does not carry serious penalties, as it allows violators simply to repent (or pretend to repent) and settle for a cease-and-desist order, and then regroup the activities slightly so as not to be caught as a repeat offender. To make cartels less obviously profitable and increase the risk and effect of public disclosure, the JFTC pushed for the introduction of a surcharge system with the AML revision of 1977. This surcharge (*kachōkin*) is an administrative punitive levy modeled after the German *Bußgeld* ("penalty money"). In lay terms, it is akin to a parking ticket: although no criminal record is established, the ticket can be expensive and thus create an incentive not to violate the rules. The surcharge system allows the JFTC to collect excessive profits gained through price cartels that are finalized as recommendation or complaint decisions; i.e., it can fine cartels without prosecuting a criminal case.

The surcharge is calculated by multiplying a percentage, as prescribed in the law, by the total amount of sales during the cartel period. Following a 1992 revision, this fixed percentage is twice as high for large firms as for small firms, and it is differentiated by sector: for large wholesalers it is 1%, for large retailers it is 2%, and for all other large firms it is 6%. The maximum cartel period to which this percentage can be applied is three years. During the 20 years since the introduction of the system in 1977, the JFTC has levied a total of ¥51.39 billion (JFTC Annual Report 1997). The largest single surcharge levied in the first half of the 1990s was the ¥6.62 billion (about $70 million at the time) charged against nine companies involved in the Chūgoku cement cartel case of 1991. Yet, in total annual amounts charged, fines are still much lower in Japan than in the U.S., and the low surcharge rates mean that usually the surcharge is less than the harm caused by a cartel (Ramseyer 1985: 636, Haley 1995: 313). The fixed percentage rate puts a limit on how much of a deterrent the JFTC can create: even if companies are found to have rigged prices by, say, 20%, a maximum surcharge of only 6% will be levied. Critics have argued this is too low, as cartelists can simply figure the 6% rate into their price scheme. The counterargument in

---

[9] Interview, JFTC, Tokyo, winter 1998. Statistics are from a database constructed from the JFTC Annual Reports between 1947 and 1997; see Chapter 5 for details.

support of the fixed 6% rule is that if this is insufficient to deter cartels, a criminal case may be appropriate (Iyori/Uesugi 1994: 260). Of course, this argument holds only if criminal cases are indeed launched.

Criminal investigations.   In cases of flagrant violations of the AML, the JFTC has two ways to pursue prosecution through the courts. First, it can file an accusation (*kokuhatsu*) with the Public Prosecutor (*kenji sōchō*), together with launching a formal administrative procedure, usually a recommendation. While the JFTC then proceeds through the adjudicative process, as described above, the Prosecutor's Office prepares a criminal case. If the defendants are found guilty of an antitrust violation in court, they will be charged a fine and may face a prison sentence. However, between 1947 and 1990, the JFTC filed a total of only six accusations, of which three were administered under SCAP in the early 1950s, and two were related to the oil cartel in the 1970s. In contrast, in the U.S. criminal proceedings became common in the 1960s, and in the 1980s, U.S. courts dealt with about 70 criminal antitrust cases a year (Iyori 1995: 84; see also Chapter 5). It is no surprise, therefore, that U.S. trade negotiators have repeatedly requested that Japan increase criminal procedures in antitrust violations, and indeed the JFTC filed four criminal accusations with the Public Prosecutor in the early 1990s (the vinyl wrap price cartel of 1992, and three bid-rigging cases). In addition, the AML was amended in 1992 to increase by 20 times the maximum fines that can be levied for criminal cartel violations. As a result, in the 1990s prosecution of criminal cases became a much more serious threat to industry, and hence a more powerful deterrent to cartel activities. Yet, in terms of frequency, the number of criminal cases prosecuted in Japan is still nowhere close to U.S. levels.

A second way of using the courts is for the JFTC to apply to the Tokyo High Court for an injunction (*sashitome meirei*), when a company or association is suspected of an activity that impedes competition so significantly that immediate action is required to preserve competition. While the JFTC does not have to provide evidence of the transgression at the time of injunction, thereafter it must launch the formal adjudicative process. In the entire postwar period, the JFTC has filed for an injunction only six times, and withdrew one of them (against the Yawata steel merger) prior to the court decision.[10] While injunctions are a very powerful tool, the JFTC shies away from them, because they bring increased public scrutiny and therefore require significantly more evidence in the recommendation than would be necessary without an injunction.

Preventive consultation.   Finally, probably the most potent and often-used tool of Japanese antitrust enforcement is the least obvious and most difficult to assess,

---

[10] Of the other five cases, two ended with a consent decision, and three resulted in a cease-and-desist order. Interestingly, all five cases involved newspaper companies, and the violations were either improper advertising or sales and pricing techniques. See JFTC Annual Report, any recent issue, statistical supplement.

and yet it has a huge impact on the overall statistics of antitrust enforcement. This tool is the "consultation system" (*jizen sōdan*), which is a form of informal, preemptive intervention. In the U.S., non-adjudicative enforcement methods are sometimes used in the form of trade practice conferences or advisory opinions on specific cases; however, reliance on informal means is neither as widespread nor as institutionalized in the U.S. as it is in Japan (Posner 1970: 370). To see how informal consultation works, consider a case where two companies want to merge. In the U.S., these two companies would announce the merger, subject to approval by the U.S. Federal Trade Commission (FTC). The FTC would then look into the situation and decide on the competitive impact of the proposed merger. In contrast, in Japan the two companies would *first* approach the JFTC quietly, and only after receiving clearance would they publicly announce the merger. Prior consultation helps save time and "face" in those cases where the JFTC rules against the merger. Thus, while the JFTC has publicly ruled against a merger only on few occasions, inferring from this that it is not stopping mergers at all would be a fallacy.

The situation is somewhat different for cartels and other AML violations, for obviously not all cartels ask the JFTC for clearance: some may not know that they are in danger of violating the law, and others may know precisely that. Regardless, the JFTC has always welcomed companies who wanted to check the legal context before initiating a joint project, establishing a specialized association, designing a new system of management guidance or a pricing formula, and the like. In 1982, this consultation system was made official, and the JFTC began publishing data on frequency and content of consultations. Beginning in the 1990s, the JFTC also prepares a separate annual report on the specifics of trade association consultations regarding cartels and unfair trade practices, including examples of cases that would have been found in violation of the AML (e.g., JFTC 1997). These data highlight the proportion of cases of collusion and market restrictions quietly solved through consultation.

Figure 4.3 compares the number of annual prior consultations of trade associations and businesses with both the informal cases (cautions and warnings) and the formally adjudicated cases (recommendations and complaints). Consultation cases clearly dominate the JFTC's enforcement statistics. In 1996 alone, there were 856 cases of consultation with trade associations, compared with 17 warnings and 61 cautions, 23 recommendations and seven complaints. Surprisingly, the JFTC found that slightly over 50% of all consultation cases would have resulted in an antitrust violation had the projects in question been implemented and subsequently prosecuted, implying that the consultation system reduces the number of JFTC cases by roughly half (JFTC 1996a, 1997).[11]

---

[11] According to the JFTC (1996a, 1997), in the mid-1990s over 50% of these consultations were requested by small- and medium-sized companies and their associations. Of all cases, about 35% were in manufacturing, while 25% were in service industries, 20–25% in distribution, and the remainder in transportation, construction, and others. Roughly one-third of all questions concerned the legality of price agreements, followed by questions on market allocation and other business restrictions.

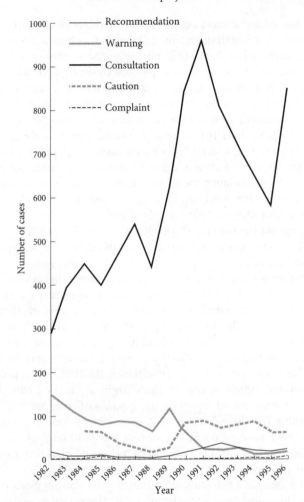

Figure 4.3. Annual Consultations as Compared to Other AML Enforcement
Source: database built from JFTC Annual Reports, 1982–1997.

   The JFTC likes this system, because *ex ante* advice uses up much less man-
power than *ex post* investigation, and thus cuts the JFTC's costs. Further, if as
sometimes argued the goal of law enforcement in Japan is not to exact penalties
but to correct behavior and allow defendants to walk if they repent, prior
consultation can be a highly effective means. In general, Japan's system of
informal regulation and law enforcement can be a strength because it allows
the regulators to go well beyond their statutory mandates in guiding corporate
behavior and enforce actions through administrative guidance; this increases
overall regulatory efficiencies (Haley 1984: 487, Upham 1987). Yet, the system
also has three major drawbacks. First, consultation is necessarily subject to a

self-selection bias in that only those associations whose actions would be easily detectable by the JFTC are likely to request JFTC advice. In contrast, powerful associations that have operated industry agreements successfully are unlikely to ask the JFTC for an evaluation of their practices. Trusting that the consultation will reduce violations and therefore keeping JFTC staff small only allows the successful cartels to thrive. Second, because the JFTC does not monitor to ensure that the cooperating firms or associations follow its advice and drop the plan, the system lacks effective deterrence. Finally, to the outside observer, the system of formal consultation increases opacity by allowing for case-by-case administrative guidance. For the JFTC, the resulting lack of public awareness of its enforcement activities frustrates attempts to increase its visibility and authority within Japan's political economy.

4.2.   The Rules of the Antimonopoly Law: Examples of Violations

'Japan has...effectively removed almost all disincentives to cartelization. A business executive considering fixing prices in Japan has practically nothing to lose....This dearth of enforceable deterrents to price-fixing has apparently led to exactly the consequences one would expect: a "cooperative" economy characterized by widespread cartelization.'

(Ramseyer 1985: 635, 637)

The AML has three major pillars, of which two are important for the purpose of studying self-regulation: (1) the prohibition of cartels, i.e., collusive activities by firms that lead to restraints of competition in particular product markets; and (2) the prohibition of unfair trade practices i.e., business behavior that reduces competition by closing competitors out of a certain market or introducing discriminating rules that benefit only a few firms. The final and third part of the law contains the prohibition of monopolies and the country's long-term industrial structure, such as through rules on mergers, cross-shareholdings, and interlocking directorships. Table 4.1 broadly outlines the content of the major sections of the law. The most important parts regarding self-regulation are Sections 3, 8, and 19. Before analyzing the actual track record of antitrust enforcement, it is helpful to see through examples how the logic of the law works and how it enables or disenables the JFTC to contain the increase in market-restricting self-regulation.

Price Fixing and Other Cartels

To the extent that self-regulation involves cartels, how easily the JFTC can prosecute cartels determines how difficult it is for industries to exercise such

Table 4.1. Overview: The Most Important Sections of the Antimonopoly Law

Section	Content
1	Outlines goal of this law: to maintain fair and free markets through prohibition of monopolies, cartels and unfair trade practices; maintain market competition
2	Defines: "firm", "industry associations", "competition", "unreasonable restraint of trade", "monopoly", "public interest"
3	Prohibits "unreasonable restraint of trade" (cartels)
6	Prohibits certain international agreements of cooperation that entail unfair trade practices or unreasonable restraint of competition
7	Cease-and-desist orders and other JFTC orders to stop or change certain practices
7(2)	Fine (*kachōkin*) on price cartels (administrative surcharge)
8(1)–(3)	Prohibits collusion and conspiracy in trade associations
8(4)	Prohibits the creation of "monopolistic situations" in highly concentrated markets
9	Limits cross-shareholdings and holding companies (revised 1996)
10 and 11	Shareholding limits on corporations and financial institutions, respectively
13	Limits interlocking directorates and dispatch of directors to other companies
15	Market concentration limits on mergers and acquisitions
18	Enables JFTC to invalidate mergers or company creation if anti-competitive
18(2)	Subjects implicit collusion and parallel price increases (through price leadership systems etc.) to JFTC notification system
19	Prohibits "unfair trade practices" as defined in Section 2; stipulates that these activities are to be further specified in "JFTC Designations" (*shitei*)
20	"Stop order" in case of Section 19 violation
21–23	AML exemptions (natural monopolies, industries with a specific industry law, special cooperatives)
24	AML exemptions of recession and rationalization cartels
25–26	Damages
	JFTC organization and rights
	Criminal procedures

self-regulation. Section 3 of the AML disallows "monopolization" and "unreasonable restraint of trade". "Monopolization" is defined in Section 2(5) as "activities by one or several firms that exclude or control the business activities of other firms, thereby restraining competition in any particular field of trade, contrary to the public interest". Clearly, the "public interest" modifier significantly compromises the effectiveness of this clause. Also, what forms a "particular field of trade" remains unclear. The term typically refers to a product market, but could be more narrowly defined as a regional sub-market or a certain stage in the production or distribution process. Likewise, the term "unreasonable restraint of trade" is subject to interpretation. As a rule of thumb, the JFTC assumes that if the largest three firms in a product market have a combined market share of more than 80%, any agreement between them would restrain competition substantially. If the combined share of the top three companies is around 50%, additional factors in the market situation need to be considered, whereas with a combined share of less than 50% the JFTC rarely finds that competition is being constrained (Iyori/Uesugi 1994: 73). In other words, if small firms without market power collude, the JFTC may not consider them to be in violation of the AML. This is in stark contrast to the U.S., where collusion such as price fixing is considered *per se* illegal, regardless of the degree of market power that results from the cartel.

An "unreasonable restraint of trade" (*futō na torihiki seigen*) is defined in Section 2(6) as, essentially, any cartel agreement of two or more firms (cf. footnote 10 in Chapter 1). Cartel activities include: fixing and maintaining price; limiting production; limiting access to technology; limiting products (e.g., through product market allocation); limiting the scope of a company's facilities (e.g., through investment adjustment); or limiting customers or suppliers (e.g., through regional market allocation or bid-rigging). Of these, price cartels are the most dominant and display the highest variety of schemes, ranging from straightforward agreements, phased-in price-hike formulas, or cost schedules to minimum or maximum retail price caps.

Reflecting the JFTC's difficulties and hesitation in launching formal cases, many cartels eventually emerge only because they are repeat offenses. One example of how some companies have ignored antitrust rules over long periods is the 1994 paint cartel. In January 1994 the JFTC ordered ten large producers of paint and their wholesalers to end price fixing for paint used on ships. The ten companies had arranged regular meetings beginning in August 1990, when oil prices increased with the onset of Operation Desert Shield in the Gulf. In the course of their meetings, the companies agreed on a price increase of 25–40% for the thinner, which is sold with the paint, and of 10–15% for the paint itself. In November 1994, the JFTC imposed a total surcharge of ¥1.85 billion for the ten firms, the third highest on record to that date. The reason for the harsh punishment was not necessarily the impudence of keeping records of all these meetings, but rather that this was a repeat case: the JFTC had issued a recommendation and cease-and-desist order to the ship paint makers in 1974, also on suspicion of price fixing. In spite of some suspicions, no further antitrust warnings occurred in the 20 years in between, but the companies' defense in 1994 that they were unaware of antitrust regulations was not too credible (*Nikkei*, January 21, 1994; *Nikkei*, November 23, 1994).

Volume cartels typically have the same effect as price cartels: by limiting the amount of goods sold, the price is driven up. Such cartels can be arranged through agreed-upon reduction of production and sales (or reduced business hours in the service industries), limits on equipment that firms can install, limits on inventory, access to raw materials, or technology. For instance, in the 1973 case of the Sanitary Ware Manufacturers Association, the association agreed to raise prices by restricting each member's monthly shipment volume. The quota for each member firm was calculated by multiplying the member's previous year's sales volume by a fixed percentage. In a similar scheme, in 1971 the Association of Methanol Formalin Manufacturers had agreed on the total annual supply of methanol in Japan, and determined the share of each member for the year (JFTC 1995).

Some volume cartels can be disguised as technology agreements or claimed to be necessitated by product specifications, and may therefore be more difficult to detect. For example, in 1994 the JFTC issued a warning to the 17 members of the Japan Radish Association (*Nihon kaiware daikon kyōkai*; total market size of about ¥20 billion) that their self-regulation on output might be violating the AML. To stem a continuing price decline of the popular side dish, the association had bought exclusive user rights to a horticulture patent from chemical companies, and had agreed on limited frequency of usage and production restrictions for each member. If a member were to exceed the production limit, it would be expelled from the agreement and thus lose access to the technology. The JFTC found the license agreement to be just a cloak to restrict production to raise prices, but issued only an informal warning (*Nikkei*, February 18, 1994). No formal investigation followed, and it remains uncertain whether the radish producers canceled the output controls or simply changed their system to maintain prices through other means.

Proving a cartel.   While in the U.S. cartels are considered *per se* illegal whatever their structure or impact, substantiating cartel activity in Japan is much more difficult. To launch a formal adjudicative process, the JFTC has to work its way through a three-step sequence. First, there has to be evidence of a joint decision by the cartel participants to do something they would not have done individually. Second, the participants actually have to follow that plan. And third, this conduct has to affect competition demonstrably.

The JFTC's biggest problem in this sequence is Step 1. Without a joint decision among the firms in question, simultaneous price increases could have been triggered by market forces. Yet, joint decisions could have been made in informal meetings, on the telephone, or even implicitly. Usually, courts accept circumstantial evidence if the JFTC can show that (a) there was a meeting, (b) limits on behavior were discussed, and (c) firms behaved uniformly afterwards. However, as discussed in Chapter 2, one part of general business practices in Japan is the large number of meetings, so that proving at which of these gatherings a cartel was discussed is difficult. Further, firms could phase in their cartel moves to make it look more random, thereby undermining the circumstantial evidence of when the initial agreement was reached.

The JFTC also runs into problems at Step 2 of the sequence: proving the actual implementation of a cartel. For the evidence to hold in court, the JFTC needs to show (a) what actions, exactly, were implemented, and (b) that there were mutually binding restrictions on the cartel participants, i.e., some kind of enforcement of the agreement. The easiest cases to uncover are those where the cartel put down penalty rules in writing or established a strict monitoring and penalty system such as excluding cartel breakers from the trade association. For instance, in a 1980 case the Association of Wire Rope Manufacturers agreed on a unified price list for each standard of wire rope. To ensure compliance, the association established a monetary deposit system. Anyone who would sell below the agreed-upon price would be punished either through exclusion from the scheme or a confiscation of the deposit (JFTC 1995). These kinds of agreement form evidence of binding rules by a cartel. However, not all cartels establish enforcement mechanisms in such obvious ways, making it often difficult for the JFTC to find evidence of coercion.

The "three-step" evidence requirement is part of the legal antitrust doctrine that developed in Japan over the postwar period. Because of this doctrine, adjudicating a formal case requires significant evidence. Without such evidence, the JFTC often has no choice but to use the informal means of a warning or caution. Because launching too many unsuccessful cases will only serve to undermine its public reputation, the JFTC prefers to use the informal route of enforcement unless there is sufficient evidence. As a result, many cases that would be brought formally in other countries are settled informally in Japan.

Implicit cartels.   A further difficulty in prosecuting price cartels arises in cases of so-called "conscious parallelism", or implicit collusion through price leadership systems. In these cases, the leading firm raises its prices, and without further discussion the other competing firms in the market follow suit. Conscious parallelism is likely to occur in oligopolistic markets where a few firms dominate the price structure and one firm is the price leader (e.g., flat glass, automobiles). Because implicit collusion undermines Step 1 of the formal case procedure, the JFTC is usually unable to prove the existence of an agreement in these cases. To strengthen oversight over price leadership schemes, with the 1977 revision of the AML a notification system was established by way of a new Section 18(2). In this system, the JFTC can order firms to report the reasons for a price increase in their industry, if (a) the combined market share of the largest three firms exceeds 70%; (b) the annual domestic sales volume in that product is higher than ¥30 billion (lowered from ¥60 billion in 1992); and (c) the base price of the commodity has increased across firms within a period of three months by a similar amount. The JFTC will study the accounts of the companies and report the results to the Diet. However, the law does not stipulate legal consequences. The notification system thus is geared not toward punishing an offender but to allowing companies to repent and change their behavior.

Since 1977, the JFTC has published an annual list of industries that fit the criteria of Section 18(2) and were ordered to explain price increases. In 1996, this list contained 87 product categories. Recent examples of cases include the completely uniform hike in prices of beer on May 1, 1994, by the four Japanese beer companies. Upon being questioned, the brewers claimed that the raise was due to an increase in taxes. Although their price hike exceeded the tax increase, the JFTC was unable to follow up on the case because it lacked evidence of either an agreement or coercion. Similarly, on March 1, 1993, the two leading producers of dry batteries increased their prices by exactly 7.1% each. They claimed that this increase was due to a decline in sales, an increase in costs, and a decrease in profits (JFTC Annual Report 1994: 146–8). Again, without whistle-blowing from within the cartel or other evidence of an agreement, the JFTC could not pursue this case. In other words, a uniform price increase itself is not considered evidence of a cartel. Because Section 18(2) provides for no real enforcement powers, implicit collusion in oligopolistic industries is not typically prosecuted and seems common.

Violations by Trade Associations: Curbing Self-Regulation

The legal situation surrounding trade associations is of particular interest for this study, because restrictions on trade association activities are the most effective means of curbing self-regulation. With the 1953 revision of the AML, rules on antitrust violations by associations were transferred from the previous "Trade Association Law" to Section 8 of the AML (see Chapter 3). Section 8 divides illegal activities by trade associations into eight broadly worded categories, including orchestrating cartels, setting up entry barriers, limiting the business conduct of association members, and engaging in unfair trade practices as a group (Wada 1990: 58).[12] Section 8(2) empowers the JFTC to issue a cease-and-desist order to an association, or if necessary dissolve it.

In 1979, the JFTC issued a first Guideline on trade associations to clarify the law. Realizing that self-regulation was increasing at a fast rate, in 1995 the JFTC further amended this Guideline to specify what kind of association activities are principally or possibly a violation of the AML (JFTC 1995). In fact, although this was not specifically stated, the primary goal of the 1995 Guidelines was to specify where the legal realm of administrative self-regulation ends and illegal activities begin. According to this Guideline, trade associations must not establish restrictions on price, quantity, investments, market access, or access to technology. Neither can they engage in *dangō* (bid-rigging), formulate quality restrictions, set exclusive standards, exchange critical information, formulate binding management guidance for their members, or exclude nonmembers from business. In short, associations must not restrict the functions and business activities of firms in their markets in any way.

Yet, even this seemingly clear-cut rule is difficult to enforce, as one of the associations' primary, and perfectly legal, functions is precisely to establish some

---

[12] In effect, Section 8(1) combines the cartel rules of Section 3 with the unfair trade rules of Section 19 (see below), with the bottom-line that trade associations must not coerce their members to engage in either of these practices. If companies that are members of an association form a cartel, the JFTC can prosecute them under either Section 3 or Section 8. In order to prosecute an association, the JFTC has to show that a binding resolution was reached in an association meeting, or at the association's office. It is usually easier for the JFTC to prove the existence of such a resolution than an agreement outside the association among competing firms, primarily because trade associations have records of meetings as well as lists of the participating members of all committees and discussion groups.

rules and restrictions within their industry. Thus, the JFTC still has to judge on a case-by-case basis whether self-regulation constitutes a "reasonable" restriction or not. For instance, while in principle an association must not limit its membership and also require that firms be members to participate in the market, there may be situations where for practical purposes membership has to be limited to allow for use of joint facilities or provide some benefit for which the association was specifically created.

The Doctors' Association offers an example of unreasonable self-regulation. In general, opening an independent practice without being a member of the local chapter of the association is not feasible for a doctor in Japan, as membership affords access to a set of necessary inroads and benefits such as being tied into hospital services or receiving certain certifications and licenses. In 1980, to restrict new entry the Doctors' Association more than doubled its dues for new members. In addition, the association agreed that applicants for new membership needed a letter of recommendation from a current member with an existing practice in the area. This made it all but impossible to open a practice in an area where the association did not want new entry. The JFTC ruled this restriction to be unreasonable, and published a special guideline to prevent the Doctors' Associations from repeating their AML violation (JFTC 1981b). The associations have reportedly modified their rules since, although there continue to be many JFTC cases involving doctors and medical practice.

The 1995 Kumamoto Taxi Association case gives an example of a joint sales company that was misused to enforce a price cartel. In Kumamoto (Kyūshū) and ten surrounding cities, 60 taxi companies agreed to raise their fares, but four member firms and three individual taxi drivers refused to join the hike. The 60 companies moved to enforce the price-hike through their joint taxi ticket vendor (*Kumamoto-shi takushi shōji*). This vendor company sells taxi vouchers to over 2,000 government and business organizations in the area, which can be used with all cars of the participating members of the local taxi associations (i.e., the organizations buy the vouchers from the joint ticket vendor at a small discount, and give them to their employees for use when working overtime or attending outside meetings). In July 1995, the Kumamoto joint voucher company decided to exclude those companies that resisted the price-hike from the joint voucher system, thus depriving them of most of their business. The JFTC looked into the case and by way of administrative guidance advised strongly that the voucher company reconsider. The company withdrew the decision to exclude the companies in September of 1995 without a formal case being launched (*Nikkei,* October 27, 1995). The case underscores that restricting business opportunities of firms in the industry is a major means of enforcing cartels, and of self-regulation more generally.

Next to setting up rules, exchanging certain kinds of information is typically the *raison d'être* for a trade association. At issue here is what kind of information can be safely exchanged without violating the AML. This uncertainty surrounding information exchange has led U.S. trade associations to include lawyers on their staff to maintain legal compliance. In Japan, lawyers in associations are extremely rare, while meetings—and the accompanying exchange of information—are much more numerous than in the U.S. If association members hold a conference or meet for seemingly idle talk, they could easily discuss forming a cartel without engaging in a formal decision-making process. The JFTC has not interfered with frequent association meetings, signaling that exchange of information is not usually considered a violation of the law. Further, many associations gather and publish data on the industry, including data on prices and possibly costs, sometimes even on behalf of the regulating ministry. If the association discloses aggregate data to its members or to the public, this may not be found in violation of the law. The 1995 Guideline on Trade Associations clearly stated that member firms must not base their own price decisions on company-based data collected by the association. Yet, not one case has yet been prepared to punish the exchange of data in trade associations. Without any precedents, it is even more difficult for the JFTC to distinguish, and thus prosecute, illegal information exchange (JFTC 1995, Kawagoe 1997: 206–8).

By far the most ambiguous area for prosecution of trade associations are activities that cross the borderline between administrative and protective self-regulation. For instance, if associations set standards or minimum quality requirements that restrict the kinds of products offered in the market or translate into restrictions of price or market access, then this is an antitrust violation. However, setting standards has long been a core activity of administrative self-regulation, often delegated by the cognizant ministry. Because it was delegated, the JFTC was unable to press antitrust issues on these practices. A subcategory of self-regulation is an activity sometimes called "self-alignment" (*jishu-chōsei*). This term refers to the association's aligning the divergent interests of members, finding consensus, setting voluntary export quotas, or guiding firms in a certain direction. Industry alignment, too, is sometimes delegated by the regulating ministry to accomplish administrative guidance or arrange voluntary export restraints. Some legal analysts have labeled self-alignment a "collusion between government and business", because the government invites industry to exchange strategic information (e.g., Wada 1990: 60). Considering these complications of official delegation, it is no surprise that the JFTC has been inhibited in looking at the activities in the 1980s and 1990s of purely private self-regulation.

"Unfair Trade Practices": Self-Regulation in the Distribution System

The primary toolkit for implementing purely private self-regulation consists of a set of activities that are legally referred to as "unfair trade practices". Closing up markets, boycotting certain competitors, or pushing price cartels through the distribution system all fall into this category. Given their relevance for accomplishing most administrative and protective self-regulation, it is worthwhile looking at these practices in detail.

Section 19 of the AML defines unfair trade practices (*fukōsei na torihiki*) as trade behavior that inhibits free competition. Specifically, this means resale price restrictions, dealing on exclusive terms, abusing a dominant bargain position, boycotts (refusal to deal or discriminatory treatment), and creating barriers to entry. As applied in the distribution system, this also includes Japan's notorious *shōkankō*, "customary trade habits". Unfair trade practices are widespread because besides the difficulties of proving their existence, the AML treats them very leniently: unfair trade practices cannot be prosecuted as a criminal offense, and neither can fines be levied. The severest possible JFTC action on a Section 19 violation is a cease-and-desist order, with little real consequences for the offender. During the Structural Impediments Initiative (SII) negotiations that began in 1989, the U.S. included "unfair trade practices" in the list of "impediments" to free trade.[13] As one outcome of these negotiations, in 1991 the JFTC announced in its new "Guidelines Concerning Distribution Systems and Business Practices" that it would henceforth consider prosecuting some unfair trade practices under Section 3, which allows for criminal prosecution and fines (JFTC 1991). However, as case analysis in Chapter 5 will show, it is still rare for unfair trade violations to be brought as a Section 3 case, and enforcement continues to be lenient.

An additional problem in prosecuting unfair trade practices is the legal ambiguity of what constitutes a violation. With the 1953 revision, the AML was watered down but provided for so-called "Designations" (*shitei*), which were formulated by the JFTC as the basis of prosecution and contained more explicit definitions of practices considered illegal. Based on the 1953 set of 12 "Old Designations", the JFTC issued a total of only 91 cease-and-desist orders in 30 years. This small number indicates that "unfair trade practices" were hardly prosecuted at all during the rapid growth years. A revision in 1982 led to the adoption of "New General Designations" (*ippan shitei*), as listed in Table 4.2. These Designations outline explicit prohibitions on retail price maintenance, boycotts, and expelling firms from a market. They describe behavior that may be legal, depending on whether firms can show that there is no "competitive damage" due to industry structure or lack of market power (Kawagoe 1997: 235).[14] Yet, the ambiguity in the nature of

---

[13] The "Structural Impediments Initiative" (SII) was launched in 1989 as an alternative to imposing "Super 301" import restrictions on many products from Japan. The premise of the SII was that Japan's system was structurally different from the U.S. system, and instead of protectionism these differences required convergence on some basic issues such as trade habits in the distribution system or antitrust enforcement. The effects of this *gaiatsu* (foreign pressure) on actual Japanese antitrust enforcement are analyzed in Chapter 5.

[14] In addition to the "General Designations", there are also six "Special Designations" (*tokushu shitei*) which separately cover six industries: canned and bottled food, department stores, newspapers, school textbooks, marine transportation, and open lottery. These six industries have been deemed special in terms of industrial structure, supplier and buyer configurations, industry concentration, and degree of collusion, and are therefore covered separately (Iyori/Uesugi 1994: 144). While these Special Designations are very important, in the aggregate picture of AML enforcement they are of secondary interest because they cover only a handful of industries. In contrast to the General Designations, the JFTC cannot change the Special Designations unilaterally; if the JFTC wants to revise the contents, it has to hold a public hearing with the industry concerned.

Table 4.2. General Designations for "Unfair Trade Practices"

Designation	Content/prohibition
1	Refusal to deal: group boycotts
2	Other refusal to deal (restrictions of trading partners, etc.)
3	Discriminatory pricing
4	Discriminatory treatment in transaction terms
5	Discriminatory treatment by a trade association
6	Sales below cost
7	Unreasonable high pricing
8	Deceptive customer inducement
9	Undue customer inducement by unjust benefits (excessive premia)
10	Unreasonable coercion (tie-in sales and reciprocal dealings)
11	Dealing on exclusive terms
12	Resale price maintenance
13	Dealing on restrictive terms
14	Abuse of dominant bargaining position or buying power
15	Interference with a competitor's transaction

Note: General Designations #8 and #9 are subject to the "Law Prohibiting Unreasonable Premiums and Representation and Other Matters" ("Premium Law").

"unfair trade practices" themselves has frustrated efforts to formulate more detailed rules, and many loopholes remain.

Shōkankō: distribution practices and retail price maintenance. The Japanese distribution system has four outstanding characteristics that combine to create a multilayered, closed system: the "standard price system" (*tatene*), rebates (*ribeeto*), return of unsold goods (*henpin*), and vertical affiliations (*keiretsu-ka*). In combination, these are called *shōkankō*—the general distribution practices. These often effectively exclude domestic and foreign competitors from markets, which is why they are widespread and form the core of self-regulation in the distribution system. While typically ineffective (and thus considered legal) if practiced unilaterally by one firm, when orchestrated through a trade association and applied with coercion, these arrangements result in "unfair trade practices". To understand the combined logic of these practices for an industry's self-regulation, it is helpful to first consider each practice separately.

The "standard price system" is commonly used in Japan, and comes in three variations, of which two are in legally "gray" areas, and one is illegal. First, the dominant practice in intermediate products and materials, such as steel, non-ferrous metals, lumber or glass, is the "after-sales price adjustment" system (*atogime seido*). The producer indicates a standard price (*tatene*) to a general wholesaler, who then indicates a standard price to a regional wholesaler, etc., but the final transaction price is determined only after the product has been sold to the end user and the actual market price been established. Based on this market price, the producer determines the margin of its wholesalers that are often specialized and exclusive (*tokuyakuten*; lit.: "special function stores"). Combined with rebates, as described next, this creates a system under which the profit structure within the entire chain of wholesalers and retailers becomes dependent on the producer. Yet, the producer's powers to squeeze the distributors' profits are counterbalanced by the producers' dependency on the specialized wholesalers: if all producers have specialized wholesalers, switching costs are very high. Through this system, most intermediate product prices are negotiated *post hoc*. The system is extremely opaque, and it is unclear to what extent intermediate product prices are fixed among producers, since actual prices are unknown. Yet, no antitrust case has been brought for after-sales price adjustment, mostly because establishing evidence of coercion is impossible. While some industries moved away from *atogime* in the 1990s, it remains the predominant pricing mechanism in many intermediate product markets.

The second type of standard price system is the "suggested retail price" (*kibō kakaku*) in end products, especially for those sold through specialized retail outlets (such as cars, electric appliances, or cosmetics). In principle, the manufacturer indicates a retail price to its wholesalers and retailers, but the retailers are free to determine the eventual price. While widely practiced in the U.S. and Europe, suggesting a retail price is even more common in Japan. According to a JFTC survey in the early 1990s, 85.5% of all manufacturers indicated a resale price for their products, and 79% set a suggested retail price (Kawagoe 1997: 345). A legal problem occurs when the producer entices or coerces the retailer to stick to the suggested price. Yet, similar to the situation with price fixing, the JFTC has to prove the existence of coercion if it wants to prepare a case, and the JFTC has had problems with this. For instance, pens and pencils cost the same across most stores and brands. In fact, pens typically have a price printed on them, such as "100" or "300" next to the producer's name. Since most stores charge the imprinted price, this is a *de facto* established price. However, the JFTC has allowed this practice for many years, because it is unaware of coercion on the retailers to charge the suggested price.[15]

The third type of standard price system is "retail price maintenance" (*saihanbai kakaku iji kōi*), and this practice is in violation of the AML except for a few specified industries. Under this system, the producer determines the final retail price (and sometimes prints it on the container) and enforces this price by monitoring the retail system and punishing violators through measures such as penalty payments or interruption of shipments. Multiple objectives are tied into maintaining prices, such as ensuring after-service or regional product availability (Telser 1960, Flath 1989). However, the practice can also be used to prevent

---

[15] Interview, JFTC, Tokyo, 1997. The uniform price structure suggests the existence of price agreements among the pen producers which are implemented through the suggested retail price. Note that the Japanese per capita use of pens is six times as high as in the U.S., so that this is a sizable industry (Mishina 1993). The JFTC has never investigated the pen industry.

discounts and to arrange price agreements.[16] In the U.S., retail price maintenance is considered *per se* illegal (meaning that no proof of negative effects on price or competition is needed to launch a case). Likewise, in Japan, it is in principle illegal for a manufacturer to restrict the sales price (JFTC 1991).

Yet, retail price maintenance continues to be widespread, because it is a most convenient tool to carry price agreements at the producers' level through the entire retail system. Because retail price maintenance reduces the noise in retailing (i.e., variations in profit margins across retail outlets), it simplifies effective monitoring of a cartel and thus reduces cheating on price-fixing agreements. Therefore, retail price maintenance in combination with producers' price cartels is quite common. For instance, the Japanese home electronics industry was largely built on this practice. Matsushita Electric Industries, the world's largest electronics manufacturer, sells brand names such as National, Panasonic, and JVC through its own vertical distribution system with roughly 25,000 exclusive retail outlets. These outlets are often forced to follow reference prices through a threat of discontinuation of shipments (Fukunaga/Chikone 1994). Sony, Toshiba and others likewise sell through exclusive retail outlets, and a reference price for the product is typically printed on the cardboard boxes in which the products are shipped. The retailers sometimes offer a discount from this reference price, creating the impression of price competition. While the JFTC has repeatedly looked at these mechanisms in the past, the courts have refused to intervene (Ramseyer 1985). One exception was a case in 1992, when the JFTC investigated the four biggest electronic firms (Matsushita, Sony, Toshiba and Hitachi) for suspicion of having agreed on a specific percentage discount off their reference prices and requiring their retailers to use this discount for the product price tags. The companies accepted the formal recommendation in 1993 and agreed to stop the practice.

There are two primary reasons why the JFTC cannot contain retail price maintenance more forcefully. First, it is rarely used in easily detectible, straightforward ways. Because suggesting a retail price is permitted, even if a producer prints a price on the product, the JFTC has to detect coercion to establish a violation of Section 19.[17] Even if the JFTC can prove coercion, it can do no more than issue a cease-and-desist order, because Section 19 violations do not carry

---

[16] For a theory of retail price maintenance, see Telser (1960). See Tirole (1988) for a discussion of economic efficiency consequences of retail price maintenance. Regardless of the economics, the practice is considered an illegal form of price fixing in the U.S. and Germany, where it is strictly prosecuted as a cartel violation.

[17] The JFTC "Distribution Guideline" (JFTC 1991) contains a long list of examples of coercion to adhere to reference prices that are theoretically illegal, including: a written or oral agreement that distributors will follow the price suggestion; initiating a new trade relationship on condition that the distributor follow the reference price; an agreement in addition to the price pledge that unsold goods must not be sold at discount prices but returned to the manufacturer; threat of retaliation should goods be sold below the reference price (stopping shipments, increasing the shipment price, or reducing rebates); and monitoring distributors through patrolling retail establishments or printing secret codes or production numbers on the end products to detect cartel breakers. All these are common practice.

more severe measures. As long as it is considered an "unfair trade practice", there are thus no true legal deterrents to retail price maintenance. Second, in the past the law has allowed for exemptions from the general rule of (a) daily use consumer products, allegedly so that the price would indicate quality (until the 1970s); (b) pharmaceuticals and cosmetics; and (c) copyrighted materials such as books and records. In the 1950s, the first of these three categories was used not only for toothpaste, soap, men's white shirts, or caramel candy, but also to allow "price alignment" in MITI-designated strategic export products such as cameras. In several subsequent reviews of the system, the list of products exempted from the maintenance prohibition was progressively shortened: by the 1970s, only consumer products under ¥1,000 could be exempted, and by the 1990s, only pharmaceuticals and copyrighted works were legally subject to retail price maintenance. However, while the exemptions were cut, the actual practice was hardly curtailed.

The second *shōkankō*, the rebate system, is often used to reinforce retail price maintenance. The original practice was simply a fixed rebate or a refund, i.e., a discount on the wholesale price, given by the producer to the retailer as an incentive to increase sales volume. Among the many varieties of rebates, two stand out as highly anti-competitive. The first are the so-called "progressive rebates" (*ruishin ribeeto*). Tied to shipments, these increase exponentially with higher volume. This creates incentives for the retailer to carry only one brand at high volume rather than several competing brands, and thus limits competition and increases the dependency of the retailer on the wholesaler or producer. This dependency in turn increases the producer's power to enforce retail price maintenance. A second type, "coverage rebates" (*kōkendo ribeeto*), are tied to the percentage of sales of the manufacturer's product in the total business of the distributor, or to the percentage of the product in total displays in the store. Again, the incentive for the distributor is to focus on one product and restrict competition for the rebate-sponsoring producer (JFTC 1991).[18] Typically, a variety of complicated schemes are used in combination. In a questionnaire conducted in the 1990s, the JFTC found that about 50% of all producers used fixed sales volume rebates for their wholesalers and retailers, while 49% used a combination of fixed and progressive rebates (Kawagoe 1997: 348).

While rebates are strictly regulated in Germany (through the "Rebate Law", *Rabattgesetz*), they are legal in both the U.S. and Japan as long as they are not tied with other mechanisms that pressure a retailer to carry only one brand. The JFTC announced in its "Distribution Guidelines" (JFTC 1991) that it is likely to

---

[18] In most cases, the producer dominates the retail system and determines the rebates. However, if the retail outlet is very large, such as a department store or convenience store chain, and the producer is tiny, the power structure is reversed and the retailer can demand a rebate from the producer. This is euphemistically called "support money" (*sanjokin*). Inappropriate "support" requests by department stores can be a violation of Section 19 and are specified in the Special Designation for the Large-Scale Retail Industries.

find these schemes in violation of the AML if they are connected to price maintenance, if the rebates are extremely high or progressive, or if the basis for calculation is unclear and used in discriminatory ways. However, rebates remain a central part of the *shōkankō*, and evidence is scarce that the JFTC is prosecuting this practice as an antitrust violation.

The third practice that supports price maintenance and may create barriers to entry is the "return of unsold goods" system, in which the retailer is allowed to return goods to the producer at no cost and thus can minimize inventory cost. About 50% of all goods sold in department stores are offered on a "return" basis, while the number is 75% for grocery stores. The actual return rate in the 1990s was more than 15% for groceries, and more than 30% for department stores (Kawagoe 1997: 352–3). While this system is not necessarily illegal, it is problematic on two counts. First, it sets incentives for the retailer to shelve only products they can return, and thus creates barriers to entry for new domestic producers and imported products. Second, the producer can use the return practice to enforce retail price maintenance, because it grants the producer leverage over the retailer.

Finally, the price setting, rebate, and goods return policies can all be part of an established system of a vertical distribution *keiretsu*—an organization of multiple layers of wholesalers and retailers that each hold one specific function in the distribution chain. This system became prevalent with the evolution and specialization of *tonya* (wholesalers) in the Tokugawa period (see Chapter 7), and even today wholesalers are called *tonya*. If they are part of a vertical *keiretsu*, these *tonya* are often exclusive dealers in one brand, similar to a franchise system. The most prominent examples are the above-mentioned exclusive retail chains for home electronics, but vertical *keiretsu* are also prevalent in the automobile, cosmetics, detergent, sports goods, pharmaceutical, photo-film, newspaper, and milk industries. It is not against the law to construct a franchise-type, exclusive distribution system, but the practices typically associated with this system, such as price maintenance, exclusive dealings, or division of sales territories, can lead to restraints of competition. Still, vertical *keiretsu* are one of Japan's traditional trade practices, and the logic of many pricing mechanisms and mutual support systems within Japan's distribution system build on these trade groups. Honoring its integral part in the distribution system, the JFTC has not launched any cases against vertical *keiretsu*.

Taken together, the *shōkankō* provide groups of producers, i.e., trade associations, with a powerful set of tools to agree on prices, allocate retail outlets and restrict entry by new competitors. *Shōkankō* form one pillar of self-regulation in that the "trade habits" help control the distribution system and thus ease the enforcement of joint rules in a product market. Because the practices have grown over the years, there is little understanding why they might be considered AML violations. Further, Section 19 of the AML does not provide for deterrents even in cases where the JFTC disallows a practice. The *shōkankō* remain widespread.

Discriminatory practices. Next to the *shōkankō*, the second large category of "unfair trade practices" contains so-called "discriminatory trade behavior". This includes boycotts (a term often used generically to describe all these practices), customer or market segment allocation, exclusive trades, dealing on restrictive terms, and abusing a dominant market position. The common purpose is to create barriers to entry. While a company can apply these techniques unilaterally, they are much more effective when implemented industrywide through the association. More than the government's trade barriers or protectionism, self-regulation is the most effective means to carry out discriminatory objectives.

Boycotts—refusing or asking others to refuse to trade with a party—can take a variety of forms. For instance, a wholesaler might place certain discounters on a blacklist if they undermine the products' price structure, or the producer may ask the wholesaler to create such a list. In a 1989 example, the Federation of Agricultural Cooperatives (*Zenkoku Nōgyō Rengōkai*, or short: *Zennō*) was found to have violated the law when it forced members to deal only with designated (i.e., *Zennō* affiliated) makers of cardboard sheets, but to refuse to buy cheaper cardboard boxes from non-affiliated makers, although they offered identical boxes (Tamura 1995: 275, JFTC 1995). In the 1991 case of the Port of Sendai Association of Lumber Importers, the association members exerted pressure on harbor companies not to handle lumber imported by nonmembers, in an attempt to prevent outsiders from importing lumber at cheaper prices. The JFTC issued a recommendation which the association accepted (JFTC 1995).

The anti-competitive effects of boycotts depend on market structure and concentration. If a market consists of many competitors, and the affected firm can find other suppliers or buyers, there is no problem.[19] However, if a concerted refusal to deal (a group boycott) results in excluding a firm from a market altogether, then this behavior can lead to substantial restraints of competition. If a group boycott is organized through the trade association, it may be a violation of either Section 19 (unfair trade practices), of Section 8 (trade associations), or of Section 3 (cartel). Before the revision of the "Distribution Guideline" (JFTC 1991), boycotts were treated only under Section 19, meaning that there was no effective deterrent and the practice was rampant. Following the SII talks with the U.S., the JFTC announced that boycotts could be considered as cartels under Section 3. However, as will be documented in Chapter 5, most boycotts continue to be prosecuted, if at all, under the lax Section 19.

Besides boycotts, companies or associations can engage in "vertical non-price constraints" in the distribution system to limit competition (General

---

[19] Because the AML grants freedom of choice among trading partners, a unilateral boycott would be a violation only if illegal means were employed to effect the boycott (Iyori/Uesugi 1994: 111). "Restraint of competition" in connection with refusal to deal is defined as one of the following situations: (1) it is difficult for a firm to enter the market even though its product is superior in price and quality; (2) it is difficult for a firm to adopt innovative selling methods to enter the market; and (3) it is difficult for a superior firm to enter a market where no active competition is taking place. The exact interpretation of "difficult" is left vague; cf. JFTC (1991).

Designation #13). Such constraints include: customer restrictions (e.g., not sell-ing to discounters); territorial restrictions (allowing wholesalers to deal in only one market); advertising restrictions (e.g., disallowing a retailer to display dis-count prices); or customer and market allocation (e.g., agreeing not to deal with the customers of another firm or to infringe on each other's sales territory). For instance, in a 1969 case of "restricting customers" involving the Tokorozawa Association of Milk Distributors, the association formed a binding agreement that no member would steal customers from other members by offering lower prices. If a switch occurred, the offending firm would return the customer to the original milk distributor. The association also extended its reach and forced non-members who had lured customers away to return them to their original distributors (JFTC Annual Report 1969).

Other types of restriction of competition are the so-called "tie-in sales" and reciprocal dealings (General Designation #10). In a tie-in sale, the seller requires buying an additional item with the purchase of one product. For instance, it is illegal for a newspaper to force its dealers to deliver the morning issue only if the customer also subscribes to the evening issue.[20] In a reciprocal deal, the purchase or sale of a product from company A to company B is combined with a reverse sale or purchase from B to A, thus restricting business opportunities of third parties in the market.

Tie-in and reciprocal sales are also often coerced by one party that is in a dominant bargaining position (General Designation #14). For instance, a large-scale retailer, such as a large convenience store chain, must not pressure its suppliers to accept the return of unsold goods, to dispatch sale personnel to the store, or to make contributions to ad campaigns.[21] Yet, while the practice is widespread, not one case involving dominant bargaining has ever been launched.

A further form of non-price vertical restraint are so-called "exclusive dealings", whereby a firm deals with a customer or supplier on condition that this customer/supplier does not deal with the firm's competitors. This is a dis-criminatory practice if it obstructs access to the product market or blocks imports of competing products. For instance, studies of the automobile industry

---

[20] This example is based on the 1955 Chūbu Nihon Newspaper case, in which the newspaper forced its dealers to tie the purchase of the morning issue into the purchase of the evening issue. The case was dropped because the JFTC could find no evidence of coercion. In a 1990 video game case, the JFTC ordered one wholesaler of video games and five secondary wholesalers not to enforce retailers in tie-in sales of a popular software: the "Dragon Quest IV" was so popular that it was often in short supply, and the wholesalers forced retailers to buy other, unpopular video games on stock together with the popular game.

[21] In August 1996, the Foods Industry Center (*Shokuhin sangyō sentaa zaidan hōjin*) published a "distribution manual" for food suppliers outlining their rights vis-a-vis large retailers such as convenience stores. According to a survey of 1,500 food producers, 90.6% had been pressured to lower their prices, 64% were demanded to pay a "distribution fee", 56% were asked to pay "sales promotion fees", 54% were forced to pay "promotion money", 50% were pushed for rebate increases, and 47% were requested to make multiple small quantity deliveries. These practices combine to squeeze the profit margins of the producers who have no leverage against the convenience store chains.

have shown that exclusive, long-term supplier relations are easier to maintain and may be beneficial to both parties (McMillan 1990). However, for antitrust purposes this exclusivity has to be completely voluntary, for two reasons. First, exclusive arrangements may restrict entry of other suppliers, including foreign firms (auto parts are a prominent example here). Second, arrangements must not be coerced by an influential supplier or manufacturer. "Influential" here means a firm that holds more than 10% of market share or is one of the largest three companies in the market segment. Whether exclusivity does indeed lead to a restraint of competition is decided by the JFTC on a case-by-case basis. The JFTC has been unsuccessful in enforcing the rules against exclusive dealing, because there are no clear legal definitions of what, exactly, constitutes coercion in an exclusive dealership. Proof of such coercion is also difficult to collect, especially if the supplier is exploited and dependent (JFTC 1991: 18–20, Kawagoe 1997: 360–6).

The final category of "unfair trade practices" closely related with self-regulation is interference by either a powerful trading partner or the trade association in the management of a firm. For instance, a manufacturer must not design a contract with a distributor that contains the right to interference in management, influence the distributor's sales prices, or restrict business activities (JFTC 1991). Trade associations may provide management guidance to their members only if it is offered individually and aimed solely to improve business operations of the member. The legal problem with management guidance is that it lends a convenient cloak for supporting price cartels or launching boycotts. Sometimes management guidance is given without the intent to form a cartel but *de facto* helps structure cooperation. For instance, in 1965 the Tokyo Association of Propane Gas Wholesalers realized that its members were charging prices that did not fully incorporate the wholesalers' costs in terms of security measures and depreciation. To help its members, the association formulated a standard cost-accounting table, which effectively suggested that all members charge the same fixed percentage over the purchase price. The association's guidance therefore amounted to price collusion on the standard wholesale price, and the JFTC found this management guidance to be a violation of the AML (JFTC 1995). Just how innocent and naive Japan's Propane Gas Wholesalers were in designing their schemes remains doubtful, however, for in the period between 1963 and 1995 they received a total of 34 informal and formal warnings and recommendations; of these, 29 cases involved local propane gas wholesaler associations.

In sum, discriminatory practices may or may not be illegal, depending on the degree of product market competition and coercion applied to them. If small firms create exclusive dealing arrangements, they are unlikely to be investigated. If two companies agree to maintain an exclusive trade relationship without designing a system of penalties, they are also unlikely to be caught, even if their actions constrain competition. Yet, if a trade association stages a group boycott, this is likely to result in effective self-regulation which may be found in violation of Section 19.

The Premium Law and self-regulation.　Besides the AML, the JFTC enforces one other law that restricts unfair trade practices. This is the "Premium Law", or the "Law Against Unjustifiable Premiums and Misleading Representations" (*Futō-keihinrui oyobi futō hyōshi bōshihō*) of 1962. This law serves three separate purposes. First, it prohibits deceptive labeling and other misguiding of consumers. This prohibition came in reaction to consumer outrage after the 1960 "fake canned beef" incident, where cans of beef were found to consist primarily of fish. Yet, rarely is the law used for serious punishment in this category (Misonō 1987: 118). The second purpose is to outlaw excessive premia or prize offerings, similar to the German "Law Against Unlawful Competition" (*Gesetz gegen den unlauteren Wettbewerb*) and the German "Rebate Law" (*Rabattgesetz*). Driven by an attempt to protect consumers from fake discount schemes and intrusive advertisements, both the Japanese and German laws prohibit or restrict the offering of discount coupons, rebates, premia and other gifts to consumers. Because U.S. companies consider such items as normal marketing practices, these restrictions have led to a discussion of what is an "excessive" premium in the bilateral trade negotiations between the U.S. and Japan, without success so far.

The third, practical, purpose of the Premium Law is to serve as a "catchall" for cases that cannot be caught through the AML, or even as a safety valve against foreign competition, as a curious example involving Pepsi-Cola Japan highlights. In this case, which underscores serious weaknesses in antitrust enforcement, Pepsi-Cola tried to undercut an ongoing price cartel in the soft drink industry to promote its product against the well-established Coca-Cola Japan. Pepsi-Cola asked its distributors to undercut the price agreement by the Soft Drink Wholesalers' Association, of which Pepsi was not a member. The association promptly complained to the JFTC that the foreign firm was undermining the industry's self-regulation. The JFTC found that Pepsi-Cola was bound by industry self-regulation, although it was not a member of the association, and threatened to employ the Premium Law to prosecute Pepsi-Cola for "unlawful competition" if it did not go along with the industry's efforts at "price maintenance". Thus, not only did the JFTC side with the soft drink cartel; it also forced nonmembers to abide with purely private and restrictive self-regulation.[22] Rather than curbing self-regulation and prosecuting cartels, the JFTC used the law to protect the soft drink industry from outside competition.

Dangō: Bid-Rigging and Contract Allocation

While the JFTC's power to curtail cartels and unfair trade behavior is limited by the AML itself, its strength is further diminished in cases where other ministries are involved. One practice where this is often the case is the so-called *dangō*. *Dangō* refers to the allocation of orders among a set of competitors combined

---

[22] Interview with industry official, 1999. The incident occurred in the early 1990s.

with price fixing to restrict competition. The word *dangō* literally means "to get together and talk"—referring particularly to trade associations or groups of firms in one industry. Because it is one form of a price cartel administered through self-regulation by trade associations, a discussion is warranted here.

Specifically, the term *dangō* has adopted the special meaning of "bid-rigging" in the construction industry. Roughly, bid-rigging *dangō* means that a group of companies prepares the bids for a public works project in a meeting prior to the auction. A price is agreed upon and the bid-winner is determined; the other bidders then propose higher prices to obscure the agreement. In industries such as public works construction, where orders recur regularly, the winner changes with each bid and every firm profits in turn. In these cases, typically all large firms in the industry are involved, and the *dangō* is organized through the trade association. In industries where future bids are uncertain, the winner may pay off the other parties to the agreement or subcontract a pre-allocated part of the job to them. In either case, the effect is that the price is higher than it would have been with truly competitive bids. *Dangō* comes in many varieties and occurs in all industries where there is procurement, public or private (Hironaka 1994).[23] What has led to the construction industries being singled out in *dangō* is that the government, as the procuring agent, is immediately involved in the process. In fact, Japan's procurement system itself may be rigged and thus invite *dangō* in the first place. This suspicion was confounded when in the early 1990s multiple cases of corruption surfaced that involved local politicians and construction companies (McMillan 1991, Woodall 1996, Krauss/Coles 1990, Yamakawa 1994).

The legal context of *dangō* unravels as follows. While the processes of the auction involving public procurement are subject to Civil Code rules, bid-rigging can also be considered an antitrust violation. *Dangō* can be violating either Section 3 (cartel, if the price is determined together with the designated winner) or Section 19 (customer allocation). If prosecuted as the latter, no punishment will be levied. Even if *dangō* is prosecuted as a cartel, the surcharge is usually lower than the profits made through bid-rigging. Following trade negotiations

---

[23] Examples abound for *dangō* outside the construction industry. In February 1995, the JFTC launched an investigation into the Medical Gas Association (*Nihon iryō gasu kyōkai*), which was suspected of forming a cartel on anesthetics and other gases used for medical purposes with the goal of raising prices through bid-rigging on hospital orders (*Nikkei*, November 28, 1995). The hospital bed leasing case involved local bed leasing associations in three areas. In 1992, the JFTC issued a cease-and-desist order to the Kinki (Osaka area) branch of the Japan Hospital Bed Association (*Nihon byōin shingu kyōkai*), and in 1993 it issued the same warning to 15 companies operating in the Okayama and Kyūshū branches of the Bed Leasing Association (*Shingu riisu kyōkai*). Both groups had met and agreed to split the lease contracts offered by newly built hospitals in the area. While there is no evidence that they actually stopped the practice, the associations accepted the inconsequential warning and apologized to the public (*Nikkei*, May 14, 1994). Bid-rigging is also common in the retail market. In early 1997, the JFTC levied a punitive surcharge from 12 department stores in Tokyo for bid-rigging in procurement of seasonal special gifts (such as graduation albums) and earthquake survival goods between 1992 and 1993. The stores agreed that one of them would win the bid for a very large order from the producers of these items, thus earning a volume discount on the purchase price. The bid-winner then sold part of the products to the other stores, thereby lowering the purchase price for all department stores involved (*Nikkei*, February 4, 1997).

with the U.S. in the early 1990s, the JFTC published a special "Guideline on Public Project Bidding" (JFTC 1994), in which it announced an increase in *dangō* prosecution. But while the JFTC has prosecuted more *dangō* cases formally in the 1990s than ever before (cf. Chapter 5), *dangō* continues unabated. The JFTC is largely unable to create effective deterrents against the practice, because the amounts of money involved are huge and fines are tiny. McMillan (1991) estimates that *dangō* may increase profits associated with public works by up to 30%, whereas the maximum surcharge for non-criminal cases is 6%, limited to three years.

To take but one example, in 1994 the JFTC found that 90% of recent public construction projects in the city of Utsunomiya (Honshū) had been contracted by *dangō*. Total projects in Utsunomiya in 1992 alone amounted to ¥28 billion, resulting in an abnormal *dangō* profit of possibly up to ¥7 billion for that one year. The Utsunomiya Construction Association (*Utsunomiya kensetsugyō kyō-kai*) had arranged for regular meetings between April 1992 and December 1993 in its offices to stop a price decline in the public construction orders of the City of Utsunomiya. The association's methods were quite standard: on the day prior to an auction, member firms determined the bid winner and bidding price. The JFTC issued a formal warning, which the association accepted, and fined 106 member firms of the association a total of only ¥1.49 billion. No criminal charges were brought (*Nikkei*, November 11, 1994, JFTC Annual Report 1995).[24]

When prosecuting construction *dangō*, the JFTC encounters two major problems. The first is that the auction system for public procurement is specifically designed to favor small- and medium-sized construction firms as part of the government support policies for such firms, so that the public procurement system itself is rigged. For instance, some auctions are open to a specific group of companies only (Kawagoe 1997: 168–70). The second problem lies with the procuring agencies, such as the Ministry of Construction for national projects, the local governments, and so-called public corporations (*tokushu hōjin*). Over time, these agencies get closely involved with the bidders, and there is evidence both of corruption and of *dangō* being initiated by the procuring agencies themselves, especially by public corporations. These are corporations primarily

---

[24] The Utsunomiya case is remarkable because it followed on the heels of promises by industry to change their behavior. Local construction *dangō* cases typically involve local chapters of the "Federation of Construction Associations" (*Nihon kensetsu gyōkai dantai rengōkai*). To protect the Federation from prosecution, *dangō* at the national level occurs in informal setups. Until 1990, the predominant shadow groups were the "*Keiei iinkai*" ("Managers' Council"), consisting of 99 firms, and its subcommittee, the "*Keiei konwakai*" ("Managers' Discussion Group"). The managers met to allocate bids in upcoming auctions every third Monday of the month at the "*Asameshikai*" (Breakfast Club). More intimate discussions were left for the "*Midori kai*" (Green Club) which met once a month for a golf outing. So well-known was the system that the U.S. finally exerted political pressure on Japan to terminate these groupings in 1990. While both groups were dissolved, this was widely considered to be just a temporary move to assuage the U.S. trade negotiators. New *dangō* cases surfaced immediately after the groups had supposedly parted. The JFTC argued that because these groups were not official trade associations and there was no evidence of coerced price fixing, the only possible AML violation they had engaged in was an "unfair trade practice" for which there was insufficient evidence (*Nikkei*, July 12, 1990).

funded with government loans to fulfil public works or national functions, such as maintaining national forests, conducting basic research, administering school lunches, or building railways, highways, and airports. A 1994 case involved the three largest manufacturers of driftwood nets for dams (synthetic fiber nets that keep driftwood and trash from entering the dam). The Water Resources Development Public Corporation (*Suishigen kaihatsu kōdan*), in charge of 25 dams, had received rigged bids from the same companies over many years. In 1994, the JFTC found that this traditional way of doing business constituted illegal *dangō*. However, the JFTC did not take any action, although it was widely suspected that the corporation had ordered the *dangō* bids (*Nikkei*, December 16, 1994).

The 1995 "sewage incident" is a similar case, but more scandalous. In March of 1995, the JFTC issued a warning to the nine largest heavy electric machinery manufacturers and 18 medium-sized subcontractors for their *dangō* activities in the bidding for electric facilities ordered by the Japan Sewage Public Corporation (*Nihon gesuidō jigyōdan*). This case raised eyebrows not only because it involved some of Japan's flagship electric companies, but also because it became clear that the public corporation had asked the firms to submit a *dangō* price *before* the auction so that it would know what kind of price levels and expenses to expect. Worse still, some defendants claimed that the public corporation requested the submission of *dangō* bids even after the JFTC had begun looking into the case in March 1994 (*Nikkei*, March 7, 1995). This impudence outraged the JFTC sufficiently to bring a criminal case in 1995. In addition to the JFTC's administrative surcharge of a total of ¥1 billion, the Tokyo High Court found the defendants guilty in 1996, and ordered fines ranging from ¥40–60 million each (roughly $500,000 at the time) as well as short prison terms for employees of the large firms and the public corporation.

These cases suggest that one primary reason *dangō* is so persistent in Japan is that *dangō* practices are invited both by the auction design itself (in skewing projects toward certain companies), and the government offices in charge of running the auctions.[25] The second major reason why *dangō* practices remain ubiquitous is the close connection between construction bid-rigging and contributions to politicians. By channeling public work projects to the large construction companies in their electoral districts, politicians cultivate ample campaign financing from the beneficiaries.[26] It is no surprise, then, that the JFTC has been unable to abolish the *dangō* system. For trade associations, this means that it is safe to *dangō* with the government. While it is too soon to tell whether the sewage case indicates a new era, the JFTC began to prosecute *dangō* violations

[25] There also may be kickbacks from the designated winner not only to the other auction participants but to the auctioneer. Several criminal cases pursued in the construction industries and local governments in Northern Japan have provided evidence for this scenario. However, these are criminal violations outside the sphere of antitrust law.

[26] See, for instance, Yamakawa (1994). During the severe recession and bad bank loan crisis of the 1990s, it became obvious that many LDP politicians were trying to preserve this vehicle for political financing through protecting large construction companies that were virtually insolvent.

much more strictly in the 1990s. As we will see in Chapter 5, however, this increased activity in *dangō* cases might imply less prosecution of self-regulation by way of unfair trade practices. As the JFTC is preoccupied with bid-rigging, boycotts are blooming.

Administrative Guidance and Antitrust Enforcement

Public procurement *dangō* is not the only area where ministries have interfered directly in antitrust enforcement; administrative guidance and officially acknowledged self-regulation are equally problematic. What can the JFTC do if a regulating ministry allows its industry to violate the AML? Especially in domestic, maturing industries, associations often have ministerial approval to restrain competition and cooperate to carry out administrative guidance. While autonomous self-regulation is difficult enough to contain, the JFTC is virtually powerless in cases of delegated self-regulation.

Invigorated by the oil cartel case of 1980, the JFTC flexed its muscles and issued its first "Guideline on Administrative Guidance and the AML" in 1981 (JFTC 1981a), complemented in 1992 by a study on "Trade Associations and Public Administration" (JFTC 1993a). The Guideline clarifies that any administrative guidance to cooperate that is not based directly on a legal provision is likely to lead to cartels, especially if directed at a trade association. Administrative guidance to collude on price or to restrict facilities, equipment, or distribution channels is even more likely to have a negative impact on competition and, therefore, to be illegal. The JFTC states very clearly that ministries must not require associations in rate-regulated industries, such as trucking, to prepare a joint proposal for price hikes, and neither should ministries ask associations to prepare statistical data on the industry that might invite anti-competitive behavior (by, e.g., asking for data on costs and thereby facilitating price collusion in that industry).

The Guideline's effectiveness, however, remains questionable, since all these activities are common practice. Industries that remain subject to special industry laws, such as those prescribing fee or rate regulation, can convincingly argue that they acted upon government order when setting up self-regulation. The situation is even more complicated when industries self-regulate illegally, but then cry for help from their cognizant ministry—often also referred to as "*kyōiku mama* ministries", alluding to the excessively devoted Japanese mother who does everything for the proper growth (education) of her child. Eager to earn a carrot from industry for future use with administrative guidance, the ministries are often willing to provide a regulatory alibi. The JFTC can cause trouble for the industries, but it cannot easily challenge the ministries.

A representative example is the cold storage cartel of 1992. This industry is subject to the Storage Industry Law (*Sōkogyō-hō*) under regulation by the Ministry of Transportation. When the use of cold storage rooms declined with the collapse of the bubble economy in the early 1990s, the members of the Japan

Cold Storage Association (*Nihon reizō sōko kyōkai*) decided to raise prices by 8.8% in April 1992. The JFTC launched an investigation in 1994, and in November 1995 issued a cease-and-desist order. The association rejected the order, arguing initially that the increase was based on individual decisions by its member firms. When confronted with further evidence, the association changed its stance and claimed that the Ministry of Transportation had agreed to the intricate mechanism for the price increase. In a rare show of strength, the JFTC remained unimpressed and filed for criminal proceedings, on the grounds that collusion is still a violation of the AML even if administered by a ministry.[27]

In the 1996 Kyūshū taxi case, the JFTC warned the local taxi associations in Kita-Kyūshū, Nagasaki and other cities on the Southern island that the joint decision by the associations to limit the number of drivers on Sundays to "increase efficiency" conflicted with the rule that associations must not interfere with their members' management decisions. The taxi industry is highly regulated and needs to file a notification for any change in prices or quantity of cars with the local bureau of the Ministry of Transportation. The taxi associations argued that the Kyūshū Transportation Bureau had identified an "oversupply" of cars on Sundays in the first place. This is dubious, because the Bureau depends on the association for data on supply and demand. Yet, the JFTC was unable to challenge the Ministry of Transportation on this case, since price effects of the reduction had not yet become visible. The JFTC issued an administrative guidance-type "caution", which the associations accepted. These cases highlight the continuing difficulties the JFTC encounters in trying to enforce the AML within Japan's regulatory system. Even if trade associations self-regulate and collude, in industries that can claim to have their ministry's blessing the JFTC remains limited in its challenging of self-regulation.

Exemptions from the AML

The AML amendment of 1953 introduced a system of "exemption" of certain cartels from antitrust rules. While Chapter 3 described the political logic behind this system, we will briefly consider the legal aspects here. There are five different types of exemption. First, special industry laws can allow cartels to supplement government regulation in a certain business. Outstanding examples are the transportation cartels, such as the taxi and trucking businesses, or the insurance premium cartel.[28] This type of exempted cartel is *de facto* a form of delegated, and thus legal, privatized regulation. Although the number of these special laws

---

[27] See *Nikkei*, December 16, 1994, November 18, 1995, and February 8, 1996. This case was still pending at the time of writing.
[28] See, for instance, the *Kaijō unsō hō* (Marine Transportation Law), *Kōkūhō* (Air Transportation Law), *Rikujō kōtsū jigyyō hō* (Land Transportation Business Law), or the *Songai hoken ryōritsu suisanshutsu dantai ni kan suru hōritsu* (Law Concerning the Non-Life Insurance Premium Calculation Association).

has been reduced since its peak period in the 1960s, in the mid-1990s there were still 34 special industry laws granting exemptions for 53 cartels (JFTC Annual Report 1997: 227).

The second type of exemption is that for small- and medium-sized enterprises. This allows cooperatives to operate cartels among small firms, particular joint sales outlets and other mutual-help ventures, to enable them to better compete with large firms. These cartels are based on the "Small- and Medium-Sized Enterprise Etc. Cooperative Law" (*Chūsho kigyō kyōdō kumiai hō*). Being exempted from many antitrust rules largely protects cooperatives from JFTC intervention when engaging in unfair trade practices or even certain types of price fixing. Although the exemption of cooperatives has received only scant attention in studies of the Japanese distribution system, it is important because most of the wholesalers and retailers that form the core of the distribution system are small-sized firms. As described in Chapter 2, most Japanese trade associations are in the distribution sector. Thus, the exemption of cooperatives from the AML is a significant limitation to the JFTC's powers to stop self-regulation in the distribution sector.

Related, but legally different, is the third type of exempted cartel, namely the export associations based on the Export–Import Trade Law (*Yushutsunyū torihiki-hō*) for the purpose of export promotion. As discussed in Chapter 3, these associations were modeled after the U.S. system of export associations introduced with the Webb–Pomerene Act of 1918. The original idea was to prevent dumping by Japanese exporters on foreign markets, but this logic was soon turned around to allow domestic agreements on price for exporting industries. While the number of export associations exceeded 100 in the 1960s, it has declined to about 35 in the 1990s.

The fourth and fifth types of exemption are probably the best-known yet smallest in number: recession and rationalization cartels based on Section 24 of the AML. Recession cartels are established by the regulating ministry to help a certain industry through short-term economic adversity. A recession cartel is legally admissible in situations when supply exceeds demand, the market price falls below the average production cost in the industry, and when the fate of large firms can be improved through the cartel. A rationalization cartel, in contrast, aims to strengthen the long-term prospects of an industry by improving production technology, product quality, and cost efficiency. The most frequent types of arrangement in this category are technology upgrade cartels and cartels that limit product differentiation (Kawagoe 1997: 215–22). Of the more than 1,000 legalized cartels in the 1960s and 1970s, recession and rationalization cartels accounted for only a minor fraction. Moreover the role of these cartels changed after the 1980 oil cartel case. Beginning in 1978, MITI preferred to rely on special blanket bypass laws to structure cartels, namely the Depressed Industries Law and the Structurally Depressed Industries Law. These laws made recession and rationalization cartels superfluous, and no AML-based cartels were newly formed in the 1990s. Indeed, recession and rationalization cartels seem to have lost their usefulness as viable tools of industrial policy. At the same time, however, the perceived need by companies of cartels was rekindled in the recession of the 1990s. As a result of the decline in officially exempted cartels and the existing high propensity to cooperate, the 1990s saw both greater opportunity and greater business needs for more autonomous self-regulation by trade associations.

4.3. Summary: The Effectiveness of the Antitrust System in Containing Self-Regulation

The Japanese Fair Trade Commission is a structurally independent but factually subordinate part of the Japanese bureaucracy. To be sure, the AML has been revised several times, the JFTC staff has been doubled, and administrative surcharges and criminal fines were increased in the late 1990s. Yet, the combination of the limitations of the AML itself and the interpretation and legal doctrine used in its enforcement have led to a preponderance of informal settlements of violations, such as "warnings" and "cautions". These are the JFTC's version of administrative guidance, as they are used in extralegal ways and depend on voluntary compliance to be effective. Over time, these limitations have left the JFTC with little authority in the marketplace, especially for containing self-regulation. Building on continuous interaction among firms in one industry and often beginning with trade-enhancing administrative measures, self-regulation provides opportunities to trade associations to go far beyond what they are legally allowed and engage in a variety of anti-competitive practices. Yet, the JFTC can interfere effectively only with the most blatant cases of protective self-regulation.

One reason for the preponderance of informal law enforcement may be that the use of shame, e.g., through negative media publicity, is an important and effective, yet cost-efficient means of antitrust enforcement. The problem with this approach is that while it may end a certain activity, it does not fundamentally alter corporate behavior. Another reason for informal enforcement lies in the tacit approval by the public of lenient antitrust enforcement. The JFTC's biggest hurdle in prosecuting self-regulation is that it has to show that the self-regulation is against the "public interest". Since this notion includes "business interests", it would be difficult indeed for the JFTC to prove that voluntary self-regulation is against the interest of the self-regulating industry. Moreover, the exemption system allows self-regulation through cooperatives. Japanese society is generally favorably inclined toward small-scale businesses, such as farmers and shopkeepers, and seems willing to tolerate a certain amount of preferential treatment even if it results in higher prices. Once exceptions are made for small firms, big business can powerfully argue that it, too, should be allowed to self-regulate.

The particular logic of the Japanese antitrust enforcement system has a huge impact on the rise of self-regulation by trade associations. There is no clause in the AML that prohibits self-regulation, unless it employs coercion. Neither is there a developed doctrine of how to treat self-regulation before the law. Most self-regulation activities, if they can be proven, are prosecuted as "unfair trade practices" under AML Section 19, reflecting a deliberate choice to treat them leniently. The JFTC can choose to prosecute collusive self-regulation as Section 3 cartels. It rarely opts to do so, partially because there is no political will to do so, and partially because to prove a cartel, the JFTC has to provide enormous amounts of evidence. Moreover, under current legal interpretation, even with conclusive evidence self-regulation is likely to be considered legal as long as it is uncoerced.

From the perspective of the Japanese firm or trade association, antitrust rules have not been a major cause for concern. Because informal admonitions are virtually inconsequential, the risks of forming a cartel or establishing a strong system of self-regulation and entry barriers in an industry are negligible. In addition, it would be truly extraordinary for the JFTC to punish a cartel or trade association severely for a first-time violation; rather, the record suggests that it is reasonable to expect the JFTC to issue informal administrative guidance first. Most violations charged with heavy fines are repeat offenses.

Without a significant change in both the legal statute and the interpretation and application of the antitrust law, the JFTC will remain unable to contain self-regulation. Even if changes happen, they will not become effective overnight. Thus, change in the AML and its application, if any, is unlikely to occur soon and fast enough to stop the ongoing increase in self-regulation. In addition to the law itself, examples of antitrust enforcement indicate that the JFTC in fact may not always be eager to curb self-regulation at all. The Pepsi-Cola case suggests that the JFTC occasionally uses the law to support self-regulation, rather than to contain it. The next chapter will show how vigorous the JFTC has been over time in enforcing its law.

5

The Evidence—Antitrust
Enforcement and Self-Regulation
in Postwar Japan

"We thought that just a little bit of price fixing should be o.k.", explained Denka's Chairman Kimura. "The employee in charge said 'no' at first, but eventually had to give in".[1] The eight companies in Japan's industrial-use vinyl wrap industry and their trade association, the Japan Vinyl Goods Manufacturers' Association (*Nihon biniiru kōgyōkai*), had been investigated by the Japan Fair Trade Commission and received 17 cease-and-desist orders in as many years. The record holder among the eight firms was Denka (short for <u>Denki</u> <u>kagaku</u> <u>kōgyō</u>), a second-tier company which according to the *Nikkei* newspaper had "many prudent gentlemen on their management".[2] Denka had received a total of ten cease-and-desist orders since the 1970s.

In November 1991, Japan's Fair Trade Commission announced that it would launch a criminal investigation into the behavior of the eight vinyl wrap companies, given their repeated violations of the antitrust law. At the time, Denka had a market share of less than 10% and was involved in a battle with Nihon Carbide and Riken Vinyl for the Number 4 position in the industry. A price fixing agreement was therefore disadvantageous to the company, and many wondered why Denka's "prudent" managers would allow themselves to get wrapped up in this cartel at a time when collusion was detrimental. President Kimura offered three explanations for the company's behavior. First, with their profits squeezed because of the recession of the early 1990s, Denka welcomed the idea of raising prices, even if that meant that they could not increase their market share for a while. Second, there was some fear that the other companies would shut Denka out of the market entirely if it did not go along with the industry's cartel. Third, no major negative repercussions were to be feared: if the past 17 years were any indication, the JFTC was likely to do no more than issue yet another cease-and-desist order. Moreover, the many members of Denka's management who had experience in arranging deals with other firms knew that while facilitating cooperation would lead to promotions, fighting a cartel might cost

---

[1] Literally, Kimura was quoted as saying: "*Kore gurai wa daijōbu darō*"; see *Nikkei*, January 28, 1992, p. 10, and *Nikkei*, May 30, 1992, p. 31, for details on this case.

[2] "*Ottori shita jenterumen ga ōi*", *Nikkei*, January 28, p. 10.

you your job. Because there was some risk to both the firm and the individual decision-maker in resisting pressure by the industry cartel, and little chance anyway to increase market share during the recession period, Denka participated in the price-fixing cartel. There were few incentives in the system to do otherwise.

When the Fair Trade Commission initiated its investigation of the industrial-use vinyl wrap industry in November 1991, the vinyl wrappers' lawyers hastened to point out that no criminal investigation had been proposed for concurrent collusive agreements in the cement, construction, or ink industries, although collusion in these industries affected consumer prices much more than industrial-use vinyl wrap. The vinyl wrappers had no reason to view their own actions as anything other than "normal", and thus felt they were being victimized. "How does this cartel damage the public interest?", asked the CEO of Mitsui Tōatsu, the industry leader, in a newspaper interview. Its lawyers proclaimed that "There is no rational reason for the criminal investigation. They are going after wrap because this industry is an easy target."[3]

The vinyl wrap case is a fairly typical example of both the activities of Japanese trade associations and their attitudes toward the antitrust law. The case raises four major issues to be analyzed in this chapter, namely: (1) the formation of cartels among competitors, almost as a default reaction during periods of recession; (2) the use of boycotts by trade associations as a means to force smaller firms to comply with cartels; (3) generally lenient enforcement of antitrust rules by the JFTC; and (4) a bias in enforcement leading to less forceful treatment of self-regulation and boycotts than of other antitrust violations. In combination, these four factors mean that JFTC prosecution of self-regulation is often informal and lax. This chapter considers these issues in both qualitative and quantitative terms, to provide insights into the Japanese conception of what constitutes an illegal cartel, and what the appropriate terms of prosecution and punishment are for various types of violation.

The empirical study of antitrust enforcement is confounded by a data dilemma that ultimately requires recourse to qualitative evidence for a complete picture of reality. This data problem is best described by way of analogy (Haley 1995). Suppose one was to conduct a comparative analysis of criminal justice systems. One would use two sets of data: the number of crimes committed, and the number of felons convicted. The ratio of the two statistics would yield an indication of efficiency in criminal justice in a country, and one could then compare this ratio with similar data for other countries. In contrast, when studying antitrust enforcement, there is only one set of data: the number of cases prosecuted by the antitrust authority. There is no independent set of statistics of all activities of collusion. This is because if the "crime" (collusion)

---

[3] *Nikkei*, May 30, 1992, p. 31. On May 21, 1993, the Tokyo High Court found eight companies guilty of criminal violation and charged each company fines ranging from ¥6 million to ¥8 million, while 15 employees received prison terms of six months to one year.

is discovered, the felons are also necessarily known. Collusion does not remain unsolved, but it may remain undiscovered. Because no data exist that indicate how many cases of illegal collusion exist but have not been prosecuted, it is difficult to evaluate the relative efficiency of antitrust enforcement across countries, or within one country over time.

Nonetheless, a data analysis of Japanese antitrust enforcement yields interesting insights, and case studies of non-prosecuted collusion can be used to supplement the data. This chapter first looks at the data published by the JFTC in its Annual Reports for the 50 years between 1947 and 1996, to analyze the pattern of antitrust enforcement throughout the postwar period and its relationship to the business cycle. Next, it addresses the question of whether Japan's antitrust authority treats some industries, such as strategic growth sectors like steel, differently from others. Again, the problem is that we cannot know the total incidence of collusion: if, for instance, the steel industry has rarely been prosecuted, this does not necessarily mean that it has rarely colluded, and neither does it reveal the degree of self-regulation in the steel industry. One way to solve this dilemma is to detect patterns in the type of enforcement; i.e., to see whether some industries are more likely to be prosecuted formally, while others face the more lenient treatment of informal settlement. Since formal cases can be costly in many ways, political pressure on the JFTC not to prosecute a certain industry may be reflected in a compromise: the JFTC admonishes the violating industry informally, but saves it the embarrassment of an official case. The data analysis shows that such patterns indeed exist. Furthermore, a comparison of formal and informal cases by industry and type of violation helps detect differences in the handling of potentially market-obstructing acts of self-regulation (such as boycotts) as opposed to indubitable cartels (such as bid-rigging). As argued in Chapter 4, the very structure and interpretation of Japan's antimonopoly law put emphasis on prosecuting price cartels over other instances of market obstruction. The case analysis supports this notion: unfair trade practices, the predominant venue of implementing self-regulation, are not prosecuted stridently.

The data analysis builds on a longitudinal database I constructed from each issue of the JFTC Annual Report (*Kōsei torihiki iinkai nenji hōkokusho*) between 1948 and 1997. In addition to the formal cases (*shinketsu*), which can be analyzed for the entire period, the database includes data on informal "warnings", which the JFTC has published beginning in 1988, and on "cautions", available since 1991. For the formal cases and warnings, I included data on the number of participating firms or trade associations; the industry; the kind of violation that I coded based on the JFTC's description of each case; and the section of the AML that the JFTC chose to use for enforcement.

The second part of this chapter complements the data analysis with case studies of self-regulation in the 1990s. Both recession and deregulation have clearly triggered an enormous increase in self-regulation. Yet, many cases of collusive self-regulation are not prosecuted by the JFTC although they are explicitly designed to restrain competition. A case study of the financial industries highlights the scope and depth of self-regulation after deregulation in the 1990s.

5.1. Data Analysis: Formal and Informal Antitrust Cases in the Postwar Period

Two major differences in antitrust enforcement between the U.S. and Japan combine to lead to a more lenient antitrust environment in Japan. First, as highlighted in Figure 5.1, in the U.S. private suits outnumber government suits by orders of magnitude (the huge increase in 1962 is attributable to the big price-fixing case in the electrical equipment industry; cf. Smith, R. A. 1961a, 1961b). In Japan, in contrast, informal cases can be seen as serving as the functional analog to private suits, which are extremely rare. Second, Japan does not typically enforce antitrust laws as criminal violations. Between 1947 and 1996, the JFTC processed a total of 1,007 cases formally.[4] Of these 1,007 cases, a mere ten (or 1%) were brought to court as criminal cases. In comparison, between 1945 and 1988 the U.S. antitrust authorities brought a total of 2,904 cases, of which 1,379 (or 47.5%) were criminal cases (Kawagoe 1997: 459–60). During the SII trade negotiations, the U.S. demanded that Japan strengthen its enforcement by bringing more cartel violations to court, and indeed four of the ten postwar criminal cases were brought after 1990.[5] Besides rarely filing criminal charges, the JFTC is also lenient in its settlement of adjudicative cases. As mentioned in Chapter 4, of the 1,007 total formal cases prosecuted in Japan in the postwar period, 77.8% were settled as "recommendations", i.e., with an administrative order such as to "cease-and-desist", while 22.2% went through the entire adjudicative system as formal complaints.[6]

Administrative surcharges (*kachōkin*; cf. Chapter 4) were levied in 190 cases (19% of all cases), and on average they were comparatively low. Between 1977, when the surcharge system was introduced, and 1996, a total of ¥51.39 billion of surcharges was levied from 3,453 companies that had

---

[4] In addition, there were four cases in violation of the Premium Law, which the JFTC sometimes includes in its official data, although these are strictly speaking not part of antitrust enforcement.

[5] Another difference in antitrust records of the two countries stems from the fact that the data for both countries include cases of collusion, such as price-fixing, as well as the so-called "abuse of monopoly power". In Japan, there was only one case of abuse of monopoly power in the entire postwar period and merger cases are typically settled informally, whereas in the U.S. merger cases constitute a large proportion of total cases.

[6] The high ratio of acceptance of all "recommendations" translates into time efficiency: since the JFTC typically requires that a respondent reply to a recommendation within ten days, cases are settled very fast, often within a month of initial filing.

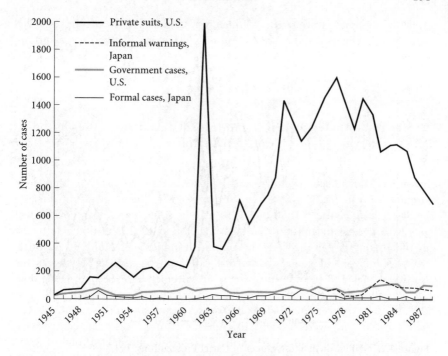

Figure 5.1. Comparison of Antitrust Cases in the U.S. and Japan, 1945–1987

Source: adapted from Kawagoe 1997: 460.

been found to have colluded illegally and made a profit in the process; this equals an average surcharge of just ¥14.9 million (or about $150,000) per company.[7] Taken together, these figures indicate that for the cases brought formally by the antitrust authorities, Japanese enforcement is much more lenient than U.S. enforcement.

Collusion during Recessions

Some observers have argued that the JFTC has increased its formal enforcement in the 1980s and 1990s, suggesting a tightening official position on collusion in Japan (e.g., First 1995, Iyori 1995). If enforcement has indeed become more strident in the 1990s, what does this imply for the shift toward self-regulation in Japan? Does an increase in formally prosecuted cases indicate an increase in self-regulation?

Figure 5.2 (similar to Figure 3.1) addresses these questions by connecting all formal JFTC cartel cases since 1947 with the annual growth rate of GNP and

---

[7] The dollar value is based on an exchange rate of ¥100 = $1. In the early 1980s, the average dollar value of the average fine levied would have been even less than $150,000 per company.

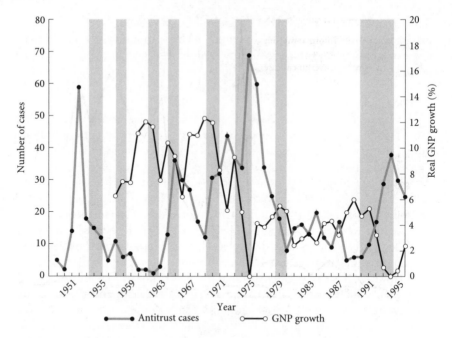

Figure 5.2. GNP Growth and Number of Cartel Prosecutions, 1947–1996

Sources: EPA 1996, JFTC Annual Reports, 1948–1997.

periods of recession (in shaded gray).[8] There are two big "blips" in the line indicating cases per year. First, in 1950, the JFTC and industry reached 59 formal settlements. This high number can be attributed to SCAP leadership in enforcing the new Antimonopoly Law. The second blip, with a total of 69 cases in 1973, is associated with the "oil shock" and the commensurate public support for the JFTC to prosecute price fixing during this period, as discussed in Chapter 3.

Figure 5.2 also shows that while the trend line in formal AML cases may be slightly increasing over time, the 1990s were not markedly different from the 1960s in the level of formal cases prosecuted per year. It seems that more important than a long-term trend is the negative correlation between antitrust prosecution and the annual growth rate: the higher the growth rate, the lower the number of cases. This suggests that companies may collude more during reces-

---

[8] Recessions here indicate the time period between the Bank of Japan's initial tightening of monetary policy through an increase in the official discount rate, and the first drop in the rate. During Japan's period of rapid growth, the official discount rate was a very effective tool to affect liquidity in the economy, and therefore an increase in this rate without doubt meant the beginning of a phase of tight money and recession. Although this changed with the opening and internationalization of the financial markets in the 1980s, the official discount rate remains a strong policy indicator. On monetary policy during the postwar period, see Patrick (1962), Schaede (1989a), Suzuki (1980).

sions. The scholars writing about an increase in prosecution in the early 1990s may have simply picked up on a periodic increase in antitrust cases during a phase of economic downturn. While the 1990s have seen an increase in cases, and possibly in self-regulation in general, there is no clear evidence that the JFTC's enforcement powers in terms of formal cases have increased compared with previous periods of recession.

The connection between recession and collusion has been explained in a game-theoretic setting by Rotemberg/Saloner (1986).[9] In revising the traditional notion that companies engage in price wars during recessions to keep whatever market share they can (e.g., Scherer 1980), Rotemberg and Saloner argue that companies are more likely to engage in price wars during boom periods and collude during economic downturns, for two primary reasons. First, cartels and other self-regulation are difficult to enforce during boom periods, when the incentive to cheat is greatest. As seen in Chapter 1, one necessary condition for a successful cartel is that the expected payoffs are constant over time so that no cartel member is enticed to forgo future cooperation for the short-term gain. However, business cycles mean that payoffs are not constant over time; i.e., boom times make cheating attractive because immediate payoffs are higher than future expected losses. Second, punishment of the cartel breaker (through boycotts or other measures) will occur only when the boom is over and companies are not operating at full capacity, i.e., when market share becomes the strategic variable. The fact that punishment is postponed increases the incentive to cheat during a boom. As a result, Rotemberg and Saloner predict, companies in a collusive industry do one of two things: they either give up on collusion during booms altogether, or else they negotiate the highest sustainable price level, which will be close to the competitive price (as otherwise the incentive to cheat becomes too high). In either scenario, competition increases during booms, while collusion is more likely to occur during recessions.

The Rotemberg/Saloner model is concerned with price levels rather than the prevalence of collusion *per se*. Tests of their model therefore use price levels as the dependent variable to show the level of collusion over time. Yet, in legal terms, if a group of firms agrees on setting prices at lower levels during a boom period, this is still a cartel regardless of the effects on competition.[10] From this perspective, collusion over time can be observed through the number of antitrust cases.

---

[9] For further theoretical studies of the relation, see Porter (1985), Bagwell/Staiger (1997), Eswaran (1997).

[10] This difference in evaluating cartels during recessions is related to the difference in emphasis that students of law and of economics put on cartel behavior. Economists are primarily concerned with the outcome of collusion, i.e., the welfare implications; therefore, if a cartel sets a price at a low level, presumably no harm is done. In contrast, lawyers—especially in the U.S. where cartels are *per se* illegal—are more concerned with the process, i.e., the fact that there is an agreement, how this agreement was structured, and whether its implementation was coerced.

Figure 5.2 suggests visually that the Japanese case supports this logic.[11] To verify the negative relationship between annual growth in real GNP and the number of cartel cases per year, the bivariate correlation between the two sets of data was computed for the 40 years between 1956 and 1996.[12] Since the hypothesis is that companies collude in reaction to an economic downturn, the JFTC cases were lagged by one year. The computation showed that the correlation is significant at the 0.05 level, with a correlation coefficient of −0.367. This result strongly suggests that, indeed, Japanese companies do collude more during recessions.

Of course, the assumption with using formal cases as a proxy for collusion is that the JFTC has been constant in its level of enforcement over time, so that the increase in the number of cases denotes an increase in collusion rather than one in enforcement activity. This assumption is complicated by the fact that data are available only for JFTC cases and not for the unknowable total incidence of collusion. But the JFTC has long been pressured not to enforce the law strictly, and it may well have found itself under short-term political influence not to enforce the law during specific periods of economic growth or downturn. If this were the case, rather than showing a decrease in collusion itself, the decrease in the number of cases during economic upswings could simply attest to the JFTC's inactivity during such periods of political pressure. This alternative explanation, however, is unconvincing for two reasons. First, given the constancy of Japan's LDP-ruled government, it seems that similar pressures would be exerted on the JFTC over time.[13] Second, if there was any short-term political pressure on the JFTC not to enforce the AML, this would be much more likely to occur during recessions when companies are suffering, bureaucrats are facing possible unwanted bankruptcies in their turf, and politicians are lobbied heavily to bail out these firms. During booms, such political pressure is likely to be much weaker. Temporary pressure on the JFTC not to enforce the AML is thus more likely to occur during recessions, reinforcing the finding that companies collude more during recessions: absent any pressure on the JFTC not to prosecute strictly, there might have been even more cases of collusion during recessions. Therefore,

---

[11] It is also possible that there is a business cycle effect in the enforcement of cartel laws. Boom periods tend to put upward pressure on prices, so that even if companies fix prices at a high level, it is difficult for the antitrust agency to argue against the companies' claim that the price increase is simply due to an increase in production costs. If product prices remain high during a recession, in spite of a general downward pressure on prices and low demand, it is easier for the enforcement agency to find evidence of cartels. Similar to price data, this "business cycle effect" in prosecution puts some limitations on the number of prosecuted cases as a proxy for collusion. However, taken together, the logic of the Rotemberg/Saloner model of limited collusion during boom periods and the strong increase of Japanese cases in periods of recession suggest that the data reveal more than just the inability of the JFTC to prosecute cartels during booms.

[12] The Japanese Economic Planning Agency did not calculate GNP prior to 1955, so that the year-on-year growth rate is available only beginning in 1956.

[13] This is very different from the U.S., where there seems to be a political enforcement pattern over time, depending on whether the administration is Republican or Democrat; see Greer (1993: 82–108) for details and data.

the data support the economic argument that firms collude more frequently and flagrantly during recessions.

JFTC Cases by Industry

The next question is whether some industries are more active self-regulators than others, and whether some industries are prosecuted differently from others. For instance, studies in the economics of industrial organization suggest that market concentration and product characteristics are important factors in facilitating cooperation or collusion among competitors, suggesting that industries where a few firms sell a homogeneous product are more likely to collude or cooperate than others. In Chapter 6, we will see in detail how these two factors affect self-regulation across industries. Here, the question is whether there are cross-industry patterns in the prosecution of self-regulation.

Tables 5.1 through 5.3 show a breakdown of all cases by industry over time, for all formal cases for the period of 1947–96, for all informal "warnings" for the period of 1988–96, and for the even more informal "cautions" for the years 1991–6. Table 5.1 highlights that the two industries most frequently prosecuted formally over time are chemicals and food and drinks, followed by machinery, construction and the kiln industries (cement, glass, and ceramics). Half the cases for chemicals (and two-thirds of those in mining/petroleum) stem from the period around the first oil shock. Curiously, the construction industry seems to have been immune from antitrust enforcement until the late 1970s, i.e., until the end of Tanaka years.[14] The most constant offenders over time with multiple formal cases reported in each decade are the petroleum, general machinery, chemicals, kiln, paper and pulp, and food and drinks industries.

Informal warnings and cautions are issued in large numbers to the construction, food and drinks and kiln industries (Tables 5.2 and 5.3). Studies of the construction (Woodall 1996) and cement (Tilton 1996) industries have attested to the widespread bid-rigging and price fixing in these sectors, so that these industries can be considered "usual suspects". The case of food and drinks is more puzzling at first sight, given the well-known political protection of farmers and fishers in Japan. Yet, there are two explanations for this finding. First, the food and drinks category covers a broad range of industries with many local chapters of small cooperatives, so that price fixing in one industry, such as soy sauce, may result in numerous separate cases, one for each local chapter. Second, some products in this category are very homogeneous, which simplifies cooperative agreements on price, distribution, and market allocation. Indeed, the most frequently cited sub-industry in the food category is milk—where consumers'

---

[14] Tanaka Kakuei, LDP politician and prime minister 1972–4, is often credited with having shaped bribery and collusion in Japan's construction industry. See Tachibana (1982), Johnson (1995), Schlesinger (1997) for accounts of his political career.

Table 5.1. Formally Adjudicated Cases (*Shinketsu* and *Kankoku*), 1947–1996, by Industry

Industry	1947–56	1957–66	1967–76	1977–86	1987–96	Grand total	in % of all cases
Food & drinks	29	28	39	21	8	125	12
Chemicals	10	10	62	9	29	120	12
All machinery*	17	12	30	10	26	95	9
Construction	1	0	7	23	62	93	9
Kiln (cement, glass, ceramics)	0	2	48	14	12	76	8
Mining/petroleum	5	1	53	11	4	74	7
Tools & miscellaneous goods**	12	8	11	16	23	70	7
Paper & pulp	5	24	19	9	7	64	6
Others	13	14	11	8	9	55	5
Propane gas	0	9	25	1	1	36	4
General machinery & machine tools	4	5	14	6	6	35	3
Small services***	9	11	14	0	0	34	3
Textiles	9	6	14	1	1	31	3
Electrical machinery/ electronic industries	7	3	8	0	7	25	2
Iron & steel	0	0	20	0	3	23	2
Tourism	10	3	5	2	3	23	2
Precision machinery	4	4	3	2	6	19	2
Transportation machinery/ shipbuilding	2	0	5	2	7	16	2
Transportation and storage	7	1	2	4	2	16	2
Pharmaceuticals	5	1	3	1	4	14	1
Retailing****	5	0	2	1	5	13	1
Banking	6	1	0	0	0	7	1
Metals	0	1	4	1	1	7	1
Marine transportation	1	5	1	0	0	7	1
Investment banking	0	0	0	0	5	5	0
Distribution*****	0	0	5	0	0	5	0
Gas	0	0	2	1	1	4	0
Insurance	1	1	0	0	1	3	0
Telecommunications	0	0	0	0	3	3	0
Trucking	0	0	1	0	1	2	0
Energy/electric power	1	0	0	0	0	1	0
Port management	1	0	0	0	0	1	0
Grand total	**147**	**138**	**378**	**133**	**211**	**1007**	**100**

Source: database built from JFTC Annual Reports, 1948–1997.

*   All machinery = sum of general machinery/machine tools, transportation machinery, electrical machinery/electronics, and precision machinery

**   Tools & miscellaneous goods = ranging from fishing hooks, golf goods, skis, toys, pens and briefcases to *tatami*, *tabi*, fans and Japanese lacquerware

***   Small services = barber shops, beauty salons, public bath houses, and dry cleaners

****   Retailing = specialized retail industry; e.g., department stores, convenience stores

***** Distribution = wholesalers covering various product items; note: specialized wholesalers are grouped by product category; e.g., the Glass Wholesalers' Association falls under "glass"

Table 5.2. Informal Settlement through Warnings (*Keikoku*), 1988–1996, by Industry

	1988	1989	1990	1991	1992	1993	1994	1995	1996	Grand total	in % of all warnings
Construction	1	0	0	7	3	4	1	5	5	26	19
Food & drinks	0	4	1	1	2	0	12	1	2	23	17
Tools & misc. goods*	0	0	0	3	3	3	2	1	0	12	9
Textiles	0	0	0	6	0	0	0	1	3	10	7
Mining/petroleum	0	0	3	1	1	0	0	0	4	9	7
All machinery*	0	0	3	7	1	0	0	1	7	19	7
Small services*	0	6	0	1	0	0	0	0	0	7	5
Electrical machinery	2	0	0	1	1	0	0	3	0	7	5
Kiln (cement, glass)	1	0	0	2	0	3	0	1	0	7	5
Chemical industry	0	0	2	1	0	0	2	0	0	5	4
Others	0	0	0	0	0	1	0	0	4	5	4
Retailing*	0	0	0	1	0	0	1	0	2	4	3
Investment banking	0	0	0	3	0	0	0	0	0	3	2
Pharmaceuticals	0	0	0	0	1	1	0	0	1	3	2
Paper & pulp	0	0	0	0	2	0	1	0	0	3	2
Telecommunications	0	0	0	0	3	0	0	0	0	3	2
Gas	0	0	0	2	0	0	0	0	0	2	1
General machinery	0	0	0	1	0	0	1	0	0	2	1
Precision machinery	0	0	0	0	2	0	0	0	0	2	1
Insurance	0	0	0	0	0	0	1	0	0	1	1
Transportation machinery	0	0	0	0	1	0	0	0	0	1	1
Transportation	0	0	0	0	0	0	0	1	0	1	1
Air transportation	0	0	0	0	0	0	0	0	1	1	1
Tourism	0	0	0	1	0	0	0	0	0	1	1
Grand total	**4**	**10**	**6**	**31**	**19**	**12**	**21**	**13**	**22**	**138**	**100**

Source: database built from JFTC Annual Reports, 1948–1997.

* = Industry categorization is explained at the bottom of Table 5.1.

brand-switching is almost entirely driven by price—followed by *tōfu*, soy sauce, bread, and canned food. Therefore, the product characteristics of the food and drinks industry may invite more cooperation.

A further interesting observation from Table 5.1 is related to "the dog that didn't bark" phenomenon; i.e., those industries that are widely suspected of close cooperation, boycotts or price fixing, but are conspicuously absent from this list. This group includes commercial and investment banking, iron and steel (except for the oil shock years), trucking, shipping and port management.[15] The fact that

---

[15] While these industries are widely considered suspect, evidence is mostly anecdotal. The investment banking industry was involved in a major scandal that broke in 1991 (see below). In the process of investigating the banks, evidence surfaced of customer allocation and other unfair trade practices. In the trucking and shipping industries, the habit of "scrap-and-build" agreements to restrict quantity has been documented widely; see, e.g., Suzuki (1995). For evidence of cooperation in the iron and steel industry through their trade association, see, among others, Lynn/McKeown (1988), Yamamura (1982), Tilton (1996).

Table 5.3. Informal Settlement through Cautions (*Chūi*), 1991–1996, by Industry

	1991	1992	1993	1994	1995	1996	Grand total	in % of all cases
Distribution & retailing	15	7	14	9	12	5	62	14
Construction	14	17	7	5	11	8	62	14
Food & drinks	5	10	16	14	5	1	51	12
Kiln (cement, glass, ceramics)	11	1	0	3	4	1	20	5
All machinery*	11	1	0	3	4	1	20	4
Textiles	2	6	0	4	2	5	19	4
Chemical industry	8	3	3	0	1	2	17	4
Transportation & storage	4	3	2	0	3	3	15	3
Small services*	1	1	2	2	4	4	14	3
Metals	3	0	6	3	2	0	14	3
General machinery	1	0	4	4	1	1	11	3
Paper & pulp	0	0	1	6	0	1	8	2
Transportation machinery	4	0	1	1	0	0	6	1
Mining/petroleum	2	0	1	1	0	0	4	1
Miscellaneous goods*	0	0	2	1	1	0	4	1
Tourism	1	0	2	1	0	0	4	1
Iron & steel	0	2	0	1	0	0	3	1
Banking	0	0	1	0	1	0	2	0
Precision machinery	0	1	0	0	0	1	2	0
Marine transportation	0	1	0	0	0	1	2	0
Trucking	0	0	0	0	1	0	1	0
Air transportation	0	0	0	0	0	1	1	0
Telecommunications	0	0	0	1	0	0	1	0
Others	17	21	17	30	12	14	111	26
Grand total	**88**	**73**	**79**	**86**	**60**	**48**	**434**	**100**

Source: database built from JFTC Annual Reports, 1948–1997.

* Industry categorization is explained at the bottom of Table 5.1.

these industries have only rarely been the subject of the JFTC's investigative interest suggests some immunity from antitrust prosecution. For instance, the iron and steel industry is sometimes called the "rice of the manufacturing industry" (*tetsu wa sangyō no kome da*), implying that it is considered crucial for national self-sufficiency, growth, and pride. The industry may therefore be afforded special political attention and protection. Another reason for antitrust immunity may be the regulation of fee schedules. For instance, the banking industry was subjected to interest rate regulation for most of the postwar period, as were insurance, taxis, trucking, and shipping. Rates were set by the regulating ministries based on recommendations by the respective trade associations. In these industries, the JFTC often suspected administrative guidance to have triggered and sanctioned collusion on rates by the companies, but it was unable to prosecute these activities because of the legal protection of uniform rates (JFTC 1981a, 1994a).

The informal cases help us understand this situation better. Recall from Chapter 4 that the "warnings" are the antitrust equivalent of written administrative guidance: while they do not have legal standing, a warning signals that the JFTC is quite serious about the issue. In contrast, "cautions" are the equivalents of oral administrative guidance and are therefore highly informal and inconsequential in legal terms. The JFTC may have no choice but to issue just a warning if there is insufficient evidence, but it may also be forced to settle informally if an industry is protected by its regulating ministry or by a politician. This results in an uneven distribution of cases across categories. For example, the category "tools and miscellaneous goods" consists mostly of strategically irrelevant, small domestic industries. Surprisingly, this group accounted for 7% of all formal cases over time, and almost 10% of the warnings in the last decade, whereas almost no informal cautions were issued to firms in these industries. In contrast, the highly protected textiles industry has only rarely been prosecuted formally, but has received 19 informal warnings in just the five years between 1991 and 1996.

The largest discrepancy between formal and informal cases is in retailing. The specialized retailing industry (department stores, supermarkets, etc.) accounts for 1% of all formal cases, 3% of all warnings, but 8% of all cautions. The difference in the distribution sector is similar, with 0% of all formal cases or warnings, but 6% of all cautions.[16] The most compelling explanation for this phenomenon is that since most retailers and wholesalers are small- and medium-sized enterprises organized in cooperatives, launching formal cases on price fixing or boycotts may be difficult. Not only do small enterprises enjoy the protection of some powerful politicians, but their cooperatives may also be exempted from the antitrust statutes, so that unless they engage in flagrant price fixing the JFTC is unable to bring a formal case.

The most important revelation from these data comes from the large number of distribution cases among the highly informal cautions. Self-regulation comprises both, price fixing and other agreements by the leading firms in an industry, and carrying out these agreements through control of the distribution system, e.g., through entry barriers or boycotts. These tools of self-regulation are "unfair trade practices", which occur at the retail end rather than at the location of manufacturing. Violations in the distribution sector are therefore often related to restrictive agreements at the manufacturing stage. For instance, if electronic equipment makers want to collude on price, they will request their wholesalers and distributors to maintain a certain price level for the product and to refuse to sell to discount stores. In this case, the self-regulation is the price collusion among the manufacturers, and the implementation occurs through boycotts

---

[16] The JFTC is not specific in its disclosure of data on cautions, which contain a large unspecified group labeled "other distribution". This means that, for instance, price fixing among fertilizer distributors could be coded as a violation in "chemicals" or in "other distribution". While this may create a bias toward "distribution" cases among the informal cautions, the large proportion of retailing and distribution cases among the cautions is nevertheless noteworthy.

and retail price maintenance at the retail level. Therefore, the fact that violations in the distribution system are not always prosecuted forcefully but are predominantly settled through an oral caution by the JFTC, suggests that the JFTC is either uninterested or ineffective in prosecuting these activities. Either way, the implementation of self-regulation is not being forcefully prevented by the antitrust authority.

JFTC Cases by Types of Violation

In prosecuting cases, the JFTC has two sets of choice to make. First, as we just saw, it has to decide whether to prosecute a case formally or settle it informally. Next, if it decides to prosecute, the JFTC has a choice among several sections of the law. As discussed in Chapter 4, self-regulation entailing retail price maintenance or boycotts can be treated either harshly as a "restraint of competition" (Section 3), or leniently as an "unfair trade practice" (Section 19). Analyzing JFTC cases by "Section 3" versus "Section 19" cases by types of violation therefore yields an additional measure of just how strictly the JFTC has chosen to prosecute self-regulation in the recent past.

Table 5.4 breaks down the major types of violation by industry for all formal cases adjudicated between 1947 and 1996. The bottom line ("Grand Total") shows that 523 of the 1,007 formal cases in the postwar period pertained to price fixing, whereas 169 were boycotts.[17] Retail price maintenance, for all practical purposes, is an extension of price fixing in that it prevents price competition at the retail end. Legally, however, retail price maintenance is treated as an "unfair trade practice" together with boycotts. Column 6 of Table 5.4 shows that the sum of retail price maintenance and boycotts yields a total of 242 cases of "total unfair trade practices". The third largest category of violations is *dangō* cases, whereas quantity cartels, improper gifts, rebates or lottery tickets and improper labeling play only a minor role in the larger picture.[18]

In looking at types of violations by industry in Table 5.4, it is not surprising to find that 58% of the *dangō* cases involve the construction industry. Most of the price-fixing violations occurred in the chemical and petroleum industries (related to the oil shock), followed by food and drinks, cement, paper, gas (in particular, propane gas) and the "small services" of barbers, dry cleaners, and

---

[17] These data may be skewed somewhat toward price fixing: in coding the data, I labeled cases that entailed price fixing plus another violation, such as a boycott, as a price-fixing violation. Likewise, when a case involved both retail price maintenance and a boycott, it was coded as retail price maintenance. The same bias applies to the informal cases, so that there is no difference in bias between formal and informal cases. However, the number of cases that apply to more than one category is rather small, except for cautions, which have a stronger bias toward price fixing.

[18] The category "Gifts and others" contains violations governed by various sections of the AML. The restrictions on gifts refers to the improper tying of a purchase to an unconnected present. In many instances, these violations are actually unfair trade practices, as they can also be considered as tie-in sales or exclusive dealings.

public bath houses. In contrast, the biggest offenders in boycotts are food and drinks, miscellaneous goods, newspapers and the kiln industries. Retail price maintenance was most often prosecuted in miscellaneous goods, food and drinks, and electronics. The category "miscellaneous goods" includes many small industries that produce daily-life goods. These used to be excluded from retail price maintenance prohibition in the 1950s and 1960s, so that this industry may have been caught in a change of legal application during the 1970s and 1980s, when the exemption of daily-life goods was gradually removed. To test this explanation, we need to look whether the JFTC has prosecuted industries differently over time.

Figure 5.3 shows the movement of types of violation, as a percentage of total violations, among the formal cases over time. While we saw earlier that the total number of formal cases in the 1990s is not in large deviation from the trend line, Figure 5.3 highlights a marked change in composition of formal cases over time. In the decade surrounding the oil shock of 1973 price fixing accounted for 75% of all cases, but it dropped to only 35% of all cases in the 1990s. In contrast, there were hardly any formal *dangō* cases between 1947 and 1976 in spite of the public construction boom before the Tokyo Olympics of 1964, whereas 39% of all formal cases in the 1990s involve *dangō*. Figure 5.3 also shows that retail price maintenance accounted for 17% of all cases in the decade between 1977 and

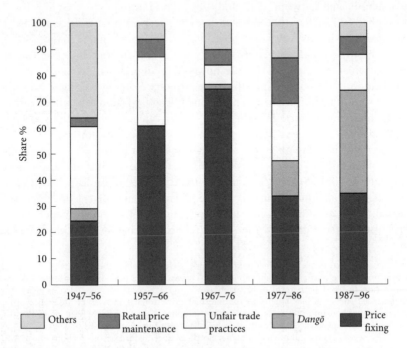

Figure 5.3. Changes in Types of Violation for Formal Cases, 1947–1996

Source: database built from JFTC Annual Reports, 1948–1997.

Table 5.4. All Formal Cases, 1947–1996, by Industry and Type of Violation

	Price fixing	Dangō	Other cartels	Retail price maintenance	Boycotts etc.	Total unfair trade practices (RPM + boycotts)	Monopoly power	Gifts & others	Protest of fine	Labeling & display	Total
Banking	1				3	3		3			7
Investment banking					4	4		1			5
Insurance	1		1					1			3
Retailing	2	3			2	2		4		2	13
Distribution	1	2								2	5
Small services	32				2	2					34
Mining/petroleum	61	4	2	2	5	7					74
Energy/power		1									1
Gas	38				2	2					40
Iron & steel	16	3	1	1	2	3					23
Metals	7										7
General machinery	19	3		3	7	10		3			35
Transportation machinery	9	2		2	1	3		2			16
Electrical mach./electronics	7			6	8	14		4			25
Precision machinery	4	3		3	6	9		2		1	19
Tools & misc. goods	22	2		22	17	39		5		2	70
Chemical industry	93	12	4	4	4	8		3			120
Pharmaceuticals	3	2	1	3	3	6		2			14

Industry										Total
Kiln	48	5			9	10		13			76
Textiles	9	8	2	4	8			3		1	31
Paper & pulp	42	2	3	7	9			8			64
Food & drinks	51	7	1	17	41	58		3	7	5	125
Construction	15	66		3	3		1	1		1	93
Transportation & storage	3	1	1	5	5	5		5		1	16
Trucking					1	1					2
Marine transportation	1			5	5	5		1			7
Port management								1			1
Telecommunications	3										3
Newspaper	10		2	9	9	9		2		2	23
Others	24	5	2	20	22	22		3		1	55
Grand total	**523**	**114**	**32**	**73**	**169**	**242**	**1**	**70**	**7**	**18**	**1007**

Source: database built from JFTC Annual Reports, 1948–1997.

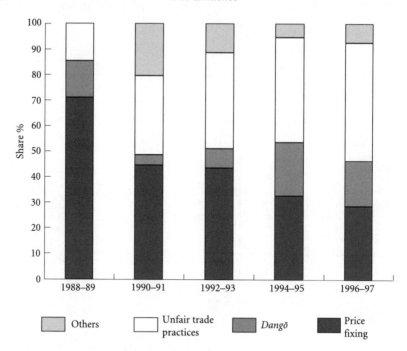

Figure 5.4. Informal Cases, by Type of Violation, 1988–1997

Note: cautions are included beginning in 1991 only.

Source: database built from JFTC Annual Reports, 1989–1998.

1986, whereas before and after that decade it was 7%. This supports the notion that the JFTC began looking into price maintenance violations in the small, "miscellaneous" industries during that decade, and it took these industries some time to adjust their traditional retail behavior to the new legal situation.

The increase in *dangō* cases and the simultaneous stagnation and even decline of cases involving unfair trade practices require some further analysis. One important reason for the increase in *dangō* prosecution may be *gaiatsu*, i.e., U.S. pressure on the Japanese government to prosecute *dangō* more forcefully, as exerted during the SII negotiations between 1989 and 1991. However, during the same SII negotiations the U.S. also pushed for more strident rule enforcement for unfair trade practices. Yet, in the 1990s the share of boycotts of all cases was down to 14% of all cases, from 22% in the previous decade. Therefore, if *gaiatsu* explains the increase in *dangō* cases over the last decade, one wonders why it has not been as effective for unfair trade practices. The explanation lies in the logic of *gaiatsu* effectiveness: it has been shown that *gaiatsu* is effective in changing Japan's ways if, and only if, there is preexisting domestic pressure for this change, so that *gaiatsu* becomes the catalyst for change. If there is no domestic interest in the issue, the foreign pressure will remain ineffective (Schoppa 1997). This explanation fits well for the construction industry, where domestic pressure to

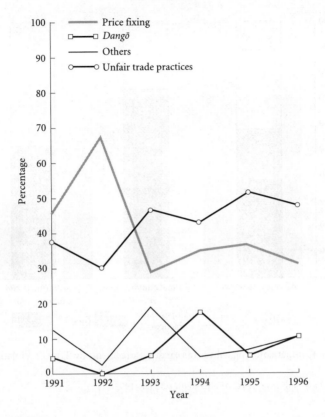

Figure 5.5. Cautions, by Type of Violation, 1991–1996
Source: database built from JFTC Annual Reports, 1992–1997.

change corruption and bribery related to public works was increasing in the late 1980s, so that *gaiatsu* helped the move toward prosecuting the construction industry. By the same logic, the fact that unfair trade practices were not prosecuted more strictly in spite of *gaiatsu* suggests that there was little existing domestic interest to do something about retail price maintenance and boycotts in the 1990s. Whatever *gaiatsu* there might have been, cracking down on unfair trade practices was not on the Japanese agenda.

Of course, it is possible that Figure 5.3 simply reflects the real incidence of violations; that is, there may be more instances of price fixing and *dangō* than of other violations. Thus, rather than a bias in prosecution the data might merely reflect the real distribution of types of violation. To test whether what we see in Figure 5.3 is a bias in prosecution or a reflection of the true incidence of cases, we need to look again at the informal cases: if the incidence of violations is similar across all cases, then the distribution by types of violation can be considered a fair reflection of actual violations. In contrast, if the composition of the informal cases is different, then this difference attests to either a legal constraint on the

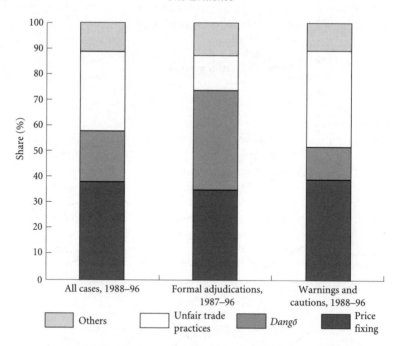

Figure 5.6. Comparison: Formal vs. Informal Enforcement, by Type of Violation, 1987–1996

Source: database built from JFTC Annual Reports, 1988–1997.

JFTC to bring certain types of cases formally, or a bias in the JFTC's choice in how to prosecute different types of violation.

Figure 5.4 shows informal cases by type of violation since 1988, the year the JFTC began publishing these data. Between 1988 and 1997, the composition of informal cases is vastly different from the formal cases: almost half (47%) of the informal cases pertain to boycotts and other unfair trade practices, while *dangō* and price fixing account for relatively smaller shares. In particular, the share of total cases represented by boycotts has increased steadily since the addition of the highly informal cautions in 1991. Figure 5.5 focuses in on the cautions by types of violation during 1991–96. Clearly, unfair trade practices account for the largest part of all cautions, and the trend in the first part of the 1990s is increasing.

Figure 5.6 summarizes the relative composition of formal and informal cases for the years 1988–96. While 39% of all formal cases are *dangō* cases, 38% of all informal cases concern unfair trade practices. Clearly, then, there is a distinctive pattern in prosecution: price fixing and *dangō* are prosecuted more strictly, through the adjudicative system and with the possibility of fines, whereas unfair trade practices are addressed with inconsequential warnings and cautions.

There are two primary reasons for this pattern. First, the lenient treatment of unfair trade practices is due to the structure of the AML itself. As discussed in

Chapter 4, Section 19 of the AML does not allow the JFTC to levy surcharges even if the case is brought formally. The leniency of the law itself hampers a strict posture by the JFTC. However, the AML does not mandate that unfair trade practices be treated only informally, and on rare occasions the JFTC has chosen to prosecute boycotts formally. This suggests a second explanation: the JFTC deliberately does not prosecute unfair trade practices to the full extent of the law. While the reasons for this may be manifold—ranging from legal doctrine and a particular interpretation of "trade habits", political pressure to protect retailing, and budget constraints that require the JFTC to focus on the seemingly bigger cases—the effect is clearly that self-regulation is not contained forcefully. Given that the application of most self-regulation requires some form of unfair trade practice, this means that self-regulation is treated leniently. A trade association pursuing self-regulation, even with the intent to restrain competition in its market, need not be overly worried about antitrust ramifications in the implementation phase.

Trade Associations and Antitrust Enforcement

To gauge the role of trade associations in self-regulation, one can calculate the relative share and weight of association cases in antitrust enforcement. Table 5.5 shows the number of trade associations involved in all cases over time, as well as the average number of firms implicated per case. Next, Table 5.6 divides all formal cases into those involving associations versus all others, and groups them by industry, thereby highlighting that trade associations are important vehicles for cooperation not only for small-firm industries but also in sectors dominated by large firms.

First, analyzing Table 5.5, the data reveal that 50% of all cases brought formally by the JFTC involve associations. In the U.S., only about 30% of all cases brought by the government involve trade associations (Greer 1993: 125). The high degree of trade association involvement in the 1950s and 1960s is striking (with, on average, 77% of all cases relating to collusion through associations). That is, when the JFTC prosecuted hardly any formal cases, most cases were directed at trade associations. Over time, however, the percentage dropped, until the 1990s, when only about one-third of all cases involved associations, comparable to the U.S. Yet, the average number of firms implicated in cases not involving associations increased from four in the 1960s to 14 in the 1980s and 1990s. In particular, in the early 1990s the number of firms per case quadrupled from an average of five to an average of 22 firms.

This increase in the number of firms per case can be explained by two concurrent forces. The JFTC decides whether to bring a case against an association or against a group of firms based on the role played by the association in the collusive agreement and the evidence at hand. The first reason for the increase in Section 3 cases (which implicate individual firms) is the stark increase in construction *dangō* cases in the 1990s. *Dangō* cases often cannot be prosecuted as

Table 5.5. Number of Formal Cases Involving Trade Associations and Average Number of Firms per Case, 1947–1996

Year	Cases with trade associations	Total number of cases	% of cases with assoc.	5-year avg.	10-year avg.	Average number of firms per case	5-year avg.	10-year avg.
1947	3	5	60			18		
1948	0	2	0			10		
1949	8	14	57	41		14	11.47	
1950	17	59	29			4		
1951	11	18	61		41%	11		9.16
1952	6	15	40			7		
1953	8	12	67			4		
1954	1	5	20	41		17	6.86	
1955	3	11	27			4		
1956	3	6	50			3		
1957	4	7	57			7		
1958	2	2	100			0		
1959	1	2	50	75		1	1.80	
1960	1	1	100			0		
1961	2	3	67		77%	1		3.02
1962	11	13	85			1		
1963	27	36	75			3		
1964	20	30	67	79		13	4.24	
1965	22	27	81			3		
1966	15	17	88			1		
1967	6	12	50			2		
1968	22	31	71			6		
1969	24	32	75	76		3	4.86	
1970	40	44	91			6		
1971	34	37	92		54%	7		5.83
1972	13	34	38			5		
1973	33	69	48			8		
1974	11	60	18	33		9	6.79	
1975	11	34	32			5		
1976	7	25	28			7		
1977	11	18	61			3		
1978	2	8	25			2		
1979	11	15	73	53		11	5.83	
1980	11	16	69			7		
1981	5	13	38		41%	6		4.93
1982	6	20	30			4		
1983	2	12	17			5		
1984	5	9	56	28		7	4.04	
1985	3	17	18			1		
1986	1	5	20			3		
1987	5	6	83			1		
1988	0	6	0			10		
1989	6	10	60	42		7	5.36	
1990	7	17	41			4		
1991	7	29	24		35%	6		13.49
1992	10	38	26			19		
1993	2	30	7			21		
1994	14	25	56	29		23	21.62	
1995	5	20	25			18		
1996	9	30	30			27		
Avg.	9.76	20.14	50					

Source: database built from JFTC Annual Reports, 1948–1997.

Table 5.6. Company Cases vs. Association Cases, by Industry, for Formal Cases, 1947–1996

Industry	Single/multiple firm cases	Industry association cases	All formal cases
Food & drinks	45	80	125
Chemicals	84	36	120
Construction	62	31	93
Kiln	40	36	76
Mining/petroleum	7	67	74
Tools & misc. goods	45	25	70
Paper & pulp	21	43	64
Others	16	39	55
Gas/propane gas	10	30	40
General machinery	28	7	35
Small services	3	31	34
Textiles	21	10	31
Electrical machinery	21	4	25
Iron & steel	22	1	23
Newspaper	13	10	23
Precision machinery	12	7	19
Transportation machinery	14	2	16
Transportation & storage	7	9	16
Pharmaceuticals	10	4	14
Retailing	12	1	13
Commercial banking	7	0	7
Metals	5	2	7
Marine transportation	2	5	7
Investment banking	5	0	5
Distribution	3	2	5
Insurance	2	1	3
Telecommunications	0	3	3
Trucking	0	2	2
Energy	0	1	1
Port management	1	0	1
Grand total	518	489	1007

Source: calculated from database built from JFTC Annual Reports, 1948–1997.

association cases because the predesignation system of public bidding predetermines the companies allowed to an auction. Even if the *dangō* usually occurs in the association, the group of bidders is not typically an exact match with all association members. If not all members of the association are involved, the JFTC has to prosecute all firms individually. Thus, the data shift toward more individual company cases, even though the role of the association remains critical.

Second, the shift to more firms per case may be related to the new Guidelines on Trade Associations that the JFTC issued in 1995 in an attempt to halt the widespread increase both in self-regulation and flagrant AML violations by trade associations (JFTC 1995). However, instead of changing behavior, it seems that the Guidelines have simply led many associations to be more cautious in keeping minutes or filing reports of meetings. While until the 1980s the JFTC could more easily find evidence of collusion in associations than for individual firms, the reverse may be true now. For instance, during interviews with various trade associations in 1995, I asked "What impact have the new Guidelines had on your behavior?" In response, a representative of the core association of an industry long suspected of price agreements explained: "Not much. We've hired a lawyer so that we don't inadvertently write things down that could be used against us." In contrast, a representative of another large trade association explained:

Oh, this Guideline has had an impact on us. Now we cannot do the things we used to do any more, such as kicking a company out of the association that doesn't get along well (*tsukiai ga warui kata*), or agreeing on the discount of the sticker price that all companies allow their retailers to offer. We can't discuss these things in the directors' meetings any more. Now they have to discuss them in subcommittees.[19]

Considered together, these developments suggest that the relative decrease in association cases does not so much indicate a decline in agreements by association member firms, as they highlight a change in the JFTC's stance and more guarded behavior by the trade associations.

Yet, the high number of formal cases involving trade associations over time alone does not indicate the relative importance of associations in the process of collusion. For instance, if all association cases pertained to small industries such as *tōfu-* or *tatami*-makers, then their relevance for the national economy would be rather low, and by extension, the role of trade associations could be considered minor. To control for this possibility, Table 5.6 breaks down trade association cases by industry, and compares it with multiple- or single-firm cases. While small industries account for a high proportion of all association cases, such as food and drinks and small services (e.g., hairdressers and dry cleaners), they are not alone. Large firms in the highly industrialized sectors, too, get caught colluding through their associations. The leaders in this group include the chemicals and kiln industries, paper and pulp, and in particular mining/petroleum. Thus, we can conclude that not only are trade associations more frequently involved in collusion than, for instance, in the U.S., but there is also no particular pattern across industries of such involvement. Most industries, broadly defined, have at one point or another been caught colluding through their trade association.

Finally, the database allows for one additional analysis of whether there is a bias in the JFTC's enforcement such that unfair trade practices—even if found to have led to restraints of competition—are not prosecuted with the strictest possible means. Such a bias can be revealed by looking at how the JFTC has chosen to prosecute different types of violation over time. Table 5.7 groups all formal cases into nine different types of transgression, such as price fixing or

---

[19] Interviews, Tokyo, summer 1995.

Table 5.7. All Formal Cases, 1947–1996, by Section of Law and Type of Violation

	Section 3	Section 8	Section 19	Others*	Labeling Law	**Total**
Price fixing	196	309	4	14		**523**
Dangō	76	37		1		**114**
Other cartels	9	17	3	3		**32**
Retail price maintenance	4	22	47			**73**
Boycotts	18	84	64	3		**169**
Monopoly				1		**1**
Gifts	16	3	12	39		**70**
Protest				7		**7**
Labeling				1	17	**18**
Total	**319**	**472**	**130**	**69**	**17**	**1007**

Source: calculated from database built from JFTC Annual Reports, 1948–1997.
* Others = other sections of the AML that rule gift-giving, international agreements, etc.

boycotts, and shows under which of the major sections of the AML pertaining to collusion and self-regulation the JFTC chose to prosecute these. The table shows that 47% of all cases relate to Section 8 (associations), 32% are cartel cases under the strict Section 3, and 13% of the cases fall under the lenient Section 19. Moreover, 59% of all price-fixing cases (309 out of 523) were prosecuted under Section 8, as were 50% of all cases involving boycotts and other unfair trade practices. Focusing in on the important issue of how strictly unfair trade practices are prosecuted, we see that only 11% of all boycott cases (18 of 169) were treated under Section 3. Retail price maintenance, although often used to implement price-fixing agreements, was mostly covered by the inconsequential Section 19 (64% of all cases); only 5% of retail price violations were treated as cartels.

Thus, the data in Table 5.7 support the overall findings of this chapter. Trade associations are involved in more than half of all formal boycott cases. Most of the unfair trade practices, and in particular retail price maintenance, are not formally prosecuted. To the extent that these practices are addressed, they are dealt with under the most lenient section of the AML. The JFTC's record of formally adjudicated cases suggests that Japan's legal doctrine is indulgent overall (as seen from a comparison of the total number of cases in the U.S. and Japan), and particularly generous in regard to self-regulation. Japan's antitrust enforcement track record suggests that self-regulation is not effectively deterred.

5.2. Case Analysis: Self-Regulation that is not Prosecuted

The analysis of antitrust cases is necessarily restricted to those activities that the JFTC has identified as violations. To complete the picture of self-regulation in

Japan, we must also look at those activities that the JFTC regards as "normal" and therefore does not prosecute, even if they may result in reduced competition. The analysis of examples and case studies is divided into two parts. It begins with examples of self-regulation across various industries, grouped by the underlying objectives of self-regulation. This is followed by case studies of the financial services industries that highlight extensive self-regulation, both administrative and collusive, in a group of industries that the JFTC has treated with benign neglect. The primary sources of information for case studies in self-regulation in the 1990s are the JFTC's consultation cases for 1995 and 1996 (JFTC 1996a, 1997), supplemented by newspaper accounts.

Protective Self-Regulation: Stabilizing Profits over Time

The most obvious way in which companies self-regulate to stabilize profits over time is to curtail competition and fix prices when faced with changes in the industry's environment, such as through a recession, a regulatory change, or import competition due to trade liberalization. At such times, companies are often willing to cooperate even if the agreement imposes limits on expansion for the future. Because it is illegal, price maintenance usually takes intricate forms, such as a fee or accounting schedule, a joint sales company with uniform prices, or standardized contracts.

For instance, in 1996 a regional cooperative consisting of small trucking companies specializing in the transportation of gravel and sand approached the JFTC with a request concerning a standard retail price system. The 1994 revision of the Road Transportation Law (*Dōrō kōtsu hō*) introduced stricter limits on overloads that increased the companies' operating costs. When some companies began selling sand and gravel at very low prices, they triggered a price collapse in the region. The cooperative took action and decided to introduce a minimum retail price system to halt the cutthroat competition: everyone had to agree to charge at least the minimum price for sand and gravel. The JFTC advised against this action (JFTC 1997: 14). While we do not know the industry's reaction to the JFTC advice in these consultation cases, it is very likely that the cooperative ultimately introduced some measure to support the industry.

This case hints at an underlying "knee-jerk" reaction to crisis that may strike one as strange: rather than letting some companies go bankrupt and thus increase market share and profit over time, the companies cooperated to ensure that all of them could remain solvent. A regional association of mahjong club owners provides another example of this attitude. Mahjong is an originally Chinese game based on small pictograph stones and dice, which in many ways assumes the social and functional equivalent role of poker in the U.S.; there are playing clubs all over the country where four players are matched and bet on their luck. These clubs are regulated by the "Law Regarding the Appropriate Management and Rules Relating to Business Affecting Public Morals" (*Fuzoku eigyō-tō no kisei oyobi gyōmu no tekiseika-tō ni kan suru hōritsu*), which required disclosure of fees and, as of 1996, set the maximum mahjong playing fee for one hour per person at ¥620.[20] In one area, competition had driven down fees to only 70–80% of the allowed maximum charge, and with the number of customers decreasing due to the recession, club owners found themselves in dire straits. The local association of mahjong club owners decided that, rather than let some of their own members go bankrupt, they would all raise their fees to the legal limit; the association would print out a price schedule and every member would post it in his club. The JFTC rejected the proposal and argued that even when a law prescribes a maximum fee limit, companies in that industry still must determine their own prices within the legal limits (JFTC 1996a: 28).

In terms of self-regulation this case is revealing for two reasons. First, it shows that while not all Japanese industries find it easy to collude on price, during recession they can often muster sufficient agreement to cooperate. The logic was that if all kept a certain number of clients, all could remain in business even with below average attendance if they all charged higher fees. Second, the story raises the interesting question of why all agreed to forming this cartel, rather than at least one of them trying to attract all players to his club with low fees, and then earn monopoly rents after the competitors had exited the market. One answer lies in the maximum price limit per player imposed on the industry by law, which reduced the attractiveness of breaking the cartel by limiting future payoffs. Moreover, the Mahjong case highlights a more general attitude that bankruptcies seemingly have to be avoided even at significant costs. Cutthroat competition during this period of severe recession would have bankrupted some mahjong clubs, maybe unnecessarily, since during boom years they all face more demand than they can accommodate. Whether driven by an attempt to maintain employment in the neighborhood, or to maintain a positive reputation as an industry and as individual businessmen, the mahjong club owners decided to pass on part of the burden of recession to their customers rather than driving some of their competitors into bankruptcy.

The All Japan Neon Sign Association (*Zen Nihon neon kyōkai*) is another case in point. This association consists of small-sized companies that design, install, run, and maintain commercial neon signs. In 1995, the association conducted a survey of its members to gauge the impact of the recession and the association's appropriate role in the 1990s. As expected, the small member firms were all facing an average decrease in sales and profits of over 20% as compared to the

---

[20] Japan has had many laws that prescribe maximum fees on goods and services; the best-known is the "Temporary Interest Rate Adjustment Law" of 1947 which set a maximum cap for the margin of certain interest rates over the Bank of Japan's official discount rate. The objective with such maximum caps differs by industry: while in finance, the goal was to lower the cost of borrowing for the manufacturing industry, presumably the objective in mahjong club regulation was to ensure that gambling was kept in reasonable bounds by limiting the profit margins of the club owners. Other industries subject to price caps through industry laws include hairdressers and public bath houses (through the "Hygiene Law") and transportation (taxis, trucking and shipping).

previous year. In response to what the association should do in this distressing situation, many members voiced a request that the association should assume stronger leadership and introduce a policy of uniform price schedules, a joint order and sales system, and joint marketing (ZNNK 1995: 25). Small companies' immediate reaction to a recession was to cooperate; the fact that they published this idea in their association's circular only highlights their limited awareness of antitrust restrictions.

Not all self-regulation is initially designed to be collusive. However, sometimes associations run into difficulties when monitoring compliance, and then have to craft additional agreements to enforce the initial one. In this way, self-regulation often begets more self-regulation, and sometimes administrative self-regulation begets protective self-regulation. For instance, in 1995 an association of manufacturers of water supply equipment (such as specially reinforced plastic pipes) realized that their members were undercutting the association's "price indication" system. It was an established "trade habit" in this industry for each company to quote a base price (*tatene*), but during the recession in the early 1990s companies had begun to undercut their own price quotations. The association argued that the price indication system was a service to buyers because it simplified price comparison with substitute products such as stainless steel pipes; hence, the collapse of the price quote system was detrimental to the buyers. The association therefore suggested that the system be reinstated by obliging every member to keep actual prices as close as possible to the quotation. The JFTC was unconvinced by the argument that the buyers, which were large construction companies, needed to be protected and advised that such a scheme would probably be illegal (JFTC 1996a: 12). Still, this case is indicative of the default approach to "price stabilization". A "base price quote" system is designed, and members' adherence to their own quotations is closely monitored; if the system collapses, the association reconvenes to structure a new agreement.

Deregulation can also trigger self-regulation aimed to stabilize profits over time. One example in this category involves a small, regional association of trucking companies. The fee schedules for the trucking business are outlined in the "Law for the Freight Trucking Business" (*Kamotsu jidōsha unsō jigyō hō*). A 1990 revision of this law had turned the former licensing system with a fixed fee schedule into a notification system under which each trucking company has to determine its own fees competitively. Whereas before, truckers could charge by weight and distance according to a prescribed rate, after deregulation they had to negotiate price with the freight shippers, who typically had bargaining power over the small truckers. In addition, new limits on overloads and increases in toll fees and gasoline taxes had driven the truckers' costs up significantly. To stabilize the foundations of the trucking business in the area, the association argued, it was necessary to launch a campaign among its members "to collect fees properly" (JFTC 1996a: 29). The JFTC advised that if the association introduced its own fee prescriptions leading to the same results as the former law, this would be a violation of the AML.

Thus, both recession and deregulation can mobilize associations to consider and reach price agreements. The fact that the JFTC consults on hundreds of price agreement requests every year suggests that associations consider it quite "normal" to discuss pricing matters when faced with changes in their business environment. Prior to deregulation, many industries were subjected to formal or informal rules on their fee structures and thus income, which provided for a stable business environment protected from price competition. With the phasing out of these rules, these industries began to face price competition to which they were not accustomed, and one immediate reaction by the incumbent firms in many industries was to curb price competition by replacing the former ministerial rules with self-regulation. In this way, by introducing a more competitive environment, deregulation triggered greater efforts at self-regulation to maintain the previous patterns of stable prices. Likewise, recession invited cooperation to stabilize prices; the costs of lower profits through stable market shares were often considered less than the benefits of stable, if lower, profits. The confluence of deregulation and recession in the 1990s thus fed into the surge in self-regulation across all industries.

Administrative Self-Regulation: Standardization and Market Rules

Administrative self-regulation has as its core activity the formulation of rules and standards among a group of companies, with the immediate goal of increasing the bargaining power of the association's members vis-à-vis large customers or increasing the industry's quality level. However, it is the case that the more homogeneous the product, the easier it is to self-regulate or collude on price or other issues (see Chapter 6 for a detailed discussion). Thus, standardizing the product or service also facilitates other forms of self-regulation, including on price.

For example, in 1996 an association of construction machinery manufacturers developed a plan to make their end products more homogeneous, presumably to help self-regulation. The manufacturers, who bought parts from general part makers for assembly, faced the problem that parts differed in specifications and thus were not easily interchangeable. The association therefore suggested the formulation of standards for the parts, which would both increase the convenience and cost-efficiency for the end user in case of repairs and lower manufacturing costs for the assemblers. Naturally, the resulting assembled product would also be more homogeneous. The association argued that the industry was not subject to rapid technological change, so that standards would not hamper innovation, and that there was significant competition among the part makers; the JFTC found no unfair trade problem with this proposal (JFTC 1997: 16).

In a similar move, in 1996 an association consisting of large- and medium-sized electronic parts manufacturers moved to standardize the boxes in which they shipped their parts. The companies realized that they sold 80% of their output through dealers. The dealers had to handle more than 100 different kinds of boxes, which increased transportation and storage costs. The association therefore designed boxes of uniform sizes that did not have an imprint of the manufacturers' logo and thus could be reused; also, uniform packaging allowed joint distribution by the various manufacturers. The JFTC found that the packaging had no impact on competition as long as the agreement was not used to boycott nonmembers, and gave the association a green light (JFTC 1997: 18). Yet, while this move was efficiency-enhancing in many ways, it also caused a potential threat of restraint of competition. First, with homogenization of the product and virtually identical packaging, price collusion was largely simplified. Second, the agreement disadvantaged importers and other nonmembers of the association who did not have access to the same packaging materials and therefore were likely to be shunned by the dealers. In general, standardization is beneficial if price competition and market access can be assured; given Japan's track record in dealing with unfair trade practices, it remains unclear whether the JFTC could in fact contain a development toward more self-regulation based on standardization.

In addition to increasing homogenization, standards are often used to increase the credibility of an entire industry by ensuring certain levels of quality and safety. However, like other standards, quality requirements can easily be used as entry barriers or to ease price agreements. For example, the introduction of the Product Liability Law (*Seizōbutsu sekinin hō; PL hō*) in 1995 triggered a move by the association representing manufacturers of door shutters to guard against liability suits. The association introduced new safety features as minimum standards, and agreed to pass the additional costs on to the buyer. The JFTC found the safety standards permissible, but advised that the price agreement resulted in an antitrust violation (JFTC 1996a: 19).

It is indeed quite common for associations to use basic safety standards to "piggyback" an additional rule, such as on price, into the agreement. A further example in this category involves the association of manufacturers of refrigeration and air-conditioning systems. As one of its functions, this association performed quality checks beyond the officially established standards in its own inspection facility. This facility was open to members and outsiders, and products that had passed the test received a sticker signaling high quality. In the mid-1990s, the association realized that some tested products were deficient although they had been certified, and many of these deficient products were manufactured by nonmembers. To maintain the signaling power of the sticker system, the association decided to restrict the inspection facility to its members only, and to allow inspectors to investigate the members' facilities and suggest quality improvements. Clearly, the possibility to bar nonmembers from access to the sticker certification could be converted into a powerful barrier to entry if membership to the association was restricted. The JFTC advised that product withdrawal had to be voluntary (JFTC 1996a: 16). Interestingly, the JFTC also alerted the association to a more straightforward solution to the problem: rather than excluding nonmembers, why not revise the inspection system? It is unlikely that this had not occurred to the association, and therefore leads one to conclude that the association's approach of creating barriers to entry rather than revising the inspection process was meant to address something other than protecting consumers from bad products. The concern about quality reputation may well have been just a pretense for excluding nonmember competitors, with the real intention to curb competition in the market for air-conditioners.

A further objective of administrative self-regulation is to protect members from swindlers. In 1995, an association of wholesalers of heat insulation materials moved to protect its members from dishonest customers by creating a blacklist. The association consisted of large- and medium-sized firms that sold heat insulation material wrapped around hot water pipes to small construction companies. Usually, the wholesalers delivered the product and received a check. During the recession of the early 1990s, some cases of fraud occurred in which the small heat insulation company received the material but disappeared before the check could be cashed. In some instances, the company changed the names of its legal representatives so that no one could legally be held accountable; in other cases, it relocated. The wholesalers' association therefore compiled a list of all construction companies specializing in heat insulation, indicating each company's creditworthiness. The JFTC found that such a list created no antitrust problem (JFTC 1997: 27), although the intent of the list was clearly to boycott certain companies.

A regional association of switchboard manufacturers tried to protect its members from price competition by introducing a rule that barred members of the association from selling at discounts. The association consisted of large- and small-scale firms that manufacture small switchboards for industrial use; the customers were mostly companies specializing in electric installation on order from large general contractors in construction. The association found that its members were in a weak bargaining position vis-à-vis the electric equipment firms and contractors who often bought in large volumes and commanded deep discounts, and asked the associations representing the two groups of buyers to exercise self-discipline in their discount requests, especially from the small suppliers. This was unsuccessful, and the switchboard makers' association therefore agreed that no member would accept orders at discount prices, which they understood to be prices below cost. The JFTC advised that the "not below cost" rule could be interpreted as a *de facto* agreement on a minimum price (JFTC 1996a: 10).

Another area where trade associations have increased their self-regulation is in the reform of the *atogime* pricing system. Partially due to government pressure to abolish the habit, and partially due to recession, various industries have moved to replace the previously widespread trade habit of after-sales price adjustment (cf. Chapter 4) with a model contract. For instance, in 1995 the association of PVC pipe manufacturers, which consisted primarily of large-scale firms, moved to revamp the industry's distribution system: selling many different kinds of pipes in small lots at undisclosed and adjusted prices had made the industry very non-transparent. The association developed a "distribution reform plan" to standard-ize the distribution of PVC pipes so that "the user can understand this market better". The association designed a model contract with pre-specified settlement conditions, including shipping conditions (minimum volume, type of shipment, delivery period) and specific routines for determining the price of pipes. In particular, the price of the product had to be firmly established at the time of ordering. The JFTC advised that it might be an antitrust violation to force members to charge fixed fees for certain services, but otherwise approved of the draft (JFTC 1996a: 24). This case is interesting on two counts. First, it suggests that many industries that have so far been characterized by *atogime*, i.e., a highly non-transparent pricing system that creates strong barriers to entry, are moving to self-regulation through model contracts. While these markets may become more transparent, entry barriers are likely to remain strong, since non-members that cannot use the model contract may face boycotts. Thus, a likely next step after deregulation of the *atogime* system is self-regulation through model contracts in intermediate product markets. Second, given this trend toward self-regulation, the reform of the *atogime* system will not make it more difficult for companies to collude on price; quite the opposite, model contracts may invite other agreements.

The PVC pipe case is by no means singular. To list but one other example, an association of special steel distributors and processors consisting mostly of small-sized firms introduced a model contract for its members. The special steel processed by these firms was used mostly in car parts, bearings, metal patterns, and machine tools. Their powerful buyers were accustomed to the old trade habits of ordering frequent small-scale deliveries, asking for specialized orders (a certain polish, etc.) at no extra fee, and after-sales price adjustments. The association moved to improve its members' bargaining power by drafting a "Trade habit reform handbook" (*Shōkankō kaizen tebiki*) which contained a model contract that specified order volume, delivery, payment conditions, and price. The JFTC advised that the model contract was not a problem before the AML as long as member firms were not forced to use it (JFTC 1997: 23). However, the association could easily use this contract to create uniform condi-tions in the industry or suggest a formula to calculate fees. As in the previous case, self-regulation in terms of standardized contracts is a likely substitute for the *atogime* system. In Chapter 6, we will look at the effects of product homo-genization on self-regulation; the data suggest that there is a very strong increase in the likelihood of self-regulation if the product becomes more homogeneous. Understanding this, associations are homogenizing their products and trade conditions to ease self-regulation for protection in the face of continuing deregulation.

Industry Case Study I: Self-Regulation in Investment Banking

While the previous examples suggest that self-regulation is widespread in manufacturing and small services, one industry where deregulation has triggered a particularly discernible increase in self-regulation is finance, including investment banking, commercial banking, and the insurance industry. Japan's regulatory environment, with its emphasis on entry restrictions and informal process regulation, has led to a bias toward self-protection by financial institutions at the expense of their small clients, and this tendency was one cause of the financial crisis of the 1990s. The financial sector continues to be subject to various regulatory changes; the following case analysis pertains to the period up to 1998.

In investment banking, governments in many countries delegate regulatory responsibility to the industry itself. For instance, in the U.S., the Securities and Exchange Act specifies so-called "self-regulatory organizations", such as registered stock exchanges and trade associations, that are in charge of designing and implementing rules on advertising, customer services, trading, and brokering. The most important of these is probably the National Association of Securities Dealers (NASD). The law is very specific in how the U.S. Securities and Exchange Commission and other appropriate regulatory agencies can supervise this self-regulation.

In Japan, the Japanese SEL (Securities and Exchange Law, *Shōken torihiki-hō*), which was modeled after the U.S. law in 1949, delegates to the Japanese Association of Securities Dealers (JASD, *Nihon Shōkengyō kyōkai*) critical functions such as formulating and monitoring rules on business ethics, stock market trading, etc. (Kanzaki 1987). During the postwar period, and especially after the takeoff of the bond and stock markets with financial liberalization beginning in the 1980s, Japanese investment banks held close ties with the Ministry of Finance (MOF) which frequently used administrative guidance to regulate the industry. This had two systemic effects. First, while there were no independent supervisory agencies, MOF's micro-management meant that the JASD's self-regulation was not autonomous; rather, the close, informal contacts made formal supervision superfluous in MOF's mind. Second, the tight relationship and overlapping interests made MOF look like a much more influential and powerful player than it was; when the system changed in the 1990s, it became clear that MOF could not in fact supervise this industry forcefully. The 1993 revision of the SEL, which came in reaction to stock market scandals and grave regulatory failure, brought a shift of the Japanese environment toward highly independent self-regulation through the JASD. As a result, since 1993 the JASD in Japan has been legally empowered to self-regulate much more independently than the NASD in the U.S.

This shift toward self-regulation was triggered by the 1993 Financial Reform Law (*Kinyū seido kaikaku hō*) which abolished, in principle, the "firewall" between investment and commercial banking by allowing cross-entry for banks and securities firms.[21] MOF initially ensured regulatory control over this process by, first, issuing licenses for entry into either market segment, and then subjecting the licensing process to numerous requirements with the idea to phase in deregulation slowly (Vogel, S. 1996). Nonetheless, the legal change made entry possible, and the number of total members of the JASD doubled from 256 in 1992 to 527 in 1995. Together with the Financial Reform Law, the SEL had been amended to allow banks to deal in securities and to define the regulatory and self-regulatory functions of the JASD. But before analyzing the JASD's new role, we need to briefly consider the concurrent subplot of the stock market scandals of the early 1990s.

The "bubble economy" ended in 1991, and while there is some debate over why and when, exactly, it ended, one factor that undoubtedly contributed to the sudden fall in the stock market was the securities scandal that broke in June 1991 (cf. Figure 5.7). When the bubble took off, after currency adjustments between the U.S. and Japan through the Plaza Accord of 1985, Japan was in the midst of a financial deregulation program that included phased-in interest rate liberalization and the introduction of new financial products in commercial and investment banking. Deregulation opened the doors for new options in corporate finance, including corporate bonds and the stock market. After years of keeping their savings mostly in commercial banks' deposit accounts, households discovered the stock market as an investment alternative. Of course, the "bubble expansion" was not without bumps, above all the October 1987 stock market crash.[22] At the time, MOF's primary concern was to keep the stock market up, mainly because it was in the process of privatizing large portions of NTT (Nippon Telephone and Telecommunications) and had already penciled the proceeds of selling NTT shares at high prices into the budget for the fiscal year. MOF therefore invited the "Big 4" investment banks—Nomura, Daiwa, Nikko, and Yamaichi—for tea at the ministry during the lunch break of October 20, and the Tokyo Stock Exchange closed its afternoon session of that day on an uptick, due to concerted buying by the large four brokerage houses of NTT stock. This incident was widely reported in the press as a testimony of Japan's financial process. However, it also undermined MOF's regulatory authority vis-à-vis the investment banks: according to the unwritten rules of administrative guidance (*quid pro quo*), the ministry now owed the industry.

The 1987 crash had also brought the message home to large investors that their stock market investments were not secure. Japan's securities firms, meanwhile, felt invincible and began to "guarantee" the principal, and often even a certain

---

[21] This "wall" was prescribed in Section 65 of the old SEL and was similar to the U.S. Glass–Steagall Act. By the 1980s, this legislation had become outdated in both countries, as new financial instruments allowed banks to circumvent the restriction; Japan moved first in abolishing the rule in 1993.

[22] On Monday, October 19, 1987, the Dow Jones Industrial Index lost 508 points, which was a decline of 22.8% and marked the deepest single day fall in the history of the NYSE so far. The waves of this drop swept around the world. The Tokyo Stock Exchange, too, opened in distress on October 20, 1987 and recorded a fall of 14.9% on that day; see Schaede (1991) for an analysis of the events surrounding the October 1987 crash.

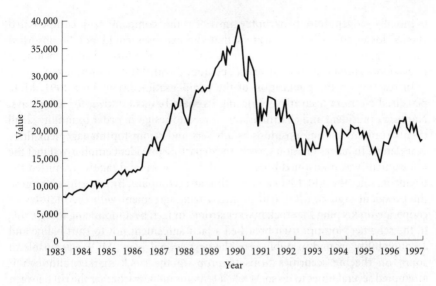

Figure 5.7. The Nikkei 225 Stock Index, 1983–1996

Source: created from Daiwa Sōken 1997.

return on the invested amount, of their most important clients by promising compensation of eventual losses. While this was probably a breach of advertising ethics, as it meant luring customers into the stock market under false pretenses, it was not illegal before Japanese law. Still, in 1989 MOF issued an administrative guidance disallowing compensation payments, but was ignored. In 1990 and 1991, Japan's securities companies paid out compensations to big clients totaling more than ¥200 billion (*Juristo*, November 1, 1991, p. 7).

In fact, compensations had occasionally been paid to large clients even through the 1980s. In those years, the securities firms had financed the payments through "churning" of small customers' accounts, i.e., unauthorized, frequent trades to produce commission income. Because brokerage commissions were regulated by law and set at comparatively high levels, securities firms could increase their profits by simply increasing trading frequency. However, by 1991 the volume of stock traded on the Tokyo Stock Exchange had dropped from an average daily volume of more than 1,000 million shares in 1988 to only 93 million shares. Since commission income accounted for more than 50% of the securities firms' revenues, they faced steep declines in profits just when their large clients were requesting compensations for their investment losses. Desperate to salvage the situation, the securities firms began to write the compensation payments off their taxes as "business expenses". The scandal broke in June 1991, when the tax authorities disallowed the tax scheme and *Yomiuri Shinbun*, the largest daily newspaper, published a list of "VIP clients" and the total amount of compensations they had allegedly received from all investment banks. Nomura Securities and Yamaichi Securities were clearly at the top of the list. Yamaichi Securities was eventually driven into bankruptcy in 1997: the company had compensated clients' losses to such high degrees that the expenses could not be absorbed into the regular accounting of the firm. Therefore, the losses had been hidden in accounts abroad for several years, apparently with MOF connivance.

In reaction to the publication of the compensation list in June 1991, MOF penalized Nomura Securities by closing its main branches down for a few days. Nomura's president and chairman were forced to resign in order to mollify small clients (only to assume positions as advisers and rejoin top management three years later). In his resignation speech, the departing president emphasized that the punishment was unjustified because MOF had known and tacitly permitted the payments since the mid-1980s and was thus an accomplice. By punishing Nomura, the president argued, MOF had broken a tacit agreement with the industry to cooperate on keeping the stock market strong. In fact, by announcing MOF's role in the scheme, Nomura itself breached a tacit agreement not to shift blame and accountability around in public. For the next several years, MOF was unable to count on the big securities firms to prop up the stock market, although it attempted several times to do so. While it remains unclear whether the rift between Nomura Securities and MOF was just a show put on to appease the public, the scandal painfully exposed MOF's inability to regulate the large securities firms.

The 1991 scandals highlight the dark side of self-regulation in investment banking. While MOF may have known about various maneuvers and machinations, it could not stop them, partially because neither the compensation payments nor the churning of small investors' accounts were, strictly speaking, illegal. These areas were covered by self-regulation, and the JASD was in charge of monitoring their members' behavior. When the scandals broke, collusion also became apparent, as Japan's big four securities had occasionally cooperated in driving up certain stocks or maintaining stock prices for mutual VIP clients.[23]

Interestingly, the response to these problems was to introduce legal reforms that gave the securities firms more self-regulatory power. As mentioned before, the Financial Reform Law of 1993 and the restructuring of the "firewall" between commercial and investment banking necessitated changes in the Securities and Exchange Law. After long discussions, the revised SEL stipulated that the JASD was to become a "licensed incorporated entity" (*ninka hōjin*) officially in charge of self-regulation.[24] In his introduction to the 1994 JASD Annual Report, JASD

---

[23] As a result of these discoveries, in 1995 the *Shōken dantai kyōgikai* ("*Shōdankyō*", Conference for Securities Associations), an industry group believed to have been the venue for these agreements, was quietly dissolved. The *Shōdankyō* used to be an "interest alignment institution" (*chōsei dantai*) for the large firms in the securities industry. It was merged with the Securities Research Institute (*Shōken keizai kenkyūsho*) where the staff took over the task of publishing the "yellow report", a monthly publication containing statistics and overview reports on Japan's securities industry. For a full account of the securities scandal of 1991, see Nakazawa/Tachiyama (1991), SCG (1991); Kurihara (1991) discusses the relationship between MOF and Nomura Securities.

[24] This is different from the legal standing of a *shadan hōjin*, as described in Chapter 2. The *shadan hōjin* also receives a license from its competent ministry, but the legal specifications are different (in general, less demanding) than that for a *ninka hōjin*.

chairman Doi Sadakane praised the revision as a "complete fulfilment of our self-regulation functions" (*"jishu kisei kinō no jūjitsu"*). As a *ninka hōjin*, the JASD has seven primary responsibilities:

1. The design and implementation of self-regulation concerning all aspects of investment banking business and stock market trading (e.g., stock trading, underwriting, bonds trading, investment advice, standards for employee uniforms, advertisements);
2. self-regulation of all business aspects related to the over-the-counter markets;
3. monitoring of all members' compliance with self-regulation through inspection of books (on top of inspections by MOF and the Bank of Japan of income statements);
4. "complaint handling", i.e., maintaining a telephone service desk for questions and complaints by stock market investors;
5. educational seminars for members' employees (e.g., in 1995, 22 courses were held on customer advertising, stock market rules, insider trading rules, business ethics, etc.);
6. management support for members, including advice on bookkeeping and accounting;
7. market research and consultation of members on foreign securities markets and their regulatory environments.

This list suggests that the JASD became a full-fledged self-regulatory body. The only critical business area not included in this list is the determination of brokerage fees, which for many years were described by MOF designation, but after a step-wise process were fully deregulated in October 1999. Although the JASD continues to be bound by the parameters of the SEL in its self-regulation, it is quite independent from MOF in implementing and monitoring its rules. Even when the JASD finds a member to be in violation of JASD self-regulation, it tries to keep MOF out of the process as much as possible, unless it detects truly criminal behavior.[25] MOF remains the cognizant ministry and as such is in charge of supervising banks. This is aimed at ensuring that banks remain within the confines of the legal and reasonable in their self-regulation.

However, the crucial missing factor is a specialized, independent supervisory agency, such as the Securities and Exchange Commission in the U.S. The absence of official process regulation vastly empowers the JASD. While the new Financial Supervisory Agency began to assume some functions of disclosure and trade inspection in 1997, the ultimate process-monitoring institution is the JASD itself.[26] The Financial Reform Law deregulated the investment industry in the

---

[25] Interview, JASD, Tokyo, September 1995. For a complete overview of JASD self-regulation, see JASD (1995).
[26] The Financial Supervisory Agency will be discussed in the next section on commercial banks. After the 1991 scandals, a "Securities Exchange Surveillance Commission" (SESC, *Shōken torihiki-tō*

sense that it abolished the "firewall" in banking by 1998. Moreover, a 1999 revision of the Securities and Exchange Law prescribed a switch from the previous licensing requirement for securities firms to a simple requirement to register with the MOF. This eliminated the last vestiges of MOF leverage through entry regulation and administrative guidance, and it further increased the investment industry's latitude in self-regulation.

Industry Case Study II: Self-Regulation and "Self-Disclosure" in Insurance and Commercial Banking

While the JASD's legal standing as an independent self-regulating agency differentiates the investment banking industry from all others, similar trends toward creating institutions of self-regulation can be observed in the life and non-life insurance industries. Insurance companies have long been regulated and protected, yet highly self-regulatory. Through the mid-1990s, premium payments and contract specifications were kept uniform by industry agreement, bolstered by a requirement that all contract changes needed MOF approval. This system eliminated most price and product competition in the industry. In addition, while MOF actively issued administrative guidance, the industry's largest companies were usually directly involved in designing, implementing and monitoring this guidance (Maya 1993, Lake 1998: 121). Deregulation in the 1990s eventually allowed cross-entry between the life and non-life insurance businesses, and parts of the market were pried open to U.S. firms through the 1994 U.S.–Japan Insurance Agreement. In response, the life insurance industry increased its efforts at self-regulation. Substituting self-regulation for previous government rules, incumbent firms upheld many of the most effective barriers to entry.

One of the most important tools of self-regulation for insurance companies was created by way of an industry-organized fund analog to "deposit insurance" for commercial banks. In commercial banking, deposit insurance is a government-run insurance scheme to guarantee up to ¥10 million of deposits; should an insured bank fail, the insurance will reimburse depositors up to that amount. Under the regulated regime, Japanese law had guaranteed life insurance customers the return of their principal in case of insolvency by a life insurance company. However, pursuant to the 1994 agreement with the U.S., the Insurance Law (*Hokengyō-hō*) was amended in June 1995, and the new law no longer

---

kanshi iinkai) was established as an appendix to MOF with the task of monitoring stock trades for insider trading and other violations of stock market rules. However, the SESC was not endowed with independent regulatory powers. Keehn (1998: 212) described the SESC as part of a system that is "the regulatory equivalent of virtual reality. Regulatory agencies appear on government charts, but they do not have independence and generally are subservient to the strategies of the economic bureaucracies." In 1997, the SESC became part of the newly established Financial Supervisory Agency, as discussed below.

includes a public guarantee of the principal. To increase creditworthiness of the industry, the Life Insurance Association of Japan (*Seimei hoken kyōkai*) created a "life insurance customer protection fund" (*hoken keiyakusha hogo kikin*). In case of bankruptcy, this fund ensures payments and allows for the transfer of contracts to solvent insurance companies; the "white knight" companies receive reimbursements from the fund to cover losses. The fund is recognized as a *kōeki hōjin* (public entity) under the law, with the life insurers' association as its official administrator.

The idea for this fund is not unique. For instance, the investment banking industry created an "indemnification fund" (*itaku shōken hoshō kikin*) as early as 1969, and after the 1993 revision of the SEL it substantially revised the fund's rules and increased its capital to ¥30 billion in 1994. What is important about these funds is that they represent the replacement of government by private initiative in serving as the ultimate bailout organization. This undermined administrative guidance toward the industry: losing the "carrot" of bailing out defunct institutions greatly undercuts the government's informal regulatory leverage. More important still, the funds can be employed to create barriers to entry into the industry. In 1995, the Life Insurance Association asked for JFTC consultation regarding membership in the fund: would it be a problem if the associations denied fund membership to newly emerging firms that are not strongly capitalized and thus pose a risk for the group? In other words, can the association use fund membership as a condition for entry, and then proscribe membership to the fund? The JFTC found that disallowing entry to a weak company was a reasonable conduct that would not inhibit competition (JFTC 1996a: 27). Thus, the association now administers a fund where membership signals creditworthiness and is thus a prerequisite for successful entry to the market, and at the same time the association judges who may join the fund. Deregulation led to delegating the administration of a bailout fund to the association, which in turn increased self-regulation in the industry.

Commercial banking, too, has been characterized by active self-regulation for many years. The ultimate umbrella organization of all banks is the Federation of Bankers' Associations (*Zenginkyō*). *Zenginkyō* has always had a major influence on the rules and regulations of commercial banking, and has long been an active lobbyist and rule administrator (e.g., Rosenbluth 1989). With the progress in financial deregulation in the 1990s, its role in guiding banks' business behavior has increased further still. While commercial banks self-regulate in many areas, ranging from agreements on non-price competition and interest rates to customer allocation, their self-regulation has become particularly notable in terms of disclosure rules during the banking crisis of the 1990s.

Without going into much legal or accounting detail, the system of disclosure rules for banks in the 1980s and 1990s can be summarized as follows.[27] Three

---

[27] For legal details, see Ochiai (1993, 1996), Yanaga (1998). In 1999, the Financial Supervisory Agency created some uniform definitions of a "bad loan" and unified the disclosure rules for purposes of bank inspection.

separate laws contain provisions for disclosure requirements by banks. First, like other companies, banks have to disclose their balance sheets, income statement, and a management report, as prescribed by Section 281(1) of the Commercial Code (*Shōhō*). Second, the Securities and Exchange Law requires that all publicly listed corporations file an Annual Report, the *Yūka shōken hōkokusho* (similar in appearance to the U.S. form 10K). However, because banks differ from manufacturing companies in the logic of assets, etc., they are exempted from most of these rules and instead are governed by special provisions contained in supplements to these laws.[28] Third, large banks are regulated by the Banking Law (*Ginkō-hō*), which requires semiannual business reports to MOF, following details specified in a MOF edict of 1982.

The relevant portion in the Banking Law is Section 21. This section demands an annual "explanatory statement" in which banks "shall publish information on assets and the general business situation for their most important offices". However, Section 21 specifically states that such disclosure is required only if it does not potentially: (1) harm the national credit order; (2) expose private information on customers; (3) inappropriately damage the bank's profits; or (4) be too costly for the bank to obtain. In other words, the law explicitly prescribes that banks should disclose only information that is not harmful to them or their customers. The law does not contain penalty provisions, and disclosure is thus completely voluntary. In fact, the law stresses "self-discipline" to "create public trust", which has been interpreted to mean that any information that could create anxiety among depositors should be withheld. Clearly, these rules do not provide for prudential banking regulation. A legal scholar has labeled the system as one not of information disclosure, but of "information management" (Ochiai 1996: 122).

An example from the 1995 bank crisis highlights the potential pitfalls of this system. As became clear when the crisis unraveled, the "most important offices" in Section 21 were defined as affiliates in which the bank held an interest of more than 5%. When the stock market collapsed in 1991, some banks had begun hiding large portions of their bad loans in small affiliates on which they did not report, and only when they defaulted in 1995 did the full extent of their hidden pockets with garbage loans surface. For instance, when Hyōgo Bank, the largest second-tier regional bank, folded in 1995, its bad loans were initially estimated at ¥1.5 trillion, or about 55% of its total loans. Just a week later it was revealed that the bank's 20 small affiliates held additional bad loans of ¥1.75 trillion; thus, while Hyōgo Bank's total deposits at the time amounted to ¥2.5 trillion, its bad loans topped ¥3.25 trillion (or $30 billion). Similar patterns appeared in the other five banks that were closed down in 1995 (Schaede 1998).

---

[28] The Commercial Code provisions are detailed for banks in a MOF edict (*shōrei*); the latest revision of the edict occurred in 1982. The Securities and Exchange Law, in Section 15, divides businesses into three categories and thus requires different treatment for banks by law; the specifics for the Annual Report can be found in Section 2 of the "Fiscal Disclosure Guidelines" (*Zaimu shohyō kisoku*) which, again, contains separate provisions for banks.

Interestingly, the banks themselves were the first to realize that the legal and MOF-designated disclosure rules were insufficient. In 1987, the members of the *Zenginkyō*, i.e., all Japanese banks, agreed on a set of "unified disclosure standards" to supplement the official requirements (*Zenginkyō tōitsu kaishi kijun*). This was pure self-regulation, and as a result banking disclosure in the 1980s and 1990s in Japan resulted in self-disclosure. Without official prudential regulation and strict disclosure rules, banks only disclosed what they voluntarily agreed to disclose. As a *Zenginkyō* representative explained in 1995:

We have our own guidelines on banking disclosure. This is a kind of self-regulation, although we do not have the power to enforce compliance. The MOF has no itemized list for disclosure; MOF operates on the basis of the Banking Law which simply requires disclosure. But what exactly banks have to disclose has been decided by the trade association, i.e., the *Zenginkyō*. This holds for other business transactions as well, such as the appropriate relation between loans and deposits. The *Zenginkyō* has designed a model ratio, based on research by one of our committees. We cannot enforce these ratios, but they are used as a base guideline. It's not necessary to monitor, anyway. Banks usually follow the association's guidelines voluntarily.

(Interview, Tokyo, September 1995)

In the mid-1990s, after the stock market bubble had burst and the severity of the banking crisis could no longer be denied, large Japanese banks were subjected to the so-called "Japan premium" in international money markets. This risk premium was charged by international lenders to all Japanese banks, reflecting the uncertainty over the situation in Japan as a whole. The "Japan premium" hurt the largest city banks more than any other constituency in the *Zenginkyō*, and the big banks pushed for an overhaul of their own Guidelines. In 1995 the *Zenginkyō* revised its self-disclosure rules by making them stricter and more comprehensive (Zenginkyō 1995).[29] Again, rather than being bound by government regulation, the banks designed their regulatory environment—in the midst of a major financial crisis.

Self-regulation in banking disclosure can easily result in self-protection. To be sure, if banks self-regulate in a system with clearly established, transparent prudential regulation, the banks' complementary activities may increase regulatory efficiency. However, if banks self-regulate in the absence of supervisory regulation, self-regulation will necessarily translate into efforts to protect the banking industry at the expense of other societal interests. To compete successfully in international markets, banks depend on creditworthiness, which rests on the reputation of the domestic regulatory system. During the 1980s, this was not a problem, because it was not apparent to the outside world that Japanese banks were operating in a regulatory vacuum; in fact, it is inconceivable to many even

---

[29] Still, the revision partially reflected the interests of smaller, regional institutions, and thus remained insufficient for signaling on international markets. Subsequently, some of the large city banks decided to temporarily adopt a set of U.S. disclosure standards in an attempt to signal their health, on top of the *Zenginkyō* rules.

within Japan that the country's famed bureaucracy would accept such regulatory slack. When the banking crisis emerged fully, MOF's reaction was to downplay it and wait for a resurgent stock market to make the problem disappear. While widely suspected of cover-ups, the Ministry itself was probably taken by surprise when the full extent of hidden loans and fraudulent schemes, including deals with the *yakuza* (mafia) and bribery, was revealed through the failure of 15 financial institutions in 1995.

When the public became increasingly upset with regulatory negligence, the government determined that it needed a supervisory agency for financial regulation that was separate from MOF and marked a clear break with existing regulation. In 1997, the Financial Supervisory Agency (FSA, *Kinyū kantoku-chō*) was founded with the task of inspecting all financial institutions. Similar to the JFTC, the FSA is part of the Prime Minister's Office, and its chief, below the rank of a ministerial vice-minister, reports to the Head of Cabinet. MOF kept its reign over entry regulation and other regulatory issues, but the FSA assumed the tasks of bank inspection and monitoring of banks' compliance with official rules. The FSA's first assignment was to discover the total amount of bad loans hidden in the banking system by conducting thorough bank inspections. Civil servants from the MOF and the Bank of Japan were transferred to the FSA, but even so the FSA was severely understaffed (Saitō 1997). For instance, when the FSA began its inspections of city banks in 1998, it had enough people to send an average of 12 inspectors to each bank for 20 days. These inspectors had to rely largely on self-disclosure, and it would have been surprising if they had identified all bad loans in such a short period (*Nikkei Weekly*, December 28, 1998).[30]

Moreover, in its first Interim Report of December 1998, the FSA declared that financial institutions "should be run on the principle of self-responsibility, with financial inspection serving as a means of supplementing this", and envisioned "self-management-style inspections" (FSA News Release, December 22, 1998). While the FSA may have envisioned a U.S.-style system of self-regulation under strict official supervision, as of 1998 it had neither the workforce nor the authority to truly set up such a system. Whether Japan's system of financial regulation can change to more transparent supervisory processes remains to be seen. Still, even if the FSA turns out to be successful eventually, self-regulation is designed to remain an integral part of the new system.

Disclosure is only one aspect of self-regulation in the banking industry. Different categories of bank—such as the regional banks, second-tier regional banks, credit unions—all have their own associations in which they meet to self-regulate. For instance, as in the investment banking and insurance industries, small bank associations have created their own "bailout funds". In 1995, when two second-tier regional banks went bankrupt and others were acutely threatened, the association used its fund to support the government in buying out bad

---

[30] For a discussion of the results of the 1998–9 inspections, see Hoshi/Kashyap (1999) and Schaede (2000).

loans of these banks to keep them afloat. As financial liberalization proceeded and more financial innovations were introduced, associations in the various bank categories took over rule-making functions, especially regarding business ethics, customer relations, and advertising. Like the investment banking industry, banks began to move away from regulatory micro-management by the MOF toward increasingly structuring the rules for their markets themselves.

The Japanese model of financial regulation, then, is a model of self-regulation without strict regulatory agencies. If markets are competitive and there is a minimum degree of supervision, the outcome may be efficient rules and good self-monitoring. However, this was not the situation in Japan in the 1990s. The scandals and the bad loan crisis demonstrated that Japan's financial industries were too collusive to self-regulate in the public interest. Their increased self-regulation meant that Japan's financial markets were dominated by the attempts of large firms to self-protect. It remains to be seen whether the new FSA will be strong enough to challenge this self-protection.

5.3. Summary: Regulation—Deregulation—Self-Regulation

Self-regulation is not a new phenomenon, and neither is it unique to Japan. However, the evidence is clear that self-regulation was on the rise in Japan in the 1990s, in both the administrative and trade-enhancing as well as the protective and collusive type. The increase came in response to a confluence of three strong factors: (1) a general move toward deregulation and market liberalization; (2) a legal environment that treats cooperative agreements and self-regulation leniently; and (3) the severe recession of the 1990s. Yet, the increase in self-regulation in the 1990s was not just a reaction to the temporary economic downturn; rather, the forces of deregulation and lenient antitrust enforcement created long-term incentives for companies to self-regulate more actively.

The JFTC has historically been unable to curb self-regulation, and there is no evidence that it intended to stop it in the 1990s. This is apparent in the fact that the JFTC chooses to prosecute cases primarily through informal settlement and consultation cases. Most of the informal cases involve unfair trade practices, which is how self-regulation typically begins. In other words, most instances of self-regulation, to the extent that they are being prosecuted at all, are settled informally. Unfair trade practices, such as retail price maintenance, facilitate the monitoring of price agreements among competing producers. Thus, if the JFTC is lenient on retail price maintenance and other unfair practices, it often condones, or even invites, upstream collusion.

Case evidence supports and complements the data results. A large number of cases suggest that most activities of self-regulation involve—directly or indirectly—some form of market restriction or barriers to entry, and some direct or indirect agreement on prices. The direct means of restraining competition include price agreements, market restrictions and boycotts, whereas the indirect means often entail a move toward standardization, which ultimately simplifies more direct cooperative agreements. For instance, when the government has abolished a regulation of price or entry barriers, many associations have tried to halt the increase in competition through the formulation of model contracts, industry-wide accounting procedures, or some safety or quality standards. All these will make the product more uniform along at least one dimension over time, and thus help the introduction of additional self-regulation. The data analysis in Chapter 6 will show that product homogeneity is a strong predictor of self-regulation; the general move toward more standards or model contracts is therefore a first step toward more self-regulation.

The very fact that self-regulation begins through some standardized or joint contract agreement makes it difficult for the JFTC to nip the newly emerging forms of self-regulation in the bud, even if it wanted to. In Japan, deregulation typically does not come as a "big bang" (though politicians may call it that). Instead, the process of deregulation, often wrought with re-regulation (the introduction of new rules), typically is one of phasing in new market rules gradually. Accordingly, trade associations do not abruptly begin to self-regulate either. Rather, in responding to the phasing in of a deregulation program, they increase their self-regulation step by step. In the initial stages, the JFTC does not seem to consider such moves to be in violation of the AML. Only time will tell whether the JFTC will eventually begin to prosecute self-regulation more stridently. In the 1990s, it had a chance to do so when the U.S., through *gaiatsu*, pushed for stricter rules on both *dangō* and unfair trade practices—but the JFTC chose to enforce only *dangō* more strictly.

Self-regulation by itself is not special to Japan. What is different in the Japanese situation is the environment in which self-regulation began to expand in the 1990s. Lenient antitrust enforcement over time has formed a system that allows for significant exchange of information and cooperation among competing firms within one industry. Moreover, the slow and predictable process of moving from regulation based on "gray" laws and administrative guidance to deregulation has granted trade associations time to structure their self-regulation. In some cases, the government has delegated regulation of certain business issues to the industry, as in the investment and insurance industries. In other cases, the associations have taken over "to protect" their members by structuring model contracts, as with intermediate product markets where the *atogime* (after-sales price adjustment) system has collapsed. Self-regulation has emerged as the rational strategy for companies and industries that face competition but no strict regulatory agencies. There are many potential positive effects of self-regulation for the incumbent firms in an industry, but also a few potentially gravely negative consequences. In some cases, self-regulation means self-protection. To evaluate the effects of self-regulation on the entire economy, the next chapter will turn to a data analysis of self-regulation by industry.

6

Data Analysis: Trade Associations and Self-Regulation

While the case studies have suggested that self-regulation is widespread and that antitrust policy is less than effective in stopping its increase, there remains a question about how prevalent such activities are, and how industries differ in the extent to which they self-regulate. If differences exist, what explains them? More important, are there predictors of self-regulation that help us determine, for example, which industries are most likely to be strongly cooperative? Understanding predictors of self-regulation also permits us to forecast the likely effects of changes in the overall economic situation or in organizational stucture on an association's activities. For instance, how is self-regulation affected if an industry agrees on standardized product characteristics? And are there organizational features of trade associations that support self-regulation and can thus be used as identifiers of such activities? The policy implications of these findings are obvious: being able to predict the degree of self-regulation in an industry using trade association data offers a new way of gauging how closed a certain product market is, and how effective it would be to push for market opening, either as a competitor or through political means. Foreign firms that want to enter Japan's markets may find it useful to analyze the existing situation of self-regulation prior to making substantial investments.

To determine the economic and organizational factors that facilitate self-regulation among companies, this chapter uses a database containing detailed information on 1,153 Japanese trade associations across 28 industries. Because data on the various aspects of self-regulation are not available for all associations, the actual sample size differs across different analyses. The chapter employs three separate sets of hypotheses, each drawing from different bodies of theory, using subsets of the data.

The chapter begins with the formulation of hypotheses, first, by building on existing theories of industrial organization which look at industry structure and product characteristics. Second, hypotheses are formulated for trade conditions that may be related to self-regulation in the manufacturing industries, namely exports, imports and the price differential between Tokyo and New York. Third, the chapter develops new hypotheses regarding the institutional characteristics of trade associations and the effect of internal organization on association activities. In the next step, the chapter introduces the database and outlines some descriptive statistics that confirm the typology of trade associations into "core" and other associations, as proposed in Chapter 2. The third part of this chapter contains the data analysis and discussion of results, which are summarized at the end.

6.1.   Predictors of Self-Regulation: Hypotheses

The Dependent Variable: Measuring Self-Regulation

Before formulating hypotheses for self-regulation, we need to define what we are trying to explain. As seen in Chapters 4 and 5, the problem with measuring self-regulation is how to differentiate properly between administrative and protective self-regulation, and how to account for the unofficial or undetected portion in either category, especially in terms of collusion. However carefully the variables are constructed, there will necessarily be a lot of "noise" in the data. Thus, throughout this analysis, it is important to evaluate results conservatively.

In constructing the dependent variable, we can employ insights gained from empirical studies of cartels, although this theory must be adapted carefully to a study of self-regulation within trade associations rather than collusion among independent firms. In so-called "structure-and-conduct" studies for the U.S., collusion is typically thought of as a formal or explicit agreement among competitors without significant individual market power to earn greater than competitive profits (Hay/Kelley 1974). Therefore, researchers sometimes use the profit rate of companies involved in collusion as an index of a collusive agreement—the higher the markup of the colluding firms, the more effective their scheme. However, two factors interfere with using profit rate here. First, U.S. studies have found that profit rate does not measure collusion particularly well, since in many cases cartels do not result in higher profits (Asch/Seneca 1976, Marvel et al. 1988, Shugart/Tollison 1998).[1] Profit rate is an even less conclusive measure of self-regulation, which is often aimed at stabilizing the market and reducing variance in profits over business cycles, even at the expense of higher profits during boom periods. Thus, even if an industry does not exhibit above-average profits, it may still actively self-regulate. Second, profit data are accessible for individual firms or for industries, but not for trade associations. To compute profit rate for an association, one needs to know the association's coverage, i.e., who the member firms are. Japanese associations were only required to disclose

---

[1] Two primary reasons have been proposed why detected cartels are often not associated with higher profits: (1) the conspiracies that actually come to light are those that were ineffective and thus faltered: cheating and retaliation are inevitable in unstable cartels but are rare in successful cartels; and (2) cartel profits are frequently dissipated by non-price competition, so that firms realize no economic profits, but only a competitive return on their investment.

this information consistently after 1995, and a test of changes in profit levels due to self-regulation is thus left for future study.

To overcome the limitations of profit rate as a dependent variable, many empirical studies of collusion in the U.S. have looked at the shared characteristics of colluding firms using official cases prosecuted by the U.S. antitrust authorities; i.e., "caught in the act of colluding" is used as the dependent variable (e.g., Hay/ Kelley 1974, Asch/Seneca 1975, Fraas/Greer 1970, Posner 1970). The difficulty with this approach is that the observable portion of collusion is a function of legal enforcement, as it reflects the types of violation that the antitrust authorities chose to prosecute. Nonetheless, for our purposes, the fact that the JFTC has either prosecuted, investigated, admonished or warned an association contains useful information about possible protective self-regulation by that association, such as agreements among competing firms to block market entry, raise prices, etc. In the database of 1,153 Japanese trade associations, a total of 152 associations (13% of the database) are known to have been investigated or admonished by the JFTC between 1980 and 1995; these associations were coded "1" to create a dummy variable called SUSPECT (Section 6.2 below explains precisely how these data were collected).

However, JFTC investigation is only one indicator of self-regulation. To construct a more robust dependent variable to index self-regulation, we can add a second measure that gauges administrative self-regulation. Being primarily rule-oriented, administrative self-regulation is often initially delegated or sanctioned by the regulator and then extended to serve the industry's needs; nevertheless, this is often described as "industrial policy". By interviewing government officials and using other indicators of regulatory involvement such as officially sponsored cartels, 300 associations (26% of the total) were identified as being actively engaged in administrative self-regulation (see Section 6.2 for data description). This resulted in a dummy variable, INDUSTRIAL POLICY, which takes the value "1" for those associations identified by the regulators as being involved in above-average administrative self-regulation.

Finally, one can combine the two markers of SUSPECT and INDUSTRIAL POLICY to gain a third, aggregate dependent variable for overall self-regulation to reveal a larger picture of how associations involved in administrative or protective self-regulation differ from associations not identified as engaged in either. This aggregate, overall variable SELFREG is indexed with the value "1" if an association was identified to engage in administrative or protective self-regulation, and "0" if an association has not been marked at all. In combining legal and collusive self-regulation, this variable allows us to gain an overall picture, whereas the sub-variables tell a more detailed story of predictors of specific self-regulatory activities.

Therefore, the overall dependent variable, SELFREG, as well as the two sub-variables of SUSPECT and INDUSTRIAL POLICY are all "1–0" variables, calling for logistic regression analysis to identify predictors of active self-regulation in trade associations. With these dependent variables at hand, the stage is now set for the hypotheses.

Economic Theories of Industrial Organization

The first question is whether there are differences in self-regulation across industries. While all Japanese trade associations engage in a certain amount of self-regulation, there may be economic factors that accentuate self-regulation of either the administrative or protective kind, which imply that some industries are more likely to self-regulate than others. What are these features in industry structure that facilitate self-regulation? Identifying specific conditions that facilitate self-regulation will allow us to forecast the likelihood that a certain association engages in active self-regulation, and it also allows an estimation of how widespread active self-regulation is likely to be across Japanese industries.

To explore industry effects on self-regulation, we can again employ the logic of "structure-and-conduct" studies in industrial organization economics, which suggest a set of industry characteristics conducive to collusion (e.g., Hay/Kelley 1974, Fraas/Greer 1977, Tirole 1988). The first and most obvious of these is the number of firms involved. Bain (1951) first suggested that the smaller the number of participants in a cartel, the less divergent the opinions among participants and thus the easier it is for firms to collude. Stigler (1964) added to this the observation that a smaller number of participants also makes it easier to detect cheating and, thus, to enforce an agreement. Translating these insights to the context of trade associations leads to the first hypothesis:

H1a: The fewer the number of member firms in an association, the more likely an association is to be actively involved in self-regulation.

However, the number of members in an association is an imprecise index, because associations vary substantially in structure and character. Association membership has a very high variance, with an average of 695, a median of 78, and a standard deviation of 3,066.[2] Fortunately, previous theory and empirical research have suggested an alternative measure that can be used to determine the effect of the number of participants on self-regulation: industry concentration. The original "small numbers" insight by Bain (1951) suggested a link between the number of members of a cartel and the degree of market concentration in

---

[2] There are some associations with more than 10,000 members, especially in the construction, printing, and real estate business. For instance, the Japan Boiler Association (*Nihon boira kyōkai*) has 17,934 members, and the All Japan Federation of Radio and TV Associations (*Zenkoku rajio terebi denki kumiai rengōkai*) has 35,000 members, presumably including subcontractors in the electronics industry as well as repair stores. Of course, these associations are primarily active in lobbying; for self-regulation, the member firms break up into smaller groups, either regionally or by more detailed product categories. In addition to high variance, the data for "regular members" do not reflect the fact that associations sometimes are members of other associations. For instance, most umbrella associations have as members only a few individual companies, but a large number of associations, and these association members may result in a high diversity of opinion. Adjusting "membership" to account for association members only increases the variance and further reduces the predictive power of this variable.

the industry. After Hay and Kelley (1974) showed, for a sample of U.S. cases, that the correlation between these two variables was negative, high, and significant, follow-up studies for the U.S. have used industry concentration as a proxy for small numbers (e.g., Fraas/Greer 1977). Therefore, we can use data for the concentration ratio instead of membership, to evaluate the effect of numbers of participants on self-regulation. The hypothesis is:

H1b: The higher the concentration ratio in an industry, the more likely is the trade association to be involved in self-regulation.

Since the data for membership and industry concentration are related, they will be used in separate analyses.

In addition to the number of participants to the agreement, empirical studies in industrial organization have shown that product characteristics may also determine the ease with which groups of firms can cooperate or collude.[3] The first of these characteristics is the degree of product heterogeneity: the more homogeneous a product, the easier it is to collude on price. There are two reasons for this. First, if the product is completely homogeneous, such as milk or gasoline, price is the primary strategic variable with which to compete, so the parties to the agreement need to discuss only one issue. Second, should one party attempt to cheat, it is easily detected, for it can only meaningfully cheat on price. Based on this logic, we can postulate that:

H2: The more homogeneous the products in an industry, the more likely the industry's association is to be involved in active self-regulation.

A second product characteristic, distinct from homogeneity, that is often considered with regard to the ease of price collusion is the rate of technological change. A rapid rate of change can destabilize or undermine a collusive agreement, because it requires frequent renegotiation to accommodate new product characteristics. In terms of self-regulation, however, rapid technological change may have the opposite effect and require more self-regulatory activity rather than less. First, in fast-changing markets, existing government rules and standards often become outdated, requiring the formulation of new rules by competing firms. Second, rapid technological change may have similar effects as new market entry with its potential to destabilize the existing hierarchy and market share among firms. For these reasons, increased technological change may trigger more efforts to self-regulate, especially by market leaders that feel threatened by new product developments. Finally, to the extent that the government supports technological change through industrial policy, there should be a positive association between technological change and the industrial policy variable. These conflicting lines of argument result in two alternative hypotheses to be tested:

[3] Many researchers have contributed to this part of the literature; see Scherer (1980) for an overview, and Hay/Kelley (1974) for an early application.

H3a: The more rapid the rate of technological change in industry, the more actively is the association involved in administrative (industrial policy-type) self-regulation.

Alternatively:

H3b: The more rapid the rate of technological change in the industry, the less likely is the association to engage in protective (collusive) self-regulation.

Because of the possibility of opposite effects, the composite variable SELFREG may not permit accurate tests of the relationship between technological change and self-regulation. Therefore, empirical tests of hypotheses 3a and 3b will be conducted using separate variables of SUSPECT and INDUSTRIAL POLICY.

The hypotheses postulated thus far are based on previous theory and research. However, there is an alternative explanation that needs to be controlled before examining the effects of the number of association members and product characteristics; that is, the behavior of a trade association may reflect its prior experience with self-regulation. For instance, associations in older industries such as coal-mining or shipbuilding, with experience in policy-induced cooperation, may self-regulate more than younger industries such as solar energy or fiber optics. While experience is difficult to measure, one proxy that can be used to represent the length, though not the intensity, of an association's prior experience is the age of the association. If, in contrast, economic factors are more important determinants of self-regulation, then the age of the association should not be significantly related with the dependent variable.

H4: The older an association, the more likely it is to be involved in self-regulation.

Trade in Manufacturing Industries

While the argument proposed in this book is that self-regulation is widespread and occurs to some extent across all industries, it is possible that trade conditions affect the degree to which associations self-regulate. The first trade activity that may predict self-regulation is exports. Exporting firms are, on average, in highly competitive product markets and hence may be assumed to engage in some administrative self-regulation but not in collusion. In contrast, primarily domestically oriented industries such as cement, glass, paper, etc., are often believed to be more active in protective self-regulation. Therefore, exports should be negatively related with self-regulation. However, it may be that exporting industries in pursuit of a sanctuary strategy are very active self-regulators. A sanctuary strategy implies that firms cooperate at home in order to create a profit cushion that enables them to compete more forcefully in international markets. Indeed, many Japanese industries have pursued such a strategy, such as through the export associations for cameras, sewing machines, and electronics in the 1960s, or in automobiles in the 1970s and semiconductors, photo-film, and steel in the 1980s. Thus, some exporting industries may in fact be active self-regulators at home. To test for this scenario, we can postulate that:

H5: The higher the exports in an industry, the less likely is the industry's core association to be actively involved in self-regulation.

A second trade statistic that may suggest active self-regulation is imports. Because Japan is poorly endowed with raw materials, many of Japan's early growth sectors were highly dependent on imports of inputs, such as pig iron, cotton, or oil. During the period of rapid growth, this import dependency enabled MITI to push for cartels as a way of allocating import quotas, such as in the steel, textile and petrochemical industries. This import dependency continues, as does MITI protection of these industries. We can therefore propose that:

H6: The higher the imports in an industry, the more likely is the industry's core association to be actively involved in self-regulation.

Finally, self-regulation, and especially collusion, should be reflected in product prices. If an industry can engage successfully in protective self-regulation, then barriers to entry should affect the level of competition in the market and thus lead to higher prices as compared with U.S. markets. If, however, all industries engage in self-regulation to create entry barriers, then prices will be higher for all products, yielding no significant differences. To test for this effect, the following hypothesis is postulated:

H7: The higher the price differential for end products between Tokyo and New York, the more active the self-regulation in that industry.

Internal Organization of Trade Associations

Besides industry and trade features, insight into the activities of a given industry may be gleaned by looking at the structure of the association itself. Said differently, are there organizational predictors of self-regulation by a trade association? To analyze the relationship between structure and function, we need to go beyond the insights of economics and develop hypotheses that build on the logic of organizational theory. As discussed in Chapter 2, a primary benefit to a company from membership in a trade association is the increase in information flow and decrease in transaction costs associated with gathering information on markets and competitors. An ongoing exchange of information is also a necessary condition for the successful implementation of a cartel agreement. Thus, trade associations that are highly active self-regulators should also be those that facilitate the exchange of information most. The question, then, is whether there are specific organizational features that indicate an active flow of information, and thus self-regulation.

The first organizational characteristic that can be used as an indicator of the volume of information flow and processing is the overall size of an association; that is, the more staff an association has, the easier it is to collect information, organize seminars, or hold meetings. This can be measured in the number of long-term employed staff (another proxy for association size is the budget, but because staff and budget are highly correlated, only staff is used here). A large staff is also associated with a higher number of dispatched (*shukkō*) employees; these *shukkō*, in turn, increase the flow of information and number of contact points across the member firms. Therefore, we can postulate:

> *H8*: The larger the staff, the more likely is the association to be involved in self-regulation.

A second indicator of the degree and intensity of information exchange may be the number of members that are immediately involved in the decision-making process. Obviously, the number of regular association members will not capture this well, since a handful of representatives could represent a large group of people. Neither does the total number of directors, i.e., member firm CEOs that are members of the associations' board, tell a complete story: again, just a few might make decisions for all. To fully capture the internal decision-making process, we need to evaluate how "tight" the association's membership is by looking at the ratio of directors to total members. For instance, consider an association with 20 members and 20 directors—here, the ratio is one, indicating that presidents of all member firms are directly involved in all agreements. In contrast, an association with 60 member firms and 20 directors has a tightness ratio of 0.33 which indicates less tightness. Tightness—how many member firms are immediately involved in making agreements relative to the size of the organization—is related to the effectiveness of interest representation and internal unity. This leads to the second hypothesis:

> *H9*: The tighter an association (the higher the ratio of directors to members), the more likely is the association to be involved in self-regulation.

Related to the ease and effectiveness of information exchange are its scope and depth. While measuring the intensity of the information flow directly is impossible, we can consider a proxy for "information sharing": the *shinboku* or friendship variable. Recall from Chapter 2 that more than 60% of all associations that answered a JFTC questionnaire considered the creation of "friendship" among the CEOs of the industries as one of their primary functions. In fact, almost 40% of all associations contained in the database have this task explicitly listed in their bylaws. To be sure, the bylaws may be just a piece of paper with little actual relevance. Yet, it is likely that the founding presidents of the association listed "friendship" as an organizational goal for a reason, and the *shinboku* objective may indeed translate into a high degree of interaction, which in turn aids active self-regulation. This can be tested by postulating:

H10: Associations that identify *shinboku* (friendship) as a primary task in their bylaws are more likely to be involved in self-regulation.

Finally, one could argue that the degree of information exchange in an association depends critically on the total number of firms in the industry, because the smaller the group, the easier it is for its members to meet, build relationships, disclose strategic details, and agree on a common agenda. To control for the possibility that all of the internal features are simply driven by the number of members, we need to include concentration. This variable indicates the number of member firms and has a lower variance than the membership variable. If the internal organizational characteristics of staff, tightness and *shinboku* truly reflect the degree of self-regulation, then the results for concentration should be insignificant. While this variable was formulated above as part of the industrial structure analysis, in order to rule out collinearity with "friendship" or staff size, the measure is included in this analysis of internal features:

H11: The higher the concentration ratio in an industry, the more likely is the trade association to be involved in self-regulation (same as *H1b*).

6.2. The Database

The database used for this analysis consists of 1,153 trade associations covering 28 industries for the years 1990–1. I compiled this database from various sources on industry characteristics and trade data, as explained below, including the most detailed Japanese directory on trade associations, the *"Dantai Meikan"* (Shiba 1991). This handbook is published biannually by a private company based on association surveys. The sample gained from these sources includes all associations that provided data on basic attributes such as the number of members, directors, and budget, or for which I could supplement this information through personal interviews and other archival sources. Given the goal of this study to compare associations across industries, the database includes only industry-specific associations; i.e., it excludes associations that span multiple industries, such as the overarching umbrella association Keidanren. The 1,153 entries represent 828 core associations, 127 cooperatives, and 76 umbrella associations. Of all associations, 851 are in the manufacturing sector, 51 are specialized associations for distribution and wholesaling, 201 are in the finance and service sectors, and the remaining 50 associations span other sectors. The categorization of industries is adopted from that used in the *Dantai Meikan*, and matches the one used for the antitrust analysis in Chapter 5 (cf. Table 6.1). The data for these 1,153 associations can be divided into three categories: structural, industrial, and functional. Not all data are available for the entire sample (e.g., industry concentration), so that the sample size differs by type of analysis.

Structural data.   The first category, structural data, refers to the defining features of the organization and allows for tests relating an organization's structure to its strategy or activities. Structural data include: budget, number of regular member firms and association members, number of directors (i.e., company represent-atives), number of staff, number of retired bureaucrats (OBs) among the staff (reported by only 68 associations), and age. Moreover, I created dummy variables for both the legal status of an association (whether or not it is incorporated as a *shadan hōjin* through a ministerial license) and for geographical scope (whether an association is national or regional). From the 37 associations that I inter-viewed, I collected data on numbers of committees, subcommittees, and *shukkō* personnel. Although the small numbers preclude extensive analyses of OBs or *shukkō*, they provide valuable qualitative insights into the functioning of associa-tions and are a useful complement to the quantitative data, as used in Chapter 2.

Industry and trade data.   To analyze the effects of industry structure on self-regulation, the database contains variables that describe an industry's market share, product characteristics, and price.[4] Industry concentration for 1990 is indexed by the combined market share of the three largest companies, yielding the variable TOP3.[5] Data were taken from JFTC data for 1990 (JFTC 1993b) and were supplemented using the Nikkei market share study for 1991(NSSS 1991). Trade data originated from two primary sources. First, I collected export and import figures (in Yen) for each industry for 1990 from trade statistics published by the Japan Tariff Association (JTA 1990). To measure possible effects of trade barriers in an industry, I collected data on the price differential between Tokyo and New York from a government price survey conducted by the EPA for the years 1993–4 (EPA 1994a).[6]

To allow for a test of economic theories of collusion concerned with product characteristics, two additional variables were created by coding product characteristics. The first of these variables gauges the degree and speed of technological change in an industry, based on 1992 U.S. data of company funds for industrial R&D performance, using SIC codes at the 2-digit level

---

[4] Because core associations represent narrowly defined industries, these data were collected for specific product categories at the 4-digit level of the Japanese commodity classification system. For the broader product representation by umbrella associations, data were collected at the 2-digit level.

[5] In contrast to the U.S., where industry concentration is typically evaluated by looking at the combined market share of the four largest firms, in Japan these data are collected for the three largest firms. Data for the Herfindahl index were also collected; however, analyses yielded very similar results for both the Herfindahl index and market share data.

[6] The price differential became a political issue in the early 1990s when it was proposed by supporters of the deregulation movement as evidence that Japanese markets are closed. The 1994 survey was particularly detailed. While other data in the database refer to the years 1990–1, the two-year time gap of the price data can be assumed to have little effect on the analysis because Japanese trade associations are rather stable over time in their internal organizational features. Moreover, if anything, the price differential between Japan's and foreign markets should have narrowed after the collapse of the bubble economy. To the extent that the time gap introduces noise, the error is on the conservative side, as the data underestimate the differential. Note that the price data are limited to end products, so that the price analysis precludes the intermediate product markets.

Table 6.1 (a). Categorization of Industries for the Variable "Rate of Technological Change"

"1" (low)	"2" (medium)	"3" (rapid)
Specialized retailing	Insurance	Commercial banking
Mining & petroleum	Metals	Investment banking
Energy	General machinery	Electrical machinery
Gas/propane gas	Transportation machinery	Precision machinery
Iron & steel	Chemicals	Pharmaceuticals
Tools & instruments	Construction	Telecommunications
Miscellaneous goods	Tourism	
Kiln (glass, cement, ceramics)		
Textiles		
Pulp & paper		
Food & drinks		
Transportation & storage		
Cargo & trucking		
Port management		
Marine transportation		

Source: based on NSF 1996.

(NSF 1996). The assumption is that the amount of corporate funds spent on research and development (R&D) is a good indicator of how technology-driven an industry is; further, it is assumed that an industry subject to rapid technological change in the U.S. will similarly be affected by technological change in

Table 6.1 (b). Categorization of Industries for the Variable "Product Heterogeneity"

"1" (very homogeneous)	"2" (slightly differentiated by quality)	"3" (somewhat differentiated: product features, quality, design)	"4" (very heterogeneous, due to brand, fashion, features, design, etc.)
Commercial banking*	Insurance	Specialized retailing	General machinery
Investment banking*	Mining & petroleum	Chemicals	Precision machinery
Energy	Metals	Iron & steel	Transportation machinery
Gas/propane gas	Kiln (glass, cement, ceramics)	Textiles	Electrical machinery
Cargo & trucking	Pulp & paper		Pharmaceuticals
Port management	Food & drinks		Tools & instruments
Marine transportation	Construction**		Miscellaneous goods
Telecommunications	Transportation & storage		
	Tourism		

Source: following Rauch (1999) for traded products; based on the consumer's perspective for services.

* After interest rate and brokerage fee deregulation in the 1990s, differentiation may become more important for these industries; for the period under discussion, banking products were not highly differentiated in Japan.

** Construction companies differentiate through engineering techniques, but within the various categories of construction (e.g., private housing, high-rise buildings, or bridges), these techniques do not differ substantially across companies.

Japan.[7] The U.S. data were used to index a variable DTECH which ranges from "1" (= little/slow; annual R&D expenditures of less than $2 billion; e.g., food or mining) to "3" (= very rapid; R&D expenditures exceeding $10 billion; e.g., telecommunications). The second variable estimates product heterogeneity, ranging from "1" (highly homogeneous products, e.g., gas or energy) to "4" (very heterogeneous products, e.g., pharmaceuticals or precision machinery). The classification of product heterogeneity was based on Rauch's (1999) categorization of products depending on whether they are traded on organized exchanges (very homogeneous), or whether there is no official price (heterogeneous). Rauch's product list was adapted to fit the Japanese industry categorization. Tables 6.1(a) and 6.1(b) present the categorization of industries for the two variables.

Functional variables. The third category of data consists of three variables indicating functional characteristics of trade associations. These variables capture the main activities of an association and allow for an analysis of the relationship between organizational or industry characteristics and an association's activities. The first of these functional data relate to the activity of friendship creation (*shinboku*). To assess friendship, I coded a dummy variable with a value of "1" if *shinboku* was explicitly mentioned in the bylaws, and "0" otherwise.

To evaluate self-regulation by an association, I constructed two additional functional variables. The first of these assesses collusion, as identified by the antitrust authority. In its Annual Report, the JFTC publishes a list of firms and associations investigated for AML infringements, such as price collusion or unfair trade practices. I coded these data for the period 1980 through 1995 for a dummy variable called SUSPECT. This takes the value "1" if an association, or more than five companies belonging to this association, was formally or informally accused of collusion during this period, and "0" otherwise. Given that Japanese trade associations are stable over time, the assumption is that if an association was found to have colluded between 1980 and 1995, the structural data of this association as of 1990–1 were a reasonable reflection of the environment in which these agreements were reached.

The second variable to gauge self-regulation is a dummy variable INDUSTRIAL POLICY, which shows whether an association has been actively involved in structuring the regulation of its industry in the 1980s and 1990s. This variable was created in two steps. First, based on a review of 53 case studies of industrial policy cartels of the 1980s, I made a preliminary categorization of those associations involved in rationalization and recession cartels. Second, I asked six mid-level Japanese government officials from various ministries to identify those associations in the data set which, in their official duties in their ministries, they believed had a role in shaping industrial policy and implementing regulation.

---

[7] Japanese R&D data are less informative for the purpose of this analysis, because they do not reveal the proportion of R&D financed through Japan's "second budget", the FILP (Fiscal and Investment Loan Program).

Specifically, I asked the officials to identify those associations that "have been actively involved in structuring programs of industrial promotion; output/ capacity reduction; cooperation on price, employees, or trade patterns; and self-monitoring (*jishu chōsei*) and self-regulation (*jishu kisei*)". While the officials agreed that this was a sufficiently precise list of criteria, they pointed out to me that *all* trade associations fulfil at least one of these functions, in particular self-regulation. Consequently, they marked only those associations in the sample that were "above-average" active in self-regulation or in their industrial policy involvement. This coding was used to categorize associations as involved in industrial policy ("1") or not ("0"). While this is a reasonable first approximation for this study, it is possible that some associations not identified by the officials might still be highly active self-regulators. Unfortunately, no more objective indicator of "industrial policy" is available.[8] However, to the extent that the officials omitted some active "self-regulators" in their categorization, this omission creates a conservative bias and, if anything, leads to an underestimation of the extent of self-regulation.

Overall, the combination of data from a variety of sources and the comprehensive data on a large sample of associations provides a unique database for analyzing the role and effects of self-regulation in the Japanese economy.

Descriptive Data: The Typology of Japanese Trade Associations

Chapter 2 began with the idea that Japanese trade associations differ in their functions, and that these differences depend primarily on size. Based on that logic, large umbrella organizations were thought to be more likely to be engaged in political activities, while core associations were proposed to be more involved in self-regulation at the industry level. To investigate this, we can test the null-hypothesis that no significant differences exist across associations with regard to size, industry characteristics, or the degree of self-regulation (as expressed in involvement in industrial policy or collusion). This analysis will provide a brief overview of descriptive statistics that distinguish among types of associations.

To examine the relationships between the various variables, bivariate correlations were computed between the three main types of association—core, umbrella, and cooperative—and their key features in terms of organization, industry characteristics, and functions. This was coded such that the focal type

---

[8] For instance, the size of imports is not a proxy for "industrial policy" involvement, because imports work both ways: while industrial policy aims to restrict imports to protect domestic markets, it also promotes imports in those industries that are highly dependent on raw materials, such as petrochemicals. Exports are not an appropriate proxy for exports either. One explanation for this is offered by Okimoto's (1989) industry life-cycle model: industrial policy is high in the infant stage of an industry, than tapers off during growth, and increases again during the stages of maturity and decline. Exports are highest during the growth stage, when industrial policy is lowest, and thus the absolute size of exports does not indicate industrial policy activity.

Table 6.2. Bivariate Correlation for Size, Industry, and Functional Variables, by Types of Association

(coded such that the association type under consideration takes the higher value)

	Sample size	Average	Standard deviation	Core associations (Core = 2, all others = 1)	Umbrella associations (Umbrella = 2, all others = 1)	Cooperatives (Coop = 2, all others = 1)
(a) Size characteristics						
Budget (in million Yen)	959	374.40	2231.70	0.03	0.004	−0.04
Regular members	1134	965.50	3066.09	−0.03	0.024	−0.07*
Association members	1131	8.38	50.60	−0.06*	0.089**	−0.56
Directors	1104	25.58	23.75	−0.06	0.15**	−0.13**
Staff	961	13.73	41.76	−0.03	0.08*	−0.07*
Shukkō	31	8.68	18.77	0.17	−0.05	−0.09
Committees	34	19.12	25.34	−0.004	0.08	−0.11
"Old Boys" (OBs)	68	1.88	2.96	0.16	−0.003	−0.18
(b) Industry characteristics						
Concentration (TOP3, in %)	500	51.01	22.09	0.12**	−0.024	−0.01
Imports (in billion Yen)	538	262.39	815.90	−0.09*	0.22**	−0.09*
Exports (in billion Yen)	538	437.67	1538.19	−0.02	0.094*	−0.07
Import ratio (in % of domestic sales)	472	3.58	7.78	−0.135**	0.045	0.19**
Price differential (New York = 100)	393	173.86	45.71	−0.06	0.14**	−0.05
Technological change (1–3)	1153	1.51	0.68	0.09**	−0.05	−0.08**
Product heterogeneity (1–4)	1153	2.61	0.97	0.01	−0.001	0.09**
(c) Functional characteristics						
National vs. regional	1153	0.40	0.96	−0.05	0.10**	−0.13*
Incorporated vs. voluntary	1149	0.52	0.50	0.36**	−0.04	−0.36**
Tightness (directors/members)	1071	0.40	0.96	0.084**	−0.09**	0.07*
Friends (shinboku)	1057	0.39	0.48	0.05	0.027	0.03
INDUSTRIAL POLICY	1153	0.26	0.44	0.07**	0.11**	−0.14**
SUSPECT (JFTC case)	1153	0.13	0.34	0.14**	−0.003	−0.12**
Age (in years, as of 1998)	1143	37.04	12.76	−0.03	0.009	0.02

$* = p < .05$, $** = p < .01$, $*** p < .001$; two-tailed significance level

of association takes a higher value than "all others", so that a negative sign indicates "less than all others". The results are summarized in Table 6.2. First, note that there are large differences across the entire sample, as indicated by the high values for standard deviations. Nevertheless, the table underscores significant differences across associations. For instance, results show that core associations are likely to be involved in industrial policy; although the coefficient is low with $r = 0.07$, the result is strongly significant ($p < 0.01$). Umbrella associations are even more involved in industrial policy ($r = 0.11$, $p < 0.01$), whereas the value for cooperatives is negative and significant ($r = -0.14$, $p < 0.01$), indicating that cooperatives are less likely to participate in industrial policy implementation than core or umbrella associations.

As for organization size, umbrella associations have significantly more associations as members, supporting the concept of a pyramidal structure of associations. Umbrella organizations are larger, have more directors, and more staff. The opposite holds for cooperatives, where all size variables are negative. The picture is less clear for core associations, suggesting a range of core associations from small to large.

For industry characteristics, the results in Table 6.2 show that the more highly concentrated an industry, the more likely its companies are to be organized in a core association ($r = 0.12$, $p < 0.01$). Thus, very large firms that dominate an industry are likely to choose as their primary organizational form a focused core association. There is also a significant negative correlation between core associations and the import ratio (the market share of imported products in an industry), showing that industries with large, dominant firms are better able to restrict imports ($r = -0.135$, $p < 0.01$). Note that the results for the trade variables (imports, exports, and the ratio of imports over exports) are stronger for the umbrella organizations, because these organizations combine the numbers for their individual member industries.

The differences across the three categories of association are most pronounced in terms of their functions. By definition, umbrella associations are more likely to be nationwide, while cooperatives are often regional. Core association are more likely to be incorporated as *hōjin*, while cooperatives are more often voluntary. Core associations are "tighter" than umbrella organizations, as assessed by the ratio of the number of directors to members; that is, core associations provide platforms for more immediate interactions among their members. Finally, the results show a significant, positive association between the "suspect" measure and core associations ($r = 0.14$, $p < 0.01$). This suggests that either core associations commit more violations, or the JFTC prosecutes core associations more actively than cooperatives, which are often exempted from antitrust regulations.

Overall, the results shown in Table 6.2 clearly reject the notion that all associations are the same and are equally likely to be involved in industrial policy and self-regulation. Rather, it seems that cooperatives, as described in Chapter 2, operate in smaller, more fragmented industries with higher imports. Core associations are more focused and involved, and also more often under scrutiny from the JFTC.

6.3. Analysis and Results

The 11 hypotheses propose sets of relationships between industry, trade, and
association characteristics and the propensity of the association to self-regulate.
Given that self-regulation as measured here is a dichotomous variable ("0" = no,
"1" = self-regulating as indexed either by JFTC prosecution or engagement in
industrial policy), the appropriate multivariate analysis needed to determine the
effects of the independent variables on the probability of involvement in self-
regulation is as follows:

$$\text{Prob }(\textit{Self-Regulation}) = \frac{1}{1 + e^{-\textit{SELFREG}}}.$$

Economic Determinants of Self-Regulation

Hypotheses 1 through 5 suggest the following analysis:

$$\textit{SELFREG} = \alpha + \beta \textit{MEMBER} + \beta \textit{PRODUCT} + \beta \textit{DTECH} + \beta \textit{AGE}.$$

In this equation, *SELFREG* is the dichotomous variable indicating self-regulation,
MEMBER indicates the number of members of the associations (*H1a*), *PRODUCT*
indicates the degree of product heterogeneity (*H2*), *DTECH* indexes the rate of
technological change (*H3*), and *AGE* is the age of the association (*H4*). To provide
a more fine-grained picture of the effects of each of the independent variables on
self-regulation, and to test the alternative hypotheses *H3a* and *H3b*, the composite dependent variable (*SELFREG*) was also disaggregated into its two component
parts (*INDUSTRIAL POLICY* and *SUSPECT*) and the same analysis conducted on
each variable; that is, the following additional logistic regressions were run:

$$\textit{INDUSTRIAL POLICY} = \alpha + \beta \textit{MEMBER} + \beta \textit{PRODUCT} + \beta \textit{DTECH} + \beta \textit{AGE}$$

and

$$\textit{SUSPECT} = \alpha + \beta \textit{MEMBER} + \beta \textit{PRODUCT} + \beta \textit{DTECH} + \beta \textit{AGE}$$

Table 6.3 presents the results of the three regressions. First, using the combined
dependent variable *SELFREG*, results are supportive of hypotheses *H2* and *H3*.
Coefficients for product heterogeneity and technological change are highly
significant. The less heterogeneous the product, the more likely is self-regulation
to occur. Also, the higher the rate of technological change, the more likely is the
association involved in self-regulation. Of course, each of these effects is
independent of the other. For instance, telecommunications, while not highly
heterogeneous (from the consumer's perspective) is certainly subject to highly
rapid technological advances. Age, in contrast, is not a significant predictor of
self-regulation overall. Neither is, somewhat surprisingly, the number of regular
members.

Table 6.3. Regression Results: Industry/Product Characteristics and Self-Regulation (with Members)

Independent variables	SELFREG		INDUSTRIAL POLICY (administrative self-regulation)		SUSPECT (protective self-regulation)	
	B	Exp(B)	B	Exp(B)	B	Exp(B)
MEMBERS	0.00	1	0.00	1	0.00	1
PRODUCT	−0.73***	0.47	−0.64***	0.52	−0.49***	0.61
DTECH	0.80***	2.23	1.09***	2.84	−0.057	0.94
AGE	0.00	1	0.01*	1.01	−0.004	0.99
N	1124		1124		1124	
Nagelkerke r²	0.14		0.15		0.047	
Significance level, goodness of fit	***		***		***	

* = p <.05, ** = p<.01, *** = p<.001; two-tailed significance levels

Note that in logistic regression results, the coefficient B indicates the change in the log odds ("odds" meaning the ratio of the probability that an event will occur over the probability that it will not) associated with a one-unit change in the independent variable. To make this same information more intuitive, the entry $Exp(B)$ (which is e raised to the power B) expresses the odds, as it shows the factor by which the odds change when the independent variable changes by one unit. If B is zero, the factor equals 1; thus if the factor is greater than 1, the odds are increased, but if it is smaller than 1, the odds are decreased. For instance, a factor of 2.23 for DTECH means that when the rate of technological change increases by one unit, the odds that self-regulation occurs increase by a factor of 2.23. In contrast, a factor of 0.47 for product heterogeneity says that if heterogeneity increases by one unit, the odds that the association is an active self-regulator decrease by more than half.

Next, the separate entries for INDUSTRIAL POLICY and SUSPECT help differentiate between industrial policy involvement and collusion. While product homogeneity is a strong indicator of self-regulation across all models, Table 6.3 suggests that the rate of technological change has no significant impact on collusion (supporting H3b), but is a strong predictor of administrative self-regulation (supporting H3a). The more "cutting-edge" an industry, it seems, the more likely is the association to be actively involved in formulating rules for the industry. Finally, the age variable is significant for INDUSTRIAL POLICY. Consistent with hypothesis H4, this suggests that older industries are more likely to be involved with their regulator in structuring market rules. Age is not a predictor of collusion.

Overall, the Japanese data support the logic and empirical findings of structure-and-conduct studies for the U.S. Product homogeneity and technological change are important predictors of self-regulation. Moreover, the findings imply that if an association moves to standardize its product (as discussed in Chapter 5), the odds of active self-regulation increase significantly. Thus, if more self-regulation is the objective, standardizing contracts is a sound strategy.

However, in contrast to the intuition that "small numbers" support collusion, the absolute number of members in an association does not carry any information about self-regulation. This may be due to the high variance of the "member" variable in the data set. To get a clearer picture, Table 6.4 shows the same analysis as above, but with market concentration, as measured by the variable *TOP3* and stipulated in *H1b*, instead of the number of association members:

$$SELFREG = \alpha + \beta TOP3 + \beta PRODUCT + \beta DTECH + \beta AGE.$$

Table 6.4 includes the results of this analysis, as well as those for separate calculations for the *INDUSTRIAL POLICY* and *SUSPECT* variables. Because concentration data are available for only a subset of the sample, the number of observations drops from 1,124 to 495. The results are very similar, but stronger than those in Table 6.3, confirming the previous findings of a dominant role of product homogeneity and technological change. However, the concentration ratio is not a predictor of self-regulation of either type. In fact, the sign is negative, indicating that, if anything, associations in *less* concentrated industries may be more active self-regulators. One possible explanation is that the higher the concentration ratio, the less important are formal agreements (e.g., Scherer 1980, Tirole 1988). Obviously, with fewer numbers, it is easier for firms to agree on self-regulation and monitor each other, making regular meetings or fixed monitoring schemes less essential. This reduces the likelihood of both detection and cooperation with the authorities. For instance, highly concentrated industries are less dependent on their cognizant ministry to structure a bargaining situation for them, e.g., through a rationalization cartel. They may also carry out

Table 6.4. Regression Results: Industry/Product Characteristics and Self-Regulation (with Market Concentration)

Independent variables	SELFREG		INDUSTRIAL POLICY (administrative self-regulation)		SUSPECT (protective self-regulation)	
	B	Exp(B)	B	Exp(B)	B	Exp(B)
TOP3	−0.00	0.99	−0.005	0.99	0.002	1.00
PRODUCT	−0.65***	0.51	−0.55***	0.57	−0.50**	0.60
DTECH	1.01***	2.77	1.08***	2.96	0.30	1.3
AGE	0.00	1	0.00	1	0.007	1
N	495		495		495	
Nagelkerke r^2	0.131		0.135		0.039	
Significance level, goodness of fit	***		***		*	

* = p<.05, ** = p<.01, *** = p<.001, two-tailed significance levels

agreements through implicit actions, such as price leadership schemes, which are difficult to detect. Therefore, while the concentration ratio is not a predictor of self-regulation, as measured here, this finding does not imply that highly concentrated industries do not self-regulate. At the same time, the results strongly suggest that even non-concentrated industries self-regulate actively.

Trade and Self-Regulation

The model testing the relationship between trade data and self-regulation is the same logistic regression model as outlined above, but this time with:

$$SELFREG = \alpha + \beta EXPORTS + \beta IMPORTS + \beta PRICE,$$

where EXPORTS and IMPORTS indicate exports and imports for the industry measured in billion Yen at the 4-digit level (*H5* and *H6*), and PRICE is the price differential between Tokyo and New York (*H7*). To test for the effects on administrative and protective self-regulation separately, again the same analysis is also run for the independent variables INDUSTRIAL POLICY and SUSPECT. Obviously, the trade logic applies only to the manufacturing sector (851 associations, or 73% of the sample). Within this group, there are federations, core associations, and cooperatives. Trade data for federations, such as the Japan Machinery Federation are collected at the 2-digit level, whereas data for core associations within the machinery industry are available at the 4-digit level, such as for the Japan Household Sewing Machine Manufacturers' Association. To avoid having the federation data overpowering the results, the analysis was limited to core associations and cooperatives only, yielding a sample of 709 associations. However, because trade data are often difficult to match with the boundaries of associations or are unavailable, the actual sample for which this analysis can be conducted is reduced to 142 associations.

Table 6.5. Regression Results: Trade and Self-Regulation in the Manufacturing Sector

Independent variables	SELFREG		INDUSTRIAL POLICY (administrative self-regulation)		SUSPECT (protective self-regulation)	
	B	Exp(B)	B	Exp(B)	B	Exp(B)
EXPORTS	0.0002	1.0	0.002*	1.0	−0.07*	0.92
IMPORTS	−0.0002	0.99	−0.0002	0.99	0.001	1
PRICE	0.007	1.0	0.004	1.0	0.02*	1.02
N	142		142		142	
Nagelkerke r^2	0.04		0.05		0.28	
Significance level, goodness of fit	NS		NS		***	

* = p<.05, ** = p<.01, *** = p<.001; two-tailed significance levels

The results in Table 6.5 show that trade variables do not explain self-regulation very well. The model's goodness of fit is insignificant, and its r^2 is small for both the industrial policy involvement and the overall self-regulation variable. Interestingly, the model fares better in explaining collusive self-regulation. Here, the data suggest that domestic industries are more likely to violate antitrust rules, and the price differential is significant. Yet, the effects are small, possibly indicating that some exporting industries, too, have been found colluding in setting up a sanctuary strategy. Thus, the analysis for SUSPECT confirms hypotheses *H5* and *H7*.

The poor fit of the trade model confirms the overall argument proposed in this book: all industries self-regulate, regardless of whether they are heavy importers or exporters. No significant differences simply mean that all industries self-regulate at some level. To be sure, the data are also quite "noisy". Industries with high imports include some of the country's flagship industries such as steel or petrochemicals. Also, given Japan's strategy of importing raw materials, adding value and then exporting the finished product, these same industries may also be active exporters, thus washing out all effects. Regardless, the results suggest that neither exports nor imports are good predictors of self-regulation.

There are several possible explanations why the price differential between Tokyo and New York is not more strongly associated with collusive self-regulation. The first concerns data limitations. For example, price data are available for internationally traded end products only and therefore exclude domestic product categories such as food items (recall that as shown in Chapter 5, self-regulation is particularly active there). The data also exclude intermediate products, such as chemicals, steel, or cement, thus not allowing for a good test of the role of industrial policy cartels. Second, again the results support the general argument that self-regulation is conducted across all industries, because prices are higher in almost all product categories in Japan than in New York. In fact, while we do not have official data on prices for homogeneous products such as glass, paper, certain chemicals, and food products, everyone who has ever shopped in Japan knows by way of anecdotal evidence that end product prices are significantly higher there than in the U.S. Finally, there may be a systemic reason why price does not clearly signal very active self-regulation, which is related to the multiple objectives of self-regulation. While the conventional logic is that companies form cartels primarily for increased profits through rigged prices, in the Japanese context, self-regulation pursues several simultaneous goals. First, companies seek stability through self-regulation. This attempt to achieve price stability could probably be measured in the variance in price movements, as opposed to relative price levels. Unfortunately, no such longitudinal data that match the product categories of trade associations are currently available, and this analysis is left for future study. Alternatively, one can consider the "hierarchy" of firms in an industry: how often does market share change visibly, and how obviously are leading firms and newcomers jockeying for positions? In most Japanese industries, in particular those dominated by a few large-scale companies, market positions have been extraordinarily stable over very long periods. Yet, to study this type of stability, one needs market share data that match trade association membership, i.e., data for all members of an association. However, Japan's trade associations have only been required to disclose the names of their member firms since 1995, making such a long-term study unfeasible for now. Again, this type of analysis is left for future study.

Overall, price data suggest that collusive self-regulation leads to somewhat higher prices, even given the generally higher price level in Japan. Domestic industries are more likely to collude than exporting industries, although the effects are small because some exporting industries engage in sanctuary strategies. The size of imports does not signal information on self-regulation.

Internal Organization of Trade Associations as a Predictor of Self-Regulation

Finally, the question is whether the internal features of an association help predict the degree and extent of self-regulation conducted by this association. Hypotheses *H8–H11* yield the following logistic regression equation:

$$\text{SELFREG} = \alpha + \beta\text{STAFF} + \beta\text{TIGHT} + \beta\text{FRIENDS} + \beta\text{TOP3},$$

where STAFF depicts the number of association employees (*H8*), TIGHT is the ratio of directors over members (*H9*), FRIENDS is a dummy variable indicating whether *shinboku* is an explicit function of the association (*H10*), and TOP3 measures industry concentration (*H11*). In addition to SELFREG, the regressions are conducted with INDUSTRIAL POLICY and SUSPECT as the dependent variables, to estimate the effects of the internal features on the separate forms of self-regulation.

Table 6.6. Regression Results: Internal Organization of Trade Associations and Self-Regulation

Independent variables	SELFREG		INDUSTRIAL POLICY (administrative self-regulation)		SUSPECT (protective self-regulation)	
	B	Exp(B)	B	Exp(B)	B	Exp(B)
STAFF	0.03***	1.03	0.03***	1.03	0.007*	1
TIGHTNESS	0.91***	2.49	0.52*	1.68	0.53**	1.7
FRIENDS	0.60**	1.92	0.85***	2.35	−0.04	0.96
TOP3	−0.016**	0.98	−0.01*	0.98	−0.007	0.99
N	363		363		363	
Nagelkerke r²	0.20		0.21		0.08	
Significance level, goodness of fit	***		***		**	

* = p<.05, ** = p<.01, *** = p<.001; two-tailed significance levels

The results reported in Table 6.6 show that the incidence of self-regulation is well explained by this model. First, the findings strongly support all four hypotheses for the composite variable SELFREG. The size of staff, standing as a proxy for the overall size of the association, strongly predicts self-regulation. While the predictive power of one additional staff member is small, the result is highly significant, suggesting that the absolute staff size matters and a staff of, say, 12 suggests less self-regulation than a staff of 24. Likewise, the "tightness" of an association, as measured by the ratio of directors over members, strongly predicts self-regulation. For every one-unit increase in the ratio of directors to members, the odds of self-regulation increase by a factor of 2.5. Moreover, the friendship (*shinboku*) demarcation is surprisingly strong as well. When this variable changes from 0 to 1, the odds of active self-regulation almost double. Market concentration, in contrast, remains comparatively unimportant and negative, as in the previous analysis of industry structure. This suggests that the absolute number of firms does not interfere with the other findings.

Looking at the separate results for INDUSTRIAL POLICY and SUSPECT, the results are similar but reveal several interesting differences. "Friendship" is the most prominent predictor for industrial policy involvement, but it is not a significant predictor for collusion. Thus, associations that identify *shinkboku* in their mission statement are very actively involved in structuring the rules for their industry. Possibly, these are competitive industries that have difficulties reaching agreements, which is why they identified the creation of friendship as an important task in the first place. In contrast, one possible reason why *shinboku* is not predictive of collusive self-regulation is that *shinboku* groups are better at avoiding detection; alternatively, industries that successfully collude do not need nice-sounding mission statements to achieve their goals.

In contrast to the split results for friendship, a tight internal organization is a powerful predictor for both rule-oriented self-regulation and collusion. The reason is obvious: the less focused an association, the more difficult it is to carry out self-regulation. Tight organization is therefore required for all types of agreement. Thus, associations characterized by a tight organization and a "friendship" mission are more likely to self-regulate than all other associations. In trying to find out whether an industry is an active self-regulator, it is helpful to consider not only product characteristics such as product homogeneity or technological change, but also the features of the trade association concerned.

Additional Analyses

Two issues remain that warrant additional analyses. The first concerns the dependent variable SELFREG, and the second tests for multicollinearity among the independent variables. As for the dependent variable, the one group of trade associations that is different from previous analyses consists of those associations that were coded "1" for both industrial policy and collusion. It is rare for an association to be involved in industrial policy and yet be admonished by the JFTC for suspicion of collusion, so this group consists of only 37 trade associations. To examine whether these associations are importantly different, I ran separate statistical analyses for them. Results show that these 37 associations are associated with industries such as chemicals and pharmaceuticals, finance, petroleum, gas, construction and trucking. On average, they were larger in terms of staff and budget, were nationwide, and above all, were more tightly organized. Conducting the above analyses using a dummy variable for these 37 associations provided equivalent results to those shown in Tables 6.3 through 6.6. More specifically, important predictors of self-regulation for this group are tightness and staff, but not trade data or industry concentration. These results simply confirm the overall pattern and do not indicate that associations engaging in both administrative and protective self-regulation are different in important ways from others.

Second, the analyses up to this point have entered the three sets of independent variables separately. This assumes that these variables are largely uncorrelated. An examination of the correlation matrix of the ten independent variables confirms that multicollinearity is indeed not a problem. For the ten variables (56 correlations), the median correlation coefficient is $r = 0.00$, with the range of extreme values extending from $r = -0.18$ to $r = 0.57$. Still, in order to examine the independent effects of these variables, all ten variables were analyzed simultaneously. It is important to recognize that this reduces the sample size considerably to $n = 107$, because of data availability. For instance, comparative price data are available for internationally traded end products only, whereas industry concentration data pertain mostly to intermediate products. Therefore, the final equation is based on a relatively small sample. The results of this analysis show that tightness is by far the most significant and strongest predictor of both administrative and protective self-regulation, followed by staff size. Exports, imports and the price differential remain unimportant. This is consistent with the previous analyses, underscoring even further the relevance of tightness in internal organization of a trade association for self-regulation.

6.4. Summary: Predictors of Self-Regulation

This chapter set out to look for possible predictors of self-regulation using industry characteristics, the trade situation, and the internal structure of an association. To do this, self-regulation was defined as consisting of two parts: an "industrial policy" component, as identified by a group of Japanese bureaucrats, and a "collusive" component, as determined by investigation of an association through the JFTC. This allowed for three different sets of analysis: activities that predict administrative self-regulation, collusive self-regulation, and both combined as compared with associations not identified to be involved in either.

The results show clearly that self-regulation differs by product characteristics and internal organization of the association concerned, but not by industry or trade characteristics. This means that all industries—whether consisting of large or small firms, whether dominated by a few large firms or fragmented, or whether in the exporting or importing sectors—are equally likely to self-regulate. This finding supports the basic argument of this book that self-regulation is increasing across the board.

Having demonstrated this, there are three strong predictors that suggest above-average active self-regulation. The first of these is product homogeneity. The more differentiated the product of an industry, the less likely are the companies in that industry to be engaged in self-regulation of either the administrative or the protective type. This suggests that the tendency toward contract and product standardization, as observed in the case studies in Chapter 5, has fueled the increase in self-regulation in the 1990s. The second strong marker is the rate of technological change in an industry. The higher this rate, the less likely are industries to collude. At the same time, rapid change requires rapid adjustment of market rules and structures, and industries subject to fast change are more likely to self-regulate in the form of rule-making.

The third strong predictor comes from the size and tightness of an association. The larger an association, measured by staff or budget, the more likely it is to be actively involved in self-regulation. Yet, size usually inhibits effective agreements. To differentiate absolute size from an effective self-regulating entity, it is essential to consider the ratio of directors (CEOs on the association's board) over total members. The higher this ratio, the more likely is the association to be active in self-regulation. In fact, "tightness" is the single strongest indicator, suggesting that to understand what is happening in an industry, studying the organization of the industry's association is critical.

Protective self-regulation is also more pronounced for domestically oriented, non-exporting industries. This supports the contention that increases in self-regulation will lead to more collusive activities by domestic firms, whereas it results primarily in more administrative activities for competitive industries. Thus, the increase in self-regulation is likely to accentuate the ongoing split, or bifurcation, of Japanese industries into two distinct segments: an efficient, internationally competitive group of industries on the one hand, and an increasingly inefficient, protected domestic segment. This bifurcation has been observed by many analysts (e.g., Katz 1998, Vogel, S. 1999). Katz (1998) argues that it will ultimately bring down the entire Japanese economy, because the inefficient sectors will either ruin or drive out the efficient ones. In this scenario, increased self-regulation would be an unhealthy band-aid that only prolongs the ills of inefficiency. However, a more optimistic interpretation is also possible: increased self-regulation means joint efforts of survival and revival. It may not work for all industries, but it may in fact have helped some of Japan's domestic industries to weather the recession of the 1990s better than they would have without cooperation. When the Japanese economy picks up again, this may result in a set of domestic industries that would no longer exist without self-regulation, thus reducing the need for imports. It is unclear what the ultimate implications of increasing self-regulation will be for Japan's economy, but some industries will surely benefit from the advantages of sharing information and formulating corporate strategies based on knowledge shared with their competitors.

Finally, this analysis allows for a rough estimation of how many Japanese industries might be actively involved in self-regulation. With 1,153 entries, the database represents about 9% of the entire population of Japanese trade associations, but a higher percentage for industry-specific associations. In looking at the "tightness" and staff size of the associations in this sample, we find that the average ratio of directors over members is 0.3, with a standard deviation of 0.47; accordingly, a tightness ratio higher than 0.8 strongly suggests active self-regulation. In the case of 10% of the associations in this sample, the tightness ratio exceeds 0.8. Moreover, more than 30% had the "friendship" objective listed in their bylaws. Finally, when focusing on the extreme values in the sample, 21% of the associations were found to represent highly homogeneous products, while 10% were identified as subject to highly rapid technological change. In sum, a conservative estimate for the years 1990–1 is that about 15% of all associations in this representative sample were extremely active self-regulators. A less conservative estimate, which looks at above-average values across the predictor variables only, is closer to 20–25%. Very active self-regulation is widespread indeed.

7

The Historical Development of Self-Regulation by Japan's Trade Associations

Japanese trade associations date back at least to the 11th century, and throughout their long history, these associations have been actively engaged in various forms of self-regulation. Initially formed by merchants and artisans trying to create markets and establish mechanisms by which to differentiate upstanding merchants from charlatans, trade associations were soon also engaged in practices such as creating barriers to entry, quality controls, or price setting. Because Japan did not have a Commercial Code until the 19th century, the creation and functioning of early markets were dependent on such self-regulation. Even after the introduction of commercial laws, the practice of self-regulation continued and eventually was institutionalized during WWII. Thus, the function of self-regulation is a feature as old as the associations themselves.

This long history of trade associations has two important ramifications for a full understanding of the present situation of self-regulation. First, while merchants have always gathered to self-regulate, there have been substantial oscillations in the extent to which the state accepted, rejected, or participated in that process. For instance, the early Tokugawa governments (17th century) and the militarists in the 1930s and 1940s were probably most actively involved in shaping trade associations. Government participation in the latter case, in fact, fed into the "developmental state" setting of the 1950s through 1970s. But there were also long interludes of less government involvement, such as the Meiji and Taishō years (1868–1924). Importantly, however, the evolution and wide swings in the intensity of government–business relationships never fundamentally undermined the significance of self-regulation, even during WWII. What we observed in the 1990s was another swing of the pendulum: after years of intensive involvement, the government was again primarily accepting self-regulation, rather than actively guiding it. In fact, limited understanding of the fundamental role of self-regulation in Japan's political economy may have led to an exaggeration of MITI's and other ministerial powers over industry in postwar industrial policy (Johnson 1982). Between 1950 and 1970, MITI was arguably more involved in industry regulation and guidance than ever before, but it could not have achieved what it did without the contribution of trade associations to policy formulation and execution.

The second important insight from the study of the evolution of self-regulation in Japan concerns the role of firmly established trade associations in economic development. Similar to the German medieval guilds (*Zünfte*) of artisans and merchants, or other organized associations in continental Europe, Japanese associations were instrumental in creating, structuring, and guiding markets throughout history (Kulischer 1928). This was obviously critical for establishing the Tokugawa economy, but more important still, these associations existed when Japan began to "take off" toward industrialization in the Meiji period (1868–1911), and to "catch up" with the West in the postwar years. When Japan's leaders set out to design a developmental strategy, they were able to rely on business input from the very beginning. In contrast, many other Asian nations have not developed firmly established, independent trade associations until the present day (MacIntyre 1994a), and contemporary political leaders are typically not interested in establishing strong business groups for fear of losing power to these diverse interests. This hampered economic development by crippling the trade-enhancing functions of trade associations and muffling the corporate voice in economic policies. In contrast, postwar Japan benefited greatly from being able to rely on an established and institutionalized process of industry involvement.

Understanding this, many Japanese government and business leaders display what may seem to be a curious interest in Japan's economic history. For instance, when the Economic Planning Agency established an inter-ministerial deliberation council to study the effects and necessities of further deregulation in 1994, they named this group "*rakuichi-rakuza*" ("Free the markets, open the associations"), following a large-scale intervention policy into self-regulation of the early 17th century (as explained below). While this may partially indicate beliefs in path-dependency by some of Japan's bureaucrats, it also suggests an important role of history in explaining or justifying current policy measures. Because economic history is relevant in the study of self-regulation, this chapter gives a detailed account of the development of Japan's trade associations. The chapter begins with a review of associations in the Middle Ages (12th–16th centuries), and then analyzes the role and structure of associations in the growing economy of the Tokugawa period (1603–1868). This is followed by an analysis of associations during the Meiji and Taishō years (1868–1924), and of the "control associations" (*tōseikai*) during WWII. A summary at the end of this chapter highlights the main points gained from this look into the past.

7.1. Early Developments: The *Za* in the Middle Ages

If the concept of a trade association is defined very loosely, the earliest such organizations in Japan can be considered to have been the *kō* or *mujin* of the

Heian period (794–1185). Through these organizations, farmers submitted dues to a group, and a few members of the group would go to the Ise shrine every year on a rotating basis to receive a blessing for their rice crop (something no farmer could have afforded on his own). The logic of this system is akin to the logic of rotating credit associations, in which each member, in turn, receives all the funds contributed by all members.[1] While the term *kō* was originally used to refer to religious groups for pilgrimages, the idea was soon adopted by merchants to monitor their trade arrangements; in the contemporary usage, the term still connotes a cooperating group of merchants (Miyamoto 1958: 63, Sheldon 1958: 72).

Toward the end of the Heian period, in the 12th century, cities began to develop in Japan, and the trade system changed significantly. Underlying this development was the formation and evolution of *shōen*, private land estates, which resulted from a government policy of encouraging private land reclamation by granting property rights to the developers of new fields. These *shōen* enjoyed a *de facto* status of extraterritoriality and thus had their own administrations. This contributed greatly to economic development, for the existence of a group of people that governed required that farmers produced surplus food to sell to the administrators. As agricultural technologies improved and the size of arable land increased, the surplus that was produced triggered barter trade, and allowed some to specialize in certain areas of workmanship. Since the availability of raw materials differed across regions, provinces began to specialize in certain products, thus creating opportunities for cross-regional trade (Miyamoto 1943: 54, Yamamura 1973). Over time, the *shōen* system also led to a classification of people by profession: among the non-farmers, those who could not enter the *shōen* administration as officials would become either warriors (*bushi* or *samurai*), or artisans who began traveling around to sell their goods in exchange for food. To facilitate the exchange, some landlords set up permanent markets in their provinces, thus creating a fixed market schedule for the traveling merchants.

The Formation of Merchants' Guilds

Before long, the merchants formed commercial guilds or *za*.[2] The first official *za* was recorded in the year 1092, when a Kyoto shrine announced the existence of a group of affiliated merchants under its patronage (Toyoda 1963: 155). *Za* were groups of artisans and merchants with closed membership (i.e., new merchants could not easily join), official standing granted by a patron, and exclusive rights of trade for specific products in their geographic area guaranteed by a patron.

---

[1] *Mujin*, also called *tanomoshi*, developed into mutual cooperatives for joint equipment purchases, etc., during the Kamakura period (1185–1333). They were extremely popular during the Tokugawa period (1600–1868), and some still exist informally today.

[2] This word comes from *zaseki* ("seat") and refers to the way in which merchants sat while conducting business.

The patron was usually a *shōen* landlord, or a temple/shrine. Until the 16th century, the Shogunate did not assume patronage over *za*, but it encouraged their independent development because it recognized the positive effects of these groups on an orderly system of production, distribution, and tax income from the provinces (Toyoda/Sugiyama 1977: 132–3). For the merchants, patronage meant a monopoly right on the production and trade of a certain good in a certain territory, which allowed them to restrain competition, block new entry and garner monopoly rents. More important still, as trade and commerce were prospering while neither civic institutions nor a feudal system had yet fully developed, groups like the *za* supplemented the missing institutional environment for trade by carrying out activities such as forging agreements on trade rules, creating barriers to entry to local markets, or establishing rules on trade credit (Miyamoto 1943: 63, Toyoda 1963: 167). In other words, in the absence of a government system of laws and regulation, the merchant groups formed to self-regulate. Thus, the *za* greatly helped the formation of markets.

The introduction of money had a positive impact on the development of Japan's economy, and it also further increased the importance of the merchant *za*. In the year 708, the first Japanese coins were minted after copper was found for the first time. However, most of the original Japanese coins disappeared during the 10th century and merchants began using Chinese coins imported through trade with China. In the 15th century, just as Chinese coins became widely recognized as currency, low-quality Japanese imitations also came into circulation. These imitation coins created a problem of asymmetric information in the process of "coin selection": when checking on coins, merchants would not accept the obviously bad ones, and suspect that the seemingly good ones might be bad as well. Of course, when finalizing a trade, everyone would try to get rid of his bad coins first and keep the good ones. This created an obvious trade hazard.[3] To overcome the adverse selection problem in coin usage, merchants engaged in repeated trade with the same group of merchants: the only way to avoid falling prey to a "bad money" transaction was not to deal with unknown merchants against whom one could not retaliate. This was accomplished by limiting transactions to members of the various *za*, since *za* membership was a long-term affiliation and bred interdependency. It thus became increasingly difficult to be a businessman and not be a member of a *za*.

As the economy and population grew, the central cities of Kyoto, Nara and Kamakura, as well as the immediate surroundings of large shrines or temples began to grow rapidly. During the Muromachi Shogunate (1338–1573), the cities developed into full-fledged markets. People of various professions formed guilds in the cities, and all members of one group lived in a certain precinct where no

---

[3] A unified currency was newly introduced by Tokugawa Ieyasu (see below) who made the *ōban*, an elliptic gold coin, the standard national currency with a fixed gold content of 68%, and determined a fixed exchange rate with smaller gold coins; silver and copper were also used as currency during the Tokugawa period (for details, see BOJ 1974, Pauer 1985, Schaede 1992).

trade other than theirs was allowed; the geographic concentration simplified intra-group monitoring. These groups came to be called *machi-za* ("city-*za*") or *ichi-za* ("market-*za*"). Markets were held in every city on fixed days of the week, and merchants would travel from market to market in adjacent cities. Merchants stood on the road and advertised their goods (*tachiba*, "standing markets"; in modern Japanese: "standpoint"). Over time, the number of products traded increased, as did the number of *za* specializing in these products across the country.[4] Dominant local *za* began to block trade by merchants from other localities. Products from other provinces were allowed to enter the market only when these goods were not produced locally (Toyoda 1963: 161, Takekoshi 1967: I: 230).

The major function of the *za* at this time was to protect the group's exclusive trading rights in a particular product line. This protection was ensured by the patron's support in expelling any contenders from outside the region, and by enforcing the separation of living quarters and businesses within the territory. The *za* members were exempted from taxes and market fees, and from tariffs when they passed through the barriers under the province's control. They were also assured that they could do business in their territory freely and safely. This protection from competition helped the various industries to grow and earn high profit margins; the *za* system thus contributed to Japan's economic growth during the 14th century.

Self-Regulation in the 16th Century

In the 15th century, the Muromachi Shogunate began to lose its political power. The Ōnin War of 1467–77, which was initially about several succession feuds in the most important regions, undermined the Shogunate's power for good. In the ensuing century, more and more provincial barriers were erected, more taxes were levied, and more people were stopped from traversing rival territories. Robbery was rampant, and there was no system of order or rule enforcement. While most of the temples lost their former influence, the *shōen* were taken over by *daimyō*, successful warriors who soon set up an army of *samurai* around them. During these turbulent times, two major changes occurred in Japan's system of trade and commerce: (1) the *za* lost their patrons and thus became independent self-regulating entities; and (2) many new merchants emerged as trade increased, and new markets were established based entirely on the merchants' own rules.

The emergence of new markets and new rules was triggered by a change in the normal mode of business during the 15th century. The system evolved from the traveling merchants' "standing markets" to one in which the merchants estab-

---

[4] The Kōfukuji, a temple in Nara, had at least 85 different *za* under its patronage in the 14th century. Some of these *za* were fairly large: in Kyoto, one merchant group reported 148 members, although 10–20 seems to have been the more usual size (Toyoda 1963: 166).

lished permanent shops where they would sit and wait for customers. These new shops were called *mise* (from *miseru*: to let see, to show), as merchants had goods on display on a regular basis. The development of fixed markets divided merchants into "traveling" and "sedentary" vendors, and thus created a functional differentiation among the *za*. The old location-specific *za* under the patronage of a landlord or temple were called "old *za*"(*honza*). Reflecting the original system, these had a strict hierarchy and hereditary membership rights, no new entry was allowed, and disputes were settled by the patron. The limits on entry forced those who wanted to start a business to form "new *za*" (*shinza*), which originally consisted of those merchants who were denied entry into the old setups. The new *za* had a more democratic, flat structure, and no limits on membership. Since these new merchants did not enjoy the patronage of some local authority, their *shinza* were completely independent in their self-regulation: they had to draw up their own rules of conflict settlement and market behavior, and they also needed to self-enforce these rules within the *za* (Toyoda 1963, Takekoshi 1967, Miyamoto 1943, 1948).[5]

However, even the old *za* were facing changes. Having lost their patrons' guidance and facing competition from the new *za*, in the 16th century the old *za* began to draft their own bylaws to establish their organizations more firmly. The first sets of official bylaws by an old *za* we know of are from 1517 in Kyoto and 1570 in Hakata. These bylaws determined the *za*'s local business areas, the kinds of business, limits to entry and other measures aimed at stemming the loss of monopoly privileges. In addition to the bylaws, the *za* established behavioral rules. One common rule was a prohibition against trade with outsiders, i.e., a boycott. The *za* merchants also held regular meetings and set policies, rules, and an internal governance code for their members. Such "*za* laws" became more frequent during the 16th century (Toyoda 1963: 172, Takekoshi 1967).

As the patrons lost power, the *za* took the regulation of markets into their own hands. For instance, the Kōfukuji (Nara) market rules included a fixed exchange rate between copper and gold, as well as copper and silver. The *za* established price limits for rice (to be revised for every harvest season), and prohibited discounts on any goods. In 1509, the Shinjuku market rules stipulated that trade was to be conducted every five days, on the 1st, 6th, 11th and so forth day of the month. The market rules also prohibited forcing a purchase or using violence to close a transaction. Goods and horses brought to the market in the morning could not be used as collateral for debt on that same day—a rule presumably intended to curb speculative deals and gambling. Merchants who had borrowed money or rice could not be pressed for it on the market day; a violator of this rule would have had his name publicly posted. Likewise, it was prohibited to enter a tavern and act violently. Anyone caught doing so was arrested and had his name posted for public censure (Takekoshi 1967: I: 373–4).

---

[5] The division into "old" and "new" *za* can be traced back to the period after the Nanbokuchō wars of the early 14th century, but the real functional differentiation is dated to the 15th century by most observers; see Yamamura (1973) and Toyoda/Sugiyama (1977) for an analysis of the early period.

Most of these rules simply aimed to keep the markets orderly. They were enforced primarily through the obstruction of future business opportunities, for publicly announcing the names of offenders was not only a measure to invoke shame. Rather, this had very practical consequences, as it made it difficult for such a merchant to find trading partners in the future, or possibly even to be admitted into the market. While the merchants could not rely on a legal system or on an authority to enforce penalties, they could employ the loss of reputation and future business as a strong deterrent to cheating.

Whereas local markets and trade were thus conducted in relatively orderly fashion, the country was in effect in a warlike state during most of the 16th century. As military leadership kept changing, and local *daimyō* took control over the formerly privately held *shōen*, the merchants not only had to set their own rules but they now also began to collect their own taxes and tariffs. Merchants took over provincial barriers that the former landlords had neglected, or built new barriers to increase their *za* revenue. While the *daimyō* were fighting battles, the merchants, through their tight associations, became politically powerful (Takekoshi 1967: I: 239).

The Three Unifiers and Trade Associations

After about a century of political turmoil, in the late 16th century the first of Japan's famed three "unifiers" (including Toyotomi Hideyoshi and Tokugawa Ieyasu), an emerging powerful *daimyō* by the name of Oda Nobunaga, began to take control over increasing parts of the country and introduced policies to curb the power of the local merchants. The most consequential of these measures was the *rakuichi-rakuza*, "free the markets, open the *za*" policy. The *rakuichi-rakuza* measures included the abolition of market taxes and fees, the revocation of the exclusive rights of *za*, and the abolition of all entry barriers by abolishing the closed membership rules. These policies were not triggered by the warlord's insights into the economic theory of free trade, but by political objectives. First, by abolishing all *za* on principle, Oda could make politically motivated exceptions and grant special rights to loyal supporters or industries he deemed important in certain territories (Miyamoto 1943: 205). Second, for unification of the country, the *daimyō* who had assumed local powers during the 16th century needed to be subjugated. Part of their power rested on the merchant *za* in their territories, as these *za* provided them with revenues and products. By abolishing the foundations of the old system, Oda undermined the standing of the merchants and of their affiliated shrines and temples, and was thus able to curb the power of the *daimyō* (Miyamoto 1978a: 45).[6] The *rakuichi-rakuza* policy

---

[6] In addition, Yamamura (1973: 457) suggests that from the perspective of the local *daimyō*, the existence of *za* (which allowed the *daimyō* to collect taxes) had become less lucrative than an increase in trade (which allowed them to collect more tariffs and duties). This shift in revenue sources lowered the resistance to Oda's policy among the local warlords.

contributed to Oda's success, who by the year 1603 had brought large parts of the country under his control. Reflecting the positive reputation that this decisive policy has earned in Japanese economic history, in June 1994 the Economic Planning Agency launched the "*Rakuichi-rakuza* Study Group" (*Rakuichi-rakuza kenkyūkai*) with the task to outline specific deregulation measures necessary to assure Japan's international competitiveness in the 1990s (EPA 1994b).

Understandably, the merchants resented the *rakuichi-rakuza* policy because it undermined their trade system, and many *za* continued surreptitiously. In addition, the new government granted exceptions to the rule, thus keeping the system of merchant associations intact. For example, the unifiers standardized the currency to unify the country, and they created new *za* to run the government's minting monopoly. These were the gold *za* (*kinza*) of 1595, the silver *za* (*ginza*; located in what is today central Tokyo) of 1598, and the copper *za* (*zeni-za*) of 1636; related to these, the *za* for scales and measures was also officially acknowledged. Elsewhere, exceptions were made from the strict *rakuichi-rakuza* rule to appease certain *daimyō*. Thus, while the new Shogunate claimed to enforce the "no *za*" policy strictly, and on paper prohibited all groups that functioned based on self-regulation, even in the capital *za* soon reemerged. The *rakuichi-rakuza* policy therefore did not result in a market free of all restrictions; instead, it led to a new configuration of the markets that centered around the castle-towns. Rather than relying on patronage by a landlord or shrine/temple, markets became based on self-regulation by merchants embedded in a more sophisticated system of rules and regulations.

In sum, the *za* constitute the first known form of self-regulation among a group of Japanese businessmen. *Za* developed in pre-modern Japan to supplement the lack of a legal and regulatory order, and to establish mechanisms that would prevent merchants from being cheated. In their initial state, *za* were monopolies meant to foster economic development; patrons protected the *za* because their self-regulation stimulated economic development, which in turn translated into political power in the provinces. Over time, entrepreneurial merchants began to challenge the monopoly system, and self-regulation through *za* became independent from political patronage. The *za* developed rules entailing mutual regulation and control, which became the main characteristics of the new trade associations in the Tokugawa period as well as of trade associations in the 20th century.

7.2. The *Nakama* of the Tokugawa Period (1603–1868)

'Merchant dishonesty was common, and almost expected, when transactions were not on a regular basis, and people preferred to do continuous business with a particular merchant whom they could know and hold responsible.'

(Miyamoto Matao, cited after Sheldon 1958: 41)

The further development and sophistication of trade associations were triggered by the rapid expansion of markets and traffic in the Tokugawa era. Without a legal system to enforce trade agreements should a counterparty renege, merchants had to rely on alternative institutions that would safeguard them against being exploited. In continuation of the *za*, manufacturers (artisans) formed guilds (still called *za*), while merchants (traders) established fixed-membership trade associations, called *nakama*, lit.: "among those who know each other". Over time, a "share" (*kabu*) system developed which served to limit entry to the associations, and trade associations generally came to be known as *kabu nakama*.

The Development of the Economy in the Tokugawa Period

The 265 years of the Tokugawa period (1603–1868) were largely peaceful and witnessed a huge rise in Japan's standard of living. The country's population expanded from 12 to 26 million people. Commercial activity flourished nationwide, thanks to a unified currency and a relatively sophisticated system of communication and information exchange. The Tokugawa Shogunate (*bakufu*) instituted a set of rules and criminal laws, which were enforced in the regions by city governors (*machi bugyō*). What really triggered the advancement of commerce, however, was the clear division of society into four separate classes.[7] At the top of the hierarchy were the emperor, the military leaders and their employees, the *samurai* (*bushi*). To enforce peace, the Shogunate forced the *samurai* to give up their swords. *Samurai* became *de facto* government officials and administrators who received a rice stipend but were not allowed to engage in commerce or manufacturing. The second echelon of society was the farmers, followed by artisans and manufacturers of products. At the bottom of the ladder were the merchants and traders. Since the military aristocracy and *samurai* (about 10% of the population) lived in the cities and castle-towns, while the farmers (84% of the population) were not allowed to leave their land, the merchants became middlemen between the producing and the consuming parts of society. They did this by shipping products from the countryside into the cities, changing rice into money, running warehouses for the *daimyō* in the large cities, and providing credit for the *daimyō*.

The regional domains (*han*) were initially quite self-sufficient. However, by the mid-17th century, the *daimyō* came to realize the benefits of product specialization and trade, and encouraged merchants to pass through their barriers. The central market hub and port was Osaka with its extended channel system. Most domains operated rice warehouses there, and more products were produced or processed here than in any other place in the country. Over time, the capital Edo (Tokyo) grew in size and importance, and the trade between the two cities was most active. Goods were transported either by land on the *Tōkaidō*, the "Eastern

---

[7] This hierarchy is referred to as "*shi-nō-kō-shō*": "samurai–farmers–artisans–merchants".

Sea highway" between the two cities, or more conveniently by boat. With increasing traffic and trade, post stations along the *Tōkaidō* grew into markets, thus furthering regional development.

This new interregional trade brought changes for the distribution system. While in the Muromachi period the pattern had been from producer to periodic markets to the consumer, it changed in the Tokugawa era into one of producer to wholesaler to retailer to consumer. The greater distances to be covered and the growth of trade and product categories required several layers of middlemen with special market knowledge. These wholesalers were (and still are) called *tonya* (or *toiya* in Osaka). At first, *tonya* were simply all-round middleman-merchants.[8] By the mid-17th century, however, they specialized, first by the products they handled, and then by their position in the distribution process. Accordingly, purchasing *tonya*, loading *tonya*, ship-owning *tonya*, and unloading *tonya* emerged. In 1697, there were 826 *tonya* in Osaka alone (Miyamoto 1978a: 41–3).

Initially, the *tonya* were brokers (*ni-uke*, "freight acceptors") rather than dealers. That is, they would not use their own money to assume positions on their own account, but they would buy, as an agent, on customers' orders. *Tonya* thus initially made money not from the spread between buying and selling price, but from fees for warehousing and transport. As trade volume continued to increase and as the *tonya* began to specialize in certain services in certain products, they began to make proprietary trades on their own accounts and accumulated some inventory; as such, they were called *shi-ire tonya* ("inventory *tonya*"). This allowed *tonya* to earn profits by speculating on future price changes, but it also exposed them to the risk of accepting bad quality shipments, and of losing the freight during transport to bad weather, robbery, or sea accidents.

The *tonya* therefore felt a need to manage their transportation system better and developed a mutual insurance system. In 1694, the Edo *tonya* formed the Federation of 10 *Tonya* Associations. The ten members were associations of merchants, each of which handled a different kind of product, which they shipped to the Osaka market regularly. The Federation then affiliated with a shippers' *tonya* association with whom they did regular business; i.e., they formed a co-dependency between several associations across various specialized *tonya* areas. In this way, the *tonya* cooperated on loss settlements that occurred during common shipments, tied captains into long-term relations to avoid dishonesty, and could negotiate group or volume shipping prices (Miyamoto 1978a: 44, Sheldon 1958: 58). Concurrently, the Osaka merchants engaged in a similar setup, the Federation of 24 *Tonya* Associations. Before long, the two federations began to cooperate, further enhancing the benefits to their members by increasing the number of cooperating firms.

---

[8] Such middlemen also existed in the Kamakura and Muromachi periods, when they were called *toimaru*. In the Muromachi years, these were special merchants employed by the military aristocracy and their retainers to serve as agents for forwarding goods and tax revenues from home provinces to the Shogunate in Kyoto (cf. Toyoda/Sugiyama 1977: 130, 134).

The Resurgence of Associations

Although the new Tokugawa Shogunate had prohibited all guilds with its *raku-ichi-rakuza* policy, merchants' associations proved too powerful and too import-ant for trade creation to be ruled out. In the course of the 17th century, the Shogunate had to reissue its prohibitions repeatedly, indicating that the forma-tion and activities of such groups continued: with the increase in trade and commerce, there were more merchants in each product or trade category and the new markets required new rules (Sheldon 1958: 50, Miyamoto 1943, 1948). In addition to the surreptitious re-emergence of associations, the Shogunate also began licensing *nakama* in industries where such associations would simplify governmental regulation; i.e., associations were allowed as a tool for public policy implementation. The two outstanding examples, in which trade associations have officially delegated regulatory functions even in the present day, are the Public Bath House (*sentō*) Association, acknowledged in 1650, and the Hairdressers' Association of 1659. Each member of these associations received a share (*kabu*), which represented a membership right and was not tradable or transferable without the group's permission. An association issued a limited number of *kabu* to restrict entry. Every *kabu* holder, or member, was required to pay a small annual fee called *myōga-kin* ("thank-you money") to the Shogunate in return for receiving membership. That meant that no one could open a bath house or beauty parlor without being a member of the association, and one could become a member of the association only with permission of the other members and by the Shogunate. We can only guess why the Shogunate adopted this scheme; in post-WWII Japan, the official explanation for restricting entry into these businesses was the goal to maintain hygiene standards.

Once the Shogunate had allowed these associations and the logic of the *kabu* system had been established, other industries claimed that they, too, needed to regulate entry for public policy purposes. The first to persuade the government of this were the money-changers (*ryōgae-ya*). As mentioned earlier, while Tokugawa Ieyasu had unified the currency, many low-quality coins remained in circulation, and it was common practice for merchants to cheat by mixing good money with bad. One of the more entrepreneurial money-changers in the early Tokugawa days opened a permanent store and worked hard to earn a reputation for honesty; once he had achieved this, other dealers joined him to form an exclusive group of money-changers with strict business rules and an ethical code, as well as mutual loan guarantees. The money-changers thus established credibility by association. However, without official recognition as a *kabu nakama* the money-changers were unable to exclude nonmembers from entering the market, and they therefore began to lobby the government for official recognition, which they were granted in 1679 (Sheldon 1958: 57).

The last decree issued to stop the *nakama* is dated 1670. After that time, the Shogunate apparently realized that "thank-you money", i.e., tax payments by associations, would significantly increase revenues.[9] With the official recognition by the Shogunate, the "trade customs and habits" (*shōkankō*) that the associations had developed undercover were accepted as official market rules. One of these customs was to prohibit business by nonmembers. The limitation of membership *kabu* was continued, although in the newly emerging groups, the *nakama* themselves, rather than the Shogunate, determined membership limits.

Internal Structure of the Nakama

Each *kabu-nakama* had its own set of rules and bylaws, which determined the "trade customs and habits" of the particular industry. The bylaws typically also contained an ethical code, obliging members to be honest. The internal structure of a typical *nakama* in the Tokugawa period was amazingly similar to that of a contemporary trade association. The highest decision-making organ was the "members' conference" or general meeting (*sōkai*), which met twice a year, in spring and in fall. The association was run by a board of directors: the standing director (who was often an employed staff person, like the *senmu riji* nowadays), the annual directors, and the monthly directors. The directors were elected officials, who typically were the heads of the most important *nakama* member firms. They met regularly at a fixed office to run the daily business, but the general meeting could replace them anytime if their performance was deemed unsatisfactory (Miyamoto 1943: 206–8, Miyamoto 1958, Takekoshi 1967: III: 245).

The work of the directors in running the *nakama* can be divided into five categories. One task was to collect taxes and monetary contributions, and pass them on to the Shogunate or the *daimyō*; usually, the required amount would be split equally among all association members. The second important task was the admission of new members. If the number of *kabu* was limited, a new applicant had to buy a *kabu* before he could become a member; the groups also usually restricted the trading of these *kabu*. If membership was open and *kabu* not limited, all members convened to discuss the trade record and quality of a new applicant. Either way, *nakama* were quite cautious in deciding whom to admit to the club in order not to jeopardize their own reputation. The third administrative task of the directors was to punish any members who had violated the *nakama* rules. The standard punishment for any offense was for the *nakama* to prohibit the member from trading for a certain period, confiscate his tools or otherwise

---

[9] A further reason for the Shogunate's policy shift was a change in the structure of the merchant class itself. In the early Tokugawa years, merchants were closely related to powerful provincial families, which were a threat to the new Shogunate. However, by the end of the 17th century, many new merchant houses, *tonya*, shippers, and money changers had developed. These were a support rather than a threat to the Shogunate, and accordingly had to be protected rather than persecuted. In addition, the more financially dependent the *daimyō* and the *samurai* became on the merchant class, the more their support for business grew.

keep him from engaging in the business.[10] The duration of such a suspension depended on the severity of the violation. The fourth task for the directors was to set prices; the rule was that the *nakama* determined the price of the service or product, and no member could change this price. Also, some *nakama* limited the quantity of output that each member could produce to curb price competition among members. Thus, by establishing limitations on membership qualification, regulating price, and sometimes regulating quantity, the *nakama* established tight protection against competition. Organizing their activities in groups also allowed merchants to enforce quality control and establish trade standards (Miyamoto 1958: 151–260, Takekoshi 1967: III: 269).

Finally, *nakama* performed a social function (Miyamoto 1958: 106). Most of them held regular Shintōist and Buddhist festivals, gave gifts to shrines and temples, and fostered a "professional" and "group spirit" among their members. This was easy, as the *nakama* members had to live in the same quarter of the city; they held their own parties, organized picnics and other entertainment. Sometimes members held joint property, possibly to reinforce a system of mutual help. The contemporary word for this task category is to create *shinboku* (friendship, mutual dependence, trust, and joint objectives; cf. Chapter 2).

The Economic Functions of Nakama

The merchants had two primary concerns in the developing markets. The first was the danger of defaults on trade agreements: cheating and reneging were prevalent in the marketplace, and there was a constant stream of "upstarts" entering the market from the countryside. Second, merchants were worried about the high variance in quality of products, services and money: as trade increased, so did product differentiation that made quality checks difficult. The solution was to gather in associations. The functions of these associations can be divided into three major categories: barriers to entry, price collusion and rule-setting.

First, as seen already, the *nakama* served to restrain competition by keeping competitors out through many entry barriers, which ranged from obvious to highly sophisticated, such as limiting entry to the association by limiting access to the living quarters. To enforce their rules, the *nakama* had a strict "refusal to deal" policy: members were not allowed to deal with outsiders, be that in their own trade or with outsiders in other product categories. Another favored barrier to entry was to demand certain quality and other standards. To be effective barriers, these standards had to be set such that only merchants who had been

---

[10] As mentioned in Chapter 5.2, this was exactly the type of punishment—maybe unusual in Western eyes—that the MOF chose to condemn Nomura Securities after the compensation scandal broke in June 1991. At the time, many foreign observers wondered why the company was not punished on the basis of legal review, rather than just having its business closed down for a few days.

in the business for a long time could actually meet them. For instance, requiring that a shipper had a certain volume before he could apply for membership meant that no aspiring shipping *tonya* could join the association. Second, *nakama* strove to ensure high profit margins through setting price limits, which were sometimes reinforced by output limitations. To curb competition among their members, many *nakama* set up a system of "fair profit" which was effectively market share allocation, either by volume or by region (Miyamoto 1943: 159, 209). In this way, all members earned a generous and stable profit margin, and yet no one had to fear encroachment on his market share by *nakama* members.

The *nakama* also formulated market rules to substitute for a legal framework. While the Tokugawa Shogunate had begun establishing a number of laws in the 18th century, most conflicts were settled through conciliation, which involved a cumbersome and costly process of appealing to the Shogunate offices (Henderson 1965). Related to the establishment of market rules were the functions of trade creation and trade facilitation. The *nakama* did this by establishing a mutual intra-*nakama* and inter-*nakama* credit and loan system. First, the *nakama*, having carefully screened all its members, guaranteed the financial standing of its members (Miyamoto 1943: 210). By rejecting weak enterprises, the *nakama* could afford to grant privileges to their members, such as easy credit and an institutional guarantee of a member's creditworthiness. Together with repeated trade, credit guarantees helped to overcome the common notion that merchants could not be trusted. Over time, stable membership across industries also allowed the merchants to establish a bookkeeping and clearinghouse system for many products. Through this system, transactions were settled on paper only, and in ten-day intervals the traders' respective "bankers" (*yarikuri ryōgae*, "matchmaking agents") would meet to compare the total sum of the book entries and settle the differences (Schaede 1989b). Thus, a short-term mutual trade financing scheme developed. By guaranteeing the entries in the books, the *nakama* backed up their members' creditworthiness and thus created new, efficient means of payment.

Finally, one last *nakama* function in the category of self-regulation was to set incentives and devise deterrents to and penalties for cheating. To protect their industries from cartel-breakers or nonmembers who were swindlers, the *nakama* used blacklisting as their primary weapon (Sheldon 1958: 56). As with the earlier *za* practice, the *nakama* would expose a charlatan and damage his reputation; hearing about his cheating, other merchants would refuse to trade with him. In cases of cartel-breaking by a member, the *nakama* used strict rules of expulsion and penalty payments. To make this deterrent even stronger, many *nakama* set up an "insurance fund" to which everyone had to contribute a sizeable amount. In the event that one member broke the rules, e.g. by undercutting prices, his contribution would be used to pay off those members who had incurred damage through his behavior. As we saw in Chapters 4 and 5, such funds remain a popular means of enforcing self-regulation to date. Given the long-term costs that distrust meant to a merchant, the *nakama* were indeed quite successful in policing their members. The combination of entry barriers, control over production, and credit guarantees for members not only resulted in effective product market controls, but outsiders could also not easily establish alternative associations: they would have had to create completely new markets and new locations, with a reputation of creditworthiness yet to be established. The protection afforded by the *nakama* to their members resulted in stable growth across many industries through the Tokugawa period.

Shogunate Policies Toward Trade Associations

In the course of the Tokugawa period, the Shogunate conducted three major reforms: the Kyōhō reform of the 1720s, the Kansei reform of the 1780s and 90s, and the Tempō reform of the 1830s. Each of these was triggered by a deterioration of the fiscal stability of the government, and each reformed, as one of its core policies, the status and activities of trade associations. The government sought, through these reforms, to utilize the *nakama* in carrying out the desired policies by guiding self-regulation. It was in this period that the pendulum of government involvement in self-regulation began to swing visibly.

The government's economic policy thinking during the Tokugawa years can be divided into two major schools: the "Confucianist" school and the "realist" school (Hall 1951: 29). The Confucianist school rested on the ideal of a large, leading class of diligent and hardworking farmers. Policy measures suggested by this school for 18th-century Japan included suppressing the merchant class and resettling warriors in the countryside and transforming them into farmers. On the other hand, the opposing "realist school" recognized the benefits of commerce and suggested that the Shogunate should adopt policies that would allow it to share some merchants' profits by encouraging their activities and taxing them a fair proportion.

The Kyōhō reform under Yoshimune, the eighth Tokugawa *shōgun*, and its economic adviser Arai Hakuseki, espoused the second approach. Although trained in the Confucianist school, Yoshimune was sufficiently pragmatic to realize that self-regulation could not be stopped and therefore was best utilized to the Shogunate's benefit (Hall 1951: 30). The reform was triggered by a major financial crisis: the problems caused by a massive fire in Edo in 1657 had been compounded by the spendthrifty ways of Yoshimune's predecessors. These predecessors had tried to resolve the slide in Shogunate finances by lowering the gold and silver content in the coins, which had led to steep inflation. What worried Yoshimune most, however, was that the price of rice had fallen relative to the general price level; since taxes, *daimyō* finances, and *samurai* stipends were all based on rice, this meant both a crisis in the farming population and lower tax revenues. The measures Yoshimune adopted included a tax and administrative reform, new sumptuary regulations for the *samurai*, and the restoration of the currency. All this still left Yoshimune with the problem of falling rice prices, and he decided to use the merchants' *nakama* to control prices.

In 1721, Yoshimune issued a decree recognizing trade associations by establishing a system of officially licensing the shares (*kabu*) of all *nakama*, and requiring merchants to join such associations. To increase revenue by taxing merchants and to control and regulate prices, the existing "undercover" *nakama* were turned into licensed associations with compulsory membership. A registration fee (*unjō-kin*) was levied for every *nakama* and every *kabu*, and an annual fee, the *myōga-kin*, which was a *de facto* business tax, was imposed on all *kabu* holders. Thus, by acknowledging the associations and making membership compulsory, Yoshimune established a system of registering and taxing merchants.[11] Next, to regulate prices Yoshimune pronounced a "price lowering decree" (*Kakaku hiki-sage rei*) in 1724. Per this decree, prices for all non-basic products were determined to fall, while prices of products made from rice, such as *sake* or soy sauce, were pegged to the rice price to halt their decline. Yoshimune had observed that the *nakama* could fix prices through collusion, and therefore sought to carry out his new price policy through them. In 1726, Yoshimune extended his decree to the *tonya* (wholesalers), who were explicitly asked to establish *nakama* in order to control prices (Hasegawa 1978: 59–60).[12]

The official recognition of the *nakama* marked a significant change in government policy. By using extant private commercial networks to create a regulatory system, the government established an institutionalized role for private sector implementation of policy measures—a system that would characterize Japan's regulatory system for centuries to come. The rules of the merchants became the primary vehicles for policy implementation.

While the Kyōhō reform buttressed government finances and stabilized economic transactions, these improvements lasted only for about 50 years. After Yoshimune, the Shogunate reverted to spending more than tax revenues warranted. During the second half of the 18th century, Japan witnessed two policy reversals that again significantly influenced the activities and role of *nakama*: the reform efforts by Tanuma Okitsugu in the 1770s, and their reversal in the 1780s through the Kansei reform.

Tanuma Okitsugu was an adviser to the *shōgun* and pursued what some observers have labeled "mercantilist" policies (e.g., Hall 1951: 30).[13] He encour-

---

[11] In addition to the newly encouraged formations, pre-Tokugawa cooperatives and *kō* (originally related to pilgrimages) were converted into *nakama* in order to receive the privileges of exclusive rights to trade and protection by the government (Miyamoto 1943: 212).

[12] Since this was not as effective in increasing the relative value of rice as Yoshimune had hoped, in 1730 he officially recognized the rice futures exchange in Dōjima (Osaka). As futures trading was considered to be gambling, and gambling was assumed to lead to higher prices, Yoshimune tried to prevent gambling in other products through the *nakama*, but invited gambling in rice through approving the futures exchange (Schaede 1989b).

[13] Tanuma was a controversial figure, due partially to his unorthodox rise to power and to his economic policies. In an era of limited upward mobility, Tanuma rose from very humble beginnings to the status of *daimyō* and, finally, Shogunate adviser. While Tanuma was an insightful politician and deal maker, he also developed a reputation for being corrupt and biased. It is said that Tanuma openly welcomed bribes and presents from merchants, in return for which he protected the interests of the *nakama* (Hasegawa 1978: 68).

aged the development of new farmland; reformed the fiscal structure of the Shogunate and set up a revolving loan fund to assist the highly indebted *daimyō*; and he sought to expand foreign trade to reap profits from import tariffs and exports of dried sea products. To bolster Shogunate finances, he actively sought to multiply the *nakama* and repeatedly increased the frequency and amount of the *myōga-kin* tax charged to the associations.

These policies triggered the rapid creation of oligopolies with exclusive rights, as it enriched merchants and their associations. Because merchants could pass a large portion of the ever-rising *myōga-kin* on to their customers by way of higher prices, consumers, and especially the *samurai*, suffered most. Thus, while the merchants prospered, the rest of the population became increasingly worse off. Resentment toward the *nakama* developed, forcing the Shogunate to make some policy changes. Tanuma was replaced as adviser by Matsudaira Sadanobu, who was a "Confucianist fundamentalist" (Hall 1951: 31). In launching the Kansei reform of 1787–93, he imposed strict austerity measures on both *samurai* and merchants; retracted sword-wearing principles granted to certain (rich) merchants by Tanuma; ordered a general cancellation of all *samurai* debt; and launched a major purge and administrative reform to eliminate corruption among Shogunate officials. Most important, Matsudaira dissolved some of the largest associations, primarily to free up trade that would bring goods into Edo. Unfortunately for the Shogunate, neither Tanuma's nor Matsudaira's reform measures could halt the continuing fiscal slide of the nation's finances. Crop failures and famines in the 1830s necessitated further measures.

The third large reform, the Tempō Reform of 1830–44 under Shogunate adviser Mizuno Tadakuni, brought about an interesting real-world experiment with market institutions, as it rested on the complete abolition of all trade associations. Mizuno judged that merchants had profited excessively from Tanuma's policies and aimed to return to the old societal hierarchy which placed merchants at the bottom. The *nakama*, Mizuno thought, were the primary reason for high prices and inflation, because their trade practices and collusion hindered competitive pricing. In an early version of antitrust policy, Mizuno argued that associations engaged in unfair trade behavior, and in 1841 he issued a decree dissolving all *nakama* (Hasegawa 1978: 84). This decree was accompanied by other reform measures, such as sending farmers from the cities back to their fields, reinstating sumptuary regulations for the *samurai*, and setting low maximum price limits on basic products other than rice.

We will never know how effective these other measures might have been, for the dissolution of the associations effectively stopped all commerce: the "reform" halted the trade-creating functions of the *nakama*.[14] While Mizuno's economic insights into the effects of collusion on price may have been correct, he certainly

---

[14] Some analysts have pointed out that not all *nakama* actually dissolved, but they now had to operate undercover. This made it very difficult to enforce trade rules and forward loan guarantees. The advanced operations of the *nakama* came to halt (e.g., Hasegawa 1978: 85).

overlooked the trade associations' functions in creating loan guarantees and efficient market organization. By disbanding the associations, Mizuno effectively toppled the pillars of the market system. The collateral for transportation, loans, and all trade-financed transactions disappeared from one day to the next, and trade rules became ambiguous. Transactions reverted to rudimentary forms without loans or other trade agreements. Many markets collapsed, and especially in Osaka and Edo, where the new policies were strictly enforced, advanced commerce came to a halt. Soon after beginning his reform, Mizuno was ousted.

Understanding the role of the *nakama* in market and trade creation, in 1851 Mizuno's successor Abe Masahiro issued a *Tonya* Reinstallation Decree. *Tonya* and *nakama* were allowed to reestablish in their old quarters, with their old rules. Simultaneously, they were also exempted from the *myōga-kin* tax. But in contrast with the earlier rules, the government did not impose limits on the number of members by predetermining the number of licenses (*kabu*) for each association. Rather, all limits on membership were abolished and rural merchants were encouraged to join the associations. Before long, the *nakama* lost their former control over the entry of new firms, and new merchants from the provinces entered the central markets in droves. Therefore, the "reinstallation" of the *nakama* in 1851 was not a continuation of the old system; instead, by opening up membership, the government undermined the old dominant position of some of the merchants and trading houses (Hasegawa 1978: 88; Miyamoto 1958: 319–56).

Unfortunately, again, it is unclear what the effects of these policies would have been, because soon after Abe had introduced his policies, the Tokugawa Shogunate was brought to fall.[15] In 1853 Commodore Perry appeared in Japan and forced an opening of harbors and commerce treaties with a number of countries by 1858. The first effect of the onset of international trade was a huge increase in domestic prices, as Japan lost control over its currency owing to the outflow of gold and copper coins triggered by foreign trade. The resulting political and institutional chaos weakened old market structures, and new export trading companies and new financial houses developed.

In 1868, the year of the Meiji restoration, the Tokugawa Shogunate ended, and with it went all its official laws and rules. While some large *tonya* and money-changers, such as Mitsui or Nomura, and some producers of defense-related products successfully turned themselves into modern businesses, many old artisans and merchants were unable to persist with open markets and international trade (Smith, T. 1955). The new entrepreneurial leaders formed alliances with the young *samurai* who became the new political leaders of the country. But while the *kabu nakama* were ordered to dissolve, many lingered on and the notion of

---

[15] The Shogunate also reversed some of Abe's market-oriented measures before they could bear fruit. In 1857, after Abe had resigned, the Shogunate reintroduced the *myōga-kin* tax to increase Shogunate revenues. The number of licenses (*kabu*) was again restricted, as the Shogunate aimed to control the merchants in a period of social and economic disorder and political upheaval (Hasegawa 1978: 88, Miyamoto 1948: 208).

the trade association remained firmly established. The heritage of the *nakama* influenced the shaping of the new business organizations of the late 19th and 20th centuries.

The *kabu nakama* system, which was not based on any economic insights by the government but developed in response to the merchants' own economic needs, had both positive and negative effects on the development of commerce in Japan. The *nakama* system supported economic development in that monopoly rents allowed *nakama* members to accumulate wealth, which they used to diversify into additional businesses such as money-changing and credit creation. Fixed prices forced merchants to compete in quality, thus constantly stimulating product improvements. Within the confines of the *nakama*, technology advances could be co-developed but kept secret from merchants in other business fields or regions. The *nakama* organization encouraged training of young apprentices, and provided financing for trade and inventory. By enabling the *tonya* to create mutual insurance schemes for transportation, the *nakama* system furthered the development of interregional commerce. Finally, by stipulating and enforcing market rules, the *nakama* system helped to overcome the mistrust prevalent among merchants; by creating institutionalized markets, the *nakama* formed the foundations of trade.

On the negative side, due to the rigid barriers to entry, reinforced by the Shogunate's seclusion policy that disallowed most foreign trade, few fresh ideas entered the merchants' groups, either through startups or from abroad. While membership in merchant groups afforded protection that resulted in wealth, their restrictive rules limited stimulation that might have come through inter-regional competition. The elaborate system of controls and restrictions translated into constant interference by the associations with private business decisions, and thus inhibited entrepreneurial opportunities. By the end of the Tokugawa period, what had been a system that spurred development and trade had turned into a handicap that slowed industrial development. Therefore, when the political system was reformed after the Tokugawa Shogunate had stumbled, the industrial system was also reorganized.

7.3. The Meiji and Taishō Years (1868 through the 1920s)

After Japan was opened through foreign trade treaties, a group of young *samurai* launched a *coup d'état*. They toppled the Shogunate, "restored" the Emperor who is known by his posthumous name Meiji, moved him and his castle to the new capital Tokyo, and formed a new central government. The domains were abolished, as the country was divided into prefectures with local governments that were dependent on the central government. Western-style ministries were formed, and they were charged in their foundation charters with the explicit task of both supporting and regulating industries. The first ministries to be established were the Ministry of Finance (*Ōkurashō*) and the Foreign Affairs Ministry (*Gaimushō*) in 1869, followed by the Ministry of Agriculture and Commerce (MAC, *Nōshōmushō*) in 1881. The Ministry of Finance was placed in charge of duties and tariffs, the budget and taxes, but it assumed a variety of additional tasks over time, including banking regulation. MAC's history was more complicated: this ministry was split into the Ministry of Agriculture (MA) and the Ministry of Commerce and Industry (MCI, *Shōkōshō*) in 1925, and MCI became the Ministry of Munitions (MM, *Gunjushō*) in 1943, until it was turned into the Ministry of International Trade and Industry (MITI, *Tsūshō-sangyōshō*) in 1947.[16]

Japan's economic development between 1868 and 1930 can be divided roughly into four phases. Between the late 1850s and 1885, the foundations of economic growth were laid by the establishment of modern, large-scale factories, and the expansion of transportation (ports) and communications (banking and postal systems) infrastructure. The period of 1885–1905 marks Japan's industrial takeoff, which was driven predominantly by textiles and the heavy machinery industry, which was spurred by the wars against China (1895–6) and Russia (1905–6). Third, the period of 1905–20 saw the development of the economic structure which still characterizes Japan today: a high degree of market concentration in the leading industries, and the dual structure (*nijū kōzō*) of a dominant but small group of very large companies and a huge number of small- and medium-sized companies and affiliated suppliers. During the first two decades of this century, the government actively supported the growth of a few large companies so that they would achieve economies of scale and thus could compete effectively with foreign firms. At the same time, the initial trade and commerce treaties with foreign countries effectively prohibited Japan from imposing tariffs or quotas. Even after these "unequal treaties" were modified, the policies of relatively free trade persisted, in spite of active lobbying by large industries in the 1920s; real change was caused only by the government's war-related restrictions in the 1930s. The 1920s was a decade of crisis, caused by the post-WWI recession, the Tokyo earthquake of 1923, and the international Great Depression. During the decade, the military became stronger, and political conflict was generally "solved" through assassinations, usually of politicians by the military (cf. Takahashi 1973: I, Umemura/Yamamoto 1989).

As one of its first actions, the new Meiji government abolished all *kabu nakama* in 1871. The official rationale was a new "free trade" policy, but in reality this policy reflected a desire by the government to influence private business agreements and control their self-regulation. The government's policy approach was to discriminate among industries: those industries that the government wanted to see grow quickly (primarily export industries) were encouraged to form associations that would help cartel agreements. Cartel agreements, in

---

[16] See Johnson (1982) for the history of this ministry.

turn, were understood as furthering the national interest (Miyajima 1986: 118, Fujita 1988: 87). Trade associations were considered synonymous with "cartels", and coordinating their activities gradually became a crucial component of public economic policy.

Business, however, was little impressed by these political stratagems. The Meiji government had no institutions in place to enforce its new association policy. Within a few months after the *kabu nakama* had officially been abolished in 1871, a group of middlemen in dyestuff trading in Osaka formed the *Eizokugumi* (lit: "permanent group"), and fish dealers in Kyoto formed the *Uonakagai Kaisha* ("fish brokerage company") with bylaws stipulating entry restrictions and market rules similar to those of the Tokugawa period. Many similar organizations emerged one after the other, and while they could not call themselves *nakama*, many of them built directly on their *nakama* predecessors. As in the earlier periods, the government had abolished the *nakama* without providing a legal and social order for business to replace self-regulation; the new Commercial Code would not be passed until 1893. Enterprises therefore still needed to establish market rules themselves. By 1886, there were at least 1,579 associations whose functions, as with the earlier *nakama*, were to protect privileges, establish trade rules, and endorse credit for their members (Fujita 1988: 88).

Reflecting the emerging industrial organization of a "dual structure" of coexisting large and small enterprises, the associations that developed after the 1880s fell into two large categories: those for small- and medium-sized enterprises, and those for large firms. Trade associations involving small merchants in one industry were usually regional and were called *dōgyō kumiai* (lit.: "same industry cooperatives"; usually translated as "local cooperatives"). Small manufacturing firms also formed regional associations called *kōgyō kumiai* ("manufacturing cooperatives"). In contrast, large firms in one industry tended to form nationwide associations that had various names such as those ending in "-*kōgyōkai*" (manufacturing association) or "*kyōkai*" (association). As seen in Chapter 2, this differentiation by name, scope, and function between small-firm cooperatives and large-firm associations still exists today. Finally, umbrella organizations for both categories, such as the Chamber of Commerce and the precursors of Keidanren and Nikkeiren, also developed in the early 20th century.

The Development of Small-Firm Local Cooperatives (Dōgyō Kumiai)

Although the local governments had implemented the central order to dissolve the *nakama* in 1871, many new local organizations emerged to organize trade. Officially recognizing the necessity of market rules, in 1877 the City of Tokyo established the *Tōkyō Shōhō Kaigisho* (Tokyo Chamber of Commercial Law), and most major cities followed suit in an effort to establish a commercial order. The primary function of these chambers was to support the establishment of local cooperatives for small businesses to foster trade though credit creation and regulation (Takahashi 1973: 76–7, Fujita 1988: 89).

The chambers led to a huge increase in the formation of cooperatives, and by 1886, there were more than 1,500 local cooperatives across the country. The central government tried to assume some control over this process in an effort to unify the country's regulatory system. The ministry in charge of associations was MITI's forerunner, the Ministry of Agriculture and Commerce (MAC). To assist the associations in improving trade conditions, in 1884 MAC issued the "Basic Regulations for Local Trade Associations" (*Dōgyō kumiai junsoku*). These Regulations stipulated compulsory membership based on a "three-quarters rule" (modified later to two-thirds): if three-quarters or more of the firms in an industry in a certain locality decided to form an association, the remaining one quarter of firms was compelled to join that association. A rule using a similar logic still lives on in today's laws for cooperatives by small- and medium-sized enterprises.[17] The idea was that establishing market rules would function only if all traders were members of the associations. Soon, the local Chambers established their own penal codes to enforce the "three-quarters" membership rule. In 1885, the central government added to these Regulations special consideration and support of associations striving to export high quality products. Over time, MAC's primary goal in regulating the associations shifted to supporting the development of a competitive export industry.

Five years after the Regulations, the government promulgated the new Constitution in 1889. In Section 22, the Constitution granted a general "freedom to move and settle". The associations therefore lost their authority to regulate their members and force nonmembers to join the group. As the legal system developed, members could have sued when coerced to join an association. To bypass this legal issue, the government drafted a new Code for Supervision of Local Cooperatives (*Dōgyō kumiai torishimari kisoku*) in 1892, which explicitly called for compulsory membership for local associations but delegated the drafting of the bylaws to self-regulation. Thus, the government solved the constitutional problem by substituting self-regulation and self-enforcement for government control. Compulsory membership effectively remained in place, but was now privately enforced.

In the 1890s, MAC began to emphasize export promotion as a policy task for associations. The ministry held regular meetings with export-industry representatives to formulate policies to improve quality in traditional industries. As a result of these deliberations the government in 1897 passed the Important Export Products Local Trade Association Law (*Jūyō yushutsu-hin dōgyō kumiai-hō*), which in some respects was a forerunner of the postwar Export Associations Law (cf. Chapter 3.1). This law allowed for the formation of trade associations,

---

[17] This rule established a precedent, as it was used as a model for many prewar, wartime, and postwar cartels (rationalization and depression cartels), as well as the 1957 Small- and Medium-Sized Enterprise Group Organization Law and the 1967 Small- and Medium-Sized Enterprise Promotional Association Law (cf. Chapter 3).

again based on compulsory membership, with the specific purpose of supporting export activities. In fact, to justify compulsory membership business representatives had argued that "preference should be given to promotion of the export business over the freedom of people" (Fujita 1988: 95). Effectively, the Export Associations Law reintroduced the old *kabu nakama* concepts of barriers to entry, limited membership, and privileges for local enterprises engaging in the same trade. The most obvious advantage for the members was that they could charge higher prices than they would have otherwise. Soon, local associations in purely domestic industries successfully lobbied to have the law extended to non-export commodities as well, and in 1900 the law was revised into the Important Commodities Local Trade Association Law. This revised law set the "compulsory rule" at two-thirds: if two-thirds of the firms in the industry wanted to form a local association, all other companies in that industry were compelled to join. Therefore, industries could apply to MAC to be deemed "important", and once so designated, they would receive government support. Both in structure and intent, this law bears a close resemblance with the 1931 Important Industries Control Law (see section 7.4) and the "depressed industries laws" of the 1970s and 1980s.

Within this emerging regulatory structure, the functions of local trade associations in the early Meiji years fell into the following broad categories: price controls; employment relations; enforcing compulsory membership; and monitoring compliance. Specifically, associations were charged with supporting the industry's growth by complementing the members' managerial resources and supporting small firms by restricting competition and ensuring certain profit margins. This included activities such as increasing product quality by sharing skills among members; conducting product inspections; sharing large-scale machinery; enlarging product markets; helping financing; mutually training apprentices; and collecting and disseminating information on related industries and foreign markets. These activities are typical functions of cooperatives overall, whose primary mission it is to support its small-firm members through cooperation and financing schemes. Yet, cooperatives also worked at restraining competition by fixing prices and allocating market shares. Not only was this perfectly legal at the time, it was also encouraged by the Meiji government (Yamazaki/Miyamoto 1988: xii, Kikkawa 1988: 53, Fujita 1988: 91).

Around the turn of the century, quality inspection of export goods became the most important of the associations' functions. Foreign trade had increased enormously, and it was apparent that in order to compete successfully in international markets, Japanese artisans and craftsmen had to improve their quality standards. In particular, maintaining the quality of raw silk exports posed tremendous problems at the time. Silk accounted for one-third of all exports, and Japan was in fierce competition with China for the burgeoning global (mainly U.S.) market for silk. In the end, Japan was successful in this competition thanks to strict quality standards and a rigorous inspection system which resulted in overall high quality and low variance. Based on this success, the Japanese government strengthened export-promotion policies, and in the 1910s, the MAC decided to actively involve small business in the nation's export drive. In 1916, the 1900 law was revised to put even greater stress on the inspection function of local trade associations. During the post-WWI recession and the Tokyo earthquake of 1923, exports by the small business and handicraft sectors declined, and the government became concerned about "excessive competition". To remedy this situation, in 1925 the Important Export Products Manufacturing Associations Law (*Jūyō yushutsuhin dōgyō kumiaihō*) merged the categories of *dōgyō* and *kōgyō kumiai* and allowed for the creation of cartels among exporting firms. This law was revived after WWII to support small firms.

In combination, the laws and rules issued in the first two decades of this century formed the foundations of small-firm cooperatives and shaped their functions to the present day. By building a support base specifically for small-sized businesses, these laws reinforced the emerging dual structure of Japanese industry, i.e., the clear demarcation between large-scale and small-scale firms. The emerging regulatory system was the result of both government policy and industry-developed regulations, with the associations remaining in charge of self-enforcement and sanctioning.

Large-Scale Trade Associations

In the early days of the Meiji period, the government established a number of enterprises in heavy machinery, mining, munitions and other progressive, high-technology industries. After the Matsukata deflation of the 1880s, which marked a period of stringent budget constraints and tight monetary policy, these public companies were sold to a few individuals, mostly the very successful, large entrepreneurs from the Tokugawa years, such as the Mitsui family. With government patronage, these new business giants grew faster than the economy as a whole, and soon the government became dependent on them for political and financial support. Big business had a growing voice in politics, and it appeared that "the tail was beginning to wag the dog" (Fairbank et al. 1965: 505). The term *zaibatsu* came into use, but in contrast to the U.S. trusts of the time, the *zaibatsu* did not so much connote a monopoly in one industry, but conglomerates whose activities spanned many different industries.

Trade associations for large firms emerged around 1900, and became prevalent in the 1920s. Most of these associations developed independent of government guidance, and their primary objectives were to regulate quality and curb "undue" competition; i.e., secure a stable profit margin. In contrast to the smaller cooperatives of the time, however, the large firms were constrained neither by rules on membership nor any other government controls on their formation. Large firms formed and joined the new associations voluntarily. Consequently, these associations were not nearly as stable as the cooperatives, and conflicts with nonmembers were frequent.[18] The first large-scale trade association to form was in banking. In 1876, before a full-fledged banking system had even developed, the roughly 150 banks established since 1868 founded the Association of National Banks. The Japan Paper Manufacturing Association in 1880, and the Japan Cotton Spinners' Association in 1882 followed suit. The primary functions of these early large-scale trade associations were to create a platform for sharing technical information and, later, to control prices (Takahashi 1973: II: 80, Lynn/McKeown 1988: 11).

Probably the most representative of these early associations was the Japan Cotton Spinners' Association (cf. Kikkawa 1988: 78, Lockwood 1954: 231, Saxonhouse 1977).[19] Cotton spinning was one of Japan's leading export industries at the time, and the association stands out as the first to organize the introduction and dissemination of foreign technology, and to develop clever stratagems to create entry barriers and increase profit margins. For instance, in 1893 the Spinners' Association formed a contract with the shipping company Nippon Yūsen Kaisha (NYK) by which NYK received all the association's shipping orders in return for (1) the refusal to transport cotton from India for enterprises that were not members of the association; and (2) a rebate on all India cotton shipments from the official freight rate for the association's members. The first condition meant a "refusal to deal" with nonmembers, and because NYK dominated the shipping line to India, this excluded nonmembers from trade in India cotton. The second condition was an early case of a joint purchase agreement to lower shipping costs through volume buying and rebates for the association's members. By the late 1920s, seven major industries had reached similar purchasing agreements. In some cases, the government supported these; for instance, the shipping line NYK received government subsidies for its services between Bombay and Japan based on the agreement with the cotton spinners (Kikkawa 1988: 67).

Besides blocking imports and new entry, fixing prices, and forming joint purchase organizations, large trade associations also supported the growth and development of the industry indirectly. First, this development function entailed securing scarce labor by preventing poaching of workers between companies and, later, by establishing association-wide provisions against strikes.[20] The second

---

[18] Fairbank et al. (1965: 566) have labeled this situation one of "semi-competitive oligopolies". They also point to a parallel of this pattern of oligopolistic haggling for influence and market share with the pattern of the oligarchic Meiji government with its entry barriers and "club" agreements. On "competitive oligopolies" formed by zaibatsu firms in various industries, see also Hadley (1970).

[19] The association went through multiple name changes over time. It was founded as the Dai Nippon bōseki dōgyō rengōkai in 1882, and eventually changed to Nihon Bōseki rengōkai in 1947; all of these names were abbreviated to "Bōren". In 1952, cotton spinning was the first industry to form an administrative guidance-based cartel (kankoku sotan). Because of its illustrious history and central role in Japan's economic history, this association is often also referred to as the "Glorious Bōren"; see Chapter 3.

[20] The prohibition of poaching other companies' employees can be traced back to the apprenticeship system of the Tokugawa era. It is possible that the Meiji period industry agreements on poaching were the precursor to the postwar system of lifetime employment which has resulted in the absence of a mid-career labor market.

function concerned promotion and extension of market size for the product. This included product examination and the division of government export subsidies among the association's members. During economic downturns, many associations also engaged in quantity restrictions for each member, in what today would be called "rationalization cartels". For instance, between 1902 and 1912, the Cotton Spinners' Association ordered its members to decrease output six times. Third, trade associations sometimes coordinated funding plans and approached banks as a group. This was particularly effective if the trade associations were in designated growth industries. During the recession after the war with China (1896–7), the Cotton Spinners' Association in 1898 received special trade financing from the Yokohama Specie Bank (Kikkawa 1988: 67). In 1920, the Iron Manufacturers' Association obtained emergency financing from five banks, while the Pig Iron Association was allotted subsidies after 1926 (Okazaki 1985). Finally, trade associations also collected and disseminated information on domestic market conditions, regulation, exports, foreign market access, as well as association-specific information such as the minutes of meetings or a summary of agreements reached within the association. Most associations began to publish a monthly bulletin for their members.

Interestingly, in many cases the associations' rules on limiting competition and fixing prices were ineffective in the 1920s. For instance, the Cement Association (*Semento Rengōkai*) was founded in 1924 after several attempts to merge the industry's leading companies had failed due to the antagonism between the two leading firms, Onoda Cement (Mitsui group) and Asano Cement (Yasuda group). The 1923 Tokyo earthquake brought an unexpected relief for the struggling cement industry, and the cement association was created at a time of high demand and limited supply owing to the destruction of Asano's main plant in Kawasaki. In 1924, the major firms in the industry agreed on market share allocations and prescribed a price range for cement. Yet, newly entering firms soon began to encroach onto the market, and had to be admitted lest they undermined the cartel. This new-firm entry watered down the quota agreement, and the system soon fell apart. Only in the 1930s, after the onset of the Great Depression, did the cartel rejoin to form several joint sale companies, which were similar in logic to the joint shipping agreements in cotton: selling all cement through one centralized company increased the bargaining power of the cement firms and served to enforce price-fixing agreements. The new cement cartel proved effective and stimulated a sharp increase in cement prices and a resultant recovery of the industry (Kikkawa 1988, Hashimoto 1985, Kimura 1995).

An early example of market protection through cartel formation is the pig iron and steel industry (Okazaki 1985, Kimura 1995). Pig iron was an industry characterized by high imports, especially from India (accounting for about 40% of the market in 1929). In contrast to the chemical industry, which simply lobbied the government for import protection through tariffs, subsidies and support for technology imports, the pig iron industry formed a price and quantity cartel that included the importers of pig iron. Adherence to cartel agreements was monitored by creating four different associations that were interdependent and rested on mutual agreements not to deal with outsiders. For instance, the five companies forming the *Nichi-man seitetsu* firms, i.e., the iron plants in Japan and Manchuria, formed the Pig Iron Cooperative (*Sentetsu kyōdō kumiai*), and agreed not to sell pig iron to nonmembers. The Steel Manufacturers' Discussion Council (*Seikō kigyō konwakai*) bridged the iron and the steel manufacturers to discuss mutually acceptable prices and, again, to agree not to sell to nonmembers. As imports continued to put these agreements under stress, in 1928 the iron manufacturers formed one joint company in charge of purchasing pig iron, the *Seitetsu kyōdō kōbaikai*. The primary purpose of this purchase company for raw materials was to control prices, i.e., to institute a controlled system of resale price maintenance. Because the importing trading companies were members of this setup, they could not undermine the cartel. That is, rather than relying on the government for protection from imports, the pig iron associations managed to tie the importers into their price cartel.

Two factors in these case histories are notable. The first is the absence of government policies for cement, which was due to the fact that the cement industry was not an exporting industry. Second, the cement cartel of the 1920s is a story of the breakdown of negotiations and distrust among members. Generally, cartels in the prewar period worked only during the recession and depression years. While there were cartels in most major industries, there was also fierce competition among the firms in these industries for market share in a fast-growing economy. The cartel was used during economic downturns and depressed prices, but as long as markets were booming, cartel members competed fiercely with each other. Colluding during recessions effectively created a safety-net for members of the association.[21]

Many cartels were unstable in the 1920s for two major reasons. First, economic growth triggered a lot of new entry into all sectors of industry, barring the newly forming trade associations from achieving complete coverage, i.e., membership of all firms in the industry. There were always outsiders, and even within the associations, some members were unwilling to bow to cartel agreements. Secondly, the free trade regime imposed by the "unequal treaties" meant that imports introduced fierce price competition. For example, the pig iron imports finally became so large that the association began to lobby for tariffs and other import restrictions. It was during the 1920s that Japanese companies learned just how detrimental imports were for domestic price and quantity restrictions. This strengthened their interest in joining associations and keeping both the importing firms and the foreign competitors out.

---

[21] See Chapter 5 for economic theories on this logic. Kikkawa (1988: 76) even argues that ultimately these cartel agreements worked to enhance competition, as output restrictions and price fixing benefited outsiders and marginal (very small) companies to stay in business through periods of recession, only to come back with an economic upswing and undermine the agreements.

The Formation of Umbrella Associations

The first federations to be established were the umbrella associations for the cooperatives formed by small companies. As early as 1791, a town assembly (*machi kaisho*) had been established in Edo as a self-governing body of merchants and bankers. This was reconstructed in 1872 into the "Tokyo Chamber" and in 1878 into the "Tokyo Chamber of Commercial Law". Around that time, a similar organization was founded in Osaka, and by 1882, 16 chambers had been established in the major trade cities of the country.

Next to establishing commercial order through harmonizing self-regulation among the various cooperatives, the chambers also served a public policy function. During the renegotiations of the "unequal trade treaties" during the 1860s, the British requested that Japan establish a system of business input into the decision-making process (Miyamoto 1978: 5). The chambers thus came to represent local business concerns and the national interests in negotiating tariff autonomy with the Western countries. The new Chamber of Commerce Ordinance of 1890 officially recognized these policy functions, and in addition defined the functions of the chambers to include encouraging trade, reporting to the government on business conditions and economic statistics, cooperating with the government on trade issues, and settling commercial disputes (cf. Miyamoto 1978, Takahashi 1973: III: 78–9).

However, the government was dissatisfied with the chambers' effectiveness in representing all business interests, as the emerging industrialists and large businesses refused to join the local cooperatives and thus were not represented by the chambers. The government therefore discontinued its subsidies and other support for the chambers to channel more funds to the new large-scale industries. By the end of WWI, the chambers had lost most of their public policy functions, and they turned more and more into self-help groups for small businesses. In their place, new umbrella organizations of the large industrialists emerged. In 1917, the precursor of Nikkeiren, the Industry Club of Japan (*Nihon kōgyō kurabu*) was founded (cf. Figure 7.1). The Club's initial purpose was to support the growth of the heavy and chemical industries, but it soon developed into a federation concerned with labor issues. To pressure the government for economic reform, a second group was founded in the Japan Economic Federation (*Nihon keizai renmei*, Keidanren's predecessor). From the beginning, the personal relations between the politicians and the *zaikai* (industrialists) were very important in driving government–business relationships, and as the Industry Club became more concerned with labor issues, the Federation emerged as the center for private–public interaction in formulating the national interest at the time. The primary function of the Federation, then, was to lobby and contribute to shaping national policy (Miyamoto 1978: 41). In 1940, both large business umbrella associations were changed to be tied into the wartime control system (cf. Figure 7.1). After WWII, they reemerged as Nikkeiren and Keidanren, while the chambers formed the Chamber of Commerce and Industry.

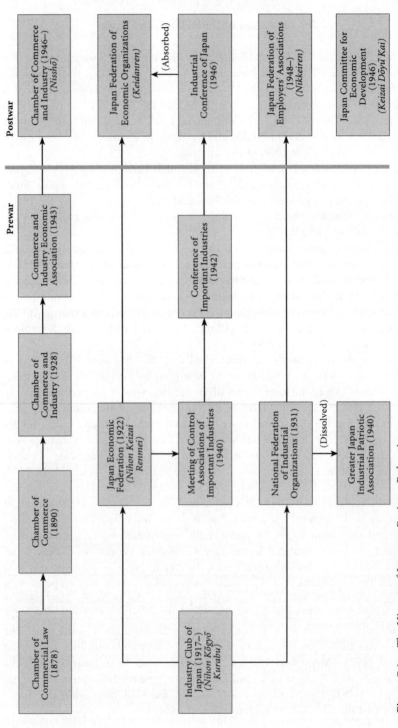

Figure 7.1. The History of Japanese Business Federations

Source: adapted from Miyamoto (1988: 4).

In sum, the Meiji and Taishō years witnessed the formation of a modern state based on a constitution, with a Commercial Code and a legal system to enforce these laws. The Commercial Code was shaped by the existing rules and trade habits as they had developed through self-regulation by *nakama* and continued by cooperatives and newly emerging trade associations. Still, the Commercial Code also meant that the primary objective of trade associations shifted from establishing and enforcing general market rules to designing industry-specific agreements and creating barriers to new entry and foreign competition. While associations for small companies focused on export promotion and mutual support, large companies used their associations as platforms for cartel agreements. These agreements tended to be stronger during economic downturns, and were mostly unstable during boom years. However, it was not until the 1930s that tight and coercive cartels became widespread in the core associations of large industries.

7.4. From 1931 to the *Tōseikai*—Control Associations During WWII

The year 1931 marked both the height of the "Shōwa (Great) Depression", and the beginning of the transition from a system of cooperation and collusion in the business sector condoned by government to a more pro-active, control-oriented wartime regime driven by government. For the small-sized businesses, the 1925 Export Associations Law was revised in 1931 into the Cooperative Law (*Kōgyō kumiai hō*), and was expanded to include domestic industries, so that all small-sized firms were encouraged to organize and agree on market share and price. The government began offering low-interest financing to local manufacturing cooperatives as an anti-depression policy, which raised the incentives for small companies to form or join associations. The number of manufacturing cooperatives increased from 82 in 1929 to 850 in 1936. While, initially, 7.2% of these cooperatives engaged in price agreements, the percentage was estimated to have reached 54% by 1936. Thus, the most common activities of small-sized manufacturers' cooperatives were to share equipment and to collude on price. Also, progressing specialization within industries demanded a differentiation of organizations. The Merchants' Association Law (*Shōgyō kumiai hō*) of 1932 created a new type of association that legally separated the distributors' from the manufacturers' associations. This division has remained in place until today: trading houses that specialize in certain products often form their own associations and are "associate members" of the corresponding manufacturers' groups (Kojima 1940: 72–87, Fujita 1988: 106).

For big business, the year 1931 also brought a major change with the new Important Industries Control Law (*Jūyō sangyō tōsei hō*). This was a "cartel support law" (Takeda 1985: 418), initially meant to help large companies overcome the Great Depression and later used to bolster the controls of the wartime economy. Indeed, one could think of it as a government order to collude on price. The initial law had a duration of five years and designated a total of 31 industries that were explicitly authorized to: (1) agree to limit production or prescribe quotas; (2) allocate market shares among large firms; (3) set price limits; and (4) oversee joint sales agencies. The designation of an industry based on the Control Law was a simple process: the ministry in charge issued the ordinance based on consultation with the Prime Minister's "Control Committee" (the precursor of the wartime Planning Board, *Keizai kikaku-in*).[22] In 1936, the law was extended for a second five-year term, but this time to introduce production and price controls in the major manufacturing industries; the law's scope was expanded to cover more than 100 industries. In 1937, the law was further amended to permit the formation of associations, and to include a "two-thirds rule" similar to that of cooperatives: if more than two-thirds of the firms in an industry agreed on price or quantitative restrictions, the remaining firms could be forced by law to abide by this agreement. By the end of 1937, a total of 1,172 trade associations of large firms operated under this law (Cohen 1958: 10).

The government tried to retain ultimate oversight over these associations by adding a clause that cartels or agreements could be modified or canceled by the competent ministry if these agreements were found to counter the national interest. Thus, an "industrial policy" clause was added to ensure that collusion in one sector would not harm other sectors. The law was revised several times, each time in an attempt to increase government power over cartel activities, as the leading politicians and bureaucrats began talking about a centrally planned economy. For instance, beginning in 1936, manufacturers were compelled to submit more detailed reports on monthly outputs. Ultimately, the government envisioned a system that rested on strict regulation of both production and distribution, and while the system did not work nearly as well as designed, the controls were strong enough to undermine the market and price mechanisms in all sectors.

At the core of the envisioned centrally planned economy were various types of so-called "central organs" (*chūō kikan*) whose prime function it was to allocate scarce resources in a certain industry and thus steer production, distribution and consumption. One example was the "national policy companies" (*kokusaku kaisha*) that bought up all goods in a certain sector such as energy, raw materials, rice, etc., and re-sold them at the government-described price (Otto 1999). For societal control, neighborhood groups (*gonin-gumi* or *tonari-gumi*) were formed to monitor adherence with rules. These groups had one watchman appointed in

---

[22] As mentioned in Chapter 3, the 1978 Depressed Industry Law allowed companies to adopt similar means to overcome the oil shock recession. Like the 1931 law, the 1978 law had a five-year limit and was extended once. Even the mechanism by which companies were designated under the law were the same. Johnson (1982: 110) considers the 1931 Important Industries Control Law to be the origin of administrative guidance, because it empowered MITI to "designate" certain industries.

every neighborhood whose task it was to closely observe and report on his neighbors' behavior (Pauer 1993, 1999). For firms, the "central organs" of control were the trade associations, which were called "control associations" (*tōseikai*). While these *tōseikai* are often assumed to have been under complete government control, there was in fact significant self-regulation still left to industry as the economy was "mobilized".

Toward the National General Mobilization Law of 1938

During the 1920s, many industries had formed new associations in order to, primarily, fix prices and thus help large companies weather business cycle fluctuations. By 1930, about 110 national trade associations had been established, of which at least 20 had formed well-functioning cartels. The real boom in cartel formation occurred during the 1930s, after the Control Law and the Small Manufacturers' Association Law had been passed and the government set more incentives for companies to form associations and devise self-regulation schemes: between 1930 and 1936, 122 new trade associations were founded, of which at least 48 were cartels (Kikkawa 1988: 61–3).

The beginning of strict economic controls occurred in 1931, when Japan rejoined the Gold Standard only to reverse that decision 11 months later. The resulting confusion over currency and exchange rates led the government to issue laws on foreign exchange controls in 1932 intended to prevent speculation and capital flight. While these did not affect domestic businesses initially, they firmly established government oversight over all foreign transactions and imports—a power the government would continue to exercise until 1965. These laws began a trend of ever more control laws that led the economy toward the wartime control system. Table 7.1 gives an overview of the most important laws of the 1930s and 1940s.

To help Japan through the Great Depression of 1931, Japan embarked on a *bona fide* deficit-spending policy in 1931 based on the classic multiplier effects of government spending.[23] Since this policy led to a huge increase in the budget deficit, in 1936 Finance Minister Takahashi Korekiyo suggested a reversal to a tight budget. But the military had very different plans of military aggression, especially in Manchuria, and assassinated Takahashi in February 1936. The new Minister of Finance, Baba Eiichi, hastened to agree with the military on a five-year plan for key industries and drafted a sizeable budget to accommodate the military (Nakamura 1983: 263). The effects of this policy change were exactly those that Takahashi had predicted: inflation, a drop in exports, and a weakened Yen that increased import prices. This necessitated stricter government rules on

---

[23] At the time, the multiplier effects were certainly not "classic"; in fact, Keynes' *General Theory* had not yet been published. While there is some discussion on whether Takahashi Korekiyo had seen a preliminary draft of Keynes' work, his 1931 measures were surely the first real-life attempt to put the insights of stimulative effects of government spending into practice (e.g., Imamura 1948).

Table 7.1. The Most Important Economic Control Laws, 1931–1945

Year	English title
1918	Military Industry Mobilization Law (first used in 1937)
1931	Important Industries Control Law
1932	Foreign Exchange Control Law
	Capital Flight Prevention Law
1937	Temporary Funds Adjustment Law
	Temporary Import–Export Grading Measures Law
	Law Concerning Implementation of the [1918] Military Industries Mobilization Law
	Temporary Export/Import Control Law
1938	General Mobilization Law
	Temporary Fertilizer Distribution Control Order
	Electric Power Administration Order
	Price Committee Order
	Workplaces Control Order
	School Graduate Use Control Order
	Coal Distribution Control Rules
1939	Rice Distribution Control Order
	Corporate Profits Distribution and Fund Raising Order
	Total Mobilization of Operations and Enterprise Investment Order
	National Draft Order
	Dividends Control Order
	Military Goods Industries and Workplaces Examination Order
	Temporary Wage Measures Order
	Mobilization Materials Use and Expropriation Order
1940	Land Transport Control Order
	Marine Transport Control Order
	Youth Employment Control Order
	Steel-Use Raw Materials Import Distribution Order
	Household Fuel Materials Supply and Demand Adjustment Rules
	Corporate Management Order
	Bank Funds Application Order
	Employee Movement Prevention Order
1941	National Labor Passbook Law
	Silk Thread Industry Control Law
	Lumber Materials Control Law
	Essential Commodities Control Order
	Trade Control Order
	Port Transport Industry Control
	National Patriotic Labor Association Order
	Corporation Approval Order
	Newspaper Companies Order
	Major Industries Control Ordinance
	Key Industries Association Ordinance
1942	Transfer and Administrative Authority Law
1943	Control Companies Ordinance

Sources: Nakamura 1983, 1989.

capital outflows and fund adjustment through two further laws in 1937 (cf. Table 7.1).[24] To channel the increasingly scarce domestic funds into key industries, the Temporary Funds Adjustment Law (*Rinji shikin chōsei hō*) was passed in September 1937 to ensure financing of the war industries and curb the manufacturing of products not considered essential for the war effort.[25] In 1937, the government passed the Law Concerning Implementing of the Military Industries Mobilization Law (*Gunju kōgyō dōin hō no tekigō ni kan suru hōritsu*) which allowed the government to expropriate private factories for military use and to prohibit consumption of goods for non-military purposes.

Full-fledged government control set in with the National General Mobilization Law (*Sōdōin-hō*) of 1938. This comprehensive government enabling act was in many ways the equivalent to the German 1933 *Ermächtigungsgesetz* that empowered Hitler to pass laws without the parliamentary checks and balances prescribed in the Constitution. In 50 articles, the *Sōdōin-hō* empowered the government to regulate production, distribution, prices, wages, trade, and labor. Section 1 stipulated that in times of war, all physical and human resources were to be centrally controlled to achieve highest efficiency for national defense. One clause prescribed complete price controls, and another effectively limited the freedom of choice of profession. Section 17 prescribed regulation of all cartels, and Section 18 ordered the formation of trade associations with compulsory membership to aid the government in monitoring firms and markets.

However, as with most Japanese laws, the text of the General Mobilization Law was vague, and the law's actual rules and prohibitions were specified through an array of ordinances, which over time affected all aspects of the economy, society and everyday life. After 1940, most controls were based not on laws, but on such orders. For instance, in 1939, employment controls and a National Empressment Order forced people to change jobs upon government order. Wage and prize freezes were issued in 1939 to curb inflation. The 1941 Major Industries Control Ordinance established input and output quotas for all military-related industries. A rice rationing system based on tickets (which soon became black market

---

[24] For instance, the January 1937 Ordinance Relating to Payments by Foreign Exchange Banks on Foreign Order required that all import payments be approved by the MOF if the balance was over ¥30,000 a month; this monthly balance was lowered to over ¥1,000 after July 1937, and to over ¥100 after December 1937. Moreover, the August 1937 Law Relating to Adjustment of Foreign Trade and Related Industries (*Bōeki oyobi kankei sangyō chōsei hō*) created an additional legal means for the government to curb exports, and the September 1937 Export/Import Control Law (*Yushutsunyū-hin rinji sochi hō*) made all trades subject to government approval. In 1938 and 1940, rules were extended to all trades even within the Yen bloc. Cohen (1958: 16) concludes that until 1941, import and export regulations were "reasonably effective", although they seem to have broken down and been circumvented by smuggling and black market activities in the 1940s.

[25] One effect of this law was that bank credit became the principal source of credit. By ensuring that all funds would flow through the banking system, and then regulating the banks, the government could command the flow of funds to designated recipients. This system was continued into the postwar period of rapid growth (1955–75) and worked as effectively then; see, e.g., Patrick (1962), Royama (1982), Horiuchi (1980), Schaede (1989a). Cohen (1958: 16–19) describes additional measures adopted during the wartime period to regulate corporate finance, accounting, and stock prices.

currency) was also introduced in 1941. Control begat control to stop the circumvention of rules. Import restrictions increased black market activities. Imports had dropped further after the outbreak of war in Europe in 1939, and the Planning Board drafted the first Materials Mobilization Plan. The system of wartime controls was firmly installed (Nakamura 1983, 1989, Ando 1987, Pauer 1999).

Self-Regulation and Wartime Economic Controls after 1940

By 1940, "an almost bewildering variety of special laws" (Cohen 1958: 22) and rules had been adopted, and trade associations came to play a special role in setting up the new system. Their specific functions as *tōseikai*, "control associations", developed as follows. While the government aimed to establish a planned economy, early attempts did not function as smoothly as envisioned. The continuing stream of new rules and ordinances had confused people, and what was perfectly legal trade one day could be a violation of some rule the next. Moreover, as knowledge about new rules spread, firms diverted an increasing proportion of their business to the black market. Besides confusion and circumvention, the system was marred by bureaucratic red tape. To see why the resulting chaos elevated the control associations to a critical position of self-regulation in this system, it is helpful to look at the typical order flow for a product.

To order a certain machine, a firm had to apply at the ministry with an explanation of purpose, use, funding, etc. Upon approval, the ministry ordered a public corporation to furnish a machine maker with the necessary input. The machine maker then manufactured and delivered the product to the firm. While not problematic in design, in practice this process was undermined by three fundamental problems. First, firms usually could not afford to wait for a machine order and therefore ordered machines up-front regardless of need; excess orders could always be sold on the black market. Second, the Army and Navy usually ignored the government budget and ordered machines as they pleased, so that private sector orders were often crowded out. Since the military refused to inform the ministries of their orders, the ministries were unable to command the order flow. The materials imported by the Navy and Army and the surplus machines manufactured because of their excess orders further fed the black market. Third, no one central government institution was in charge of supervising the regulatory mechanism. Instead, various ministries were responsible for the industries in their regulatory domain. For instance, while the Ministry of Commerce and Industry (MCI) oversaw most of the military-related production, important industries such as foodstuff, fertilizer, and transportation were outside its domain (Cohen 1958: 64).

In this chaotic situation, the government—as it had done several times in previous centuries—encouraged self-regulation: by empowering associations to ration and control, the government intended to regulate and monitor the order flow by simply controlling the associations. The initial plan for the control associations (*tōseikai*) was drafted by Hoshino Naoki, former MCI bureaucrat and chief of the Cabinet Planning Board, as well as Minister-without-Portfolio in the Second Konoe Cabinet in 1940. Hoshino envisioned uniform policies across all industries, carried out through *tōseikai* in each industry that were to be headed by a director appointed by the government and imbued with dictatorial authority. This plan, however, was drafted without the input of industry, and was met with a surprisingly violent outcry. The Japan Economic Federation (Keidanren's predecessor) led the attack on the government. The opposition focused not only on the control scheme but also criticized the government's distribution system and the red tape wound around raw materials, machine and other orders. The government had gone too far, and business was adamant.[26] Until 1940, the government's measures had always benefited at least one part of the business community, and thus did not evoke protest. Setting up control institutions run by government officials with dictatorial powers, however, united the *zaikai* and created an unsurmountable obstacle to the plan.

Swiftly, the Planning Board chief was replaced by Ogura Masatune. Ogura had been the Director-General of the Sumitomo holding company, and his appointment was clearly a move by the government to appease the *zaikai* (Cohen 1958: 30–1).[27] The Key Industries Associations Ordinance of September 1941 was a compromise in which the *zaikai* fared much better than the government. The agreement was to form associations that were run by the business leaders, were governed primarily by self-regulation, albeit in the "national interest", and had compulsory membership (something big business wanted). The resulting control associations were thus very different from the originally envisioned government-run control agencies: they were empowered to introduce their own rationing rules, monitor compliance themselves, and design sanctions. By the time the *tōseikai* took over, the government had in some ways less power over industry than before establishing them, especially given that the chief of the Planning Board was now a businessman (Johnson 1982: 153, Hadley 1970: 12, Nakamura 1974).

Under the new system, the *tōseikai* formed the center of the control system for each industry. The 1941 Key Industries Association Ordinance (*Jūyō sangyō dantai rei*) supplemented the general cartel formation order of the 1938

---

[26] Cohen (1958: 28) cites a Japan Economic Federation statement as saying that the "industrial expansion plan...has no composite basis...hence the unsmooth distribution of necessary materials and equipment, red tape procedure, and...conflict between various control institutions". The *Oriental Economist*, the famous critical English-language business magazine, in its January 1941 issue expressed surprise over the sharp reaction: "For the past several years...no matter what policy the government was enforcing, [these businessmen] have hardly stirred, much less offered, any protest....But they now seem to have recovered their senses and to have gotten up enough courage again to dare to criticize the government" (page 6).

[27] Curiously, this same Ogura became Minister of Finance in the Third Konoe Cabinet, and one of his protégés at the time was Hyūga Hōsai, who in 1965, as president of Sumitomo Metals, revolted against a MITI-administered output reduction cartel in steel; see Johnson (1982: 268–71).

Mobilization Law and commanded that all industries related to military procurement (i.e., almost all industries, since production of so-called "luxury products" had been all but ruled out at that point) create such a control association. This led to an enormous increase in associations, since there was now an association for almost every product category. The explicit mission of the *tōseikai* was to allocate raw materials and set prices in line with government orders. The large *tōseikai* also included administering resource allocation and distribution in their portfolio. Since membership was compulsory, no company could avoid the controls. According to SCAP documents, by the end of WWII there were at least 1,538 nationwide control associations, and 6,588 local cooperatives (Cohen 1958: 32, Hadley 1970: 368).

The control associations were not regulated by one single government agency. Rather, every *tōseikai* was placed under the jurisdiction of the ministry in charge of regulating its particular industry. As today, the bylaws of every association had to be approved by the ministry in charge. While the president of each association had to be appointed by the cognizant minister, he was nominated by the member firms and was almost without exception the president of the company with the largest market share in the industry. Johnson (1982: 152) infers that this meant that control associations became "utterly dominated by the *zaibatsu*" firms. While this may have been true in some cases, the *zaibatsu*, especially Mitsui and Mitsubishi, were in fierce competition for market share, which often foiled the agreements necessary for effective cartels. More important than the *zaibatsu* dominance was the fact that the government did not dominate the *tōseikai*. *Tōseikai* rules were not new, but often were based on attempts at cooperation in the same industries in the 1920s, and on the more formal cartels after 1931. The two primary differences made by the 1941 Ordinance were that (a) because of compulsory membership, the associations' power over their industries was increased; and (b) the government's goals for the cartels had shifted from supporting exports to rationing and allocating materials for military production.

The specific functions of the *tōseikai* were to collect from all members the estimates for capital, material and labor requirements for the following quarter; adjust these estimates to form a consolidated industry-wide request for raw materials; and submit this request to the ministry in charge. Ministries would then consolidate all requests and draft a unified plan that formed the basis of an industry's total allocations and quotas. Subsequently, the *tōseikai* had to sub-allot and implement the quota. The associations themselves were to manage production and distribution in the industry. Yet, even this system left the government dissatisfied with the controls over the nation's overall distribution system. In an attempt to curb black market activity, the government endowed the *tōseikai* with official enforcement authority, thus effectively turning the associations into "private-interest governments". The 1942 Transfer and Administrative Authority Law gave the *tōseikai* authority to issue permits relating to the provisions of the Mobilization Law of 1938 and its uncountable ordinances, the import–export laws and the various laws on finance. To ensure that the *tōseikai* would be sufficiently powerful to enforce such authorizations, the law stated that control associations were to be considered official agencies; resisting a *tōseikai* order was thus illegal.

While the government's intent with the Transfer and Administrative Authority Law was to control business more forcefully, in effect the empowerment of the *tōseikai* simply increased self-regulation by trade associations. Because the Meiji-period laws, including the Commercial Code, were largely irrelevant during the wartime years, associations could draft their own rules and enforce them as they pleased. In doing so, they were not bound by explicit government orders, other than that their rules had to be in the "national interest" in the broadest sense. The only forces that counterbalanced the power of the *tōseikai* in the markets were the Army and Navy, which usually bypassed the associations and ordered from the companies directly. The government, on the other hand, was unable to control industry: the Cabinet Planning Board could not regulate market structures and order flows, the Prime Minister was unable to control the ministries, and the ministries were unable to control the associations (Cohen 1958: 59).

This situation displeased Tōjō Hideki, who had become Prime Minister in 1941. He launched several attempts to increase the Prime Minister's powers over business. In 1943, the MCI was remodeled into the Ministry of Munitions (MM) to concentrate economic regulation in one ministry. Tōjō himself became the Minister of the MM, in addition to being Prime Minister and War Minister. Yet, in spite of Tōjō's attempts to concentrate power in his office, unified control was never achieved. The MM's bureaucrats did not dare to refuse orders placed by business for fear of being accused of obstructing the war effort; for them, giving in to business demands was by far the easier route than trying to reestablish full government authority (Cohen 1958: 65, 70). In 1943, Tōjō issued a new Control Companies Ordinance. While Tōjō's intention was to regain influence over business, in fact the ordinance only legitimized many practices that most leading industries had long since adopted. The new "control companies" were joint stock companies owned jointly by the firms in one industry, with the task of centralizing purchases, sales, and distribution of commodities and administering the inventory.[28] In the process of setting prices, the control companies often incurred losses. The 1943 Ordinance allowed the control companies to ask the government for reimbursement of their losses. The idea behind this centralized purchasing system was to support munitions production by keeping input prices low. Yet,

---

[28] These "control companies" (*tōsei gaisha*) were public corporations, similar to the postwar *tokushu hōjin*. A variety of such corporations were formed in the 1930s. One type were so-called *eidan*, which administered plant construction and conversion to military use, or for raw materials imports and stockpiling management. These included the "Industrial Facilities Corporation" (*Sangyō setsubi eidan*) and the "Essential Material Supervision Corporation" (*Jūyō busshi kanri eidan*); both were run by bureaucrats from the leading ministries. Further, so-called "policy companies" (*kokusaku kaisha*) bought up all supplies of rice, synthetic fuel, minerals, coal lumber, fertilizer, silk and many more, and then allocated these products at preset prices (often subsidized) to designated firms in designated industries (see Cohen 1958 for a detailed description of these processes and the problems they created).

this did not curb the power of the *tōseikai*. Tōjō needed the *zaikai* and their military supplies, and to ensure continued production he was better off catering to the large companies' needs than imposing rules upon them that they would reject.

With the control companies in place, the distribution process regulated by a *tōseikai* typically functioned as follows. An association would submit a plan on input requirements and production schedules for a period to the MM, which the official would rubber-stamp. The "raw materials control company" for the industry then purchased the inputs and sold them to the member firms according to prescribed market share quotas. Upon completion of production, a "product control company" purchased all the finished products, other than those directly sold to the military; the control companies operated on a fixed percentage commission they received on volume. Prices were predetermined, so that the only uncertain variable in this process for the companies was the availability of raw materials. Finally, the product control company sold to a centralized wholesalers' purchasing company which would then allocate quotas to a set of consuming industries or a centralized retailers' company (cf. Cohen 1958, Nakamura 1974, Hadley 1970). In this way, the entire system ultimately rested on the control of purchases and sales, and these controls were implemented and monitored by the trade associations. It is therefore not surprising that after the transition to the postwar system, among the various regulatory mechanisms and layers of rules, those within the distribution systems remained the strongest, and should prove to be the hardest to regulate, and deregulate, even in the present day.

Nakamura (1983: 290) summarizes the logic of Japanese wartime controls in the following seven steps: (1) the government's aim of military expansion required channeling limited funds toward designated industries; economic control thus originated in financial controls; (2) limited foreign reserves necessitated import restrictions to ensure that scarce funds be spent on imports with immediate relevance to military manufacturing; (3) these military imports had to be paid for by exports, so that export promotion policies were designed to sustain high raw material imports; (4) "Materials Mobilization Plans" channeled resources to military-related goods and the export sector; (5) to curtail the production of consumer goods and prevent prices from rising, price controls and policies aimed to "adjust" demand and supply were set up; (6) to ensure proper implementation of the Materials Mobilization Plans, some organizational design was needed to oversee the distribution of goods; (7) finally, labor had to be policed through national conscription and labor mobilization.

This regulatory algorithm placed the *tōseikai* squarely in the middle of the control process. The organizational design that Japan's militaristic regime chose to enforce the economic rules was the *tōseikai* system. Yet, these *tōseikai* were not dependent on the government, but rather empowered to formulate their own rules within the control framework. *Tōseikai* were therefore not so much regulatory tools as they were authorized institutions of industry self-regulation: they were based on compulsory membership, had governmental authority to enforce their own rules, and performed regulatory functions that usually rest with the government. Moreover, as for sanctioning and punishing cartel-breakers, the associations were autonomous in their self-regulation.

Some observers have argued that the primary difference between Japan's wartime and postwar economic system is the shift from a military to a trade dominance objective (e.g., Noguchi 1995, Gao 1997). In this view, Nakamura's seven-step algorithm explains well the postwar situation if we simply substitute the word "export" for "military", with the institutions remaining largely the same as those employed during the War. Thus, the government's goal to expand exports required channeling scarce resources to strategic sectors, while quantity and price controls helped steer supply and demand. At the center of this system—before, during and after WWII—were the trade associations. While subjected to varying degrees of government intervention and guidance, throughout Japan's economic history, self-regulation has been a dominant regulatory tool, and trade associations have played an integral regulatory role. Not surprisingly, after WWII they continued this role, albeit under modified political and legal parameters.

7.5. Summary: Self-Regulation in Japan's Economic History

Throughout the development of Japan's economic system, self-regulation has been a hallmark of trade association activities. Initially, trade associations arose to fulfil the basic economic need of establishing markets. Over time, these activities expanded into rule-setting, and self-regulation became a core activity of associations. Private rule-setting was so effective that it came to be used for, or instead of, government regulatory policies. Trade associations have thus always played a central role in both trade creation and business regulation.

Japan's modern-day trade associations grew out of the *za* which emerged in the 12th century. During the Middle Ages, these *za* formed under the patronage of landlords or local temples/shrines. The *za* performed one central economic function in this early period: they organized and maintained markets in fixed locations. The development of stable markets facilitated institutionalized trade. While market rules were rudimentary, the *za* established a system to keep unknown merchants out of regional markets and thereby reduced the local merchants' risk of being cheated into accepting low-quality coins or products.

During the Tokugawa period (1603–1868), trade associations became much more sophisticated. The *kabu nakama* were instrumental in strengthening markets by establishing credit guarantees. The advent of a secure trade credit system significantly enhanced methods of exchanging goods. The *nakama* also created market rules and organized timetables for markets. Their strict internal organizational rules provided for institutionalized processes of rule enforcement. During the second half of the Tokugawa period, the Shogunate began to use the *nakama* organization for its own policy purposes, as self-regulation for the first time became an important tool for the Shogunate to implement and enforce rice price policies and other regulatory measures.

The Meiji and Taishō eras (1868–1925) marked a period of rapid industrialization in Japan. Before Japan pronounced its first Commercial Code in 1893, trade associations had formed resembling the old *nakama* to organize markets for small companies. However, around the end of the 19th century, companies differentiated by size, and growing businesses received substantial government support to drive forward the nation's effort to "catch up" with Western nations in technology and organization of production and business. In the early 20th century, large firms began to establish their own associations. While the associations for small firms primarily engaged in mutual assistance and financing, those for large companies in the growth sectors were platforms for organizing technology imports and crafting cooperative and collusive arrangements. Yet, in an environment of fast growth, fierce competition often made cartels unstable. In these cases, the government attempted to step in and promote cartels, as it considered inter-firm cooperation an effective means to avoid duplicate investment and encourage optimal allocation of resources.

The Important Industries Control Law of 1931 made it easier for the government to direct industry-wide agreements, and it also marked the initiation of the wartime economy. The government aimed to erect complete economic guidance to support military production. However, the system was not as effective as its designers had hoped, partially because the regulatory authorities were not sufficiently centralized. To ensure compliance with the scheme, the government again turned to trade associations for assistance. Each narrowly defined industry was asked to establish a "control association", *tōseikai*. The *tōseikai* were charged with monitoring their members' production as well as the distribution of products. Ironically, rather than increasing government control over business, the *tōseikai* system allowed associations to assume more and more independent self-regulatory functions. Self-regulation within the industry, by these powerful associations, became one pillar of the wartime economic control system.

Over the course of history, the Japanese government has tried various policy approaches to self-regulation. During the Tokugawa period, attempts to abolish trade associations to curb their self-regulation (and thus to diminish merchants' power) proved disastrous. In instances when the government attempted to control trade associations, either through high taxes or constraining rules, self-regulation was not significantly hampered. Whatever turn history took, and whatever measures the government chose to adopt, self-regulation remained one of the integral features of Japan's political economy. Over time, trade associations thus cemented their place within Japan's political economy. Firmly established processes of business participation in economic policies significantly enhanced the viability of postwar industrial policy. It also meant that Japanese industries could not be fooled easily: they would rather self-regulate than succumb to unfeasible government rules.

8

The Implications

8.1. The New Dominance of Self-Regulation in Japan's Regulatory System

Japan's system of political economy and regulation is unlikely to converge with the U.S. system, at least in the medium run, because changes brought about by deregulation are not leading to the adoption of a more transparent, accessible system. Instead, the supposedly market-opening effects of deregulation are being offset by increasing self-regulation through trade associations. Self-regulation refers to a system whereby the leading firms of an industry, through their association, design the rules of trade for their industry and enforce these rules through self-designed sanctions. The primary objectives of self-regulation are to "self-promote", i.e., to increase firms' competitiveness, or to "self-protect", i.e., to shield an industry from competition. The resulting "cooperative system" in Japan is markedly different from the Anglo-Saxon market model as it allows incumbent firms to contain competition. It also deviates from continental European patterns where industry, while influential, has less power in the regulatory processes than in Japan.

Self-regulation has been the most important function of Japanese trade associations throughout history. Even during the postwar period of rapid growth, there was plenty of self-regulation by industry. In this period, the regulating ministries were usually involved, either directly in the decision-making process or more indirectly through encouragement and recognition of industries' activities. It is precisely because of this ministerial involvement that many Japan scholars have long argued that Japan is characterized by a high degree of bureaucratic power. Because the self-regulatory process and the interests of the government (bureaucrats and politicians alike) were intertwined at many stages of the process, it has always been difficult to determine unambiguously whether bureaucrats were acting as agents of industry, or industry was shaped to the interests of government. However, the underlying, constant mechanism that has been driving Japanese regulation is self-regulation by industry; what differs over time is the involvement of bureaucrats in this process. With an increase in official deregulation and the decline of bureaucratic influence over industry in the 1980s and 1990s, it has become apparent just how important self-regulation is for a complete understanding of Japan's political economy.

The notable increase in the relevance of self-regulation was triggered by the confluence of deregulation and recession in the 1990s. Deregulation contributed to the increase in self-regulation because it exposed Japan's lack of process, or supervisory, regulation. The Japanese regulatory system has long focused on entry regulation, which was abolished gradually beginning in the 1980s. Yet, stepwise deregulation was not complemented by the introduction of new process supervision, i.e., the monitoring of incumbent companies on a day-to-day basis. Throughout the period of rapid growth, ministries had administered entry into Japan's most important industries and markets, through either specific industry laws or a vast array of permits, licenses, notifications, approvals and other administrative requirements for opening a line of business. Once a firm had entered a business, it was expected to stay in close contact with the ministry that would invoke situational regulation through the largely informal and extralegal mechanisms of administrative guidance. Hence the institution of the ministry-*tan*, a company or association employee in charge of dealing with the cognizant bureaucrats on a daily basis. When scandals involving various ministries led to a toning-down of the *tan* system in the 1990s, and process supervision through frequent contacts with the regulators was therefore severely curtailed, the new void in continuous oversight was not filled by new supervisory agencies. At the same time, in some industries deregulation of entry permits progressed through the 1990s, creating a perceived need by incumbent firms to increase their own barriers to entry and take over a more general regulatory function. Trade associations filled the regulatory void by advancing their own systems of monitoring member firms through increased self-regulation.

The recession of the 1990s further increased the trend toward more self-regulation. The theoretical insight that companies have more incentives to cooperate or collude during recessions has been borne out by the data for many countries; the movement of antitrust cases over time suggests that Japan is no exception here. The worse the economic downturn of the 1990s became, the more industries met in their associations to consider ways of cooperation that would help dampen the negative impact of recession. While large firms typically attempted to bolster profits through coordinated "price maintenance", small firms strove to survive through cooperation along multiple dimensions, as the case studies in Chapter 5 have highlighted. For instance, in industries where deregulation and recession had undermined the system of *post hoc* price determination (*atogime*), associations tried to supplement the mechanism through standard contracts and unified pricing structures.

Even when the recession of the 1990s ends and the economy eventually recovers, a significant reversal in self-regulation is unlikely, because, once instituted, a system of self-regulation is inherently stable and difficult to repress. To see why self-regulation will continue to be a dominant and persistent part of Japan's regulatory system, it is important to understand the systemic and institutional differences between self-regulation through trade associations and collusion through cartels. The critical distinction is that self-regulation is a continuous process, whereas cartels are typically formed and then disbanded. While all cartels build on self-regulation, self-regulation does not build on a cartel and it may not constitute a cartel. Cartel members gather for the specific purpose of fixing price. Firms that do not otherwise interact gather solely to agree on how to restrain competition among each other. Cartels are typically unstable, as there are multiple potential causes of breakdown. Most often, cartels are undermined by one member who finds it more advantageous to go it alone and undercut the cartel to make a short-term profit at the expense of the other firms.

In contrast, self-regulation is an institutionalized, ongoing process. The best way to analyze the activities that constitute self-regulation is to differentiate between administrative (rule-oriented) and protective (collusive) self-regulation. Administrative self-regulation is legal and often efficiency-enhancing in that it helps to facilitate trade, create markets, structure trade agreements, establish industry standards, and many more. In contrast, in protective self-regulation associations use their power to set rules for their industries to establish restraints to competition. This can happen through concerted efforts such as boycotting nonmembers (preventing their entering the market); dividing markets up geographically so that each member is a local monopolist; setting standards so high that only incumbent firms can possibly achieve them; or tabulating accounting schedules that constitute *de facto* price fixing. The dividing line between the two sets of activities is not always clear, which explains why the Japanese antitrust authority has not been successful in containing self-regulation to trade-enhancing activities: collusive practices are often piggybacked onto other association activities. Moreover, in the 1950s and 1960s many competition-restraining activities were allowed or even actively encouraged by the ministries in charge of fostering and regulating their industries. Over time, some of these activities became ordinary "trade habits", leaving Japan's Fair Trade Commission without a body of legal doctrine upon which to build for strict antitrust enforcement.

Self-regulation is a staple activity of trade associations. The process of formulating self-regulation is institutionalized in the trade association, so that meetings, committees, and elections of leading officers are all clearly grounded on well-established rules. Japanese trade associations are very stable, both in terms of existence and membership; member turnover or dissolutions are extremely rare. Member firms convene at various levels of management position, in frequent meetings organized through numerous standing committees. Most important, trade associations engage in a variety of activities: they lobby politicians and bureaucrats and channel political contributions; they are involved in regulation and policymaking processes; and they represent their industry vis-à-vis other constituencies. Because some association activities are critical to each firm's survival, exit from an association is not an easy or even viable option for a firm discontent with self-regulation. Firms thus typically remain association members over the long run, and go along with self-regulation, even if they are occasionally disadvantaged by it.

The multitude of activities thus bolsters the stability of self-regulation. If the association also forms a temporary cartel, this is unlikely to undermine other, ongoing self-regulation by the industry. Yet, without the institutionalized mechanisms of self-regulation, a cartel is unlikely to be stable. Therefore, throughout the postwar period most cartels were formed and orchestrated in the hallways of the relevant trade association. Trade associations are at the heart of all self-regulation, and of most cartels. Given the strong benefits that accrue from regular interaction among competing firms, self-regulation is unlikely to decline after the end of the 1990s recession. While firms may see fewer incentives to cooperate on price or may want to renegotiate some restrictive portions of self-regulation installed in the 1990s, their associations will remain in place, as will the basic makeup of self-regulation.

8.2. The Evidence

Two sets of evidence are required to support the argument of an increasing role of self-regulation in Japan's political economy: legal and economic. Regarding Japan's legal system, the question is whether the increase in protective self-regulation can be stalled or halted through antitrust enforcement. In economic terms, the issue is whether all industries self-regulate in similar ways, or whether there are systemic differences in self-regulation that allow for an evaluation and forecast of the relevance of self-regulation for Japan's overall economy.

Japan's legal and doctrinal development in antitrust has centered around the prevention or prosecution of illegal price cartels and *dangō* (bid-rigging), although owing to the large amount of evidence required for the JFTC to launch a formal case, even price fixing is often settled informally. In contrast, as shown in Chapters 4 and 5, so-called "unfair trade practices" have long been a subordinate concern of the JFTC. Unfair trade practices include boycotts and refusals to deal with certain companies, retail price maintenance and restrictive practices in the distribution system, and other means to bar new entry to the industry and prevent price competition. These practices are at the very core of self-regulation, for they assist downstream implementation and monitoring of agreements among upstream manufacturers. One telling example is the network of exclusive retail outlets in the electronic appliances industry, where even discount prices—to the extent they occur—have often been orchestrated jointly by the manufacturers. The database of all postwar antitrust cases constructed for this study allowed for an in-depth comparison of formal and informal JFTC cases, which documented that unfair trade practices are predominantly settled informally. Moreover, the published records of the JFTC's highly informal consultation program point to a marked increase in self-regulation by both large- and small-firm associations in the 1990s. Yet, in spite of the widespread occurrence of such practices, efforts to restrain them remain muted. Even egregious cases that are prosecuted formally do not carry punishment, because the measure prescribed by law in such cases is an inconsequential "cease-and-desist" order. While the JFTC could choose to prosecute serious "unfair trade practices" as cartels and thus raise the stakes significantly, it has in the past only rarely opted to do so.

It is important to note that there is a choice in how to enforce antitrust rules, and in all countries with antitrust legislation this choice is necessarily political. Over time, the political stance on how to deal with antitrust violation results in a pattern—the so-called "legal doctrine". Japan's FTC has little going for it in this department: throughout the postwar period, industrial policy and protection of producer interests took political precedence over the letter of the antitrust law. Thus, even when the basic concepts and effects of industrial policy began to be questioned in the 1980s, there was no body of case precedents or shared public notion of the benefits of strict antitrust prosecution. Even in the 1990s many in Japan submit that, in principle, cooperation is a good thing, including cooperation among competing firms. In this environment, it is no surprise that JFTC action against seemingly minor moves such as "unfair trade practices" remains tentative.

Furthermore, private antitrust suits in Japan are extremely rare, so that the legal "market mechanism" does not take over where the government balks. Japanese law does not know treble damages, and the process of a private antitrust claim is prohibitively cumbersome and expensive. This makes the JFTC the only institution to launch antitrust cases, and opens all doors for political influence of antitrust enforcement. In contrast, in the U.S. antitrust cases can originate through three different channels: at the federal level, at the state level, and through private litigation. This curtails political control and yet results in significant deterrents to potential cartels. Even at times when the political climate favors more business cooperation, companies always face the possibility of being sued by their current competitors or companies attempting to enter the business. For Japan, relying on only one actor in antitrust enforcement with no legal doctrine supporting active prosecution means that self-regulation faces only very few legal deterrents. Since there is no discernible political move within Japan to change the system toward more proactive antitrust enforcement, true changes in the legal situation cannot be expected any time soon.

Moving on to the evidence in economic terms, the critical question is whether there are patterns of self-regulation that help us to understand its prerequisites, supporting conditions, and economic effects. In spite of all the obstacles that such a study necessarily encounters—the fact that collusion is typically kept secret being only the most annoying of them—analysis employing a database of 1,153 trade associations, combined with industry data and information from the database of JFTC cases, has yielded surprisingly strong results. The major insight from this analysis is that self-regulation differs by product characteristics and internal organization of the association, but not by industry characteristics.

All industries, whether consisting of large or small firms, being exporters or importers, being highly concentrated or not, or being mature or newly emerging, are equally likely to engage in self-regulation of one type or the other.

While industry structure *per se* does not affect the incidence of self-regulation, product characteristics have a significant impact. Supporting economic theories of collusion, Japanese industries dealing in more homogeneous products are more likely to be actively involved in protective self-regulation. Product homogeneity facilitates cooperative agreements and monitoring of compliance, because manufacturers cannot easily bypass the agreement through product modifications. Based on similar logic, industries subject to rapid technological change are not as likely to collude, because the constant change in product specifications makes agreements difficult. At the same time, however, Japan's high-technology industries are very active in administrative self-regulation: if industry standards are changing fast, official regulation is often too slow to adapt to market needs, and therefore it is in the interest of manufacturers to organize their own market rules. A further indication of very active self-regulation in an industry lies in the very structure and organization of the trade association. The more tightly organized an association, the more likely it is to be engaged in orchestrating, formulating, and implementing self-regulation. "Tight organization" refers to the representation of member firms on the board: naturally, if only every third member sends an official to association board meetings, agreements are much more difficult to implement than if every member is represented. Therefore, the ratio of directors (company presidents on the board) over total members is a telltale sign of an association's cohesiveness and ability to self-regulate.

One variable that does not flag self-regulation is the price differential between Tokyo and New York. This may be surprising if one expects that self-regulation, in particular of the collusive type, should result in above-normal prices. Yet, the price data support the general notion that self-regulation occurs across all industries: prices are higher in most product categories in Japan than in New York. Moreover, protective self-regulation is to be found in more homogeneous products, such as glass, cement, paper, certain chemicals, or certain types of steel; for none of these industries are price data easily observable, and more extensive research is left for further study. Yet, there are also systemic reasons why "price" does not clearly signal very active self-regulation, which are related to the multiple objectives of self-regulation. While companies that form a cartel are primarily interested in increased profits through rigged prices, the more constant and long-term self-regulation pursues a number of simultaneous goals. First, companies seek stability through self-regulation. For instance, many associations for small-sized companies, especially in the service sector, arrange for mutual help through self-regulation, as outlined in Chapter 5 for mahjong clubs, neon sign or *tatami* makers, bath house owners and hairdressers. The economic logic here is that mutual support in hard times is a group insurance that will make everyone better off over time; the insurance premium manifests itself in lesser profits for the individual entrepreneur by agreeing on stable, unchanging prices and market shares over time.

Another rationale behind self-regulation is to support a sanctuary strategy among large, exporting firms. This refers to a strategy under which large exporting companies create a profit cushion through domestic cooperation and price agreements, and then use these profits to undercut foreign competitors on world markets. Allegations of such strategies have been brought against, among others, Japan's camera manufacturers in the 1960s, the electronic industries in the 1970s, the car assemblers and semiconductor companies in the 1980s, as well as the photographic film and steel industries in the 1990s. Self-regulation is the obvious tool to implement a sanctuary strategy, as it allows for simultaneous moves toward enhancing exports, shielding domestic markets, and pushing agreed-upon prices through a distribution system with exclusive wholesalers and retailers to ensure retail price maintenance.

In sum, the insights from the JFTC and trade association databases are that self-regulation is on the rise, there is no political will to stop this development through antitrust enforcement, and the practice is widespread across all industries. The effects of increased self-regulation are most visible in industries with homogeneous products or in industries that are subject to changes in the environment, such as technological progress, where updated rules are pertinent for business success. Self-regulating trade associations are more tightly organized than others; indeed, it is quite easy to know a self-regulatory association when one encounters one.

8.3. Implications for Japan's Economy

The effects of the increase in self-regulation differ by industry: some industries will benefit from it, whereas others will suffer. Overall, the greatest pitfalls of collusion are inefficiency and sloppiness. If a group of companies sets price limits and otherwise constrains competition, eventually these companies are likely to become cost-inefficient and lose their competitive edge. However, not all self-regulation is collusive, and not all collusion or cooperation must necessarily lead to inefficiency. Instead, self-regulation may allow companies to optimize their investment and production schedules such that, over time, self-regulation may increase their ability to compete. If companies convene regularly and exchange information, they are better able to make informed business decisions and avoid duplicating efforts, such as in research and development. If they discuss their investment plans, or even allocate product markets among themselves, they can optimize the allocation of total resources within the industry. If they agree to keep dividend payments low, they can lower their cost of capital. Companies can also avoid becoming inefficient even if they cooperate strategically. In addition to benchmarking domestic companies, they can benchmark their competitiveness against their best foreign competitors. They can collude on price or control the distribution system, but encourage competition in quality, design, etc. If they employ a sanctuary strategy, they can increase profits at home while selling their products at highly competitive prices in world markets.

To be sure, not all Japanese companies benefit in these ways from self-regulation. Instead, self-regulation is likely to exacerbate the already apparent bifurcation of Japanese industry into export-oriented, efficient industries on the one hand, and primarily domestic, inefficient industries on the other. Exporting industries use self-regulation to increase their international competitiveness and to self-promote, while domestic industries use self-regulation primarily to self-protect. Thus, export-oriented, efficient industries benefit from the shift away from government micro-management toward more independent self-regulation. While companies in these industries self-regulate for structuring the domestic market, they are unlikely to agree knowingly to self-regulate in ways that will limit their international competitiveness. For instance, Japan's automobile makers meet frequently and discuss the structure of their domestic dealerships, and possibly even discuss some investment plans, but they are not very likely to limit their own market share expansion either in Japan or abroad through any kind of collusive agreement (other than to the extent prescribed by voluntary export restraints). Likewise, home electronics manufacturers may agree on price on the domestic market, as was revealed in an antitrust case in 1992, but they will be careful not to cooperate in areas that are strategically sensitive.

In contrast, many domestic industries self-regulate not so much to increase their individual and joint international competitiveness, but rather to create tight barriers to entry, subdivide and allocate the market, and collude on price. Many industries in this category, such as cement and other basic materials, have long been protected by the government through import protection and domestic policy measures, and are known to have colluded for many years (e.g., Tilton 1996). Likewise, the Large-Scale Retail Law has long protected retailing, and self-regulation will allow small stores to continue to benefit from the old rules even as they are being deregulated on paper (Upham 1996). Thus, as the government withdraws from micro-managing some of these industries, they will increase efforts at self-protection, and without an external competitive threat these industries are unlikely to become more efficient in the process. However, not all domestic industries must necessarily suffer from more self-regulation: through joint efforts at survival and revival, many companies that would have gone bankrupt without cooperation were able to weather the severe recession of the 1990s. When the economy recovers, Japan's economy can thus build on a sector of domestic industries which might have been wiped out in a more competitive environment, reducing the need for imports of basic and intermediate products. Helping its companies through recessions and avoiding bankruptcies have long been two of Japan's basic policies; in the 1990s, these efforts shifted partially into private hands, but that did not make them any less effective.

One important implication of self-regulation is that it buttresses the inherent stability and long-term viability of large-scale Japanese firms. The increase in self-regulation reflects a preference among Japanese firms for a lower variance in profits in the long run over higher profits in the short run. In fact, this particular preference is one fundamental reason why the propensity for inter-firm cooperation is generally high in Japan. The reasons for this attitude are numerous and have been studied elsewhere. To mention only a few, these include: the general notion that the primary goal of a company is not to maximize shareholder value in the short run but to create value over time and offer stable, long-term employment (Nikkei 1991, Takeuchi 1991, Schaede 1994); related to this, the managerial constraints caused by the system of lifelong employment for a significant portion of the workforce and the *keiretsu* system (Odagiri 1992, Lincoln/ Nakata 1997, Gilson/Roe 1993, Gerlach 1992); a system of "patient capital" whereby the stock market does not measure a company's achievements based on quarterly earnings but on long-term gains (Porter, M. 1992, Lightfoot 1992); and, most basically, the recent history of having had to steer companies through the aftermath of WWII that is still in the immediate memory of many contemporary Japanese CEOs and has created a general conservative attitude and aversion to variability and uncertainty over time (e.g., Tsuru 1993, Abegglen 1984, Nakatani 1984).

Accordingly, when Japanese companies self-regulate, they often do so in an attempt to make their business environment more stable, predictable, and understandable. Short-term profit maximization is not necessarily their goal. To fully appreciate the objective function of the typical Japanese CEO, we need to understand self-regulation as a mechanism that serves to minimize risk; a conceptualization of price fixing just as a means to increase profits misses the larger and more enduring aim of most Japanese companies. Cooperation with competitors through trade associations is the dominant business practice in most Japanese industries. By stabilizing the business environment, the increase in self-regulation will allow large Japanese firms to continue their long-term, risk-minimizing approach to corporate strategy. Sharing critical information in times of crisis will allow major companies to survive recession and structural downturns, even with the fading relevance of industrial policy. As a result, large firms in Japan's leading industrial sectors will remain viable, forceful competitors in international markets in the long run.

8.4. The Stability of the System in the Medium Term

Of course, the Japanese government could decide to change the system. The JFTC could begin to prosecute violations involving "unfair trade" through a more rigorous interpretation of the Antimonopoly Law, or the law could be revised.

The government could create regulatory agencies, such as those in the U.S., to fill the regulatory void. Or, foreigners could enter the Japanese market in large numbers and undermine the current system. The question, then, is how long will the system of cooperative capitalism based on self-regulation last in Japan?

For a change to occur in the antitrust system, there would have to be a widespread recognition within Japan that this cooperative system, and the protective self-regulation it entails, is a bad thing. Currently not one powerful constituency in Japan's political landscape favors fundamental change, but there are many strong opponents to it. Even legal scholars and the JFTC, who would prefer stricter rules on cooperation among competing firms, see no legal problem with self-regulation unless it is coerced. In fact, certain industry laws, such as the Securities and Exchange Law, have recently been revised to allow for more, rather than less, self-regulation. When the U.S. trade representative pushed, by means of *gaiatsu*, to increase the antitrust enforcement in cases of *dangō* and unfair trade practices, Japan accepted the first piece of advice but ignored the second. Newspapers do not often comment on the practice, and it is rarely criticized in public. There is no obvious movement against self-regulation in Japan.

In more systemic terms, there is a surprisingly precise answer to the question of how long it would take for Japan's government to fill the existing regulatory void, if it were to address the issue seriously. Of course there is always uncertainty about the future, but barring major calamities, it can be assumed with some confidence that it will take at least 25 years, and probably longer, before Japan will develop independent regulatory agencies with effective powers. The reason for this lies in the structure and logic of Japan's civil service and its promotion system. In the Japanese system, bureaucrats are hired at age 22 and are promoted slowly through the ranks, until the best of the group assume leading positions in the ministry or agency. There is typically no mid-level entry into civil service careers. While ministries differ in the extent to which they empower young officials to make decisions, it usually takes about 25 years for a bureaucrat to reach a position with any real decision-making power. Meanwhile, a new agency will effectively be run by *shukkō*, seconded officials from other ministries. These dispatched officials only stay with the agency for, on average, two years and therefore never really adopt the mindset of that agency. Only when the people who were originally hired by the agency reach executive positions can independent decision-making be expected.

The JFTC itself is the best example of how this process plays out over time: when the JFTC was founded in 1947, it was staffed with private businessmen, repatriated employees from the Manchurian Railways, and *shukkō* from MITI and other ministries, who had their industries' interests more at heart than antitrust. It took until the late 1970s before the JFTC scored its first major victory. But even through the 1990s it has remained an integral part of the overall political processes of Kasumigaseki (the bureaucracy) and Nagatachō (the politicians) by way of having its chairman position customarily staffed by former leading officials from the Ministry of Finance. Therefore, even 50 years after its establishment, the JFTC is not a fully independent regulatory agency. Naturally this was not so much due to the JFTC's desire to be dependent, but rather based on a political decision to keep the antitrust watchdog on a tight leash. Similarly, if the government were to create new regulatory agencies, these would be likely to remain subservient to the existing system.[1] The very structure of the civil service system and promotion is unlikely to change.

A further reason why supervisory agencies are unlikely to assume widespread process regulation lies in the logic of Japan's political system. Japan has long maintained that unlike in the U.S. presidential system, in a parliamentary system there is no provision for independent regulatory agencies, because the parliament is the ruling body. Using this argument, Japan in 1952 abolished all of the supervisory agencies created by the U.S. and transferred their functions to the industrial ministries; examples include the Radio Regulatory Commission (modeled after the Federal Communications Commission) and the Securities and Exchange Commission (modeled after the U.S. commission of the same name) (Krauss 2000). This political stance explains both the absence of regulatory agencies in Japan and the continuing resistance to creating them.[2]

Another potential force for undermining the system of cooperation and self-regulation is foreign entry. Until the 1980s, there were significant constraints on foreign direct investment into Japan, both political and economic. In 1998, the legal constraints to FDI were removed, and more foreign firms have found inroads to Japan's markets, especially in the area of banking and finance. Nonetheless, while the various legal changes combined with the recession and the depressed stock market of the 1990s could trigger change by inviting foreign takeovers and by making Japan's markets more accessible, there are two strong reasons why increased foreign participation is unlikely to affect the overall system of self-regulation, at least in the medium run. First, a foreign firm that begins operations in Japan will either be excluded from the association due to restrictive self-regulation, or it will become a member of the association and thus be included. If it is excluded, the foreign firm will pose no serious threat to the rule-making of the association.[3] If it is included, it can shape the self-regulation of the industry, but there is no obvious reason why the foreign firm would want to undermine it (other than maybe when self-regulation entails price fixing). In

---

[1] This applies also to the Financial Supervisory Agency (FSA), which was founded in 1997 to accelerate the regulatory clean-up of Japan's banking crisis. In the case of the FSA, some of the new mid-level officials are long-term *shukkō* from the Ministry of Finance, and it may be in their interest to adapt to the new regulatory logic of the agency. Nevertheless, it will be difficult to shed the previously acquired skills of informal regulation.

[2] Interestingly, Japan's argument may have been just a cloak to resist U.S. changes and empower the industrial ministries. Other countries with parliamentary systems have independent regulatory agencies; e.g., Germany's banks are regulated by both the central bank and a *Bundesaufsichtsamt* (Federal Supervisory Agency for the banking system).

[3] If the foreign firm is dominant in its industry, it may be able to undermine the domestic industry's rules as an outsider; knowing this, the Japanese association is likely to admit the foreigner to prevent the disruption. Therefore, associations are likely to exclude those foreign firms that are unlikely to undermine the industry's rules from the outside.

the case of a regulatory void, rules by the trade association may be preferable to no rules, and entry barriers and other restrictions are as welcome to the foreign firms as they are to the domestic ones, as long as the foreigners are part of the in-group. Second, even if a foreign firm is opposed to self-regulation it may not have a choice in the matter, as happens when self-regulation means access to the distribution system. Thus, the biggest foreign effect on association agreements will most likely be a possible shift toward more administrative and less protective self-regulation in that industry. It is also important to note that while easier market access to Japan has frequently been hailed in the media in the late 1990s, the import ratio in most industries in Japan remains far below 10% of total sales. There are still only very few industries where foreign firms play a dominant role.

Examples of industries where foreigners have participated in self-regulation in the past support this reasoning. The two most representative cases are the chemicals and auto tire industries. In the chemical industry, several European and U.S. companies have long been members of the Japan Chemical Trade Association (JCIA, *Nihon kagaku kōgyō kyōkai*). These companies have typically gone along with industry agreements, even if they were occasionally amazed by the extent of cooperation.[4] The Automobile Tires Trade Association has one foreign member, Michelin, who acquired second-tier tire maker Okamoto in the 1980s. The Michelin representative director sent to association meetings throughout the 1990s was a former Okamoto official. Interestingly, the tire industry has also been investigated repeatedly for suspicion of collusion since then. While Michelin may or may not have been a beneficiary of these price agreements, the foreign firm was clearly no hindrance for the association to structure protective self-regulation.

Even in the financial services sector, self-regulation is unlikely to be undermined seriously by foreign competitors. To be sure, in the 1990s foreign banks have become important players, but they are still not allowed to join the important domestic associations as full members. In trust banking, after a U.S.–Japan agreement in the early 1990s to allow U.S. asset managers to enter the Japanese market, these firms were asked to become members of the Trust Bank Association (*Shintaku kyōkai*). Subsequently, as one foreign bank representative put it, "we had absolutely zero control over how to price our products, because the association was running the business" (Interviews, summer 1998). Whereas in investment banking, the foreign community has largely ignored the agreements made by their Japanese competitors, an example where foreign firms happily went along with self-regulation is the non-life insurance industry: after years of lobbying and *gaiatsu* to open the Japanese market to U.S. insurance companies, once these companies were admitted into the market, they began to lobby *against* further deregulation. Clearly, the remaining barriers to entry and opaque rules through self-regulation were as much in the interest of the foreign

---

[4] Interview with a German member firm, 1997.

incumbent firms as of the domestic ones. Thus, overall there is reason to believe that it would take several simultaneous and fundamental changes to create an environment where foreign firms could and would effectively undermine domestic self-regulation across a large number of industries.

8.5. Self-Regulation in Theory and Comparative Perspective

To analyze what Japanese trade associations do, several theories of inter-firm cooperation and the generic functions of associations within a political economy have been considered throughout this book. As for theories in economics, the Japanese case underscores most concepts of collusion developed theoretically and empirically in the U.S. First, the Japanese case confirms the notion that companies collude more during recessions. This is important when evaluating the development of antitrust enforcement in Japan over time. While the number of JFTC cases increased in the 1990s, only the future long-term record will tell whether this increase was due to a more active stance taken by the JFTC, or simply a temporary reflection of the extended recession. Second, the data analysis confirmed the economic concepts about industry structure and cooperation: those Japanese trade associations that were highly active self-regulators were all characterized by industry characteristics supportive of cooperation, such as product homogeneity. In response to deregulation many Japanese trade associations have attempted to standardize their products, services or contracts. Because product homogeneity significantly increases the likelihood of self-regulation, this trend toward standardization is a harbinger of even more self-regulation.

As for political science and sociology, the Japanese case illustrates that while the concept of "private interest government" (PIG) is helpful for a first approach to the study of trade associations, it builds on the restrictive condition of delegation of power by the government to industry. This creates serious limitations for a full analysis of associations. First, in a dynamic context, associations may initially be authorized by the government to assume certain regulatory tasks but over time extend these, especially in industries that undergo rapid technological change. This introduces the difficulty of having to determine where the PIG function ends and private activity begins, and creates a bias toward overestimating the power of government. Second, even in static terms, associations engage in rule-making, joint activities, etc., without explicit government authorization. Setting aside the issue of the legality of such practices, to fully account for these activities within a political economy a concept broader than the PIG notion is needed. Self-regulation is such a concept, and although it is necessarily less precise than the PIG concept, it is more useful in defining and explaining the entire spectrum of trade association activities within a political economy.

Some legal scholars have recently suggested a concept of self-regulation as an alternative to the strong "regulatory state" situation in the U.S. and other Anglo-American market systems (Ayres/Braithwaite 1992). According to this concept, the state sets incentives for industries to engage in administrative self-regulation, but supervises the legality of these rules. This is markedly different from Japan, where associations also self-supervise and self-enforce, and thus construct a more complete system of self-regulation. Moreover, the Ayres/Braithwaite model builds on the assumption of a strong regulatory state, with existing precedents and a large legal machinery—a condition that does not exist in Japan. Nevertheless, the empirical evidence from Japan highlights one of the most obvious difficulties in the model of U.S. self-regulation: how to juggle the dual, and mutually contradictory, necessities of leaving regulation to the regulatees while supervising the legality of their activities. Japan has not addressed this issue, and as a result self-regulation leads to regulatory priority of producers' self-interest over other societal interests.

The issue of self-regulation obviously begs for a comparative discussion. Most certainly Japanese associations are not unique in performing self-regulation, and a full evaluation of the Japanese situation will only be possible after an extensive study of self-regulation in other countries. The goal of this book was to shed light on the specific Japanese case, leaving the study of other countries to further research. However, even without the benefit of in-depth knowledge of other systems, the following issues can be flagged for a comparative research agenda. First, the argument proposed here is that, in contrast to the Anglo-American "competitive system", Japan has a "cooperative system" more similar to the continental European/Asian style. How, then, do Japanese trade associations compare to those in Germany and France? The legal systems, including that of antitrust law, of Germany and Japan have been compared in the literature (Haley 1984, 1998b, Herdzina 1991). There are indeed significant similarities, beginning with government-sanctioned recession and rationalization cartels (which may originally be a German concept) and the role of trade associations in the policy-making policies (Willeke 1980, Kromphardt 1987, Henning 1991). However, the extent to which German associations self-regulate has not yet been empirically studied. Likewise, while France and Japan are said to share similar industrial policy approaches, we do not know how trade associations in the two countries compare (e.g., Zysman 1983, Cohen/Gourevitch 1982).

A second comparative question is how Japan compares to other Asian countries in terms of self-regulation. Is self-regulation a future model for those countries that emulated some of Japan's concepts of industrial policy? Answers to this question need to rely not only on a careful differentiation of Asian countries as to how similar their business environments, legal systems and government policies really are, but also on a study of the role of institutions in economic development and in a country's political economy. For instance, trade associations in Indonesia are a rather recent phenomenon, and are more utilized by the government for purposes of political control than for regulatory participation (MacIntyre 1994a, b). In Thailand, the 1980s saw the emergence of associational activity, both at the industry level and as peak organizations. Some of these associations are slowly beginning to play a role in policymaking processes, but they are not nearly as firmly established, stable and involved as Japan's associations (Laothamatas 1992, 1994). Korea, while often compared with Japan, has long been characterized by much stronger and more authoritarian political leadership, and its trade associations have mostly been mere vehicles to implement policies from above, rather than actively shaping them from below (e.g., Moon 1994, Amsden 1990, Haggard 1990, Kim 1997). Taiwan's government similarly has long treated trade associations as top-down control mechanisms, and strict regulation and control have suppressed real business input in economic policymaking (Noble 1998, Wade 1990). Thus, while Japan may resemble other Asian countries in its emphasis on cooperation, it differs along the critical dimension of having a long history of strong, independent trade associations. As Chapter 7 has shown, trade associations in Japan are firmly established institutions involved both in their own rule-making and the country's political decision-making process. They cannot be easily abolished, captured, co-opted, or otherwise turned into instruments for convenient use by the government.

Moreover, the extent to which a country's trade associations engage in self-regulation critically depends not only on their relationship with the government, but on the broader system of comparative government–business relationships and the legal situation. While Japan adopted many European laws in the 19th century, and some critical U.S. laws in the 20th century, the Western influence on law differs across countries in Asia. Likewise, the role of the state in local economies, the extent of import protection, the interaction between government and business executives, the system of antitrust enforcement, and the political system all combine to determine the relative influence and regulatory authority of trade associations in Asia. A serious comparative analysis of self-regulation in Asia thus would have to build on detailed analyses of these factors for the individual country, and possibly industry case studies to determine how institutional factors and country policies play out in different economic scenarios (e.g., Doner 1991, 1992).

Finally, the move toward highly active self-regulation in Japan has not just been systemic, but was partially triggered by external shocks: the process of deregulation combined with increased incentives to cooperate during the extended recession of the 1990s. This confluence of forces is particular to Japan, and it is thus not a logical necessity that other Asian countries adopt self-regulation after they have "caught up" and achieved development. There is nothing intrinsic to the notion of the developmental state that necessarily leads to self-regulation by associations; self-regulation is one possible outcome after the developmental state has achieved its goals. However, a system of industry self-regulation may be a viable option for some Asian countries, and the Japanese case suggests that it is not a foregone conclusion that this route would make a country less economically powerful overall.

8.6. Implications for U.S.–Japan Relations

After the burst of the "bubble economy" in the early 1990s, and particularly with the "Asian economic crisis" of the late 1990s, the U.S. stance vis-à-vis Japan shifted from one of awe, jealousy and an intense effort to gain market access to one of disregard and even contempt. While in the 1980s, Japan's companies were hailed as examples of world-class management and leadership, once the U.S. economy was again stronger than Japan's, those management styles were suddenly considered inefficient. An accurate evaluation of Japanese business clearly lies in between these two extreme viewpoints, and ought to be differentiated by industry. Yet, one result of the pendulum swing toward downplaying the prowess of Japanese business was a diminished political interest in the U.S. in pushing for an opening of Japan's markets in the 1990s: not only was the U.S. economy doing well, making foreign market access a secondary issue, but the targeting policies of the first Clinton administration had also largely failed and were not replaced by other tools of *gaiatsu*. Thus, with the temporary decline in *gaiatsu* in the mid-1990s, foreign pressure on Japan to revise its antitrust enforcement in regard to unfair trade practices lessened. The route to self-regulation was made more viable without the counteracting force of *gaiatsu*.

When the effects of the 1990s recession eventually fade, Japan's economy will reappear on the U.S. radar screen. Yet, regardless of any deregulation programs the Japanese government may announce, most markets are unlikely to become more open, since self-regulation will have increased to fill any voids left. Of course, some Japanese industries may decide to open their markets and structure their rules accordingly. However, as of the late 1990s such "open" industries were few and far between in Japan, and in many industries self-regulation was specifically used to ensure that the distribution system remained difficult to penetrate for new competition. While discount stores and mail order companies were quite successful in opening inroads to the Japanese consumer during the late 1980s, many of these new forms of outlet were hit hardest during the 1990s recession. Much more than in fashionable consumer items, however, the distribution system in intermediate products, such as flat glass or paper, continue to be dominated by Japanese distribution practices that often result in barriers to new competition, foreign and domestic alike. Coordinated through trade associations, these practices have proven effective in aligning exclusive wholesalers to the few dominant incumbents. Likewise, the feasibility of more foreign acquisitions and takeovers as well as direct investment in Japan will depend on the rules determined by industry, as self-regulation empowers incumbent firms to decide on market entry: only if the incumbents do not fear a threat of having their rules undermined will they stop creating major barriers to deter entry. It seems unlikely that foreign entry alone will be strong enough to undermine the system.

Just as incumbent firms can influence how open markets are to foreign acquisitions, they can also determine the shape of post-deregulation domestic markets.

Through the 1970s and 1980s, the Japanese government removed most of its import tariffs on manufacturing goods, and in the late 1980s it also eradicated some of the most notable non-tariff trade barriers (Lincoln 1988, 1990, Balassa/Noland 1988). However, many of these non-tariff trade barriers were in fact set up by the trade associations and continue in this form in spite of official trade liberalization measures. This makes it difficult for the U.S. government to put pressure on Japan to open its markets: if rules are not based on a law or official regulation, how much can the government change about them? Self-regulation affords the Japanese ministries an excuse for why they cannot change the situation: the government can claim that it is not responsible and not accountable for an industry's behavior. The U.S. trade negotiator's counterargument might be that to the extent that self-regulation creates barriers to entry, it should not be permitted. To this, the Japanese reply will continue to be that the Japanese system is different and that foreign firms need to work harder to learn how to do business in Japan. Little change, indeed, can be expected in U.S.–Japan trade negotiations.

The shift toward self-regulation also facilitates a defense of Japanese trade practices in the larger international arena, as became apparent in the Eastman Kodak versus Fujifilm case. In 1995, Kodak had filed a complaint against the domestic practices of its major competitor, Fujifilm, in which it argued that the Japanese government had adopted measures to support Fujifilm's attempts to keep its domestic markets closed and control prices. When Japan refused to enter bilateral negotiations, the case was brought to the World Trade Organization (WTO). In 1998, upon careful deliberation a WTO panel ruled that Kodak's evidence was insufficient to prove willful obstruction of market access by the Japanese government through specific regulation of the photo-film market. The WTO panel was probably correct in this finding, because most of the barriers that Kodak had encountered were based on self-regulation, and government's role was rather limited. However, because antitrust policies were not considered by the WTO at the time, Kodak could not have made the claim of self-regulation and had no choice but to exaggerate the role of government intervention and protection to make its case. Therefore, self-regulation fell into legal no-man's-land: under the international legal regime of the 1990s, self-regulation could not easily be challenged by Japan's trading partners.

Overall, then, the increase in self-regulation means that deregulation does not necessarily lead to more open markets in Japan. Some product markets might open up, while others will remain closed, depending on several variables. These include: the nature of competition in the industry; the structure of the distribution system and product characteristics (i.e., the ease with which the market can be kept closed); the degree and speed of deregulation (e.g., remaining laws in related industries); and the extent of re-regulation and retrenchment of the cognizant ministry (i.e., the number of licenses, permits and approvals required in spite of the fact that the basic business law has been deregulated). While trade negotiations can impact some of these variables in some industries, changing the entire package will be difficult.

The evidence presented here also suggests that there is no convergence with the U.S. system in sight. Japan is unlikely to change the general logic of its political economy and market micro-structures toward the Anglo-American competitive market approach. Of course, some Japanese companies may opt to open up, adopt international accounting standards and take other actions needed to compete successfully in foreign markets. However, the overall structure of the Japanese market will not converge with the U.S. model in the foreseeable future. The Japanese economic system has been built on cooperation: throughout history, the basic assumption underlying trade association activity was that inter-firm cooperation would further economic growth and thus was good for Japan.

This basic assumption of the cooperative system is also reflected in Japanese linguistics. The Japanese antitrust law states that a cartel can be "in the public interest". Accordingly, the Japanese word *karuteru* ("cartel") denotes an officially sanctioned cooperative agreement among a group of competing firms, and the connotation is not negative. To add to this word the notion of illegality requires the additional denominator of "shadow cartel" (*yami karuteru*). Japan may have an antitrust law that was originally based on U.S. legal thought, but the interpretation is vastly different. As long as this difference in interpretation persists, Japan's economy will work differently from that of the U.S. As one MITI official commented to me:[5] "I think what you describe is correct. But do you have to use the word 'cartel' in your analysis? Americans will necessarily misunderstand that. What we do is not illegal. It's the system."

[5] Tokyo, March 1995.

REFERENCES

Abegglen, James C. 1984. *The Strategy of Japanese Business*. Cambridge, MA: Ballinger.

Akagi, Tsuruki. 1978. *Gyōsei sekinin no kenkyū (A Study of Administrative Tasks)*. Tokyo: Iwanami Shoten.

Aldrich, Howard, Udo H. Staber, Catherine R. Zimmer, and John J. Beggs. 1990. Minimalism and Organizational Mortality: Patterns of Disbanding among U.S. Trade Associations, 1900–1983. In *Organizational Evolution—New Directions*, ed. Jitendra V. Singh: 21–52. London: Sage.

Aldrich, Howard and Udo H. Staber. 1988. Organizing Business Interests—Patterns of Trade Association Foundings, Transformations, and Deaths. In *Ecological Models of Organizations*, ed. Glenn Carroll: 111–26. Cambridge, MA: Ballinger.

Aldrich, Howard, Catherine R. Zimmer, Udo H. Staber, and John J. Beggs. 1994. Minimalism, Mutualism, and Maturity: The Evolution of the American Trade Association Population in the 20th Century. In *Evolutionary Dynamics of Organizations*, ed. Joel A. C. Baum and Jitendra V. Singh: 223–39. Oxford: Oxford UP.

Almond, Gabriel A. 1970. A Comparative Study of Interest Groups and the Political Process. In *Political Development: Essays in Heuristic Theory*, ed. Gabriel A. Almond: 51–76. Boston: Little, Brown and Co.

Almond, Gabriel A. 1990. Pluralism, Corporatism, and Professional Memory. In *A Discipline Divided: Schools and Sects in Political Science*, ed. Gabriel A. Almond: 173–88. Newbury Park, London: Sage Publications.

Amsden, Alice H. 1990. *Asia's Next Giant: South Korea and Late Industrialization*. Oxford: Oxford UP.

Anchordoguy, Marie. 1989. *Computers, Inc.—Japan's Challenge to IBM*. Cambridge: Harvard University Press.

Anchordoguy, Marie. 1997. Japan at a Technological Crossroads: Does Change Support Convergence Theory? *Journal of Japanese Studies* 23, no. 2: 363–97.

Ando, Yoshio. 1987. *Taiheiyō sensō no keizaishi-teki kenkyū (An Economic-Historic Analysis of the Pacific War)*. Tokyo: Tōkyō Daigaku Shuppan-sha.

Ariga, Michiko and Luvern V. Rieke. 1964. The Antimonopoly Law of Japan and Its Enforcement. *Washington Law Review* 39: 437–78.

Asch, Peter and Joseph J. Seneca. 1975. Characteristics of Collusive Firms. *Journal of Industrial Economics* 23: 223–37.

Asch, Peter and Joseph J. Seneca. 1976. Is Collusion Profitable? *Review of Economics and Statistics* 58: 1–12.

Ashby, W.R. 1956. *An Introduction to Cybernetics*. London: Chapman and Hall.

Axelrod, Robert. 1984. *The Evolution of Cooperation*. New York: Basic Books.

Ayres, Ian and John Braithwaite. 1992. *Responsive Regulation: Transcending the Deregulation Debate*. Oxford: Oxford UP.

Bagwell, Kyle and Robert W. Staiger. 1997. Collusion over the Business Cycle. *Rand Journal of Economics* 28, no. 1 (Spring): 82–106.

Bain, Joe S. 1951. Relation of Profit Rate to Industry Concentration: American Manufacturing, 1936–1940. *Quarterly Journal of Economics* 65 (August): 293–324.

Balassa, Bela and Marcus Noland. 1988. *Japan in the World Economy*. Washington DC: Institute for International Economics.

Barnett, William P. and Glenn R. Carroll. 1987. Competition and mutualism among early telephone companies. *Administrative Science Quarterly* 32: 400–21.

Baron, David P. 1995. Integrated Strategy: Market and Nonmarket Components. *California Management Review* 37, no. 2: 47–65.

Baron, David P. 1997. Integrated Strategy and International Trade Disputes: The Kodak-Fujifilm Case. *Journal of Economics and Management Strategy* 6, no. 2: 291–346.

Baum, Joel A.C. and Jitendra V. Singh, eds. 1994. *Evolutionary Dynamics of Organizations*. Oxford: Oxford UP.

Beason, Richard and David E. Weinstein. 1996. Growth, Economies of Scale, and Targeting in Japan (1965–1990). *Review of Economics and Statistics* 78, no. 2 (May): 286–95.

Berger, Suzanne. 1981. Introduction. In *Organizing Interests in Western Europe: Pluralism, Corporatism, and the Transformation of Politics*, ed. Suzanne Berger: 1–23. Cambridge: Cambridge UP.

Berger, Suzanne and Ronald Dore, eds. 1996. *National Diversity and Global Capitalism*. Ithaca: Cornell UP.

Bisson, Thomas A. 1954. *Zaibatsu Dissolution in Japan*. Berkeley: University of California Press.

BOJ (Bank of Japan, Nihon Ginkō chōsa-kyoku), ed. 1974. *Nihon no kahei* (*History of Japanese Currency*). Tokyo: Tōyō Keizai Shinpō-sha.

Calder, Kent E. 1988. *Crisis and Compensation: Public Policy and Political Stability in Japan, 1949–1986*. Princeton: Princeton UP.

Calder, Kent E. 1989. Elites in an Equalizing Role: Ex-Bureaucrats as Coordinators and Intermediaries in the Japanese Government–Business Relationship. *Comparative Politics* 21 (July): 379–403.

Chandler, Alfred D. Jr. 1990. *Scale and Scope: The Dynamics of Industrial Capitalism*. Cambridge: Harvard University Press.

Cohen, Jerome B. 1958. *Japan's Postwar Economy*. Bloomington: Indiana UP.

Cohen, Steven S. and Peter A. Gourevitch, eds. 1982. *France in the Troubled World Economy*. London: Butterworth.

Coleman, William D. 1988. *Business and Politics—A Study of Collective Action*. Kingston: McGill-Queen's UP.

Crawcour, Sydney. 1997. Kōgyō iken: Maeda Masana and His View of Meiji Economic Development. *Journal of Japanese Studies* 23, no. 1: 69–104.

Czada, Roland. 1994. Konjunkturen des Korporatismus: Zur Geschichte eines Paradigmenwechsels in der Verbändeforschung (The Conjunctures of Corporatism: On the History of a Paradigmatic Change in the Theory of Organized Interests). In *Staat und Verbände* (*State and Associations*), ed. Wolfgang Streeck, PVS—Politische Vierteljahreszeitschrift Vol. 35, Sonderheft 25/1994: 37–64. Opladen: Westdeutscher Verlag.

Daiwa Sōken. 1994. *Kisei kanwa de gyōkai wa kō kawaru* (*How will deregulation change business?*). Tokyo: Nihon Jitsugyō Shuppan-sha.

Daiwa Sōken. 1998. *Shōken handobukku* (*Securities Handbook*). Tokyo: Daiwa Sōken.

Dick, Andrew R. 1992. The Competitive Consequences of Japan's Export Cartel Associations. *Journal of the Japanese and International Economies* 6: 275–98.

Dick, Andrew R. 1993. Japanese Antitrust: Reconciling Theory and Evidence. *Contemporary Policy Issues* 11, no. 2: 50–61.

Dick, Andrew R. 1994. Explaining the Stability of Cartel Agreements. *UCLA Working Paper.*

DiMaggio, Paul J. and Walter W. Powell. 1983. The Iron Cage Revisited: Institutional Isomorphism and Collective Rationality in Organizational Fields. *American Sociological Review* 48: 147–60.

Dolbear, F.T., L.B. Lave, G. Bowman, A. Lieberman, E. Prescott, F. Rueter, R. Sherman. 1968. Collusion in Oligopoly: An Experiment on the Effect of Numbers and Information. *Quarterly Journal of Economics* 82, no. 2: 240–59.

Doner, Richard F. 1992. Limits of State Strength: Toward an Institutionalist View of Economic Development. *World Politics* 44, no. 4: 398–431.

Doner, Richard F. 1991. *Driving a Bargain: Automobile Industrialization and Japanese Firms in Southeast Asia.* Berkeley: University of California Press.

Dore, Ronald. 1986. *Flexible Rigidities: Industrial Policy and Structural Adjustment in Japan 1970–1980.* London: Athlone Press.

Dore, Ronald. 1987. *Taking Japan Seriously: A Confucian Perspective on Leading Economic Issues.* Stanford: Stanford UP.

Ebata, Tetsuo. 1990. *Kanryō daikenkyū (A Detailed Study of Bureaucrats).* Tokyo: Chikuma Shobō.

Encarnation, Dennis J. 1992. *Rivals Beyond Trade: America versus Japan in Global Competition.* Ithaca: Cornell UP.

EPA (Economic Planning Agency Japan, Keizai kikakuchō), ed. 1994a. *1994nen kakaku repooto (Price Report 1994).* Tokyo: Government Publication.

EPA (Economic Planning Agency Japan, Keizai kikakuchō), ed. 1994b. *Rakuichi rakuza kenkyūkai chūkan hōkoku (Interim Report by the Rakuichi-Rakuza Study Group).* Tokyo: Government Report.

EPA (Economic Planning Agency Japan, Keizai kikakuchō), ed. 1996. *Keizai hakusho (Economic White Papers).* Tokyo: Government Printing Office.

Eswaran, Mukesh. 1997. Cartel Unity over the Business Cycle. *Canadian Journal of Economics* 30, no. 3: 644–73.

Evans, Peter B., Dietrich Rueschemeyer, and Theda Skocpol, eds. 1985. *Bringing the State Back In.* New York: Cambridge UP.

FAIR (Foundation for Advanced Information and Research), ed. 1991. *Japan's Financial Markets.* Fair Fact Series II. Singapore: Look Japan Publishing.

Fairbank, John K., Edwin O. Reischauer, and Albert M. Craig. 1965. *East Asia: The Modern Transformation.* Boston/Tokyo: Houghton-Mifflin/Tuttle.

Fallows, James. 1994. *Looking at the Sun: The Rise of the New East Asian Economic and Political System.* New York: Pantheon Books.

Feldman, Gerald D. and Ulrich Nocken. 1975. Trade Associations and Economic Power: Interest Group Development in the German Iron and Steel and Machine Building Industries, 1900–1933. *Business History Review* 49: 413–45.

First, Harry. 1995. Antitrust Enforcement in Japan. *Antitrust Law Journal* 64, no. 1: 137–82.

Flath, David. 1989. Vertical Restraints in Japan. *Japan and the World Economy* 1: 187–203.

Fletcher, W. Miles. 1996. The Japan Spinners' Association: Creating Industrial Policy in Meiji Japan. *Journal of Japanese Studies* 22, no.1: 49–76.

Fraas, Arthur G. and Douglas F. Greer. 1977. Market Structure and Price Collusion: An Empirical Analysis. *Journal of Industrial Economics* 26, no. 1: 21–44.

Friedman, David. 1988. *The Misunderstood Miracle: Industrial Development and Political Change in Japan.* Ithaca: Cornell UP.

Fujita, Teiichiro. 1988. Local Trade Associations (Dogyo Kumiai) in Prewar Japan. In *Trade Associations in Business History*, ed. Hiroaki Yamazaki and Matao Miyamoto: 87–113. Tokyo: University of Tokyo Press.

Fukunaga, Hiroshi and Kyoko Chinone. 1944. Taking on the System. *Tokyo Business Today*. May 1994: 4–12.

Galbraith, Jay. 1973. *Designing Complex Organizations*. Reading MA: Addison-Wesley.

Gao, Bai. 1997. *Economic Ideology and Japanese Industrial Policy: Developmentalism from 1931 to 1965*. Cambridge: Cambridge UP.

Gerlach, Michael L. 1992. *Alliance Capitalism—The Social Organization of Japanese Business*. Berkeley: University of California Press.

Gilson, Ronald J. and Mark J. Roe. 1993. Understanding the Japanese Keiretsu: Overlaps between Corporate Governance and Industrial Organization. *The Yale Law Journal* 102, no. 4: 871–906.

GMAJ (The Glass Manufacturers' Association of Japan). 1994. *The Glass. Technology and Communication*. No. 34. Winter 1994.

Gourevitch, Peter A. 1982. Making Choices in France: Industrial Structure and the Politics of Economic Policy. In *France in the Troubled World Economy*, ed. Steven S. Cohen and Peter A. Gourevitch: 1–20. London: Butterworth.

Greer, Douglas F. 1993. *Business, Government, and Society*. New York: Macmillan. 3rd edition.

Hadley, Eleanor M. 1970. *Antitrust in Japan*. Princeton: Princeton UP.

Haggard, Stephan. 1990. *Pathways from the Periphery*. Ithaca: Cornell UP.

Haley, John O. 1984. Antitrust Sanctions and Remedies: A Comparative Study of German and Japanese Law. *Washington Law Review* 59: 471–508.

Haley, John O. 1986. Administrative Guidance versus Formal Regulation: Resolving the Paradox of Industrial Policy. In *Law and Trade Issues of the Japanese Economy—American and Japanese Perspectives*, ed. Gary Saxonhouse and Kozo Yamamura: 107–28. Seattle and London: University of Washington Press.

Haley, John O. 1991a. Japanese Antitrust Enforcement: Implications for United States Trade. *Northern Kentucky Law Review* 18, no. 3: 335–66.

Haley, John O. 1991b. *Authority without Power: Law and the Japanese Paradox*. Oxford: Oxford UP.

Haley, John O. 1995. Competition and Trade Policy: Antitrust Enforcement—Do Differences Matter? *Pacific Rim Law and Policy Journal* 4, no. 1: 303–25.

Haley, John O. 1998a. Culture, Competition and Deregulation: Japan's Challenge to International Harmonization of Competition Law. In *Comparative Competition Law: Approaching an International System of Antitrust Law*, ed. Hanns Ullrich: 93–104. Baden-Baden: Nomos.

Haley, John O. 1998b. Error, Irony, and Convergence: A Comparative Study of the Origins and Development of Competition Policy in Postwar Germany and Japan. In *Festschrift für Wolfgang Fikentscher, zum 70. Geburtstag*, ed. Bernhard Großfeld, Rolf Sack, Thomas M.J. Möllers, Josef Drexl, and Andreas Heinemann: 876–918. Tübingen: Mohr Siebeck.

Hall, John Whitney. 1951. The Tokugawa Bakufu and the Merchant Class. *Occasional Paper, Center for Japanese Studies* 1: 26–33.

Hanano, Akio, Haruhito Tetsune, and Yoshinori Morita. 1991. *Zaisei tōyūshi (Fiscal and Investment Loan Program)*. Tokyo: Tōyō Keizai Shinpō-sha.

Hannan, Michael and Glenn R. Carroll. 1992. *Dynamics of Organizational Populations: Density, Competition, and Legitimation*. New York: Oxford UP.

Hannan, Michael and John H. Freeman. 1989. *Organizational Ecology*. Cambridge, MA: Harvard UP.

Harari, Ehud. 1988. The Institutionalization of Policy Consultation in Japan: Public Advisory Bodies. In *Japan and the World*, ed. Gail Lee Bernstein and Haruhiro Fukui: 138–61. New York: St. Martin's Press.

Hasegawa, Shin. 1978. Kinsei-chū/kōki no shōgyō (Trade in the Second Half of the Tokugawa Period). In *Nihon shōgyō-shi (A Business History of Japan)*, ed. Teiichirō Fujita, Matao Miyamoto, and Shin Hasegawa: 48–96. Tokyo: Yūhikaku.

Hasegawa, Shin. 1985. Satsuki-kai: Jūdenki karuteru (The "Satsuki Group": The Heavy Electric Machinery Cartel). In *Ryō-daisenkan-ki no Nihon no karuteru (Japan's Cartels in the Interwar Period)*, ed. Jūrō Hashimoto and Haruhito Takeda: 273–322. Tokyo: Ochanomizu Shobō.

Hashimoto, Jūrō. 1984. *Daikyōkō no Nihon shihon-shugi (The Japanese Economic System during the Great Depression)*. Tokyo: Tōkyō Daigaku Shuppan-kai.

Hashimoto, Jūrō. 1985. Semento Rengōgai (The Cement Federation). In *Ryō-daisenkan-ki no Nihon no karuteru (Japan's Cartels in the Interwar Period)*, ed. Jūrō Hashimoto and Haruhito Takeda: 127–68. Tokyo: Ochanomizu Shobō.

Hay, George A. and Daniel Kelley. 1974. An Empirical Survey of Price Fixing Conspiracies. *Journal of Law and Economics*, April 1974: 13–38.

Henderson, Dan Fenno. 1965. *Conciliation and Japanese Law in Tokugawa and Modern, Vol. I*. Seattle: University of Washington Press.

Henning, Friedrich-Wilhelm. 1991. *Das industrialisierte Deutschland, 1914–1990 (The Industrialized Germany, 1914–1990)*. UTB. Paderborn: Schöningh.

Herdzina, Klaus. 1991. *Wettbewerbspolitik (Competition Policy)*. UTB. Stuttgart: Gustav-Fischer Verlag.

Herrigel, Gary. 1996. *Industrial Constructions: The Sources of German Industrial Power*. Cambridge: Cambridge UP.

Hicks, John R. 1935. Annual Survey of Economic Theory: The Theory of Monopoly. *Econometrica*, no. 3: 1–20.

Hilferding, Rudolf. 1981 (first published 1910). *Finance Capital—A Study of the Latest Phase of Capitalist Development*. London: Routledge and Kegan Paul.

Hironaka, Katsuhiko. 1994. *Sore demo dangō wa nakunarai—"Dairi dangō" no jidai ga yatte kita (Why Dangō Will Not Disappear—The New Era of "Delegated Dangō")*. Tokyo: Tōyō Keizai Shinpō-sha.

Hirschmeier, Johannes and Tsunehiko Yui. 1975. *The Development of Japanese Business, 1600–1973*. London: Allen & Unwin Ltd.

HKKK (Heiwa keizai keikaku kaigi). 1977. *1977–nenpan Kokumin no dokusen hakusho (The 1977 White Paper of National Monopolies)*. Tokyo: Ochanomizu Shobō.

Hollingsworth, J. Rogers and Leon N. Lindberg. 1985. The Governance of the American Economy: The Role of Markets, Clans, Hierarchies, and Associative Behavior. In *Private Interest Government*, ed. Wolfgang Streeck and Philippe C. Schmitter: 221–54. London: Sage.

Honjo, Eijiro. 1935. *The Social and Economic History of Japan*. Kyoto: Maruzen Company, Ltd.

Honsho, Jirō. 1993. *Dokyumento Keidanren—Zaikai shūnōjin no honne (Documentary on Keidanren—The Truth about the Zaikai's Leaders)*. Tokyo: Kōdansha Bunkō.

Horiuchi, Akiyoshi. 1980. *Nihon no kinyū seisaku (Monetary Policy in Japan)*. Tokyo: Tōyō Keizai Shinpō-sha.

Hoshi, Takeo, Anil Kashyap, and David Scharfstein. 1990a. The Role of Banks in Reducing the Costs of Financial Distress in Japan. *Journal of Financial Economics* 27: 67–88.

Hoshi, Takeo, Anil Kashyap, and David Scharfstein. 1990b. Bank Monitoring and Investment: Evidence from the Changing Structure of Japanese Corporate Banking Relationships. In *Asymmetric Information, Corporate Finance, and Investment*, ed. R. Glenn Hubbard: 105–26. Chicago.

Hoshi, Takeo, Anil Kashyap, and David Scharfstein. 1991. Corporate Structure, Liquidity, and Investment Evidence from Japanese Industrial Groups. *The Quarterly Journal of Economics*, February: 33–60.

Hoshi, Takeo and Anil Kashyap. 1999. *The Japanese Banking Crisis: Where Did it Come From and How Will it End?* Cambridge, MA: NBER Working Paper #7250.

Hotta, Tsutomu. 1994. Zenekon oshoku no ōsureba konzetsu dekiru. (How Bribery in the Construction Industry could be Extinguished). *Chūō Kōron*, January, 82–91.

Ichinose, Tomoji. 1989. *Gendai kōkyō kigyō ron (An Analysis of Public Corporations)*. Tokyo: Tōyō Keizai Shinpō-sha.

Iida, Shigeru. 1985. *Shōwa dōran-ki no Nihon keizai bunseki (An Analysis of the Japanese Economy During the Recessions of the Early Showa Period)*. Tokyo: Shinhyōron.

Imamura Takeo. 1948. *Takahashi Korekiyo*. Tokyo: Jiji Tsūshin-sha.

Inoguchi, Takashi and Tomoaki Iwai. 1987. *"Zoku giin" no kenkyū: Jimintō seiken o gyūjiru shūyakutachi (The Zoku-giin: The Group of Major People in Charge of Leading the LDP)*. Tokyo: Nihon Keizai Shinbun-sha.

Ishikawa, Tsuneo. 1985. *Gendai no kinyū seisaku (Japan's Contemporary Monetary Policy)*. Tokyo: Tōyō Keizai Shinpō-sha.

Ito, Daiichi. 1991. Government-Industry Relations in a Dual Regulatory Scheme: Engineering Research Associations as Policy Instruments. In *The Promotion and Regulation of Industry in Japan*, ed. Stephen Wilks and Maurice Wright: 51–80. New York: St. Martin's Press.

Iyori, Hiroshi. 1986. Antitrust and Industrial Policy in Japan: Competition and Cooperation. In *Law and Trade Issues of the Japanese Economy: American and Japanese Perspectives*, ed. Gary Saxonhouse and Kozo Yamamura: 56–82. Seattle and London: University of Washington Press.

Iyori, Hiroshi. 1995. A Comparison of U.S.–Japan Antitrust Law: Looking at the International Harmonization of Competition Law. *Pacific Rim Law and Policy Journal* 4, no. 1: 59–91.

Iyori, Hiroshi and Akinori Uesugi. 1994. *The Antimonopoly Law and Policies of Japan*. N.Y.: Federal Legal Publications, Inc.

JASD (Japan Association of Securities Dealers; Nihon Shōkengyō kyōkai), ed. 1995. *Teikan, Kisoku (Bylaws and Rulebook)*. Tokyo: Nihon Shōkengyō kyōkai.

JFTC (Japan Fair Trade Commission), ed. 1977. *Dokusen kinshi seisaku 30 nenshi (A 30 Year History of Antitrust Policy)*. Tokyo: Ōkurashō Insatsukyoku.

JFTC (Japan Fair Trade Commission), ed. 1981a. *Interpretations Concerning the Relation Between the Antimonopoly Act and Administrative Guidance.* Tokyo: Government Report.

JFTC (Japan Fair Trade Commission), ed. 1981b. *Ishakai no katsudō ni kan suru dokusen-kinshi-hō jō no shishin (Antimonopoly Act Guidelines for Activities of Doctors' Associations).* Tokyo: Government Report.

JFTC (Japan Fair Trade Commission), ed. 1991. *The Antimonopoly Act Guidelines Concerning Distribution Systems and Business Practices.* Tokyo: Government Report.

JFTC (Japan Fair Trade Commission), ed. 1993a. *Jigyōsha dantai no katsudō to dokusen kinshi-hō-jō no shomondai—yori akareta katsudō o mezashite (Trade Association Activities and Problems under the Antimonopoly Act—In Pursuit of More Open Activities).* Tokyo: Government Report.

JFTC (Japan Fair Trade Commission), ed. 1993b. *Shūyō sangyō ni okeru ruiseki seisan shūchūdo to Haafindaaru shisū, Heisei gannen/ni-nen (Concentration of Production and the Herfindahl Index in Major Industries for 1989 and 1990).* Tokyo: Government Report.

JFTC (Japan Fair Trade Commission), ed. 1993c. *Shūyō sangyō ni okeru ruiseki shukkō shūchūdo, Heisei gannen/ni-nen (Concentration Ratios for Shipments in Major Industries for 1989 and 1990).* Tokyo: Government Report.

JFTC (Japan Fair Trade Commission), ed. 1994a. *Interpretations Concerning Administrative Guidance under the Antimonopoly Act.* Tokyo: Government Report.

JFTC (Japan Fair Trade Commission), ed. 1994b. *Kōkyōteki na nyūsatsu ni kakaru jigyōsha oyobi jigyōsha dantai no katsudō ni kan suru dokusen kinshihō-jō no shishin (The Antimonopoly Guidelines Concerning the Activities of Firms and Trade Associations in Relation to Public Bids).* Tokyo: Government Report.

JFTC (Japan Fair Trade Commission), ed. 1995. *Jigyōsha dantai no katsudō ni kan suru dokusen kinshi-hō no shishin (The Antimonopoly Guidelines Concerning the Activities of Trade Associations).* Tokyo: Government Report.

JFTC (Japan Fair Trade Commission), ed. 1996a. *Jigyōsha dantai no katsudō ni kan suru shūyō sōdan jirei, Heisei 7–nen (Report on the Most Important Consultation Cases for Trade Associations in 1995).* Tokyo: Government Report.

JFTC (Japan Fair Trade Commission), ed. 1996b. *Gaishi-kei kigyō kara mita waga-kuni jigyōsha dantai no katsudō ni kan suru chōsa hōkokusho (Report on the Behavior of Japanese Industry Association from the Perspective of Foreign Enterprises in Japan).* Tokyo: Government Report.

JFTC (Japan Fair Trade Commission), ed. 1996c. *Kōsei torihiki iinkai no soshiki kyōka: Jimu sōkyoku-sei no dōnyu to jūten kadai. (The Strengthening of the JFTC Organization and the Introduction of the "General Affairs Office" System).* Tokyo: Government Report.

JFTC (Japan Fair Trade Commission), ed. 1997. *Jigyōsha dantai no katsudō ni kan suru shūyō sōdan jirei, Heisei 8–nen (Report on the Most Important Consultation Cases for Trade Associations in 1996).* Tokyo: Government Report.

JFTC (Japan Fair Trade Commission), ed. various years. *Kōsei torihiki iinkai nenji hōkoku (JFTC Annual Report).* Tokyo: Ōkurashō Insatsukyoku.

Jijichō (Ministry of Home Affairs), ed. 1996. *Heisei 6–nenbun seiji shikin shushi hōkoku no gaiyō (An Outline of the Political Funds Report for 1994).* Tokyo: Government Report.

Johnson, Chalmers. 1974. "The Reemployment of Retired Government Bureaucrats in Japanese Big Business". *Asian Survey* 14, November: 953–65.

Johnson, Chalmers. 1978. *Japan's Public Policy Companies*. Washington: American Economic Institute.

Johnson, Chalmers. 1982. *MITI and the Japanese Miracle— The Growth of Industrial Policy, 1925–1975*. Stanford: Stanford UP.

Johnson, Chalmers. 1989. MITI, MPT, and the Telecom Wars: How Japan Makes Policy for High Technology. In *Politics and Productivity: How Japan's Development Strategy Works*, eds. Chalmers Johnson, Laura Tyson, and John Zysman: 177–240. New York: Harper Business.

Johnson, Chalmers. 1995. *Japan: Who Governs? The Rise of the Developmental State*. New York: Norton.

JTA (Japan Tariff Association), ed. 1990. *Nihon bōeki geppō (Japan Exports and Imports, Commodity by Country)*, Vol. 12. Tokyo.

Kahler, Miles. 1996. Trade and Domestic Differences. In *National Diversity and Global Capitalism*, ed. Suzanne Berger and Ronald Dore: 298–332. Ithaca: Cornell UP.

Kanazawa, Yoshio. 1963. The Regulation of Corporate Enterprise: The Law of Unfair Competition and the Control of Monopoly Power. In *Law in Japan—The Legal Order in a Changing Society*, ed. Arthur von Mehren: 480–506. Cambridge, MA: Harvard UP.

Kanzaki, Katsurō. 1987. *Shōken torihiki hō (The Securities and Exchange Act)*. Tokyo: Seirin Shoin.

Kaplan, Eugene J. 1976. Perspectives on Government-Business Interaction in Japan. In *Asian Business and Environment in Transition*, ed. Ashok Kapoor: 323–37. Princeton: Darwin Press.

Katz, Richard. 1998. *Japan—The System That Soured: The Rise and Fall of the Japanese Economic Miracle*. Armonk NY: M.E. Sharpe.

Katzenstein, Peter J., ed. 1978. *Between Power and Plenty: Foreign Economic Policies of Advanced Industrial States*. Madison: University of Wisconsin Press.

Kawagoe, Kenji. 1997. *Dokusen kinshi-hō— Kyōsō shakai no feanesu (The Antimonopoly Law—The Fairness of a Competitive Society)*. Tokyo: Kinzai.

Keehn, E.B. 1998. The Myth of Regulatory Independence in Japan. In *Unlocking the Bureaucrat's Kingdom—Deregulation and the Japanese Economy*, ed. Frank Gibney: 204–19. Washington: The Brookings Institution.

Keidanren (Keizai Dantai Rengōkai), ed. 1978. *Keizai dantai rengōkai 30-nenshi (A 30 Year History of Keidanren)*. Tokyo: Toppan Insatsu.

Keidanren (Keizai Dantai Rengōkai), ed. 1993. *1993 nendo Keidanren no iken—yōbō-tō (Opinions, Expectations, etc. for 1993)*. Tokyo: Keidanren.

Keidanren (Keizai Dantai Rengōkai), ed. 1994a. *Datsu kisei shakai ni muketa—Jikkō aru kisei kanwa suishin keikaku no sakutei o motomeru (Toward a Society Freed from Regulation—Requesting Implementation of Effective Plans to Support Deregulation)*. Tokyo: Keidanren.

Keidanren (Keizai Dantai Rengōkai), ed. 1994b. *Seiji shikin kanren shiryō (Reports on Political Funds)*. Tokyo: Keidanren.

Kernell, Samuel. 1991. "Conclusion: The Primacy of Politics in Economic Policy". In *Parallel Politics: Economic Policymaking in Japan and the United States*, ed. Samuel Kernell: 325–78. Washington: The Brookings Institution.

Kester, W. Carl. 1991. *Japanese Takeovers: The Global Contest for Corporate Control*. Boston: Harvard Business School Press.

Kikkawa, Takeo. 1988. Functions of Japanese Trade Associations Before World War II: The Case of Cartel Organizations. In *Trade Associations in Business History*, ed. Hiroaki Yamazaki and Matao Miyamoto: 53–83. Tokyo: University of Tokyo Press.

Kim, Eun Mee. 1997. Big Business, Strong State: Collusion and Conflict in South Korean Development, 1960–1990. Albany: State University of New York Press.

Kimura, Takatoshi. 1995. *1920 nendai Nihon no sangyō bunseki (Analysis of Japan's Industries in the 1920s)*. Tokyo: Nihon Keizai Hyōron-sha.

Kocka, Jürgen. 1978. Entrepreneurs and Managers in German Industrialization. In *The Cambridge Economic History of Europe, Vol. VII (1), The Industrial Economies: Capital, Labour and Enterprise*, ed. Peter Mathias and M.M. Postan: 492–598. Cambridge: Cambridge UP.

Koh, B.C. 1989. *Japan's Administrative Elite*. Berkeley: University of California Press.

Kojima, Seiichi. 1940. *Nihon senji chūsho kōgyō ron (An Analysis of Small and Medium Enterprises During the War)*. Tokyo: Chikuma Shobō.

Komiya, Ryutaro. 1988. Introduction. In *Industrial Policy of Japan*, ed. Ryutaro Komiya, Masahiro Okuno, and Kotaro Suzumura: 1–22. Tokyo: Academic Press.

Komiya, Ryutaro. 1990. *The Japanese Economy: Trade, Industry, and Government*. Tokyo: University of Tokyo Press.

Krasner, Stephen D. 1978. *Defending the National Interest: Raw Materials Investments and U.S. Foreign Policy*. Princeton: Princeton UP.

Krasner, Stephen D. 1984. Approaches to the State: Alternative Conceptions and Historical Dynamics. *Comparative Politics* 16: 223–46.

Krauss, Ellis S. and Isobel Coles. 1990. Built-in Impediments: The Political Economy of the U.S.–Japan Construction Dispute. In *Japan's Economic Structure: Should it Change?*, ed. Kozo Yamamura. Seattle: Society for Japanese Studies.

Krauss, Ellis S. 2000. *NHK: Broadcasting Politics in Japan*. Ithaca: Cornell UP.

Kreps, David M. 1990. *Game Theory and Economic Modelling*. Clarendon Lectures in Economics. Oxford: Oxford UP.

Kromphardt, Jürgen. 1987. *Konzeptionen und Analysen des Kapitalismus (Concepts and Analyses of Different Forms of Capitalism)*. UTB. Göttingen: Vandenhoeck.

Kulischer, Josef. 1928. *Allgemeine Wirtschaftsgeschichte des Mittelalters und der Neuzeit (General Economic History of Middle and Modern Ages)*. München/Berlin: von Oldenbourg.

Kurihara, Shigeru. 1991. *Nomura Shōken ni naibu kakumei wa okoru ka (The Possibility of an Internal Upheaval at Nomura)*. Tokyo: Dai-Ichi Kikaku Shuppan.

KZJK (Kinyū zaisei jijō kenkyū-kai), ed. 1986. *Kinyū jiyūka to En no kokusaika (Financial Deregulation and the Internationalization of the Yen)*. Tokyo: Kinyū zaisei.

Lake, Charles D. II 1998. Liberalizing Japan's Insurance Market. In *Unlocking the Bureaucrat's Kingdom: Deregulation and the Japanese Economy*, ed. Frank Gibney: 116–41. Washington: Brookings Institution Press.

Laothamatas, Anek. 1992. *Business Associations and the New Political Economy of Thailand*. Boulder: Westview Press.

Laothamatas, Anek. 1994. From Clientelism to Partnership: Business–Government Relations in Thailand. In *Business and Government in Industrialising Asia*, ed. Andrew MacIntyre: 195–215. Ithaca: Cornell UP.

Lightfoot, Robert W. 1992. *Note on Corporate Governance Systems: The United States, Japan, and Germany*. Boston: Harvard Business School.

Lincoln, Edward J. 1988. *Japan: Facing Economic Maturity.* Washington, D.C.: The Brookings Institution.

Lincoln, Edward J. 1990. *Japan's Unequal Trade.* Washington D.C.: The Brookings Institution.

Lincoln, James R. and Yoshifumi Nakata. 1997. The Transformation of the Japanese Employment System. *Work and Occupations* 24, no. 1: 33–55.

Lockwood, William W. 1954. *The Economic Development of Japan—Growth and Structural Change.* Princeton: Princeton UP.

Lynn, Leonard H. and Timothy J. McKeown. 1988. *Organizing Business—Trade Associations in America and Japan.* Washington: American Enterprise Institute.

Machlup, Fritz. 1952. *The Political Economy of Monopoly— Business, Labor and Government Policies.* Baltimore: Johns Hopkins UP.

MacIntyre, Andrew, ed. 1994a. *Business and Government in Industrialising Asia.* Ithaca: Cornell UP.

MacIntyre, Andrew. 1994b. Power, Prosperity and Patrimonialism: Business and Government in Indonesia. In *Business and Government in Industrialising Asia,* ed. Andrew MacIntyre: 244–67. Ithaca: Cornell UP.

Marburg, Theodore F. 1964. Government and Business in Germany: Public Policy toward Cartels. *Business History Review* 38: 78–101.

Marvel, Howard P., J.M. Netter, and A.M. Robinson. 1988. Price Fixing and Civil Damages: An Economic Analysis. *Stanford Law Review* 40: 561–75.

Matsubara, Satoru. 1995. *Tokushu-hōjin kaikaku (The Reform of Special Corporations).* Tokyo: Nihon Hyōronsha.

Matsushita, Mitsuo. 1993. *International Trade and Competition Law in Japan.* Oxford: Oxford UP.

Maya, Yoshio. 1993. Seimei hoken gaisha wa genten ni kaere—Riyōsha fuzai no sōgō kinyū kikan-ka ron (Life Insurance Companies Ought to Return to their Roots: How Turning into General Financial Institutions Would Leave Them Without Clients). *Ekonomisuto,* March 23: 18–23.

McAffee, R. Preston, and John McMillan. 1992. Bidding Rings. *American Economic Review* 82, no. 3: 579–99.

McCubbins, Mathew D. and Gregory W. Noble. 1995a. Perceptions and Realities of Japanese Budgeting. In *Structure and Policy in Japan and the United States,* ed. Peter F. Cowhey and Mathew D. McCubbins: 81–115. Cambridge: Cambridge UP.

McCubbins, Mathew D. and Gregory W. Noble. 1995b. The Appearance of Power: Legislators, Bureaucrats, and the Budget Process in the United States and Japan. In *Structure and Policy in Japan and the United States,* ed. Peter F. Cowhey and Mathew D. McCubbins: 56–80. Cambridge: Cambridge UP.

McKean, Margaret A. 1993. State Strength and the Public Interest. In *Political Dynamics in Contemporary Japan,* ed. Gary D. Allinson and Yasunori Sone: 72–104. Ithaca and London: Cornell UP.

McMillan, John. 1990. Managing Suppliers: Incentive Systems in Japanese and United States Industry. *California Management Review* 32, no. 4: 38–55.

McMillan, John. 1991. Dangō: Japan's Price-Fixing Conspiracies. *Economics and Politics* 3, no. 3: 201–18.

McMillan, John. 1992. *Games, Strategies, and Managers—How Managers Can Use Game Theory to Make Better Business Decisions.* Oxford: Oxford UP.

Mishina, Kazuhiro. 1993. *Tombow Pencil Co. Ltd.* Boston: Harvard Business School.

Misonō, Hitoshi. 1987. *Nihon no dokusen kinshi seisaku to sangyō soshiki (Japan's Anti-monopoly Policy and Industrial Structure)*. Tokyo: Kawa shobō shinsha.

Miyajima, Hideaki. 1986. Shōwa kyōkō-ki no karuteru to seifu (Cartels and the Government during the Great Depression). In *Kindai Nihon no keizai to seiji: Nakamura Takafusa sensei kanreki kinen (Politics and Economy of Modern Japan: Festschrift for Professor T. Nakamura)*, ed. Akira Hara: 265–98. Tokyo: Yamagawa Shuppan-sha.

Miyamoto, Mataji. 1943. *Nihon Shōgyō-shi (A Business History of Japan)*. Tokyo: Ryūginsha.

Miyamoto, Mataji. 1948. *Kinsei shōgyō keiei no kenkyū (Trade and Management in the Tokugawa Period)*. Kyoto: Daihasshū Shuppan KK.

Miyamoto, Mataji. 1951. *Nihon kinsei tonya-sei no kenkyū (The Wholesaler-Merchant System of the Tokugawa Period)*. Tokyo.

Miyamoto, Mataji. 1958. *Kabunakama no kenkyū (Research on kabunakama)*. Tokyo: Yūhikaku.

Miyamoto, Matao. 1978. Kinsei zenki no shōgyō (Trade in the First Half of the Tokugawa Period). In *Nihon shōgyō-shi (A Business History of Japan)*, ed. Teiichirō Fujita, Matao Miyamoto, and Shin Hasegawa: 14–47. Tokyo: Yūhikaku.

Miyamoto, Matao. 1988. The Development of Business Associations in Prewar Japan. In *Trade Associations in Business History*, ed. Hiroaki Yamazaki and Matao Miyamoto: 1–45. Tokyo: University of Tokyo Press.

Moon, Chung-in. 1994. Changing Patterns of Business–Government Relations in South Korea. In *Business and Government in Industrialising Asia*, ed. Andrew MacIntyre: 142–66. Ithaca: Cornell UP.

Morison, Elting. 1966. *Men, Machines, and Modern Times*. Cambridge, MA: MIT Press.

Muramatsu, Michio, Mitsutoshi Ito, and Yutaka Tsujinaga. 1986. *Sengō no atsuryoku dantai (Pressure Groups in Postwar Japan)*. Tokyo: Tōyō Keizai Shinpō-sha.

Muramatsu, Michio and Ellis S. Krauss. 1987. The Conservative Policy Line and the Development of Patterned Pluralism. In *The Political Economy of Japan, Vol. 1: The Domestic Transformation*, ed. Kozo Yamamura and Yasukichi Yasuba: 516–54. Stanford: Stanford UP.

Muramatsu, Michio and Ellis S. Krauss. 1990. The Dominant Party and Social Coalitions in Japan. In *Uncommon Democracies: The One-Party Dominant Regimes*, ed. T.J. Pempel: 282–305. Ithaca: Cornell UP.

Murphy, R. Taggart. 1996. *The Weight of the Yen*. New York: W.W. Norton & Company.

Nagasawa, Eiichirō. 1989. *Shadan hōjin, zaidan hōjin no unei jitsumu (Specifications for the Administration of Incorporated Entities)*. Tokyo: Dōbunkan Shuppan.

Nagasawa, Eiichirō. 1996. *Shadan hōjin, zaidan hōjin no setsuritsu jitsumu (Specifications for the Establishment of Incorporated Entities)*. Tokyo: Dōbunkan Shuppan.

Nakamura, Takafusa. 1974. *Nihon no keizai tōsei: senji sengō no keiken to kyōkun (Japan's Controlled Economy: Experience and Lessons from the Wartime and Postwar Years)*. Tokyo: Nihon Keizai Shinbun-sha.

Nakamura, Takafusa. 1983. *Economic Growth in Prewar Japan*. New Haven: Yale UP.

Nakamura, Takafusa. 1985. *Nihon keizai—sono seichō to kōzō (The Japanese Economy: Its Growth and Structure)*. Tokyo: Tōkyō Daigaku Shuppan-sha.

Nakamura, Takafusa, ed. 1989. *"Keikaku-ka" to "minshū-ka" (The Planned Economy and Democratization)*. Tokyo: Iwanami Shoten.

Nakazawa, Kei and Akira Tachiyama. 1991. *Nomura Shōken Sukandaru no Kenshō (An Investigation into the Nomura Scandal)*. Tokyo: Kenyūkan.

Nakatani, Iwao. 1984. The Economic Role of Financial Corporate Groupings. In *The Economic Analysis of the Japanese Firm*, ed. Masahiko Aoki: 227–58. Amsterdam: North-Holland.

Nikkei (Nihon Keizai Shinbun-sha), ed. 1991. *Zeminaaru gendai kigyō nyūmon (Introduction to Modern Japanese Corporations)*. Tokyo: Nihon Keizai Shinbun-sha.

Nikkei (Nihon Keizai Shinbun-sha), ed. 1994. Shingikai no uchimaku: shikumi mareru yōron (Inside the Shingikai: A Structural Survey). *Nikkei Bijinesu*, September 12: 12–24.

Noble, Gregory W. 1988. The Japanese Industrial Policy Debate. In *Pacific Dynamics: The International Politics of Industrial Change*, ed. Stephan Haggard and Chung-in Moon: 53–95. Boulder, CO: Westview Press.

Noble, Gregory W. 1998. *Collective Action in East Asia: How Ruling Parties Shape Industrial Policies*. Ithaca: Cornell UP.

NSF (National Science Foundation), ed. 1996. *National Patterns of R&D Resources: 1996*. Arlington, VA: NSF Report: 96–333.

Noguchi, Yukio. 1995. *1940–nen taisei (The 1940 System)*. Tokyo: Toyo Keizai Shinpō-sha.

Nonaka, Ikujiro and Hirotaka Takeuchi. 1995. *The Knowledge-Creating Company—How Japanese Companies Create the Dynamics of Innovation*. New York, Oxford: Oxford UP.

NSSS (Nikkei Sangyō Shinbun-sha), ed. 1991. *'92 Shijō senyūritsu (1992 Market Share Data)*. Tokyo: Nihon Keizai Shinbun-sha.

Ochiai, Seiichi. 1993. Ginkō no furyō saiken disukuroojaa (The Disclosure of Bad Loans Held by Banks). *Jurisuto* 1030, September 15: 16–23.

Ochiai, Seiichi. 1996. Ginkō disukuroojaa rippō no arikata (How to Introduce Legislation on Disclosure in Commercial Banking). *Jurisuto* 1095, August 1–15: 121–7.

Odagiri, Hiroyuki. 1992. *Growth through Competition, Competition through Growth: Strategic Management and the Economy in Japan*. Oxford: Oxford UP.

Okazaki, Tetsuji. 1985. Sentetsu kyōdō kumiai (The Pig Iron Association). In *Ryō-daisen-kan-ki no Nihon no karuteru (Japan's Cartels in the Interwar Period)*, ed. Jūrō Hashimoto and Haruhito Takeda: 19–37. Tokyo: Ochanomizu Shobō.

Okazaki, Tetsuji. 1994. The Japanese Firm under the Wartime Planned Economy. In *The Japanese Firm—Sources of Competitive Strength*, ed. Masahiko Aoki and Ronald Dore: 350–78. Oxford: Oxford UP.

Okimoto, Daniel I. 1989. *Between MITI and the Market—Japanese Industrial Policy for High Technology*. Stanford: Stanford UP.

Otto, Silke-Susann. 1999. National Policy Companies and their Role in Japan's Wartime Economy. In *Japan's War Economy*, ed. Erich Pauer: 124–44. London: Routledge.

Ozaki, Robert S. 1972. *The Control of Imports and Foreign Capital in Japan*. New York: Praeger.

Patrick, Hugh T. 1962. *Monetary Policy and Central Banking in Contemporary Japan*. Bombay.

Patrick, Hugh T. 1967. Japan 1868–1914. In *Banking in the Early Stages of Industrialization—A Study in Comparative Economic History*, ed. Rondo E. Cameron: 239–89. London: Oxford UP.

Patrick, Hugh T. and Thomas P. Rohlen. 1987. Small-Scale Family Enterprises. In *The Political Economy of Japan, Vol. 1: The Domestic Transformation*, ed. Kozo Yamamura and Yasukichi Yasuba: 331–84. Stanford: Stanford UP.

Pauer, Erich. 1985. Episodes from Asian Monetary History: Iron versus Copper Coinage in Premodern Japan. *Asian Monetary Monitor* 1985, March/April: 23–37.

Pauer, Erich. 1993. *Nachbarschaftsgruppen und Versorgung in japanischen Städten während des Zweiten Weltkrieges* (*Neighborhood Groups and Food Provision in Japanese Cities during WWII*). Marburg: Marburger Japanreihe Bd. 9.

Pauer, Erich. 1999. A New Order for Japanese Society: Planned Economy, Neighborhood Associations and Food Distribution in Japanese Cities in the Second World War. In *Japan's War Economy*, ed. Erich Pauer: 85–105. London: Routledge.

Pempel, T.J. 1998. *Regime Shift: Comparative Dynamics of the Japanese Political Economy*. Ithaca: Cornell UP.

Pfeffer, Jeffrey and Gerald Salancik. 1978. *The External Control of Organizations: A Resource Dependence Perspective*. New York: Harper & Row.

Porter, Michael E. 1992. *Capital Choices: Changing the Way America Invests in Industry*. Washington: Council on Competitiveness.

Porter, Robert H. 1985. On the Incidence and Duration of Price Wars. *Journal of Industrial Economics* 33, no. 4: 415–26.

Posner, Richard A. 1970. A Statistical Survey of Antitrust Enforcement. *Journal of Law and Economics* 13: 365–419.

Prestowitz, Clyde V. Jr. 1988. *Trading Places: How We Are Giving our Future to Japan and How to Reclaim It*. New York: Basic Books.

Procassini, Andrew A. 1995. *Competitors in Alliance: Industry Associations, Global Rivalries, and Business-Government Relations*. Westport, Connecticut: Quorum Books.

Ramseyer, Mark. 1982. The Oil Cartel Criminal Cases: Translations and Postscript. *Law in Japan* 15: 57–78.

Ramseyer, Mark. 1983. Japanese Antitrust-Enforcement After the Oil Embargo. *American Journal of Comparative Law* 31: 395–430.

Ramseyer, Mark. 1985. The Costs of the Consensual Myth: Antitrust Enforcement and Institutional Barriers to Litigation in Japan. *The Yale Law Journal* 94, no. 3: 604–45.

Ramseyer, Mark. 1992. The Antitrust Pork Barrel in Japan. *Antitrust* 6, Summer 1992: 40–3.

Ramseyer, Mark and Francis McCall Rosenbluth. 1993. *Japan's Political Marketplace*. Cambridge, MA: Harvard UP.

Rauch, James E. 1999. Networks versus Markets in International Trade. *Journal of International Economics* 48, no. 1: 7–35.

Rinchō (Rinji gyōsei kaikaku suishin shingikai), ed. 1990. *Gyōkakushin Zenshigoto* (*A Full Account of the Gyōkakushin*). Tokyo: Gyōsei.

Rosenbluth, Frances McCall. 1989. *Financial Politics in Contemporary Japan*. Ithaca: Cornell UP.

Rotemberg, Julio J. and Garth Saloner. 1986. A Supergame-Theoretic Model of Price Wars during Booms. *American Economic Review* 76, no. 3: 390–407.

Rotwein, Eugene. 1964. Economic Concentration and Monopoly in Japan. *Journal of Political Economy* 72: 264–80.

Rotwein, Eugene. 1976. Economic Concentration and Monopoly in Japan—A Second View. *Journal of Asian Studies* 36, no. 1: 57–77.

Rōyama, Shōichi. 1982. *Nihon no kinyū shisutemu* (*The Japanese Financial System*). Tokyo: Tōyō Keizai Shinpō-sha.

Saijō Nobuhiro. 1986. *Kinyū jiyūka to ginkō/shōken* (*Commercial/Investment Banking and Financial Deregulation*). Tokyo: Shihon shijō kenkyūkai.

Saitō Makoto. 1997. Kinyū kantoku-chō no soshiki to kinō: Gyōseihō sajiki kara miru makuai-geki (The Organization and Functions of the Financial Supervisory Agency:

Watching a Multiple-act Theater from the Skybox of the Administrative Law). *Jurisuto* 1119, September 15: 9–15.

Samuels, Richard J. 1987. *The Business of the Japanese State: Energy Markets in Comparative and Historical Perspective*. Ithaca: Cornell UP.

Saxonhouse, Gary R. 1977. Productivity Change and Labor Absorption in Japanese Cotton Spinning, 1891–1935. *Quarterly Journal of Economics* 91, no. 2: 195–219.

Saxonhouse, Gary R. 1979. Industrial Restructuring in Japan. *Journal of Japanese Studies* 5, no. 2: 273–320.

SCG (Shōken chōsa guruupu K). 1991. *Dokyumento: Shōken fushōji jiken (The Securities Scandal: A Documentation)*. Tokyo: Dai-Ichi Kikaku Shuppan.

Schaede, Ulrike. 1989a. *Geldpolitik in Japan 1950–1985 (Monetary Policy in Japan, 1950–1985)*. Marburg: Marburger Japan-Reihe.

Schaede, Ulrike. 1989b. Forwards and Futures in Tokugawa-Period Japan: A New Perspective on the Dojima Rice Market. *Journal of Banking and Finance* 13: 487–513.

Schaede, Ulrike. 1990. *Der neue japanische Kapitalmarkt— Finanzfutures in Japan (The New Japanese Capital Markets: Financial Futures)*. Wiesbaden: Gabler.

Schaede, Ulrike. 1991. Black Monday in New York, Blue Tuesday in Tokyo: The October 1987 Crash in Japan. *California Management Review* 33, no. 2: 39–57.

Schaede, Ulrike. 1992. *Geld ist Spiel, Zeit ist Geld, Geld regiert die Welt?—Zum Phänomen "Geld" in der japanischen Gesellschaft (Money is Game, Time is Money, Money Rules the World—The Phenomenon of "Money" in Japanese Society)*. Tokyo: Deutsche Gesellschaft für Natur- und Völkerkunde Ostasiens, OAG Aktuell.

Schaede, Ulrike. 1994. Understanding Corporate Governance in Japan: Do Classical Concepts Apply? *Industrial and Corporate Change* 3, no. 2: 285–323.

Schaede, Ulrike. 1995. The "Old Boy" Network and Government–Business Relationships in Japan. *Journal of Japanese Studies* 21, no. 2: 293–317.

Schaede, Ulrike. 1998. MOF, Money, and the Japanese Banking Crisis of 1995. In *Die Rolle des Geldes in Japans Gesellschaft, Wirtschaft und Politik*, ed. Angelika Ernst and Peter Pörtner: 95–128. Hamburg: Mitteilungen des Instituts für Asienkunde.

Schaede, Ulrike. 2000. *The Japanese Financial System: From Postwar to the New Millennium*. Boston: Harvard Business School Case.

Scherer, F.M. 1980. *Industrial Market Structure and Economic Performance*. Boston: Houghton-Mifflin.

Schlesinger, Jacob. 1997. *Shadow Shoguns: The Rise and Fall of Japan's Postwar Political Machine*. New York: Simon and Schuster.

Schmitter, Philippe C. 1979. Still the Century of Corporatism? In *Trends Towards Corporatist Intermediation*, ed. Philippe C. Schmitter and G. Lehmbruch: 7–52. London: Sage Publications.

Schoppa, Leonard. 1997. *Bargaining with Japan: What American Pressure Can and Cannot Do*. New York: Columbia UP.

Schwartz, Frank. 1993. Of Fairy Cloaks and Familiar Talks: The Politics of Consultation. In *Political Dynamics in Contemporary Japan*, ed. Gary D. Allinson and Yasunori Sone: 217–41. Ithaca: Cornell UP.

Schwartz, Frank. 1998. *Advice and Consent: The Politics of Consultation in Japan*. Cambridge: Cambridge UP.

Scott, W. Richard. 1995. *Institutions and Organizations*. Thousand Oaks, CA: Sage.

Senō, Akira. 1983. *Gendai Nihon no sangyō shūchū* (*Market Concentration in Contemporary Japan*). Tokyo: Nihon Keizai Shinbun-sha.

Sheldon, Charles David. 1958. *The Rise of the Merchant Class in Tokugawa Japan 1600–1868—An Introductory Survey.* New York: Russell & Russell.

Shiba KK, ed. 1991. *Zenkoku kakushū dantai meikan* (*All Japan Associations Directory*). Tokyo: Yokoyama Insatsu KK.

Shugart, William F. and Robert D. Tollison. 1998. Collusion, Profits, and Rational Antitrust. *The Antitrust Bulletin*, Summer 1998: 365–74.

Smith, Richard Austin. 1961a. The Incredible Electrical Conspiracy—Part I. *Fortune*, April 1961: 132–80.

Smith, Richard Austin. 1961b. The Incredible Conspiracy—Part II. *Fortune*, May 1961: 161–224.

Smith, Thomas C. 1955. *Political Change and Industrial Development in Japan: Government Enterprise, 1868–1880.* Stanford: Stanford UP.

Smitka, Michael J. 1991. *Competitive Ties—Subcontracting in the Japanese Automotive Industry.* New York: Columbia UP.

Sōmuchō (Prime Minister's Office), ed. 1992. *Kisei gyōsei no kaizen o mezashite* (*Improving the Regulatory System*). Tokyo: Government Report.

Sōmuchō (Prime Minister's Office), ed. 1994. *Shingikai sōran Heisei 6 nen pan* (*Compendium on Shingikai 1994*). Tokyo: Ōkurashō Insatsukyoku.

Sōmuchō (Prime Minister's Office), ed. 1995. *Tokushu hōjin sōran Heisei 7 nen pan* (*1995 Compendium of Public Corporations*). Tokyo: Gyōsei kanri kenkyū sentaa.

Sone, Yasunori. 1993. Conclusion: Structural Political Bargains: Government, Gyokai, and Markets. In *Political Dynamics in Contemporary Japan*, ed. Gary D. Allinson and Yasunori Sone: 295–306. Ithaca: Cornell UP.

SSKK (Sekiyū kagaku sangyō kihon mondai kyōgikai shōkankō iinkai), ed. 1995. Sekiyū kagaku sangyō kihon mondai kyōgikai shōkankō iinkan hōkoku: Shōkankō no zeisei o mezashite (*Towards an Improvement of "Trade Habits": A Report by the Trade Habits Subcommittee of the Deliberation Council on Basic Problems in the Petrochemical Industry*). Tokyo: Government Report.

Staber, Udo. 1987. Corporatism and the Governance Structure of American Trade Associations. *Political Studies* 35, no. 1987: 278–88.

Staber, Udo and Howard Aldrich. 1983. Trade Association Stability and Public Policy. In *Organizational Theory and Public Policy*, ed. R. Hall and R. Quinn: 163–78. Beverly Hills: Sage.

Stigler, G. 1964. A Theory of Oligopoly. *Journal of Political Economy* 72: 44–61.

Streeck, Wolfgang. 1994. Einleitung des Herausgebers, Staat und Verbände: Neue Fragen. Neue Antworten? (Editorial Introduction, State and Associations: New Questions. New Answers?). In *Staat und Verbände* (*State and Associations*), ed. Wolfgang Streeck, PVS—Politische Vierteljahreszeitschrift, Vol. 35: 7–34. Opladen: Westdeutscher Verlag.

Streeck, Wolfgang and Philippe C. Schmitter. 1985a. Community, Market, State—and Associations? The Prospective Contribution of Interest Governance to Social Order. In *Private Interest Government—Beyond Market and State*, ed. Wolfgang Streeck and Philippe C. Schmitter: 1–29. London: Sage Publications.

Streeck, Wolfgang and Philippe C. Schmitter, eds. 1985b. *Private Interest Government—Beyond Market and State.* London: Sage.

Suzuki, Yoshio. 1980. *Money and Banking in Contemporary Japan.* New Haven: Yale UP.

Suzuki, Yoshio. 1995. *Kisei kanwa wa naze dekinai no ka?* (*Why Deregulation Won't Happen*). Tokyo: Nihon Jitsugyō Shuppan-sha.

Tachibana, Takashi. 1982. *Tanaka Kakuei kenkyū zenkiroku* (*A Complete Report on Tanaka Kakuei*). Tokyo: Kōdansha.

Takahashi, Kamekichi. 1973. *Nihon kindai keizai hattatsu-shi* (*A History of Japan's Modern Economic Development*). Tokyo: Tōyō keizai shinpō-sha.

Takeda, Haruhito. 1985. Sōkatsu to tenbō (Summary and Perspectives). In *Ryō-daisenkanki no Nihon no karuteru* (*Japan's Cartels in the Interwar Period*), ed. Jūrō Hashimoto and Haruhito Takeda: 411–22. Tokyo: Ochanomizu Shobō.

Takekoshi, Yosoburo. 1967. *The Economic Aspects of the History of the Civilization of Japan.* London: Dawsons of Pall Mall (3 volumes).

Takeuchi, Hirotaka. 1991. The Japanese System of Corporate Governance: Will Stakeholders Remain Silent? Working Paper, Tokyo: Hitotsubashi University.

Tamura, Jiro. 1995. Foreign Firm Access to Japanese Distribution Systems: Trends in Japanese Antitrust Enforcement. *Pacific Rim Law and Policy Journal* 4, no. 1: 267–76.

Telser, Lester. 1960. Why Should Manufacturers Want Fair Trade? *Journal of Law and Economics* 3: 86–105.

Tilton, Mark. 1995. Informal Market Governance in Japan's Basic Materials Industries. *International Organization* 48, no. 4: 663–85.

Tilton, Mark. 1996. *Restrained Trade: Cartels in Japan's Basic Materials Industries.* Ithaca: Cornell UP.

Tirole, Jean. 1988. *The Theory of Industrial Organization.* Cambridge, MA: MIT Press.

Tōyō Keizai, ed. 1995. Shingikai de nanika okonawarete iru no ka: Kōkyō ryōkin kaikaku no ura, shingikai da ga, sono mae ni shingikai no kaikaku koso hitsuyō da (What is Happening at the Shingikai? Behind the Reform of Public Moneys are the Shingikai, but Prior to this Reform, We Need to Change These Very Shingikai). *Shūkan Tōyō Keizai,* July 15: 72–5.

Tōyō Keizai Shinpō-sha, ed. 1994. *Nihon no jinmyaku to kigyō-keiretsu* (*Japan's Personal Relations and Corporate Keiretsu*). Tokyo: Tōyō Keizai Shinpō-sha.

Toyoda, Takeshi. 1963. Za to dosō (Za and dosō). In *Iwanami kōza Nihon rekishi—Chūsei 2* (*Iwanami Series—Japanese History, Middle Ages 2*), ed. Iwanami Shoten, Vol. 6: 155–86. Tokyo: Iwanami Shoten.

Toyoda, Takeshi and Hiroshi Sugiyama. 1977. The Growth of Commerce and the Trades. In *Japan in the Muromachi Age,* ed. John W. Hall and Takeshi Toyoda: 129–44. Berkeley: University of California Press.

Tsuda, Tatsuo. 1990. *Zaikai—Nihon no Shihaishatachi* (*The Zaikai—The Men Who Dominate Japan*). Tokyo: Gakushi no yūjin.

Tsujinaka, Yutaka. 1988. *Rieki dantai* (*Interest Groups*). Tokyo: Tōkyō Daigaku Shuppan-sha.

Tsujinaka, Yutaka. 1996. Interest Group Structure and Regime Change in Japan. *Maryland/Tsukuba Papers on U.S.-Japan Relations,* Maryland.

Tsuru, Shigeto. 1993. *Japan's Capitalism: Creative Defeat and Beyond.* Cambridge: Cambridge UP.

Tushman, Michael L. and Charles A. O'Reilly. 1997. *Winning through Innovation: A Practical Guide to Leading Organizational Change and Renewal.* Boston: Harvard Business School Press.

Uekusa, Masu. 1987. Industrial Organization: The 1970s to the Present. In *The Political Economy of Japan, Vol.1: The Domestic Transformation*, ed. Kozo Yamamura and Yasukichi Yasuba: 469–515. Stanford: Stanford UP.

Umemura, Mataji and Yūzō Yamamoto, eds. 1989. *Kaikō to isshin* (*The Opening and the Restoration*). Tokyo: Iwanami Shoten.

Upham, Frank K. 1987. *Law and Social Change in Postwar Japan*. Cambridge: Harvard UP.

Upham, Frank K. 1993. Privatizing Regulation: The Implementation of the Large-Scale Retail Stores Law. In *Political Dynamics in Contemporary Japan*, ed. Gary D. Allinson and Yasunori Sone: 264–94. Ithaca: Cornell UP.

Upham, Frank K. 1996. Privatized Regulation: Japanese Regulatory Style in Comparative and International Perspective. *Fordham International Law Journal* 20, no. 2: 396–511.

Uriu, Robert M. 1996. *Troubled Industries: Confronting Economic Change in Japan*. Ithaca: Cornell UP.

Vartabedian, Ralph. 1997. The Rising Tide of Corporate Political Donations. *Los Angeles Times*, September 21.

Vestal, James. 1993. *Planning for Change: Industrial Policy and Japanese Economic Development, 1945–1990*. Oxford: Oxford UP.

Vogel, Ezra F. 1979. *Japan as Number One: Lessons for America*. New York: Harper & Row.

Vogel, Steven K. 1996. *Freer Markets, More Rules—Regulatory Reform in Advanced Industrial Countries*. Ithaca: Cornell UP.

Vogel, Steven K. 1999. Can Japan Disengage? Winners and Losers in Japan's Political Economy, and Ties that Bind them. *Social Science Japan Journal* 2, no. 1: 3–21

Wada, Tateo. 1990. Jigyōsha dantai no kinō (The Functions of Trade Associations). *Jurisuto 950*. February 15: 57–62.

Wade, Robert. 1990. *Governing the Market—Economic Theory and the Role of Government in East Asian Industrialization*. Princeton: Princeton UP.

Washio, Akio. 1996. Political Donations not Catching. *Japan Times*, Oct. 1996.

Weick, K.E. 1969. *The Social Psychology of Organizing*. Reading MA: Addison-Wesley.

Weidenbaum, Murray L. 1990. *Business, Government, and the Public*. Englewood Cliffs, NJ: Prentice Hall.

Weinstein, David E. 1995. Evaluating Administrative Guidance and Cartels in Japan (1957–1988). *Journal of the Japanese and International Economies* 9, no. 2: 200–23.

Whittaker, D, Hugh. 1997. *Small Firms in the Japanese Economy*. Cambridge: Cambridge UP.

Willeke, Franz-Ulrich. 1980. *Wettbewerbspolitik* (*Competition Policy*). Tübingen: J.C.B. Mohr (Siebeck).

Willmott, Hugh C. 1985. Setting Accounting Standards in the U.K.: The Emergence of Private Accounting Bodies and their Role in the Regulation of Public Accounting Practice. In *Private Interest Government*, ed. Wolfgang Streeck and Philippe Schmitter: 44–71. Beverly Hills: Sage.

Woodall, Brian. 1996. *Japan Under Construction: Corruption, Politics, and Public Works*. Berkeley: University of California Press.

Woodruff, Christopher. 1998. Contract Enforcement and Trade Liberalization in Mexico's Footwear Industry. *World Development* 26, no. 6: 979–91.

World Bank, ed. 1993. *The East Asian Miracle—Economic Growth and Public Policy*. Oxford: Oxford UP.

Yamakawa, Yukio. 1994. *Watashi wa warui kensetsu gyōsha* (*I am a Bad Construction Guy*). Tokyo: Deeta hausu KK.

Yamamura, Kozo. 1967. *Economic Policy in Japan: Growth Versus Economic Democracy.* Berkeley: University of California Press.

Yamamura, Kozo. 1973. The Development of Za in Medieval Japan. *Business History Review* 47, no. 4: 438–65.

Yamamura, Kozo. 1982. Success that Soured: Administrative Guidance and Cartels in Japan. In *Policy and Trade Issues of the Japanese Economy—American and Japanese Perspectives*, ed. Kozo Yamamura: 77–112. Seattle and London: University of Washington Press.

Yamamura, Kozo. 1997. The Japanese Political Economy after the "Bubble": Plus Ça Change? *Journal of Japanese Studies* 23, no. 2: 291–331.

Yamazaki, Hiroaki and Matao Miyamoto, eds. 1988. *Trade Associations in Business History—The International Conference on Business History 14.* Tokyo: University of Tokyo Press.

Yanaga, Masao. 1998. Disukuroojaa no jūjitsu/kōsei torihiki ruuru (Fair Trade Rules and Fulfilment of Disclosure Rules). *Jurisuto* 1145, November 15: 21–6.

Yayama, Taro. 1998. Who Has Obstructed Reform? In *Unlocking the Bureaucrat's Kingdom*, ed. Frank Gibney: 91–115. Washington: The Brookings Institution.

Yeomans, Russell Allen. 1986. Administrative Guidance: A Peregrine View. *Law in Japan* 19: 125–67.

Yoshida, Jinbu. 1964. *Nihon no karuteru* (*Japan's Cartels*). Tokyo: Tōyō keizai shinpō-sha.

Young, Michael. 1991. Structural Adjustment of Mature Industries in Japan: Legal Institutions, Industry Associations and Bargaining. In *The Promotion and Regulation of Industry in Japan*, ed. Stephen Wilks and Maurice Wright: 135–66. New York: St. Martin's Press.

Zaisei chōsakai (Fiscal Study Group), ed. 1994. *Kuni no yosan 1994* (*The 1994 Budget for Japan*). Tokyo: Hase Shobō.

Zenginkyō (Federation of Bankers' Associations of Japan), ed. 1995. *Ginkō to ginkō kyōkai* (*Banks and the Bankers' Associations*). Tokyo.

ZNNK (Zen Nihon neon kyōkai, All Japan Neon Association), ed. 1995. Tokushū: Gyōmu kaikaku ankeeto (Administrative Reform Survey Special Issue). *NEOS*, 32 (December): 3–26.

Zucker, Lynn G. 1983. Organizations as Institutions. *Research in the Sociology of Organizations, Vol. 2*, ed. S. B. Bacharch: 1–47. Greenwich, CT: JAI Press.

Zysman, John. 1983. *Governments, Markets, and Growth.* Ithaca: Cornell UP.

INDEX